PIMLICO

592

5

Libraries

LONGMATE, N.

The workhouse: a social history

Charges are payable on books overdue at public libraries. This book is
due for return by the last date shown but if not required by another
reader may be renewed - ask at th
the last date and the details shown a

THE WORKHOUSE

A Social History

———

NORMAN LONGMATE

With a New Foreword by the Author

PIMLICO

Published by Pimlico 2003

2 4 6 8 10 9 7 5 3 1

Copyright © Norman Longmate 1974

Norman Longmate has asserted his right
under the Copyright, Designs and Patents Act 1988
to be identified as the author of this work

First published in Great Britain by Maurice Temple Smith, 1974

Pimlico edition 2003

Pimlico
Random House, 20 Vauxhall Bridge Road,
London SW1V 2SA

Random House Australia (Pty) Limited
20 Alfred Street, Milsons Point, Sydney,
New South Wales 2061, Australia

Random House New Zealand Limited
18 Poland Road, Glenfield
Auckland 10, New Zealand

Random House South Africa (Pty) Limited
Endulini 5A Jubilee Road, Parktown 2193, South Africa

Random House UK Limited Reg. No. 954009

A CIP catalogue record for this book
is available from the British Library

ISBN 0–7126–0637–8

Papers used by Random House UK Limited are natural,
recyclable products made from wood grown in sustainable forests.
The manufacturing processes conform to the environmental
regulations of the counry of origin

Printed and bound in Great Britain by
Mackays of Chatham

Foreword to the Pimlico Edition

Since this book was first published, much has changed in the world of workhouse history. In 1974 many people still had personal memories of the institution, as inmates or employees, and a far larger number could recollect the dread among their parents and grandparents of ending up there or in the hospital or old people's home that now commonly occupied the premises, around which an aura of hatred still lingered.

But already by 1974, workhouses were becoming hard to find. As soon as premises could be found which lacked such associations, former workhouses were demolished wholesale and those that now remain were saved rather by a new enthusiasm for preserving the past than by any special regard for social history. Housing developers, so often painted as the enemies of conservation, have proved the saviours of much property under threat. The sensible principle has been accepted that it is better to keep an ancient building in some form, even if used for a totally different purpose, than to see it swept away. A classic example, which I came across while following my other interest, military history, is supplied by Fort Picklecombe, completed in 1872 as part of the defences of Plymouth, as described in *Island Fortress* (Pimlico edition 2001). This splendid waterside building was given up by the military in 1956 and ingeniously reshaped inside, to provide 'luxury apartments', largely used as holiday homes. The arched roofs of the gun galleries now provide curved ceilings for spacious sitting-rooms and the balconies on which the guns were run out now shelter sun-bathing civilians.

The 'swords into ploughshares' principle is less easily applied to workhouses, often inconveniently sited and deliberately designed to look repellent. Given the hostility which still surrounds them it is more surprising that so many have survived than that most have disappeared. Those 'listed' as of outstanding historical or architectural interest cannot easily be radically altered or demolished. Of those of which fragments, or whole buildings remain, identification can today be difficult, even to the knowledgeable eye. The former workhouse at Richmond in Surrey, for example, on a site used to house the poor even before 1834, stands close to Richmond Park in a highly prosperous area. The former gatehouse is still identifiable, on one side of attractive gold-tipped gates, which now prevent access except to the owners of

the expensive houses and flats within, armed with a security code. Two of the former blocks remain but are altered almost out of recognition. The only clues to the original purposes the site served are the modern buildings nearby which house sheltered homes and a day centre for the elderly. The buildings which formed the workhouse and those added close by form St George's Square. To 'end up' there is a proof of affluence.

The most notorious workhouse of all, which I describe in Chapter 10, Andover in Hampshire, illustrates the same process even more dramatically, for here the original layout has been retained and the date the building, still recognisably the same, was opened, 1836, remains inscribed over the pediment. The recent history of the Andover workhouse is typical of many others less well known. It became, after losing its original role, St John's Hospital for the elderly, then an annexe to the nearby Cricklade College and Icknield School. In 1997 the 2.5 acre site was offered for sale, with the 'listed' workhouse in its centre. It was duly sold and has been admirably developed. The brickwork of the former wards is immaculate, a flight of gleaming white steps leads up to the front door, which is crowned by an elegant fanlight and flanked by grassy banks. The neatly paved area at the front is separated from the road by neatly cropped lawns and a hedge. The only admonitory note is struck by a sign which warns: 'Strictly No Parking. Residents Only'. With the station – 65 minutes by fast train to London – only a short walk away, properties at what is now The Cloisters are in heavy demand. I enquired about one advertised for sale but found it had already been bought.**

The best known of English workhouses, that in which Oliver Twist 'asks for more', in the eponymous novel published in 1837–9, never existed, though it is based on fact, and is clearly of the pre-1834 'parish' type. Charles Dickens returned to the attack in 1864–5 in *Our Mutual Friend*, in which an old woman dies by the roadside rather than enter 'the union'. The location is not identified but one supposedly fictional workhouse can be identified with certainty, that at 'Casterbridge', featured by Thomas Hardy in *Far from the Madding Crowd*, published in 1874. One of the scenes in this typically gloomy story portrays a young woman, Fanny Robin, ruined and betrayed by the evil Sergeant Troy, making her sad way to Damer's Road, Dorchester, where she sees the workhouse as her only refuge. She staggers the last mile or so with the help of a large dog, and is duly taken in; the dog, despite her

---

* This two roomed flat had been on offer at £95,000. One to let cost £500 a month. No doubt these figures will have changed by the time this book appears.

concern for him, is 'stoned away'. Fanny dies in childbirth during the night and, to save the expense of a brass plate, her name is chalked on the cover of her coffin. Hardy acknowledges, however, that this particular economy was later abandoned and gives a surprisingly sympathetic description of the building, referring to its 'picturesque appearance' as 'masses of ivy grew up, completely covering the wall', though 'the grim character of what was beneath showed through'. This was the reason that so many workhouses were destroyed but 'Caster-bridge' survived, to become a hospital, an old people's home and, today, offices and a children's nursery.

Amid the general picture of destruction and alteration one gleaming exception stands out. Today, as was not possible in 1974, one can visit a workhouse which looks much as it did in 1834. Southwell is not merely the sole survivor. It is in a sense the mother of all workhouses, for, though opened just before the introduction of the New Poor Law, it became to a large extent, in both its architecture and its principles, a model for all those that followed.

The origins of the workhouse at Southwell (sometimes pronounced Suthall) are described in Chapter 3. Opened in 1824 at a cost of £6,596 to serve the 49 parishes of the Thurgaton Hundred, it was retained to become the 'deterrent' workhouse for the enlarged Southwell Union, of 60 parishes, with minor extensions to the original buildings made by the Poor Law Commissioners' favourite architect, Sampson Kempthorne – see Appendix. Over the years numerous minor changes were made. In 1871 a separate infirmary was built behind the main building and a maternity ward, for local mothers as well as inmates, was later added. In 1914 better accommodation was provided for children and additional space for elderly women in a separate building, known as Greet House, a name increasingly used in place of the already hated 'workhouse' for the whole institution. Over the years a separate washhouse, piggeries, a stable block for the guardians' horses, cells for recalcitrant vagrants, a new mortuary, were all added. By 1948 the largest group occupying the site were old people requiring medical care or simply shelter. For a time it housed homeless families in 'bed sitter' type accommodation. Eventually all these residents left and Southwell Workhouse stood empty and, though 'listed', was threatened with demolition by developers, wishing to use the site for housing. Happily, it was sold instead to the National Trust for £250,000, though the cost of restoring the building and opening it to the public was put at £4.5 million.

But the problem was not merely financial. As the *National Trust Magazine* acknowledged in Summer 1998, 'acquiring a building for an overt educational purpose rather than for its aesthetic qualities does mark something of a departure for the Trust'. Fortunately it was decided to add this example of an unloved institution to its portfolio of stately homes and other historic properties, and the National Lottery Fund generously contributed half of the estimated cost.

Little description is needed of this new, if unusual, treasure for it can, and should, be visited. 8 miles from Newark (itself one and a half hours by train from London) 13 from Nottingham, near the centre of England, Southwell is readily accessible. The weary pauper trudging reluctantly towards it would have appreciated the bus that now runs from Newark. I arrived, most inappropriately, by taxi, on a cold February day, with a bitter wind sweeping across the bleak winter landscape. Standing in the high-walled exercise yard at the rear of the building one could still sense something of the despair which must have afflicted the newly arrived applicant for relief, and overwhelmed him as he went inside.

The wards and staircases are still as they were, revealed and, where necessary, restored rather than replaced. One can walk on the original hardwood lime-ash floors, inspect the surviving iron hooks for hanging clothes, find oneself unable to see out of the high windows, or through the opaque glass in the children's schoolroom. Greying stone and authentically peeling paintwork apart, the property is immaculate inside and out, as was the original workhouse. The one commodity of which it was never short was labour.

Southwell is a fine example of social archaeology and visiting it illustrates vividly the principles which lay behind it. It left me with two dominant impressions. The first was the effectiveness of the 'classification' policy, which successfully prevented any contact between different categories of inmate. Several storeys, and windowless, bricked-off staircases divided the damp and gloomy laundry in the basement, where the unmarried mothers and other able-bodied women toiled, from the bare and cheerless 'infirm' men's ward on the second floor.

My second lasting memory when I made my way out, with vast relief, as in a Victorian novel, to the piercing wind buffeting the walls, was of the great contrast, deliberately emphasised by the architect, between the accommodation and way of life of the workhouse inmates and of those who ruled them. At Southwell, as was usual, the master's home was in the centre of the building and formed its core. On the ground floor was his office and the boardroom. Above, his sitting-room, from which he could keep all the outside yards and vegetable gardens under observation. Only in the brick-screened 'hole in the ground' lavatories in the corner of the yard could the pauper escape from this perpetual scrutiny. Adjoining the master's sitting-room were his bedrooms and, no doubt added after 1834, a Victorian

WC. It was not merely that the master's accommodation was far more spacious and better decorated than the rest of their workhouse but that they seemed to belong to a totally different world.

Superior even to the master were the guardians and here, too, Southwell is revealing. The paupers reached the reception block at the back through an iron gate, like cattle filing into a field. The guardians arrived through an arched stone gateway leading on to a gravel path at the front of the building. There they passed through an impressive door into a wide, high-ceilinged hall, used, no doubt, not merely for meetings but for substantial meals, where they were waited on by the inmates.

In restoring the buildings at Southwell, the National Trust has also opened up the guardians' archives, admirably preserved by the local authority, and supplemented them by 'oral history', recordings made by people who lived in or visited the workhouse in the days of its glory.

It is helpful to read a Victorian recipe for making gruel by the pint:

> Take a spoonful of oatmeal, stirring with one third of a pint of milk. Make up the rest with water, and boil up three or four times, stirring often.

The carefully maintained punishment register is equally revealing:

24 April 1852
Rachel Revill: Breaking a window purposely   8 hours in the lock-
                                              up and gave her
                                              1 lb of potatoes in
                                              lieu of pudding for
                                              dinner.

The recorded memories of one man born in the workhouse tell their own story:

> I used to see my mother, but only in the distance. We used to be on the other side of the railing, we could see them come out, shout to them. They used to wave back but ... they weren't allowed to go across and talk to you.

A local GP testifies to the effectiveness of the 'separation' policy:

> The architectural arrangements were such that ... staircases all sort of crisscrossed. So it worked out that somebody at the top was unable to communicate with the next room, unless they

went down three flights of stairs and right the way back up the other three flights.

The opening of the workhouse at Southwell is not the only sign of renewed interest in the subject. I describe in Chapter 16 the work of Dr Joseph Rogers, 'the hero of workhouse reform', and was delighted to attend, in 1996, the unveiling of a plaque to him on his former house at 33 Dean Street, Soho. A constant advocate of better care for the mentally ill, Dr Rogers would, I suspect, have been delighted to know that when the great Victorian asylum at Colney Hatch in Hertfordshire was converted into housing, excellent soundproofing was advertised as one of its attractions. At last the padded cells against which he campaigned had proved their value.

This second Foreword ends where the first began, at the former workhouse in Newbury which awakened my interest in social history. A 'listed' building which has received many more modern, but unlisted, accretions, the result today is an uneasy mixture of Victorian brickwork and twentieth-century glass and wood. Here is one site which might well have been cleared to provide purpose-built premises for the wide range of facilities it now accommodates. Today it certainly demonstrates the proliferation of welfare services, each meeting a specific need, as the original founders of the workhouse had intended and as the Minority Report of the Royal Commission on the Poor Law in 1909 recommended. Behind the main entrance stands a sign, unthinkable in either the 1830s, when the workhouse was built, or the 1930s, when I first saw it: 'Welcome to Sandleford Hospital'. Beside it are a proliferation of notices pointing the way to Health Promotion, Physiotherapy, the Elderly Rehabilitation Unit, the Learning Disability Service and the Day Nursery. Close by, in the area where the 'casuals' – see Chapter 19 – once waited for admission are some twenty-first-century amenities: a Pupil Referral Unit; the offices of a housing association and, perhaps still approached with trepidation, a Driving Test Centre.

I owe, finally, a word of thanks to the reviewers who gave a kindly reception to the first edition of this book, to the correspondents who have urged me to get it back into print, and to the publishers who have made this possible. I am grateful to those who have helped me with fresh information or in other ways: Professor Keith Allen; Mr Robert Fennell; Mrs Elizabeth Longmate; Dr Ruth Richardson; and the Test Valley Borough Council, responsible for the Andover area.

NRL
July 2002

Foreword

I grew up in the shadow of the workhouse. The drab council estate
—since demolished—which was my home as a child was separated
only by a main road from the local workhouse and everyone living
on the estate was constantly aware of its grim presence. We knew
nothing of its history, but, researching for this book many years later,
I discovered that it was a very typical specimen of its kind, which had
been erected in 1836 to house three hundred and fifty paupers. The
cost, £5,332 19s., had proved a bargain: a century later it was still
serving its intended purpose of terrorising the poor, even though
the union system, of which it was part, had vanished in 1930, the year
I first saw the building. Officially it now had another name, but to us,
and to the sad, ragged tramps who shuffled towards it past our doors,
it was still 'the workhouse'—feared, hated and menacing. People
on the estate who were down on their luck (as many were in 1930)
still spoke of 'ending up across the road' and we all regarded the
inmates, elderly, often bent figures mainly, whom we could see sun-
ning themselves on the ugly iron balconies that decorated the cheerless looking building, with a mixture of superiority and sympathy.

The staff of the workhouse were automatically loathed, irrespective
of their merits, while the workhouse master's daughter, about the same
age as myself, whom I secretly thought attractive, was lucky if insults
were not shouted at her as she walked home from school; a different
one, of course, from ours.

These experiences first roused my interest in the subject of
this book, but it was only while writing other books on the Victorian
period that I discovered that there was no existing history of the
workhouse and decided to try to fill the gap. Some of the material
published here has already appeared in the Programme, *Christmas
Day in the Workhouse*, broadcast on BBC Radio 4 in December
1971, in the *Observer* Magazine in August 1972 and in a radio programme for schools, *Poverty and Welfare*, in January 1973. All
of these have brought a number of letters from interested readers
or listeners and the last-named, which was largely about the
Andover workhouse scandal described in Chapter 10, caused one
woman, who had grown up in Andover, to recall how although her

... parents and their remaining brothers and sisters died happily at a good age, cared for by us, their children ... the 'workhouse' fear was still with them and with many of their generation. Both my parents (born in the 1870s) had a terror of the place. When we passed it on walks my mother and father, though by then travelled and self-educated people, still spoke with bitterness of the things done there in the past. As children in the 1920s we still ran past its high walls in superstitious fear.

After many years away I regarded the tales as mere legend, but some years ago I returned to nurse for a brief period in the now bright and decorated 'St John's Hospital'. But the old corridors and chapel, mortuary and yards remained and, on night duty, doing rounds at night across the yards and blocks, one had a presence of evil... Once when Sister wanted the old mortuary tidied up and varied records removed for repainting and modernising the building, I volunteered and glancing at the records of births and rapid deaths of infants in the past century I knew it wasn't all imagination... I tried to get further information locally but... the subject of the workhouse was strongly tabooed.

Apart from such correspondents, who have encouraged me to explore the subject as fairly and thoroughly as I could, my thanks are due to the following, who supplied me with information or suggested sources of material: Miss Margaret Holmes, County Archivist of Dorset; Mrs Elizabeth Cockburn of Hilfield Manor near Dorchester, who lent me her manuscript article on the Cerne Abbas workhouse; Miss Enid Porter, Curator of the Cambridge and County Folk Museum; the staff of the County Record Office, Bedford; Mrs Constance Mullineux of Worsley, Lancashire, author of a monograph on a Lancashire union, *Pauper and Poorhouse*; Mr W. H. Devereux, Borough Librarian of Swinton and Pendlebury, Lancashire; and the Information Division of the Department of Health and Social Security. I am particularly indebted to Mr Richard Wildman of Bedford, a former president of the Cambridge University Victorian Society, who photographed for me various surviving workhouses and wrote the essay on workhouse architecture which appears as an Appendix. Mrs Jessie Peters of Swinton kindly supplied the photographs of the children's ward at Salford workhouse, taken by her father: a reminder of how short a gap separates us from the workhouse era.

NRL

1 Whipped to Death

> The poor may be whipped to death and branded
> for rogues...before any private man will set
> them to work or provide houses for labour.
> *Stanleye's Remedy*, 1646

Any traveller riding down the dusty or muddy lanes of Southern
England between 1835 and 1840, or rattling in the mail coach along
the fine new turnpike roads, could not have failed to notice the vast
new buildings which seemed to be springing up everywhere. In market
towns they dwarfed the surrounding shops and cottages; in the depths
of the countryside they stood gauntly in hitherto untilled fields or on
desolate stretches of waste land. Usually they consisted of a bleak, two-
storey block, built round a courtyard, with vegetable gardens lying
behind it. At the front there was a narrow gate, guarded by a porter's
lodge, with a large bell hanging above it, and the premises were invariably surrounded by a high wall.

Glancing at the new buildings as one succeeded another at intervals
of twenty miles or so, a visitor new to England might have supposed
that the whole of the English countryside had been swept by some
gigantic crime-wave and that these were vast jails, run up hastily to
accommodate a whole army of prisoners. If he had stopped to talk to a
labourer in the fields, or had gossiped with the ostler at the inn, this
impression would have been confirmed. The building he had seen
would have been referred to with a dread and loathing that Newgate, or
the notorious House of Correction at Coldbath Fields, could not have
equalled, and the very name of the intrusive new establishment would
have been spoken with reluctance. 'The union house', 'the union' or
most commonly of all, 'the house', was how the working class described
it, or more ominously 'the Bastille' or 'old Basty'. It was not until
time had made the new building familiar, and sun and rain had helped
the raw white stone and cheap red brick to mellow into the landscape
that those 'lower orders' for whom it was intended began to describe
it by its correct name, 'the workhouse'—a name still evocative of fear
and disgust among the old.

The workhouse represented a bold, ruthless and in some ways successful attempt to solve a problem almost as old as society itself, pauperism: the state of needing to be supported by the rest of society. No one expected it to cure poverty, the mere fact of being poor, for this was universally accepted as the common condition of most of mankind. Those who needed assistance from society to survive fell into two distinct groups: the 'impotent' poor unable to maintain themselves such as the very old, the very young, the sick, the crippled, the blind and the insane; and the 'able-bodied' poor, who merely lacked work and hence wages.

During the Middle Ages no formal provision for either category was attempted, those in need being supported by their family or neighbours, or by the church, but the growth of towns in the later Middle Ages and the dissolution of the monasteries in 1536 disrupted this simple system. From the accession of Edward VI in 1547 onwards a new law affecting some section of the poor was passed every few years. One of the earliest, in 1552, instructed the clergy to preach fund-raising sermons, to enable the 'aged, impotent or lame' to be provided for in 'tenantries, cottages and other convenient houses, to be lodged at the costs and charges of the said cities, towns, boroughs and villages, there to be relieved and cured by the devotion of good people'. As for the physically fit, it tended to be assumed then, and later, that they were idle only from choice, for: 'If any man or woman, able to work, should refuse to labour and live idly for three days, he or she should be branded with a red hot iron on the breast with the letter V and should be judged the slave for two years of any person who should inform against such idler.'

Later laws followed a similar pattern. By an Act of 1572 anyone soliciting alms without a magistrate's licence to beg or, if he came from another parish, who failed to wear 'some notable badge or token both on the breast and on the back of his outermost garment', was to suffer 'burning through the gristle of the right ear'. In 1597 a new provision was added that any 'sturdy beggar' caught should be 'stripped naked from the middle upwards, and be whipped until his body was bloody and be sent from parish to parish, the next straight way to the place of his birth'. Both whipping beggars out of the parish and 'badging' the poor, usually with 'blue and yellow bays pinned upon their sleeve and breast', rapidly became popular practices, destined to survive for nearly three centuries.

But the Elizabethan laws were not merely deterrent. In 1576 the justices in every area were ordered to buy or hire buildings and to equip them with 'wool, hemp, flax, iron... that youth might be accustomed and brought up in labour and... may not have any just excuse in saying that they cannot get any service or work'. These 'houses of industry' seem to have been non-residential and though they contained the seeds of the future workhouse, the term itself had not yet come into use. 'Workhouse' at this period was a poetic synonym for 'workshop', the womb, for example, being described in 1548 as 'an heavenly workhouse' and the liver in 1581 as 'the workhouse of thick and gross blood'. It was not until 1652 that the word was first used in its modern sense and not until the nineteenth century that it finally supplanted such rivals as 'poorhouse' and 'parish-house'.

By the end of her reign Elizabeth's Parliaments were feeling their way towards a comprehensive policy for poor relief and in 1597 a new Act called upon every parish to appoint 'overseers of the poor', with the twin duties of finding work for those without it and of building 'parish-houses', described as 'hospitals and alms-houses', on waste land for the use of those unable to support themselves. The overseers, or if they refused to help, the justices, could also be appealed to for relief in sudden emergency, funds for the purposes being provided by a rate levied on all property-owners. Here lay the basis of all welfare legislation for the next two hundred and fifty years and in 1601 all the measures passed piecemeal in the previous half century were consolidated into one major statute, commonly known as the Elizabethan Poor Law, or by its official title, 'the 43rd Elizabeth', which, periodically re-enacted, was to remain basically unaltered until 1834, though not for want of suggestions for improving it. The author of *Stanleye's Remedy* in 1646, for example, set out *The Way to reform Wandering Beggars, Theeves, Highway Robbers and Pick-pockets, wherein is shewed that Sodom's Sin of Idleness is the Poverty and Misery of this Kingdom; by some Well-Wishers to the Honour of God and the Public Good, both of Rich and Poore.*

'The poor', pointed out Stanleye, 'may be whipped to death and branded for rogues... before any private man will set them to work or provide houses for labour... I have heard the rogues and beggars curse the magistrate unto their faces for providing such a law to whip and brand them and not provide houses of labour for them; for surely many would go voluntarily to workhouses to work, if such houses were provided for them.'

In his *New Discourse on Trade,* in 1669, Sir Josiah Child advocated the appointment of 'Fathers of the Poor', who, by a levy of fifty per cent on the takings of play-houses, would finance 'workhouses, hospitals and houses of correction', where 'the girls may be employed in mending the clothes of the aged; in spinning, carding and other linen manufactures and the boys in picking oakum, making pins, rasping wood, or other manufactures'. The purpose of such establishments, explained the author, was not to make profits but to provide useful occupation, 'the great business of the nation being ... to keep the poor from begging and starving and ensuring such as are able to labour that they may be hereafter useful members of society'.

Many schemes were far less practical. *The Grand Concern of England Explained*, in 1673, ascribed the prevailing unemployment and the size of the poor rate, estimated at £840,000 a year, to the increase in the number of stage coaches, 'an ignoble, base and sordid way of travelling'. If these were suppressed by law, the resulting demand for grooms for horses would, it was claimed, speedily solve the unemployment problem. The writer of *England's Improvement by Sea and Land*, in 1677, was more ambitious, aiming not merely 'to set at work all the poor in England', but 'to out-do the Dutch without fighting, to pay debts without money, to prevent unnecessary suits in law' and even 'to prevent fires in London'. The grand panacea to accomplish all this was, it seemed, to expand the textile industry and develop iron manufacture in the Forest of Dean.

Some writers already advocated the use of the workhouse, described in one pamphlet in 1677 as a 'working almshouse', where even abandoned children of four or five, now costing their parishes two shillings a week, could earn threepence a day, and a practical venture on these lines, reported by Thomas Firmin in *Proposals for the Employing of the Poor, especially in and about London*, in 1678, attracted great attention. Firmin set up a warehouse in Aldersgate which supplied flax to the local poor for spinning and dressing, at a rate of payment of threepence or fourpence a day. 'By which experiment', he wrote, 'I perceived that the only way to provide for our poor ... is to provide such work for them as they may do at their own home, which, though never so mean and homely, is more desired than any other place; and the way which several persons have proposed, of bringing them to a public workhouse, will never affect the end intended.' Firmin did, however, make a distinction between the incorrigibly idle and the deserving unemployed, acknowledging that for 'vagrants and sturdy beggars who have no habitation, and must be held to their labour as galley-slaves are tied to their oars . . . workhouses are very necessary. But for such poor people as have habitations of their own and who . . . would take pains at home it is altogether unreasonable and unprofitable to force them to a public workhouse'.

The other most influential pamphlet of the period was anonymous but was probably by the leading jurist, Sir Matthew Hale. The famous '43rd Elizabeth' was, the author declared, 'a good provision for the impotent poor if duly executed. But the plaister is not as large as the sore; there are many poor who are able to work if they had it, and [received] reasonable wages'. He urged that parishes should be legally compelled to provide work for the unemployed, with several combining together in a union, to set up a common workhouse. But nothing came of this suggestion, or of an even more forward-looking one made in an official report to the Board of Trade in 1697, which recommended compulsory free education for all pauper children aged from three to fourteen, with free school meals, in the shape of 'water gruel, which may be prepared by the fire in the school room'.

Apart from the great '43rd Elizabeth', the outstanding legacy of the seventeenth century to later generations of English poor was the '13th Charles II', better known as the Act of Settlement and Removal of 1662, possibly the worst law ever passed by a British Parliament. Ever since the fourteenth century 'impotent' beggars had been forcibly sent back to their place of birth and under the Elizabethan Poor Law of 1601 anyone applying for poor relief outside his native parish was returned to it, or if it was unknown, to the last place where he had lived for at least a year. In 1662 the law was changed to give a newcomer the right to a 'settlement', and thus the right to poor relief and immunity from being sent away, in any place where he had lived unchallenged for forty days. During this period, however, he could, on complaint being made to the churchwardens, and upheld by two justices, be ordered back to his last place of settlement, unless he could prove, by renting a property worth £10 a year, that there was no danger of his becoming chargeable to the poor rates. As the average labourer's cottage was valued at fifty shillings a year, or less, only a man of some substance was safe from removal. In fact, almost anyone—however industrious and law-abiding—who moved to seek work or to better himself could now be sent back to the very place he had tried to escape from.

This was bad enough but the new law was made even harsher in 1686 when it was ruled that the vital forty days could only begin once

notification of arrival had been given to the overseer of the poor and
again in 1692, when it was decided that the forty days were to date from
the time of public announcement in church of the newcomer's arrival.
A person thus faced the agonising dilemma of advertising his arrival,
and risking immediate deportation, or keeping quiet about it, and
leaving himself liable for years afterwards to be betrayed and forcibly
removed.

Under the same Act of 1692 it became possible to acquire a settlement in various other ways, such as paying rates, holding parish office,
becoming indentured as an apprentice, or, most important, 'by service',
which meant working for the same employer for at least a year, a concession often evaded by engaging a man for only 364 days at a time.
Women could, after 1692, obtain a settlement by marriage; legitimate
children, in the official phrase, 'followed' their mother's settlement,
and illegitimate ones took that of their birthplace. In all these compli-
cated provisions lay the seeds of future confusion and endless legal
argument, for the various members of a family might have different
settlements. 'This single clause of a short Act of Parliament', wrote
the great economist Adam Smith in *The Wealth of Nations* in 1776,
'has occasioned more doubts and difficulties in Westminster Hall',
where the law courts were then situated, 'and has been more profitable
to the profession of the law than any other point in English juris-
prudence'. About the nature of the law he had equally little doubt. 'To
remove a man who has committed no misdemeanours, from a parish
where he chooses to reside, is an evident violation of natural liberty
and justice...There is scarce a poor man in England...who has not,
in some part of his life, felt himself most cruelly oppressed by this ill-
contrived law of settlements.'

In 1795 the Law of Settlement was amended to ensure that no one,
however poor, should be removed until he or she actually became a
charge on the rates, apart from pregnant, unmarried women, who were
potentially the most expensive, and hence the most unpopular, of all
paupers. At the same time the justices were empowered to suspend a
removal order until a sick person was fit to travel, a concession
extended in 1809 to the sufferer's family. But mere age did not count
as infirmity within the meaning of the Act; in 1834 there was widespread public criticism of the treatment of a poor old man of ninety
who was sent back to Steyning in Sussex from Bristol in midwinter
with 'neither rug nor coat to cover him', and, on changing coaches in
London, had to be taken to St Bartholomew's Hospital 'in the most

pitiable state from the effects of filth, cold and want of nourishment, having travelled three days and three nights', the doctors advising that 'to have taken this poor old creature on his journey . . . would have been fatal'.

Three years later, however, occurred an even worse case involving a man called William Withers, who had become crippled with rheumatism while en route from Bristol to London, and been forced to spend six weeks in the parish workhouse at Walcot, Bath. In April 1837 he was sent back to Clerkenwell travelling 'outside' on a coach 'on the windward side' despite 'a considerable fall of snow and a severely cold wind'. The journey began at six in the evening and by half way, 'at Newbury about one o'clock in the morning,' Withers had to be lifted off the coach and 'helped into the tap-room' where 'the waiter . . . humanely gave me a glass of brandy and water which was held up to my mouth to swallow'.* By the end of the journey Withers had lost the use of his hands and feet—and then, in bed, a permanent invalid at Clerkenwell, he learned the absurd truth that the removal order was, the court decided, invalid on technical grounds, and he would have to be sent back to Walcot before he could legally be removed from it. Meanwhile Clerkenwell, being legally entitled to pass on the bill for his support to Walcot, treated him royally. 'Whatever he asks for he has', *The Times* reported. 'If he fancies fish, flesh or fowl, he is supplied with them. He smokes a great deal, and has two pots of porter a day, besides two glasses of gin or wine, as he thinks proper.' This cheerful bulletin cannot have made very happy reading in Bath, for the Walcot overseers now faced a bill for £500 legal costs, plus the original removal expenses and five shillings a week for Withers' support until he either died or was fit to be returned to them so that he could again be sent back to London—this time legally.

Clerkenwell was not the only place that was generous to other parishes' paupers and to an underpaid parish doctor a patient, who had hitherto received only the scantiest medical attention, suddenly became, on being sentenced to be removed, someone to be cherished. The perpetual curate of the parish of Hinton Charterhouse, near Bath, for example, was understandably bitter against 'the absurd law of settlement', after someone who 'for some trivial reason belonged to the parish' was ordered to be brought back there from his real home in London, his departure being postponed while he was ill. 'For six

*The inn concerned was probably *The Pelican*, the birthplace forty years before of the Speenhamland system (see Chapter 3).

weeks boxes of pills and mixtures were daily inflicted without inter-
mission', 45 mixtures being prescribed in 43 days, plus 17 boxes of
pills. 'The man, his wife and daughter, were then sent down by coach,
in care of a parish beadle, like criminals in the custody of a policeman,
and delivered up, in due form, to the overseer of Hinton, together
with the doctor's bill, which amounted to £6. 12*s*. and the charges
for maintenances, £2 16*s*., in all nearly £10 . . . As soon as this man
and his family were set at liberty they returned to seek their
maintenance as before.'

The actual expenses of removals, despite a not ungenerous scale of
allowances paid to the escorting officers—Middlesex in 1846 paid
7*s*. 6*d*. for 'delivering' a deportee more than ten miles, plus 4*d*. a mile
for transport—were only a minor part of the overall bill. Where the
money really melted away was in the law courts, for to win a case became
to many parishes a matter of honour. The Law of Settlement, the first
historian of the Poor Laws observed in 1764, had already 'led to a
greater quantity of litigation and hostile divisions than any other law
on the statute book—aye, or than all the other laws from the time of
Magna Carta put together'. 'Everything was deemed fair in resisting
or enforcing a claim of settlement', wrote one of the first Poor Law
Commissioners appointed in 1834. 'The most astute counsel and
attorneys exercised their wit and exhausted their learning, much no
doubt to the advancement of their own professional reputation; but . . .
with serious cost to the parish.' This was often serious indeed. The
125 inhabitants of the tiny parish of Hermitage in the Cerne Abbas
union faced around this time a legal bill of £112 after successfully
challenging in the courts an attempt by the neighbouring village of
Minterne Magna to unload onto it responsibility for a woman with
five children, while Minterne Magna had to pay equally heavy costs,
plus those of maintaining the family concerned until the children
grew up.

Some unions on principle fought every case up to the highest level,
assembling witnesses from every corner of the country. In 1815, when
removals and associated legal expenses over the whole country cost
£287,000, there had been appeals against the initial judgement in no
fewer than 4,700 cases while in one case, involving a widow, in 1826,
enough was spent, one of the lawyers noted, in bringing witnesses
from Lancashire, Wiltshire and Hampshire by stage-coach and in
payments to members of his profession, 'to have established the poor
woman and her family in a comfortable way of livelihood' wherever

they wished to live. In fact they were forcibly removed from Lancashire to London, then sent to Salisbury, then back to London and finally to Southampton, 'the place of settlement of her husband's grandmother some fifty or sixty years ago'.

In 1846 the law was amended to prevent the removal of any widow within twelve months of her husband's death, but even this humane concession was evaded. The parish authorities of Canterbury around 1866 decided to remove a pregnant woman and her small child before she became a widow, when her husband, then under sentence of death, was executed for murder. Grief-stricken mother and small infant were thereupon heartlessly driven off to London while the husband was still in the condemned cell, and dumped in the workhouse of St Paul's, Covent Garden, where the husband had been born, which made it his wife's place of settlement by marriage. There they stayed until the kindly workhouse doctor, deeply shocked by the case, published an account of it in the press, which raised £25, enough to send the woman back to her real home in Canterbury, where, seven years later, she was, he found, still doing well in service.

In 1847 both Houses of Parliament had formally resolved 'that the Law of Settlement and Removal is generally productive of hardship to the poor and injurious to the working classes, by impeding the free circulation of labour', but no legislative action had followed.

In one case in the 1850s, published in the *The Times* (a constant opponent of Poor Law abuses throughout the period) a hitherto respectable carpenter, who had himself paid poor rates in the wealthy West End parish of St George's, Hanover Square, was ruined by a fire and was sentenced under the Law of Settlement to move back into the depths of rural Sussex, where, in the days of his prosperity, he had rented a cottage worth £10 a year while working for a local member of the aristocracy. Only a public appeal by his former employer's wife, a duchess, saved him from being returned there in disgrace as a pauper.

In the following decade a Poor Law Inspector drew attention to the experiences of another tradesman who had lost his job just before he had lived long enough in the same place to become irremoveable. He was ordered back to his native county, and even though, before he could be moved, he had recovered his old job and ceased to draw relief, he was still carried off forcibly from the place where he had both a home and work to a place where he had neither, being, said the Inspector, 'like a madman with rage'.

Few laws can have been so constantly and convincingly criticised, so violently abused; few can have been more self-evidently unreasonable and unjust, yet few have lasted so long. Incessantly attacked, universally reviled, the Law of Settlement endured because those who were its victims lacked the power to change it, and those who had the power to repeal it lacked the will. Even the most dim-witted, precedent-bound Victorian MP must have known in his heart, so overwhelming and unanimous was the evidence, that the Law should long ago have been abolished, but there were, as with every reform, always reasons why it should not be done this session and Parliament eased its collective conscience by steadily shortening the qualifying period of residence needed to escape removal. It was cut to five years in 1846, to three in 1861 and to one in 1864. Beyond this MPs refused to go and although many parishes sensibly agreed between themselves not to carry out the law, even as late as 1907 more than 12,000 people were being removed each year—a classic example of how the evil that bad law-makers do lives after them.

Besides revealing the reluctance of governments to remedy an acknowledged injustice, the Law of Settlement had an important consequence: its existence caused the better-off classes to accept that if the poor were to be legally tied to their native place, society must accept responsibility for supporting them there, perhaps in some central institution. The corollary to the Law of Settlement was the workhouse.

2 Much Oppressed

> From want of proper regulations and manage-
> ment...workhouses have not had the desired
> effect, but the poor in many places instead of
> finding protection and relief have been much
> oppressed thereby. *Preamble to Gilbert's Act*,
> 1782

By the end of the eighteenth century local government in England was
in an almost impenetrably tangled state. The basic unit for most acti-
vities remained the parish and almost any form of communal enter-
prise, involving several parishes even in the same town, required a
private Act of Parliament to set up a special body solely for this purpose.
Within a single city, lighting and paving, sewerage and water supply
might be controlled by a network of separate, and perhaps conflicting,
authorities and coping with poverty was sometimes almost an afterthought. Thus the statutory basis for the administration of poor relief
in Leeds was a single clause in a private Act providing powers for
lighting and cleaning the streets.

The pioneer city in setting up an effective workhouse was probably
Bristol, where the parishes combined under a special Act to create a
single authority, the Corporation of the Poor. The initiative was taken
by a merchant called John Cary, who in 1698 opened the 'New Workhouse' on what were for the time enlightened principles. He began by
operating systematic visiting of all those on 'out-relief', receiving
weekly allowances in their own homes. 'Where we found them oppressed, we stood by them,' wrote Cary. 'For some we provided clothes,
for others work. When they wanted houses, we either paid the rent or
became security for it.' He also brought together a hundred orphan
girls who were taught spinning, to make them self-supporting, given
'wholesome diet and good beds to lie on' and had 'leave to walk on the
hills with their tutresses, when their work was over, and the weather
fair ... We offered good nourishment ... beef, peas, potatoes, broth,
pease-porridge, milk-porridge, bread and cheese and good beer (such
as we drank at our own tables), carrots, turnips, etc...and bought the
best of every sort.'

Cary was enthusiastic about the results claiming that 'our old people are comfortably provided for; our young children are well looked after...our boys and girls are educated to sobriety and brought up to delight in labour...' During the next few years similar establishments were opened in several other cities. The first person to think of the workhouse as a deterrent, rather than, like Cary, as a place of shelter, seems to have been Matthew Marryott, a country gentleman of Olney in Buckinghamshire, who pointed out that 'the advantage of the workhouse to the parish does not arise from what the poor people can do towards their own subsistence, but from the apprehension the poor have of it'.

Parliament was sufficiently impressed by Marryott's success in carrying out his ideas to pass in 1723 an Act sponsored by Sir Edward Knatchbull, and often known by his name, which authorised any parish to set up its own workhouse. Within a few years one hundred and fifty parish workhouses had been opened, though larger places, seeking to combine their parishes to build a joint workhouse, still had to go through the burdensome procedure of obtaining a private Act, of which more than a hundred were passed between 1601 and 1834, while another eighty general Acts concerning various aspects of the Poor Law, all introduced by private members, were passed during the same period. Almost every place that opened a workhouse reported at first immense savings from the new system. Bradford, in Wiltshire, having built a workhouse in 1727, claimed by 1731 to have cut its poor rates from £800 to £400. At Beverley, in Yorkshire, a local resident recorded how:

> ... on opening the workhouse notice was given to the poor that the weekly pension was to cease and that such as were not able to maintain themselves ... might apply to the governors of the workhouse. The result of this was that though before the opening of the house 116 persons received the parish allowance, not above eight came in at first and in the subsequent Winter [1727-8] the number in the house never exceeded 26, although all kinds of provisions were very dear and the season was sickly.

Already the word itself was acquiring a special significance. 'A workhouse,' wrote a Maidstone man around 1727, 'is a name that carries along with it an idea of correction and punishment and many of our poor have taken such an aversion to living in it, as all the reason and argument in the world can never overcome.' A book published in 1725 gave details of more than a hundred successful workhouses and in 1735, despite Parliament's reluctance to order any parish to do anything, William Hay MP carried through the House of Commons a Resolution 'that it is necessary for the better relief and employment of the Poor that a public workhouse...hospital...house of correction, be established...in each county', although a subsequent Bill never achieved a third reading.*

Additional impetus was given to the workhouse movement by the publication in 1753 of a pamphlet by the magistrate and novelist, Henry Fielding, *Proposal for making an Effectual Provision for the Poor*, which advocated creating in Middlesex, and, if successful there, in every county, an enormous workhouse for 5,000 inmates, the discipline becoming stricter the further you went inside. Thus anyone who could produce a pass testifying that he was 'an honest industrious person . . . incapable at present of procuring work in this neighbourhood' would be accommodated overnight in the comfortable outer buildings; long-term unemployed would live, under stiffer conditions, in 'the county house', further inside the walls, while the incorrigible idlers, estimated at 600 of the 5,000, would be pushed further on still into the 'house of correction' inside the inner courtyard. Fielding planned to hire out the resident paupers, rather like a prison chain-gang, to any willing employer within twenty miles, a pauper being forced to remain with him for a year, though his wages would be compulsorily saved to provide him with a small nest-egg on his release.

This ingenious scheme was never tried out, but the idea of large workhouses, covering several parishes, began to gain ground. The reason was not hard to understand: even as late as 1831 nearly 7,000 of the 15,000 parishes in England and Wales contained fewer than 300 people, and another 5,400 had under 800. These small and isolated rural communities, where a literate man was a rarity, were clearly far too small to support an effective workhouse of their own. As early as 1697 the philosopher John Locke, then working as a Civil Servant, had suggested in a pamphlet *A Report of the Board of Trade to the Lords Justices respecting the Relief and Employment of the Poor* 'Hundred Houses', each serving several parishes and run by a board of representatives from each parish. Several similar Bills were introduced into Parliament, only to be dismissed as invading the sacred right of each locality to run its own affairs. A few determined

---

*The same Resolution condemned the Laws of Settlement as 'very difficult to be executed, vexatious to the poor and of little advantage to the public'.

members persisted, however, and in 1756 a local Act led to the setting up of a new authority to serve 28 parishes in Suffolk, its aims being neatly set out in a pamphlet published ten years later:

> We propose to incorporate to administer proper comfort and assistance to the sick, infirm and aged, introduce sobriety and virtue among them, and in an especial manner to render their children useful to society by acquainting them with their duty towards God and man, whence many are saved from an untimely end and all of them enabled to acquire an honest livelihood and so not remain any longer a burden and reproach to our county. We incorporate, too, to ease the respective parishes in their rates and also to feed and clothe the objects of their care with that plenty and decency that their wants and situation can reasonably require . . . Our design, too, is to invite gentlemen to attend to the state and conduct of the poor—a concern which, however weighty and important in itself . . . is not . . . regarded by them in the separate parishes . . . seeing that but very few owners of any fashion live where their estates are situated, and . . .whenever it happens that they do reside there, the indelicacy and rudeness of parish meetings oblige them never to come to such assemblies.

So, in June 1756, fifty clergy and squires assembled at an Ipswich inn to launch the new-style workhouse on its way, under the chairmanship of a famous and gallant sea-dog, Admiral Vernon, the local MP, who generously donated a site for the workhouse on Nacton Heath and lent £1,000 to set the scheme under way. Two years later the 'Nacton House of Industry' proudly opened its doors and all the paupers and vagrants of the district, not over-willingly, shuffled inside.

'The poor came to us', claimed the founder of the scheme, 'in a most miserable and filthy condition; they were clothed in rags, and some of them, the children especially, almost literally naked. We expected and were prepared for this so that, to prevent the introduction of vermin, before they were admitted they were shaved and cleansed thoroughly by washing in warm water, and then all new clothed throughout from head to foot.' Another observer, writing eight years later, was almost lyrical about the results. 'Many children', he wrote, 'are rendered useful who otherwise would have figured nowhere but in a landscape of Gainsborough's . . . lying upon a sunny bank half naked, with their bundles of stolen wood by their sides.' And not merely were the poor better cared for; within four years

£2,000 had been saved and the poor rates had been cut by half. Other places, particularly in East Anglia, hastened to obtain Acts to build their own 'Hundred Houses'. By 1776 eight, housing from 150 to 350, were in operation in Suffolk and Norfolk alone, the inmates being employed, according to the locality, in making fishing nets and ropes or corn-sacks and plough-lines.

As so many writers complained in so many periods, however, the poor seemed strangely ungrateful for the benefits lavished upon them. When several parishes in the Woodbridge area of Suffolk ceased in August 1765 to pay out-relief and instructed the former recipients to seek food and shelter in the new workhouse, they made instead 'a riotous appearance at the *White Hart* at Wickham Market when the Directors of the Hundreds . . . were assembled for the execution of their Poor Act. A very large body of them, consisting of some hundreds of men, women and children, armed with cudgels and such weapons as they could procure, surrounded the house, threatening destruction to all those who should interest themselves in the building and establishment of a House of Industry'. After doing £500 worth of damage to one workhouse, the mob was finally confronted at Nacton by a force of dragoons, summoned by the magistrates, which charged and scattered them. The lesson proved effective and enduring. Local opposition to the workhouse ceased for a generation and fifty years later one commentator could still write, as though describing a tourist attraction, 'Suffolk is famous for its workhouses. Most of the estates of the nobility and ancient families appear to be embellished with one.'

Apart from the workhouse, designed to cope with all categories of the local poor under one roof at public expense, there were by the end of the century in the London area alone, excluding the great voluntary hospitals, more than a hundred charitable establishments of various kinds, including alms-houses with places for 1,300 old men and women, lying-in hospitals for poor mothers, and a 'Magdalen House for the admission of seduced females'. The most famous of all was the Foundling Hospital, opened in 1741 thanks to the efforts of a retired sea-captain, Thomas Coram, who had been shocked at seeing the bodies of unwanted infants 'who had been murdered and thrown upon dunghills'. The 'Foundling' was soon overwhelmed with applicants, especially after 1756 when Parliament voted it £10,000 on condition that any new-born baby was automatically admitted.

In March 1760, following wholly unjustified charges of mismanagement and immorality on the part of the governors, the Parliamentary grant was withdrawn and, soon afterwards the last child, baptised as Kitty Finis, was admitted. But 'the Foundling' left behind it one valuable legacy in the shape of an increased concern for unwanted children, especially on the part of one of its governors, Jonas Hanway, an eccentric, multi-purpose reformer, mocked by his contemporaries and best remembered by posterity for pioneering the use of the umbrella. A self-made business man, he devoted himself to innumerable causes, from campaigning against the evils of tea-drinking to urging the need for a police force, but his most enduring and honourable obsession was the protection of the unwanted child. In London, he discovered, seven out of ten children taken into parish care died before the age of two; the average for the country as a whole was three out of ten. Many metropolitan parishes did not even keep a register of such children since the turnover was so vast.

Hanway's revelations led to two new laws. One, in 1762, known as 'The Act for keeping poor children alive', required parishes to maintain proper records of all children admitted to their workhouses, so that at least the death rate in the most unhealthy institutions and the identity of 'nurses' whose charges invariably died would be known. The other, still called 'Hanway's Act', in 1767, laid down that all children in the public care between the ages of two and six should be moved at least three miles out of London and that any babies taken into care in parishes should be sent out to the country within a fortnight of their birth, unless being breast-fed by the mother. Each parish was also required to appoint a number of 'noblemen and gentlemen' to serve as 'guardians of the parish poor children', both while they were in the workhouse and later, at the age of seven or eight, when they were found employment outside. Their fate in the expanding mills of Lancashire and Yorkshire is too well-known to need recounting here. A Preston man, born in 1794, recalled seeing in childhood the workhouse apprentices from the neighbouring factory in church on Sunday 'crooked-legged, becoming deformed with having to stop the machinery by placing their knees against it'.

The other method used in the eighteenth century to dispose of workhouse children was to apprentice them to private employers, either by requiring each ratepayer in turn to accept one for at least a year, under penalty of a £10 fine or, more commonly, by offering a premium of up to £10 to anyone who would take a child off the parish's hands. The former system often led to an unwilling ratepayer, saddled with an unwanted mouth to feed, doing his best to reclaim his investment in overwork and general maltreatment, while the dangers of the premium system were later eloquently pointed out by a Poor Law official:

A parish apprentice is regarded as a defenceless child, deserted by its natural protector and whose legal Guardian, the parish, is only anxious to remove the burden of its maintenance, at the least possible cost . . . The premiums offered with the children proved an irresistible temptation . . . Ten pounds or twenty pounds was wanted to pay a pressing demand, to avoid a warrant of distress for rent due or a bill for their stock in trade . . . The class of tradesmen to whom the children were apprenticed were generally petty tradesmen of a low caste, who were usually unscrupulous in their neglect of their duties to the children . . . means were often taken to disgust the child with his occupation and to render his situation so irksome as to make him abscond. It will appear from the evidence that many children have been thus driven to ruin.

While Hanway was campaigning in London for the rights of the workhouse children, another philanthropic reformer, a typical 'country gentleman' from Staffordshire, Thomas Gilbert, was pouring out a stream of pamphlets on his particular remedy for pauperism. Although he, too, found time to draft many ingenious schemes, from charging road-users extra on Sundays, to heavily taxing dogs, Gilbert's dominant interest was to carry through a Bill to authorise any group of parishes to unite for poor relief purposes and to build a common workhouse. 'It has been my study in forming this Bill', he wrote in 1775, 'to see the poor well accommodated and treated with great humanity, but kept under a strict conformity to the rules and orders of the house, to encourage good behaviour, sobriety and industry, by proper rewards.'

Gilbert, who had entered Parliament in 1763 at the age of 43, finally carried his scheme through the House of Commons in 1775, only to see it narrowly rejected by the Lords. But, in an amended form, it finally became law in 1782. 'From want of proper protection and management . . . workhouses have not had the desired effect, but the poor in many places instead of finding protection and relief have been much oppressed thereby', complained the preamble. The Act authorised the merging of parishes for poor relief purposes wherever two-thirds of the rate-payers were in favour; any parish within ten miles of the workhouse, which was supposed to be in every sense the hub of the union, being eligible to join. It was adoptive only—there was no

compulsion on parishes to form unions and, a most important
exception—it was not intended to apply to the able-bodied who were
to be found work, or given relief outside. By its author's death,
in 1798, very few 'Gilbert unions' had been formed, though by 1834,
they numbered 67, covering 924 parishes, or about 1 in 16 of all those
in England and Wales.

The vast majority of workhouses continued, therefore, to serve
individual parishes and many, no doubt, resembled the one described
by the poet George Crabbe, son of an Aldeburgh schoolmaster,
in 1783:

> Their's is yon house that holds the parish poor,
> Whose walls of mud scarce bear the broken door;
> There, where the putrid vapours, flagging, play,
> And the dull wheel hums doleful through the day,
> There children dwell who know no parents' care,
> Parents, who know no children's love, dwell there!
> Heartbroken matrons on their joyless bed,
> Forsaken wives, and mothers never wed,
> Dejected widows with unheeded tears,
> And crippled aged with more than childhood fears;
> The lame, the blind, and far the happiest they!
> The moping idiot and the madman gay.

The most comprehensive picture of the condition of the workhouse
at this time was provided by a baronet, Sir Frederick Eden. He was
shocked by the complaints of high prices heard on all sides in 1794-5,
and by the small-scale riots which often accompanied them, when
desperate labourers' wives stole from market stalls the goods they
could not afford to buy or left behind the price they considered fair.
Eden made enquiries from well-placed correspondents all over the
country and published the results in 1797 in *The State of the Poor*,
a vast, 3-volume work which went into astonishing detail about
hundreds of parishes. Eden was content to pass on the information
he collected, modestly remarking that 'to offer detailed plans of
reform...much exceeds my abilities'. The result was a Doomsday
Book of working-class life, outside the workhouse as well as in it.

That the workhouse could be a decent place was shown by the
report on the one in Liverpool, which housed 1,120 people from a
population of 55,000:

The workhouse...is in many respects constructed upon an eligible plan. The old people are provided with lodging in a most judicious manner: each apartment consists of three small rooms, in which are one fireplace and four beds, and is inhabited by eight or ten persons. These habitations are furnished with beds, chairs and other little articles of domestic use that inmates may possess; who thus being detached from the rest of the poor, may consider themselves as comfortably lodged as in a secluded cottage. The most infirm live on the ground floor; others are distributed through two upper stories. They all dine together in a large room ...The children are, principally, employed in picking cotton, but are too much crowded together, 70 or 80 work in a small room. About 50 girls are bound apprentice to a person who attends in the house and employs them in sprigging [i.e. embroidering] muslin. The house receives ... from 1*s*. 6*d*. to 2*s* 6*d*. a week, according to their proficiency.

Few workhouses were as well run as this. At Oxford, Eden's reporter commented, 'The house is exceedingly dirty' and 'in many respects the very reverse of what a house of industry ought to be. No regular quarters appropriated to the sick, aged or infirm; nor nurseries for the children. The sexes strongly intermixed in their eating, sitting rooms and also in their [work] shops and exercise grounds; nor any separation between their wards and sleeping grounds.' This was an important point, if idle paupers were to be prevented from quietly taking things easy during working hours.

At Norwich, where 700 paupers were housed under 'dark and confined' conditions in a former monastery, forty beds were crowded into each room and the occupants had to queue up for their food and take it back to eat on their beds, while the workhouse in Louth, in Lincolnshire, only built in 1791, was almost as ill-equipped:

The house is not erected on a good plan; the only entrance to the house yard etc. is through a door not 4 feet wide and only 8 feet high, which is very inconvenient for the taking in of hay, or bringing out manure etc. The stair-case is narrow and steep. There are no regular working rooms or detached apartment for the reception of the sick. There is one large lodging-room for the men and another for the women, each containing 14 beds, which are partitioned from each other by deal-boards at each end and on one side; the view of a sick neighbour is thereby in a great measure obstructed, but to a feeling mind the sense of hearing must frequently convey very disagreeable ideas . . .

Discipline in these small local workhouses varied from the ferocious to the non-existent. At Kendal and Kirkland, in Westmorland, where in 1793 there were 143 in the workhouse out of a population of 8,000, anyone caught smoking in his room was liable to 'six hours in the dungeon' while the penalty for not wearing your pauper's badge, marked 'KK Poor', was four hours confinement there. 'Persons convicted of lying', the same rules laid down, were 'to be set on stools in the most public place of the dining room, while the rest are at dinner, and have papers written on their breasts with these words written thereon, INFAMOUS LYAR, and shall lose that meal'. At the other extreme were places like Alsford, in Lincolnshire, where the workhouse had only fifteen occupants, half of them under fifteen years old and the rest elderly. 'As an old woman, who is almost a pauper, is the governess of the house,' reported a local resident, 'she is opposed by clamorous competition for power and is scarcely able to retain the reins of government, much less to enforce good order and industry.'

On the whole it was in very small workhouses such as this that conditions were worst and the constant throwing together of so many different types of pauper must have made life miserable for them all. It is hard not to feel sorry for the fourteen inmates of the tiny workhouse at Buckingham, 'consisting of women, children and old men, some of whom are insane', or for the solitary man at Winslow, who shared the building with fifteen old women and children. At Wetherall, in Cumberland, a brand-new workhouse, open for only a month, contained seventeen children and only seven adults, among them a blind labourer of 40, a lame man of the same age, an 88-year-old farmer, 'L.P., a spinster', who had had 'two bastard children' and 'was already rather idiotish' and 'N.G. aged 52. She became a little insane in consequence (it is supposed) of her husband who was a blacksmith, having deserted her'.

Two facts emerged clearly from Eden's great survey: that few of those in the workhouse could support themselves; and that society was failing in its duty to provide them with a decent and civilised place of shelter. By this time the earlier faith in the workhouse was already shaken, due to the disagreeable discovery that it cost far more to support a pauper inside the workhouse than outside. Often a pauper, living at home and helped by relations, would settle for a shilling a week parish allowance to stay out of the house, while to maintain him inside, allowing for clothes and medical attention as well as food and shelter, cost at least 2s. 6d. to 4s. a week and often more. Paying off the capital cost of the building, or the interest on the loan used to build it, could also prove a crippling burden and many of those who had helped to provide one of the grandiose East Anglian 'Hundred' houses in the mid eighteenth century lived to regret it. The House of Industry for Mitford and Launditch, in central Norfolk, for example, which had taken two years to build, and cost £10,000 plus £5,400 for furniture and equipment, was still saddled with a £10,000 debt twenty-four years later. In 1764-41 parishes near Clavering in Essex, had proudly 'incorporated' by private Act and borrowed £7,000 for this purpose. Thirty years later, with the house still partly unpaid for, the new union's paupers were costing it £2,261 a year, while their earnings amounted to only £189.

It had often been argued that the real value of such large and impressive workhouses lay in discouraging people from entering them, but here, too, disillusionment soon replaced the first high hopes, as, following an initial drop, the number of paupers, and the cost of the poor rates, both began to rise again. At Witham, in Essex, the opening of a workhouse had cut the poor rates by half, to £230; by 1785 they had soared to £2,899. At Hemel Hempstead, expenditure, reduced in 1722 to £388, had climbed by 1785 to £966. In mid century the universal claim had been that the poor rates were halved by building a workhouse. Now it was clear that over the long term they had, instead, doubled, trebled or increased tenfold. Even the ambitious, pioneering 'Hundred House' at Nacton near Ipswich had failed to fulfil its early promise. Within a year of its opening out-relief had begun to creep back; by the end of the century food and materials were almost openly being stolen from the union, cash was being embezzled, and costs were soaring. The reason was a loss of interest, and hence of supervision, on the part of the local gentry. When meetings of the Directors and Guardians were summoned at the workhouse often from 28 parishes no one turned up at all. Only when the management committee met at the hospitable *White Hart* at Wickham Market, could a bare quorum be scraped together, the very hostelry, ironically, where the rioters protesting at the founding of the workhouse had once held the first Directors imprisoned.

3 The Road to Ruin

Unless some efficacious check be interposed...
the amount of the assessment will continue, as
it has done, to increase... producing thereby the
neglect and ruin of the land. *Report of the Select
Committee on the Poor Laws*, 1817

On 6 May 1795 — twenty 'discreet persons' of the county of Berkshire
— justices, clergy and landowners — met at the *Pelican* inn at Speenhamland in Newbury to debate how to relieve the prevailing distress.
They concluded that current wages were often inadequate even to
support a man in work and ought to be made up out of the poor rates to
a basic minimum, fixed according to the price of bread and the size
of his family. When the large 'gallon' loaf, weighing 8 lb 11 oz, cost
1s. 0d., it was estimated that he needed 3s. 0d. for his own support,
plus 1s. 6d. for every other member of the family; when the loaf cost
1s. 4d. he was entitled to 4s. 0d. for himself, plus 1s. 10d. for each
dependant, and so on. The allowance varied by 3d. to the man and 1d.
to his family for every 1d. the price of a loaf rose or fell beyond
a shilling.

There was nothing particularly new about the Speenhamland
scheme, or Berkshire Bread Act, as it was known, but never before had
a single scale, which prevented trouble-making variations between
parishes and individuals, been so rapidly and widely adopted. Some
counties still favoured different, and usually less generous, scales of
their own, but the principle was almost universally accepted. The
'bread money' rapidly came to be regarded as the poor man's right, his
compensation for the enclosure of his common land, and for being
chained by the Act of Settlement to his own parish, even when it had
no work for him. In 1796 Parliament, fearing the spread of revolutionary sentiments from France to Britain, repealed as 'inconvenient
and oppressive' and 'injurious to the comfort and domestic situation
and happiness of...poor persons' all restrictions on 'out-relief', and
empowered the magistrates to countermand the refusal of any
parish overseer to relieve any applicant they considered deserving.
Soon, almost everywhere, 'out-relief', formerly granted reluctantly,

at least to the able-bodied, was both given as a duty and demanded as a right. Within a generation, from being the rare exception, it became the almost universal rule.

Quite apart from its allegedly harmful effect on the recipient—and the automatic subsidising of wages removed all incentive for the labourer to ask and the farmer to concede a living wage—the Speenhamland system soon proved exceedingly expensive. In theory the vestry which ran each parish, chosen by election or virtual self-appointment from among the better-off ratepayers, had every reason to keep payments from the rates down, but in practice all too many profited by being generous. Thus,in the town of Morpeth eleven of the twenty members of the Select Vestry were connected with the licensed trade and well aware that much out-relief ended up across their own bar counters.* 'Relief in kind', designed to prevent such abuse, benefited those grocers, bakers and shoemakers who sat on the vestry and who granted the poor 'tickets' on their own, or their friends' shops, while landlord vestrymen rarely favoured sending rent-owing families into the poorhouse, preferring to make the payment of the arrears a first charge on any allowance they were given. The Overseers of the Poor, responsible for the day-to-day administration of relief on behalf of the vestry, were even more open to corruption or, occasionally, intimidation.

In one Kent village the overseer received no salary, but was recompensed for his trouble, an official investigator discovered, through the resulting 'perquisites of his office. The poor-books were kept on the counter of the village shop, owned by his brother, and applicants for relief were told "Apply at the shop", where they were also informed of the decision of the vestry, which met at the public house'. The paupers were, 'dealt with at the vestry according to their docility at the shop', where prices were up to 40 per cent above those elsewhere, and the same man owned fourteen cottages, occupied by paupers, for which, in his capacity as overseer, he paid himself £46 10s. a year rent, while the poor rates were collected by his servant, going from door to door, his wages being charged to the parish. †

Many overseers were uneducated, the parish books being kept instead by the overseer's wife or sister. The official already quoted

*A Select Vestry had wider powers than an ordinary vestry, and its membership and the right to vote for it was restricted to the wealthier ratepayers.
†Following the reforms of 1834, this overseer was dismissed, and eventually committed suicide.

described one such unpaid helper, 'a fine healthy, blooming girl of eighteen. As her plump, red finger went down the items it was constantly clearly its official duty to lay aside a profusion of long black corkscrew ringlets, which occasionally gambolled before her visitor's eyes.' Her spelling did not match her charms; the two longest lists she maintained were headed 'low women' and 'hilly jittimites', a phonetical rendering of 'illegitimates'. 'These impressed accountants', the same investigator found, 'were often grossly illiterate and in many cases dressed in hob-nailed shoes and common smock-frocks... scarcely able to read or write.' One overseer assured him that his parish *had* no population, the word being new to him, and when asked for the paupers' dietary proudly led his visitor to the workhouse dining room and pointed to the table. The reaction of one parish to proposals for reform was this admirably forthright letter, long preserved in the Poor Law Board's archives:

It will never do us any good to alter the law in our parish as our parish is very small and there is no probability of alter our kearse at all. There is no persons fitter to manage the parish better than ourselves. T.T., Oversear.

Even in parishes which were basically well run traditional extravagances could, under such administration, easily creep in. One parish account book, inspected in the 1830s, contained a recurring item, 'For sparrows 2*s*. 6*d*'. The paupers were paid fourpence a dozen for shooting the birds and, miraculously, their bag always came to just this amount. Britwell, Shropshire, went one better, with the mysterious entry: 'For birdkeeping, moles and sparrows, £20', while the explanation of the overseer of another parish for the regular charge of 1*s*. 0*d*. for tolling the church bell was that 'The clerk is a dreadful man and always threatens to fight me, whenever I wants to drop that 'ere charge!' More puzzling, and still unexplained, was this striking entry in another parish's books: 'To John Bell for cutting his throaght 12*s*.'

Not infrequently, boredom or distaste had led the few responsible inhabitants of a place to allow all the power to fall into the hands of one man. One of the government's Assistant Commissioners, appointed to enquire into the state of the Poor Law in 1832, recorded verbatim this conversation in a parish in south-eastern England:

'Who is the overseer?'
'Mr Parker'.

'Who is the assistant overseer?'
'Mr Parker'.
'Who collects the rate?'
'Mr Parker'.
'Who determines on the rate?'
'Mr Parker'.

and so on through every parish office. The versatile Mr Parker, in addition to his duties as overseer (a post he had held for 36 years) was village constable and master of the workhouse, and in private life a farmer and a butcher. He was a self-made man with, it turned out, no faith in education and not a child in the workhouse could read or write. 'Why', he explained, 'it be a thing quite injurious. When I finds a promising child I sets him to work.'

Where no willing Mr Parker existed, the job of overseer was often taken on by the leading ratepayers in rotation and sometimes two overseers served turn and turn about with results that could be ludicrous. At Newbury, where each was in charge for alternate fortnights, one employed a baker friend to supply the workhouse with bread, while his successor cancelled the contract and ordered the paupers to bake their own. One, anxious to separate the different categories of inmates, ordered various alterations to the building; his rival, no believer in classification, had them removed, the master of the workhouse, understandably bemused, commenting: 'I left the wall standing and when I came back after an absence of forty-eight hours it was clean gone.'

Occasionally overseers behaved in an extraordinarily high-handed way, as at Effingham, Surrey, in 1814, where after forcing a pauper called Henry Cook to marry a woman from Slinfold whom he had seduced and made pregnant, the parish decided, when both wife and child ended up in the workhouse, that the simplest and cheapest long-term solution would be for Cook to sell his wife:

The overseers accordingly directed Chippen to take her to the town of Croydon on the next market day, where, as...previously arranged, the husband met them. The wife was then sold by the husband to one John Earl for one shilling. The following receipt was written out on a 5s. 0d. stamp and attested by Daniel Cook, the brother of the husband, and Chippen, the governor of the workhouse:
Received by John Earl, the sum of one shilling in full for my lawful wife, by me...Henry Cook. 17 June 1815.

Earl and his bride-to-be were then sent, at public expense, to his native parish, Dorking, where they were married, the Effingham overseers generously providing a leg of mutton for the wedding breakfast. Here the couple lived happily together for some years, acquiring eight children, until, on discovering that his marriage was not legally valid, Earl deserted the family. Eventually the woman and her children ended up back in Effingham, their parish of settlement by the woman's legal marriage to Henry Cook. Here, in 1836, they were still living on poor relief, the parish now having nine mouths to feed instead of the original two.

At Cambridge when one parish tried to force a pauper to marry a girl he had made pregnant, there was an 'unseemly wrangle at the alter as to terms', the prospective groom, not very gallantly, offering to marry the girl or not, according to whether his parish or hers paid him best. Equally embarrassing scenes were not uncommon, especially after 1809 when the magistrates, on the unsupported word of a pregnant woman, could order the man she named as the child's father to support it if he refused to marry her.

A Berkhamsted vicar described how he had 'repeatedly known instances of men being apprehended under a bastardy warrant, carried off to a surrogate for a licence and brought to church, in the same morning, to be married...I have seen the handcuffs removed from the man at the church door as I approached...with the constable and overseer as witnesses to the marriage.' There were even more outrageous cases where some totally innocent man was accused, as in this story recounted in 1836, about events that had taken place a few years earlier:

> At Barnstaple...a clergyman of high character for piety and usefulness one morning received a visit from a woman apparently large with child. She opened the conversation by calling attention to her rotund appearance and told him that unless he made her a handsome allowance she would swear the child to him... Distracted and alarmed for his reputation he consented to pay the demand and appointed her to call on his solicitor... The solicitor, a shrewd man, at the appointed time secreted two women in a small room divided from the place of interview by a folding door. The woman arrived and commenced the negotiation...The lawyer expressed his doubts of the cause producing the appearances; might it not be dropsy? The female was indignant at the suggestion. The lawyer, however, doubted,

and before she was aware of the intention, handed her through the folding-door into the presence of the two women...His gravity was presently disturbed by repeated peals of laughter and the two women rushed in with a large pillow, and the threatening mother, in very slender figure. The same pillow had been hawked about at other houses with better success.

The power the magistrates had formally been given in 1796, and had long enjoyed in practice, to reverse decisions made by the parish overseers, was based on the belief that, as men of education, social standing and integrity, remote from the pressures of everyday village life, they could be trusted to prevent injustice and extravagance. In fact, however, they often proved merely gullible, as the Rev. Thomas Spencer found on taking up his living as perpetual curate of the village of Hinton Charterhouse near Bath in 1826:

> The applicant for relief would first endeavour to work upon the feelings by a pathetic tale; and, if narrated by a female gin-drinker, it would be accompanied with many tears. If this failed there would be a joke to put the overseer in a good humour; and lastly threats of revenge, to make him afraid. If the overseer continued unmoved in a few days a summons would reach him from the magistrates, which confided...triumph to the pauper; who, remaining an hour or two at each public house on the way, told how the justices had ordered him more allowance for doing nothing than others could earn by hard work.

The Rector of Little Massingham, Norfolk, where nearly half the 150 inhabitants were on out-relief, was equally critical of the magistrates who, at about the same date, addressed to 'The churchwardens and overseers of the poor' a peremptory order to provide relief for 'a healthy strong young man' who had appealed to them after the parish had turned his request down. 'The bearer, Thomas------, complains to me for want of relief from you. As he seems to be in a distressed situation, if you do not satisfy him you must meet him here tomorrow morning by nine o'clock.'

'To the magistrates the old poor laws gave power such as no aristocracy before ventured to assume', wrote one critic a few years later:

> They sat as mediators between the employers and the employed and decided what the one party should pay and the other receive. They could indulge their love of power without appeal

and their benevolence without expense. An active county magistrate in a pauperised district, fond of business, influence, and popularity became the terror of the overseers, the idol of the labourer for twenty miles around.

So troublesome was the whole business of administering poor relief that many places, from the early eighteenth century onwards, 'farmed' their poor out to a private contractor. Advertisements in local newspapers invited competitive tenders under the heading 'The poor to let', though there was considerable variation in the categories covered, some contractors undertaking to maintain only the 'outdoor' poor, others only the 'indoor', while many agreements specifically excluded children or cripples or lunatics. Although the system clearly lent itself to abuse, the terms were rarely over-generous. At Chalfont St Peter, Buckinghamshire, for example, in 1812, the 'farmer' promised to provide 'comfortable and sufficient lodging and washing, and...good and sufficient meat, drink and every other article necessary' for all those sent to the workhouse, to pay 'such sums of money as the church-wardens and overseers or any justice of the peace...shall...direct and appoint' to those on out-relief, to supply free midwives for women in labour, education for the workhouse children and free burial for the parish dead. For all this he received only £812 a year, though the parish provided the workhouses and paid an extra 1s. 6d. a week for any illegitimate child admitted.

At Faringdon, in Berkshire, the contractor in 1832 undertook to supply 'good meat dinners three days at the least in each week' and 'mutton or such other diet as may be suitable' for the sick in the poor-house, but his annual fee, £2,200, was still £600 a year less than the parish had formerly spent. He kept costs down by enforcing strict discipline and hard labour in the workhouse, which discouraged applicants, while firmly refusing out-relief to able-bodied bachelors.

But in most places out-relief to all categories of pauper grew remorselessly between 1795 and 1834, provoking scores of indignant pamphlets to be penned in country vicarages. From Norfolk the Rev. C.D. Brereton pointed out that of 21 inhabitants of Little Massingham buried in recent years no fewer than 11 had had the letter 'P', signifying pauper, marked in the parish burial register after their names, but even this posthumous mark of disgrace had failed to shame the living into saving for their old age.

From Hinton Charterhouse in Somerset, where half the population of 734 were on relief, supported by only 100 ratepayers, the Rev.

Thomas Spencer publicly repudiated his previous illusions about the deserving poor. 'These paupers', he discovered, 'formed the great support of the lowest grade of beer-houses; there they spent their evenings in noisy revelry'—so that their 'loud singing and mirth' kept awake the sober, early-to-bed ratepayers who paid for their drinks. Far from the overseer terrorising the paupers, here it was the paupers who lorded it over the authorities. 'I no longer wondered,' wrote Spencer, 'that the parish money was bestowed plentifully upon the sturdy and able-bodied and that small sums were given to the sick and bed-ridden. The latter ... were the only cases in which the overseer dared to practise economy. Thus to the strong man was given 2*s*. to 12*s*. a week; and to the helpless poor from 1*s*. to 2*s*. 6*d*. a week.' The rural magistrates were equally critical of the practice of supplementing wages, or the Speenhamland system, than which, protested a Dorset magistrate, 'a more unjust, a more impolitic, a more illegal, a more destructive measure, never was devised . . . In a few more years, this . . . demoralising system, which was creeping slowly and steadily round the land, would have insinuated itself into every cottage and have completely changed the character of the English peasantry.'

Even more harmful than making up the income of a man in work, most parishes believed, was allowing him to be completely idle and much ingenuity was expended in trying to keep the unemployed occupied. Under the 'roundsman' system, able-bodied men on out-relief were sent round the ratepayers, who, if they had nothing useful for them to do, often ordered them to dig holes and then fill them in, or to deliver 'letters' of blank sheets of paper. To prevent their paupers earning money on the sly some parishes compelled them to stay on public view, producing such curious entries in the parish accounts as this one in an Oxfordshire village: 'Paid for men and boys standing in the pound six days £6 7*s*. 0*d*.'

The overseer for Princes Risborough in Buckinghamshire, where in 1834 a hundred able-bodied men were on relief, described with shocked surprise how 'The paupers used to stand about in the market place. I have often seen them slink behind and get away on seeing a farmer or any person coming who they thought was going to employ them.' At Pollington in the West Riding of Yorkshire, the overseer admitted that paupers put to repair the roads 'work only four hours per day ... they sleep more than they work, and if any but the surveyor found them sleeping they would laugh at them'.

One young Oxford undergraduate, spending the long vacation of

1828 at a friend's home in the village of Deddington, found his faith in his fellow men sadly shaken:

> Some time after breakfast we daily noticed a number of men of all ages creeping rather languidly past the window . . . There were forty of them, no doubt the same day after day. I followed them. In less than a mile they stopped at a large and rough stone-quarry, formed themselves into groups, sat down, talked. After a time they rose and set to work. This was well after ten o'clock . . . Starting long before four o'clock, I met them returning to the town.

After taking Orders, the same man, now perpetual curate of the Warwickshire village of Moreton Pinkney, was disturbed at 11.15 one night by a loud noise from the inn, a quarter of a mile away, and hurried there, ready to reprove his wayward parishioners:

> Then came a voice from the parlour, 'Oh come in, take a seat, Mr Mozley, we are glad to see you'. I walked in and found twenty or thirty farmers. This was the monthly apportionment of the paupers, that is, the whole labouring population, among the larger ratepayers. All the former had assembled at the door, or the yard behind, or in the offices, on in front to hear their fate. The appropriation was sometimes equally disagreeable to the master and to the man, and it was no uncommon thing to begin or terminate a month's association with a fight on the green.

In some places there was a formal auction of unemployed labourers, like a slave market. At Ash, in Kent, this took place every Thursday and the best men, 'knocked down' for a promised wage of 12 shillings a week, cost the parish nothing, but those who fetched only eight or ten shillings had their income made up from the poor rates.

The clinching argument, which by 1830 had convinced almost every clergyman, MP, magistrate and landowner that a drastic change in the Poor Laws was overdue, was the soaring cost of the poor-rates. Parliament had been staggered when, on Thomas Gilbert's insistence, the first national returns had been called for in 1776, revealing a total expenditure in England and Wales of £1,531,000, excluding charges for other services often bracketed with them. By 1783 the total had reached £2 million, by 1803 more than £4 million and by 1832 £7 million. This was not really a frightening sum—it equalled only about 10s. per head of the population—while the often-repeated statement that the whole labouring population was being 'pauperised' was also untrue; over the whole country about one person in ten was living wholly or partly on poor relief, but many of these were old or infirm. More serious was the unequal incidence of the rates; in an agricultural county, like Sussex for example, they reached 23*s*. 0*d*. in the pound, or twice the national average.

Farms, the public was told, could not be let because of the burden of the poor-rates, and whole villages were being abandoned. This too, was a wild exaggeration. The only example ever quoted was Cholesbury in Buckinghamshire, where after the poor-rates had risen from £10 to £367 in one generation, the farmers had given up their farms, the parish overseer had closed his books, and the poor, abandoned by their masters, had assembled outside the rector's door demanding food. Cholesbury was wholly exceptional—its five farms had clearly been inadequate to support its 140 inhabitants—but the dramatic myth, as so often, was preferred to the prosaic truth, and even kind-hearted people began to believe at last that something was seriously wrong in rural England.

The factor which finally prompted the governing classes to tackle a situation which had long been called intolerable was probably the widespread agricultural riots which occurred all over the southern counties in the autumn and winter of 1830. By continental standards they were a very tame affair. There was a good deal of machine-breaking, a general demand for a modest increase in wages, some damage to property, a few stones thrown—and little more. The whole movement was easily put down, and the numerous transportations, and the handful of hangings, which followed, left the countryside apparently quelled for good. Was this not the moment, many citizens now asked, with the Napoleonic wars safely over and the danger of revolution averted, to call a halt to pampering the poor, before further demands were made at the point of the pitchfork and the blazing torch?

Behind the unspoken desire to teach the poor a lesson, lay a more fundamental fear, that unless stern action were taken, the population must rise to a point where the land could no longer support it. This fear had exercised a morbid fascination over the minds of the governing classes ever since 1798, when the clergyman Thomas Malthus had proved to his own satisfaction and theirs, that poor relief was bound in the long run to be disastrous, since it encouraged the poor to marry and have children whom they could not hope to feed. Society should instead, he urged, be forcing labourers to marry late and have fewer children. A few of Malthus's contemporaries kept their heads, like

William Cobbett, who published in 1831 a satirical play, *Surplus Population*, ridiculing his ideas, but most readily succumbed to the alarmist doctrines advanced in the *First Essay on Population*, convincing themselves that it was their duty to treat the poor harshly now to save the country from future starvation.

But though Malthus and his disciples were the real long-term enemy, to the half-starved labourer in the villages the immediate cause of his sufferings seemed to be the recently invented reaping and threshing machines and in 1830 these were the first target of the rioters almost everywhere. The Industrial Revolution had meant, too, the loss of the small-scale out-work—button-making, paper-box making, lace-making—which had enabled many farm labourers' families to supplement their income from small-town manufacturers now driven out of business. Finally, the labourer's deepening poverty and sense of despair were made worse by the policy of enclosures.

Between 1760 and 1810 about five million acres of common fields were legally appropriated and fenced off by private landowners, robbing the labourer not merely of the right to grow crops, graze cattle or gather fuel on them, but destroying the last shreds of his economic freedom. To some respectable citizens this seemed indeed an advantage. 'The use of common land by labourers operates upon the mind as a sort of independence', complained one Shropshire resident in 1794, preventing 'that subordination of the lower ranks of society which in the present times is so much wanted'.

For nearly twenty years after 1815 Parliament constantly debated the problem of rural pauperism, even considering, without result, such forward-looking ideas as contributory old age pensions from the age of fifty, and a statutory minimum wage. In 1817 a Select Committee on the Poor Laws reported, as expected, that they were ruining the country and that 'unless some efficacious check be interposed... the amount of the assessment will continue, as it has done, to increase till it shall have absorbed the profits of the property on which the rate may have been assessed, producing thereby the neglect or ruin of the land... and the utter subversion of that happy order of society so long upheld in these kingdoms'. Despite this dramatic warning no legislation followed, and when one MP, ahead of his time, proposed a graduated income tax to be used solely for poor relief, Lord Castlereagh dismissed the idea on the grounds that 'from it's not having been done up to the present day... there was some difficulty hanging about it'.

In 1821, another MP, cast in the same reactionary mould as Castlereagh and like many self-styled 'reformers' of the Poor Laws eager in fact to see them abolished altogether, proposed a Bill to limit the poor rate in the future to the level it had reached in the previous year. predicting that 'Unless some attempt were made to stem the torrent, they must at no distant period absorb all the land in the kingdom.' He wanted to end all relief, except to the old or sick, leaving the able-bodied man and his family to take their chance of starvation, but Parliament was not convinced, though in the following year another MP proposed a more gradual reduction in parish aid, acknowledging that suddenly to 'pluck such large means of subsistence from the very mouths of the poor...would be...most unwise and...dangerous'.

The findings of a Select Committee on Labourers' Wages, appointed in 1824, revealed, however, that in the worst-paid county, Dorset, a man in full employment earned no more than 6s. 0d. or 7s. 0d. a week, which made subsidising the income of men in work unavoidable. 'In some counties, as in Bedfordshire', admitted the Committee, 'this payment usually begins when the labourer has a single child, wages being so low that it is utterly impossible for him to support a wife and child without parish assistance.'

Amid such a generally gloomy picture anyone with a more cheerful tale to tell was sure of a ready hearing. Although there was later some dispute as to whom was first in the field, the real pioneer in trying out the remedy which was soon to be applied everywhere seems to have been the Rev. Robert Lowe, who on becoming rector in 1818 of Bingham, near Nottingham, found that he had inherited a 'completely pauperised' village, where 'the poor were... masters... turbulent, idle, [and] dissolute' and 200 of the 1,600 population were idling their days away on the parish pay-roll. Within a few years Lowe had totally tamed his parishioners and cut the poor-rates by three-quarters, having 'devised means for rendering relief so irksome and disagreeable that none would consent to receive it who could possibly do without it'. The 'irksome and disagreeable means' consisted in virtually abolishing out-relief and offering instead food and shelter in the workhouse, where conditions were made so strict that soon all its former occupants, apart from a dozen or so senile, sick or insane people with nowhere else to go, had voluntarily moved out. Lowe urged upon his cousin and fellow clergyman and magistrate, the Rev. John Becher, at nearby Southwell, the adoption of the same 'system of forcing able-bodied paupers to provide for themselves through the terror of a well-disciplined workhouse'.

The Bingham experiment was now repeated on a far larger scale at Southwell, where Becher invited a retired sea captain already living in the parish, George Nicholls, to take over as Overseer of the Poor and to apply the same principles. The results were equally striking for soon the recipients of out-relief among the 3,000 inhabitants of Southwell numbered no more than eleven, mainly widows, for very few applicants accepted the alternative of 'indoor relief'. So satisfied was Becher with what had been achieved that in 1823 he called a meeting of all the local gentry and overseers, who decided to form a new Thurgarton Union under Gilbert's Act, uniting 49 parishes, with a combined population of 14,000. The union spent more than £5,000 on putting up a brand-new workhouse, opened in 1824, which 'conducted upon the principles of salutary restraint and strict discipline'. Economy and discomfort were the watchwords. The paupers shuffled about the garden in wooden-soled clogs, since 'They are more economical' and 'If tendered for sale they excite suspicion', while no recreation of any kind was provided, the only reading matter being tracts supplied by the Society for Promoting Christian Knowledge. In his pamphlet, *The Anti-Pauper System*, published in 1828, Becher drew a moral that was to be widely quoted by other reformers: 'The advantages resulting from a workhouse must arise not from keeping the poor in the house but from keeping them out of it.'

spread rapidly, largely as a result of *Eight Letters on the Management of our Poor...in the Two Parishes of Southwell and Bingham*, which appeared in a Nottinghamshire newspaper in 1822 and were then reprinted as a 70-page pamphlet. The author, *Overseer*, of whom much more will be heard, was in fact George Nicholls. His thesis was already familiar but it was argued with conviction and authority, in blunt outspoken language, free of the cumbrous classical and biblical quotation, and sly gibes at other authors, in which so many writers on the Poor Laws indulged. 'Poor houses—not to be made too comfortable', ran the heading to Letter No. 111, which urged that 'instead of yielding to the impulse of our feelings, by giving relief whenever the semblance of distress approaches us, the overseers must resolutely refuse all parochial aid, excepting...relief to the aged, infirm and impotent.'

For the able-bodied meanwhile, only the workhouse was to be available, run in the strictest possible way:

The poorhouse ought to be so . . . conducted as that the labouring part of the community might not behold it better furnished, better provided, more comfortable than their own homes. They should not, in Winter, see all its chimneys cheerfully smoking, when their own homes are cold . . . nor all comforts . . . pervading the abode of the pauper, when their own habitations presented scenes of want and wretchedness . . . The dread of a poorhouse has decreased in about the same ratio that pauperism has augmented . . . owing to the humane and well-meant endeavours to improve these receptacles, which are now so very generally converted into abodes of comfort and even of apparent elegance . . . I wish to see the poorhouse looked to with dread by our labouring classes and the reproach for being an inmate of it extend downwards from father to son . . . Let the poor see and feel that their parish, although it will not allow them to perish through absolute want, is yet the hardest taskmaster, the closest paymaster and the most harsh and unkind friend they can apply to.

Here was the classic statement of the philosophy behind the deterrent workhouse and in many a country rectory or squire's mansion, on many a rural magistrates' bench, it awoke an approving echo. It was now to be seen whether it would prove equally influential among the politicians at Westminster.

4 Doing their Duty

His Majesty's Ministers thought it their imperative duty as a government to apply themselves at once to this question. Lord Althorp introducing the *Poor Law Amendment Bill*, 18 April 1834

In November 1830 the High Tory Duke of Wellington, having rashly declared that the state of parliamentary representation in England was already perfect, was forced to resign. He was succeeded as Prime Minister by a moderate Whig, Lord Grey, whose government was preoccupied with the struggle for the great Reform Bill until June 1832, when it at last became law. Four months earlier, in February, the government had announced the setting up of a Royal Commission on the Poor Laws, drawn from both parties. The Tories were only too happy to co-operate in changing the law, especially since, as Sir Robert Peel later confessed, had they tried to do so themselves they would probably have failed.

The Commissioners, drawn from both parties, ultimately numbered nine. The chairman, Charles Blomfield, Bishop of London, who afterwards became a great campaigner for sanitary reform, was ably supported by another bishop who was an authority on the Poor Laws, the veteran MP, Sturges Bourne, who had presided over the Select Committee of 1817, and the most respected economist of the time, Nassau Senior, still only forty-two, who as a young man in his twenties, witnessing the abuse of out-relief in his father's Wiltshire parish, had there and then 'resolved to reform the English Poor Laws'.

Dominating the Commission were the ideas of the famous political thinker Jeremy Bentham, who died in 1832, and his disciples, known as 'the philosophic radicals'. Bentham believed that normally the citizen could best serve both his own needs, and those of society, by pursuing a policy of self-interest, but that in some areas government must take a more positive role, as in caring for the sick or insane. He thus made a sharp distinction between the able-bodied, who not merely could but should be left to support themselves, and the 'impotent poor', on whose behalf government must intervene, probably through a new 'Indigence Relief Minister' responsible to Parliament. Like many reformers Bentham worked out his schemes in meticulous detail, preparing blueprints for a model circular workhouse-cum-prison known as a 'panopticon', and personally designing the paupers' beds.*

On no one did Bentham's opinions make more impact than on a young freelance journalist called Edwin Chadwick. His occupation earned him such insults as Mr 'penny-a-liner' Chadwick. If Malthus and Bentham created a climate of opinion in favour of making the Poor Law harsher, Chadwick was the zealous and resourceful administrator who translated their ideas into orders and regulations. He is probably the most important figure in the history of the workhouse: the institution, as it developed in the late eighteen thirties, reflected not merely his acute and tidy mind, but also his personality, austere, unlovable and inhumane. Perhaps his childhood, with a father who suffered a series of misfortunes in business before settling down as a provincial editor, and a stepmother (his own mother having died while he was small) had left its mark. Perhaps he was influenced by the fact that, coming from a socially dubious background of writers and Radicals, and lacking a university education, he was never accepted by his superiors as one of themselves.

Self-opinionated, unbelievably industrious (he regularly worked twelve hours a day and rarely took holidays), totally lacking in any capacity for self-criticism, Chadwick had both the defects and the virtues of the self-made man. At eighteen he had started his career as a clerk in an attorney's office; at twenty-three he bravely decided to read for the Bar, while supporting himself by writing secretly—such was the scorn in which the newspapers were held—for *The Times* and other publications. His great opportunity came when he made the acquaintance of John Stuart Mill, then a junior civil servant and later the outstanding 'utilitarian' philosopher. Mill introduced him to Jeremy Bentham, whose personal assistant and favourite protégé he rapidly became.

In 1832, shortly before Bentham's death, Chadwick was offered a temporary post in the civil service, as one of twenty-six Assistant Commissioners, or special investigators, appointed by the recently created Royal Commission 'to make a diligent and full inquiry into the

*See Appendix.

practical operation of the Laws for the relief of the poor in England
and Wales...and to report whether any, and what, alterations,
amendments or improvements may beneficially be made in the said
laws'. Most of the Assistant Commissioners were young barristers
or ex-officers, each of whom was eager to make a name for himself.
But none carried out more devotedly than Chadwick his printed
instructions to 'communicate with the clergy, magistrates and parish
officers...to be present at vestry meetings and at the petty sessions
of magistrates'; none more faithfully and voluminously complied with
the requirement to 'keep a full daily journal of his proceedings and give
to the Central Board, at least once a week, a sketch of his proceedings';
none was more whole-heartedly steeped in the Benthamite beliefs
which most of the Commission shared. Within a year, Chadwick, now
aged thirty-three, had been promoted 'from the field' to become a
Commissioner himself; within two he had become, as will be mentioned later, the key figure in the greatest reshaping of the Poor Law
since Tudor times, and the builder, if not the architect, of the
Victorian workhouse system.

Before 1832 even the most basic facts about local conditions were
unknown in Whitehall; the first census had not been taken until 1801,
while the registration of births and deaths had still not begun. Now
the Assistant Commissioners, eager, able and determined, penetrated
into 3,000 parishes and townships, about one in five of all those in
the country, conducting what the minister chiefly responsible
described as 'the largest, the most comprehensive, the most important'
official enquiry every undertaken, and sending back to London a
flood of information that eventually filled twenty-six volumes
totalling 13,000 large pages.

The Assistant Commissioners were expected to establish two basic
points: that out-relief was ruining the country and demoralising the
labouring classes, and that the only obvious alternative to it, the
workhouse, was ineffective if every petty parish was left to run its
own. These charges were not hard to substantiate, as one stern critic
of the old Poor Law, Sir Francis Head, was soon reporting from East
Kent:

> A considerable number of poor-houses . . . are composed of old
> farm-houses, more or less out of repair. Some are supported by
> props—many are really unsafe—several, lying alone in a field, seem
> deserted by all but their own paupers—some stand tottering in a
> boggy lane, two miles from any dwelling and in many cases they

are so dilapidated, that it seems a problem whether the worn-out, aged inmate will survive his wretched hovel, or it him.

But while these workhouses were too mean for their purpose, others were too grand:

The River Workhouse, which is on the old Dover Road, is a splendid mansion ... 'delightfully situate' and fit for the residence of a 'county member' or 'nobleman of rank'. Modestly retired from the road it yet proudly overlooks a meandering stream, and the dignity of its elevation, the elegant chasteness of its architecture, the massive structure of its walls, its broad double staircase, its spacious halls, the lofty bedrooms and its large windows, form altogether 'a delightful retreat', splendidly contrasted with the mean little rate-paying hovels at its feet ... To be sure, it is not yet paid for—though many of its aged paupers, unable to reach its summit ... prefer to live 'cheap and nasty' in a shed which adjoins it ...

In Suffolk, another official observer, Dr James Phillips Kay, (later better known as Sir James Kay-Shuttleworth, the educational reformer) was equally struck by the 'palatial character' of one of the surviving 'hundred-houses':

The hundred-house eclipsed some of the neighbouring mansions ... I wandered through lofty and spacious rooms and halls, well-lighted, clean, well-ventilated, but almost untenanted. In the dining-hall the tables were arranged for the guests; in the chapel the benches were prepared for the worshippers. On every side I beheld an apparatus intended to produce some great result. The yards were surrounded by extensive workshops; large rooms in the main building were filled with machinery but the only busy thing in the establishment was the spider, which had spun its web on the spinning wheels. There were two large enclosures without the building ... 18 acres of grounds were attached to the house, on which five cows, eight pigs and a flock of fat poultry were kept. There was a monastic character of quiet and plenty about the establishment. Nevertheless, this house contained only a few aged and decrepit men and women in the corners of some of the spacious rooms, and some sturdy paupers who lounged on the sunny benches in the yard, watching a group of children at play.

A particular target of criticism by most reformers, including Chadwick, was 'the general mixed workhouse', which catered for every type of pauper. As Sir Francis Head explained, after a tour of the Kentish workhouses:

> In the smaller ones minute classification has been found impossible; all that is effected is to put the males of all ages into one room and all the females into another. In either case, the old are teased by the children, who are growled at when they talk and scolded when they play, until they become cowed into silence. The able-bodied men are the noisy orators of the room; the children listen to their oaths and, what is often much worse, to the substance of their conversation, while a poor idiot or two, hideously twisted, stands grimacing at the scene or, in spite of remonstrances, incessantly chattering to himself. In the women's hall, which is generally separated by only a passage from the men's, females of all ages, of all shapes, live with infants, children and young girls of all ages.

One result of this throwing together of different types of inmate, complained Head, was that those who had nothing wrong with them were far too comfortable, as in another workhouse he visited where he found 'a room full of sturdy labourers . . . in hobnailed half boots and dirty smock-frocks... sitting round a stove with their faces scorched and half-roasted. As we passed them they never rose from their seats and had generally an over-fed, a mutinous and an insubordinate appearance.' Far from reforming the poor, Head protested, the workhouse was itself promoting immorality. He inspected one where adolescent boys and girls 'were, strange to say, separated only till dusk', and others where 'the rooms were divided, but they met together, when it so pleased them, in the yards.'

'We often', Head complained, 'found a large attic in the roof, used as a dormitory for the "able-bodied labourers and their wives". Each bed was separated from its neighbour by an old blanket. The beds were identified with letters of the alphabet and, as Head pointed out with heavy irony, 'if husband A should happen unintentionally to make a mistake, the posting of his shoes at the end of the wrong bed—might perchance throw B, C and D and the rest of the connubial alphabet all wrong'. But the real objection to allowing married couples to stay together in the workhouse was that it helped to make life there tolerable:

'As soon as the workhouse life shall become wholesomely repulsive,' Head summed up, in a classic statement of Malthusian doctrine, 'the rude, amorous ploughman will pause a little before he contracts a marriage which must ere long make him its inmate; whereas if (as in the old system) it were to offer him not only the blooming girl of his heart, but heavy lumps of savoury foods, the warm bribe, like the bride, must be irresistible.'

Yet while the workhouse was far too luxurious to deter the able-bodied, it was also failing to provide a comfortable place of shelter for the elderly and infirm. In one workhouse Head discovered:

> . . . a group of worn-out men, with nothing to do, with nothing to cheer them, with nothing in the world to hope for, with nothing to fear; gnarled in all sorts of attitudes, they look more like pieces of ship-timber than men. In another room are seen huddled together in similar attitudes a number of old, exhausted women, clean, tidy but speechless and deserted . . . in large, airy bedrooms we found men and women all bed-ridden. As we passed between two ranges of trestles almost touching each other, nothing was to be seen but a set of wrinkled faces which seemed more dead than alive. Many had been lying there for years; many have been inmates of the poorhouses for fourteen, fifteen or eighteen years; few seemed to have any disorder. They were wanting nothing, asking for nothing, waiting for nothing, but their death. In the Coxhead United workhouse we found the following group seated round a small fire:
>
> David Kettle, aged 99
> William Pipson, aged 90
> John Hollands, aged 90
> Edward Baldwin, aged 76
> John Latherby, aged 75

They were all learning towards the lad Latherby who in a monotonous tone of voice was very slowly reading [a] prayer to them... On our taking the pamphlet from his hands to copy the words . . . the five men never altered their attitudes, but during the whole operation, sat like the frozen corpses which in Napoleon's retreat from Moscow were found still in the attitude of warming their hands round the white, dead embers of their departed fire.

To prepare public opinion for a major change in the law Lord Brougham, the Lord Chancellor, the driving force behind the movement for Poor Law reform, commissioned the leading woman political writer of the time, Harriet Martineau, to write a series of *Poor Law*

Tales based on material sent in by the Assistant Commissioners. She was a natural choice for the assignment, for she had already published an immensely successful series of short novels on similar lines, entitled *Illustrations of Political Economy*, the underlying message being that 'The plea... that every individual born into a state has a right to subsistence from the state is false. All encouragement to the increase of population should be withdrawn.'

The *Poor Law Tales*, despite similarly impeccable Malthusian sentiments—Miss Martineau was a great admirer and personal friend of Malthus*—did little for her reputation, while Brougham defaulted on his personal share— £25—of her promised fee of £100 a story. (She had, perhaps, little cause for complaint since it was her constant thesis that misfortune ennobled the character.) In all Harriet Martineau's stories everyone who resorted to outdoor relief came to a disastrous end, and only those who bravely endured a period in the workhouse retained any chance of ultimate prosperity. She even denounced 'the gift of coals and blankets to the poor at Christmas' as encouraging them to multiply beyond their means, describing the whole Poor Law as 'a gangrene of the state'. To the modern reader it seems hard to believe that her badly-written and blatantly biased stories can ever have exerted much influence, but they were certainly widely read and helped to make their author a popular celebrity, besieged by crowds wherever she went.

Far more substantial, it seems likely, was the impact of the Assistant Commissioners' reports, which were sent down by despatch box to Lord Brougham, at his country seat in Westmorland, as soon as they arrived in London, and eagerly scanned by him every night after dinner, for colourful and quotable passages. (His days at this period were spent in walking on the Lake District hills with a London journalist to whom he held forth on his desire to raise 'the poor man out of the degradations of poverty'.) In 1833 a volume of *Extracts* from the reports was published and, with the help of a secret government subsidy, fifteen thousand copies were distributed, to great effect. Not merely were doubting Whigs won over but even convinced Radicals. The tailor Francis Place, at sixty-two the elder statesman

---

*Their friendship was furthered by the curious fact that Malthus's voice was one of the few she could hear clearly without using an ear trumpet; she had been almost deaf since the age of 18 and was in 1832 a confirmed, and somewhat soured, spinster of 30.

of the working-class movement, was persuaded by the argument that only the abolition of out-relief could restore the labourer's self-respect and make him fit to rule himself. If appointed to enforce a sterner Poor Law, 'I would' he wrote to Harriet Martineau, 'help to carry it on with all my heart and soul'. That great apostle of liberty, the philosopher John Stuart Mill, also succumbed to the government's propaganda campaign. The evidence, he told the writer Thomas Carlyle, 'showed the thing to be unspeakably bad'.

In March 1834 the 300-page *Report of the Royal Commission* was published, after being drafted by Chadwick and rewritten by Nassau Senior. Its key proposal was 'that except as to medical attendance ... all relief whatever to able-bodied persons or to their families, otherwise than in well-regulated workhouses . . . shall be declared unlawful, and shall cease'. To administer a new Poor Law, in which out-relief was restricted to the old and other 'impotent' poor, the Commission proposed the merging of all the parishes in the country into a number of unions, on the lines of the existing 'Gilbert unions', with each run, like them, by a committee elected by the ratepayers, to be known as Guardians of the Poor. Each parish, however small, would choose at least one Guardian, and the unions would be supervised by a Central Board of Commissioners, appointed by the government but not directly responsible to Parliament.

The heart of each union was to be the workhouse, which should in future be the sole form of relief for the able-bodied. It was only from fear of the workhouse, one Assistant Commissioner was quoted as believing, that 'new life, new energy, is infused into the constitution of the pauper; he is aroused like one from sleep...He surveys his former employers with new eyes. He begs a job—he will not take a denial—he discovers that everyone wants something to be done. He desires to make up this man's hedges, to clear out another man's ditches, to grub stumps out of hedgerows for a third...He is ready to turn his hand to everything.' To achieve this happy result, insisted the *Report,* 'the first and most essential of all conditions was that the able-bodied inmate's 'situation on the whole shall not be made really or apparently so eligible as the situation of the independent labourer of the lowest class'. Realising that the conditions under which the 'independent labourer' often lived meant that the workhouse inmate might be better fed, clothed and housed than he was at home, the Commissioners planned to make his life unpleasant in other ways, as George Nicholls had so successfully done at Southwell. The pauper would be forced to undergo such indignities as wearing a prison-style uniform, be subjected to the hardest and most tedious labour human ingenuity could devise, and, above all, be separated from his wife and children, for in the new union workhouses 'rigid classification' was to be the rule. Nor could the labourer sacrifice himself to save his family. Relief granted to any member of it, the *Report* advised, should count as relief to all and they must either enter the workhouse together or stay outside and starve.

Finally the *Report* proposed, not before time, a major simplification in the laws governing settlement and illegitimacy: the parish of settlement of all legitimate children born after the introduction of the New Poor Law would be their birthplace; those born out of wedlock would, as in the past, 'follow' their mother's settlement. The whole responsibility of supporting such children would, the *Report* recommended, now fall on the mother 'and any relief occasioned by the wants of the child shall be considered relief afforded to the parent', which meant that both unmarried mother and baby must either starve or enter the workhouse together.

The fathers of illegitimate children, on the other hand, were now to escape scot free, since, advised the Commission: 'All acts which punish or charge the putative father shall, as to all bastards born after the passing of the intended act, be repealed.' This was not, as was later alleged, a particularly blatant example of sex discrimination, but a recognition of the fact pointed out by Malthus that one could always identify the mother of an unwanted child and that the more a woman had to lose, the more firmly would she resist a would-be seducer.

Even before the *Report of the Royal Commission* had been published, a Bill, largely drafted by Nassau Senior, had been prepared to give effect to its recommendations. The Cabinet approved it within a fortnight and at a series of meetings during the following month, many of which Edwin Chadwick attended, the rest of the government was won over. Curiously enough the only real opposition came from some aristocratic ministers, who feared a 'rural rebellion' if, as planned, out-relief to the able-bodied was everywhere abolished on a fixed date in 1835, and it was therefore agreed instead to taper it off, union by union, as each became ready for the great reform. Even more curiously, the real driving force behind the change was the one minister with an outstanding reputation as a friend of the poor, Henry, Lord Brougham.

Brougham, who was fifty-six in 1834 and at the height of his

powers, was a man of outstanding intellectual ability. He had
written a major scientific paper in his teens, had helped to found
The Edinburgh Review, the most influential literary and political
magazine of the century, in his twenties, had become a nationally
famous barrister at thirty, after successfully challenging the
Orders in Council which crippled British trade during the Napoleonic war. Two years later he was an MP and, before long, the
leading orator in the House of Commons. He was hailed as a popular
idol after championing the cause of Queen Caroline against the
disreputable George IV, and was on the side of every popular and
progressive cause: the abolition of slavery, child labour and military
flogging, the reform of the penal system, the encouragement of trade
unions and popular education. A contemporary described him as 'a
titled tribune of the people' and his reputation for eccentricity— *Punch*,
in a pun on his name, described him as 'a vehicle for progress, though
...rather shaky about the pole'— probably did him no harm among
his working-class supporters, always indulgent to aristocratic foibles.*

In 1832, with the last great measure he had sponsored, the Reform
Bill, safely on the statute book, Brougham turned his restless energy
and towering talents to an equally far-reaching reform of the Poor
Laws and he became the government's chief spokesman on the subject
in the House of Lords, over which he presided as Lord Chancellor.
But the real battle was expected to be fought in the House of Commons,
where the Bill was introduced on 17 April 1834 by the Chancellor
of the Exchequer, Lord Althorp. He took the now familiar line that
the existing state of affairs had 'most of all...been injurious to the
labouring classes themselves' and that therefore the government had
'thought it their imperative duty...to apply themselves at once to
this question'. Some people, he admitted, felt that all state assistance
to the poor should be abolished, but 'so long as we were accessible, not
only to the feelings of religion but to the dictates of humanity', this
was impossible. The Bill was, however, a major reform which would
repeal or amend nearly 500 existing Acts. Althorp pointed out that
100 parishes already had a deterrent workhouse, either under private
Acts or as members of 'Gilbert unions' and he defended the proposed
Central Board on the grounds that it would be exempt from 'local

*He was, for instance, said to have played 'Hot and cold', a form of 'Hunt the
slipper', with the Great Seal at a country house party, and had a disturbing
habit of asking visitors 'You don't think I'm mad, do you?'

prejudices and local feelings', though any 'general order' it made would only come into force after being laid before MPs for forty days.

In this, and subsequent debates, it was in fact the 'unconstitutional' or 'despotic' powers of the new Commissioners, and the introduction of the dangerous new idea of centralised control, that came in for most criticism. One speaker did complain that the Bill seemed 'to treat poverty as a crime' and another objected to 'enclosing men whose only offence was unavoidable poverty within the walls of a workhouse' but he spoke, *Hansard* recorded, 'amidst much noise and interruption'. The second reading was carried by 299 to 20, the third by 187 to 50, the only major amendment, which removed the Commissioners' powers to dissolve existing unions, being of no benefit to the poor though potentially troublesome to the new Commissioners.

In the Lords the Bill had an even easier passage and it was hardly necessary for Brougham to speak, as he did, for four hours, commending to their lordships the joys of 'laborious poverty' compared to 'wealthy idleness'. The Lords responded by carrying the second reading by 76 to 13. The Bill even survived the fall of the government, though on a different issue, and the replacement of Lord Grey by Lord Melbourne, whose usual reaction to ministers proposing new legislation was 'Oh, why can't you leave it alone?' 'Never did a great measure pass through Parliament more easily, we might say more triumphantly', commented Nassau Senior. 'All parties united to give force to the principle and perfection to the details of a measure which they felt to be essential ... to the welfare ... of the country.'

Almost the only prominent political figure to denounce it, in fact, was William Cobbett, who undertook, in an *Open Letter*, to support the Tory Sir Robert Peel if he would campaign for 'a repeal of the Poor Law Bill, complete and entire'. His offer was not accepted and Cobbett's course was now almost run, for a year later, in June 1835, he died.

The Government triumphed despite the almost united opposition of the national press, which had little time to rouse opinion before the Bill had been hustled through Parliament. The hostility of the newspapers was unexpected. According to Harriet Martineau, after the Bill's first reading 'ministers went home to bed with easy minds, little imagining what waited them at the breakfast table. It was no small vexation to me, on opening *The Times* at breakfast on the 18th, to find a vehement and total condemnation of the new Poor Law. Everybody in London was asking how it happened.'* One rich Whig MP was so infuriated that, on the very morning the 'Thunderer' unmasked its guns, he hurried out and bought for £15,000 the ailing *Morning Chronicle* to put the government's case.

The Times's attitude was blamed by many ministers on Brougham, who was said to have had a violent quarrel at Brooks' Club with its editor, Thomas Barnes, or to have offended him by contemptuously tearing up a note from Lord Althorp asking 'Are we to make war on *The Times* or come to terms?' The real explanation was probably that *The Times*'s proprietor, John Walter, personally disliked the Bill and believed that it would be unpopular among the country magistrates. But despite the opposition of *The Times*, incomparably the most important upper- and middle-class paper of the day, and of Cobbett's *Political Register*, the most widely circulated among the working class, the Bill went remorselessly on. On 13 August 1834 Cobbett delivered one final onslaught on the 'poor man robbery Bill', but he spoke in vain. The next day the Poor Law Amendment Act received the royal assent and became the law of the land.

The Times's first attack on the Bill in fact came on 19 April. On 18 April it reported the previous day's debate without comment.

5 Mr Chadwick's Cold Bath

I felt I was embarked in a great cause...My heart was in it. George Nicholls, Poor Law Commissioner, c. 1834

Even before the Poor Law Amendment Act was on the statute book the government had selected the three Poor Law Commissioners who would introduce and supervise the new system. As nominal chairman they chose a country gentleman, Thomas (later Sir Thomas) Frankland Lewis, a 53-year-old former Tory MP educated at Eton and Christ Church. He had always been interested in Poor Law questions, but was no innovator, and one of his colleagues, no revolutionary himself, found him 'so much of the old school and so averse to incur the responsibility of any forward movement that we had great difficulty in dragging him along'. Serving with Lewis, who in 1839 was succeeded by his son, a far abler person and a future Home Secretary, was a 37-year-old Whig barrister, John (later Sir John) Shaw-Lefevre, who had emerged from Eton and Cambridge, in the view of a contemporary, 'clear-headed...industrious...a man of the world', and with him the other member of the team found himself able to work 'with perfect confidence and satisfaction'. This third Commissioner, who really dominated the work of the Commission, was that same Captain George Nicholls whose work as overseer at Southwell had already made him a national figure.

Nicholls was the real 'father of the Victorian workhouse'. Unluckily for its future inmates he was, like Chadwick, just the type of largely self-made man who was unlikely to feel much sympathy with any of life's casualties. The son of a Cornish farmer who had died when the boy was eleven, leaving the family far from well off, Nicholls went to sea in 1791 when he was fifteen, to make his fortune serving as a midshipman with the East India Company. By 1816 he was rich enough to 'swallow the anchor' and settle down ashore, moving to Southwell in 1819, with the results already described.

His achievements there led to his being offered the post of superintendent, jointly with the engineer Thomas Telford, of the building of the Gloucester and Berkeley ship canal, and after this assignment was finished, in 1827, he became manager of the first provincial branch of the Bank of England, at Birmingham, at £1,700 a year. By 1832, when the great Poor Law enquiry began, he was regarded both as a sound, no-nonsense business man and as the great authority on all matters concerning poor relief. One Assistant Commissioner spent several days picking his brains and the parishes at Southwell he had reformed were among the few given a clean bill of health in the 1834 Report.

When Lord Melbourne approached him about becoming a Poor Law Commissioner in a flattering letter—'I see no-one I should pronounce more likely to fill it [the post] with firmness and discretion'—Nicholls, who was happily settled in Birmingham, wished to decline and was only won over by the doubling of the original salary of £1,000 a year, and by a personal appeal to his patriotism. From the government's point of view it was an excellent appointment. There was nothing dangerously clever about Nicholls; the average, rate-paying business man could readily identify with him. To his biographer, the chairman of a rural union, he seemed late in life 'a well-knit, alert old man, with keen grey eyes, under extremely bushy eye-brows, rather austere... Serious he certainly was, and earnest... There is hardly a suggestion of a joke of his own making... His bent was matter of fact.' He was a 'single-minded man, with a strong sense of duty to his God and his neighbour'.

Nicholls's taste in entertainment was simple. He liked straightforward, easy-to-follow tunes, and the novels of Sir Walter Scott and Frederick Marryat. When taken to a performance of *Don Giovanni* he spent his time studying the libretto, shutting the book with a disapproving snap and remarking, 'What a shocking state of society!'

The new Commissioner was clear from the first what he wanted to do and, looking back later in life, he acknowledged that his experiences as an overseer had permanently shaped his thinking. At first, he wrote, 'We contemplated the workhouse as little more than an instrument of economy, calculated to lessen the parish expenditure by a reduction of the poor-rates'; only later were 'the full consequences ... imposed on the working classes by a well-regulated workhouse ... understood and appreciated. We then saw that it compelled them ... to be industrious, sober, provident, careful of themselves, of their parents and children... The workhouse thus acted instead of ... that law of necessity wisely imposed by Providence upon mankind ...

The pauper is subjected to so many disagreeable circumstances that the desire to escape from these constantly urges him on to renewed exertion'.

The Poor Law Commissioners lost no time in getting to work. After being sworn in at noon on 23 August 1834, they held their first board meeting that same afternoon in their temporary offices in Whitehall Yard, from which they moved a few weeks later to more spacious premises at Somerset House. Here everyone from the Commissioners downwards worked long hours. Nicholls was devoted to his two daughters—the death of the elder, at seventeen, in 1835, inflicted a lasting wound—but that autumn and winter they saw little of him. 'The duties I was performing', he later wrote, 'were, I believed, of the greatest importance. I felt that I was embarked in a great cause to the furtherance of which all my faculties should be devoted...'

The administrative and clerical staff of the Commission had an equally busy and demanding life, for their immediate superior was the indefatigable Edwin Chadwick. Chadwick was bitterly disappointed not to be appointed a Commissioner himself. The Cabinet turned him down on the grounds that his 'station in society' was too low. He was instead made Secretary to the Commission, at £1,200 a year, and consoled himself by behaving as though he actually were a Commissioner. Quarrelsome, self-important, disloyal when convinced he was right, unshakable to the point of obstinacy, too clever to ignore, too useful to dismiss, Chadwick was an intolerable subordinate, and a far from agreeable superior. His appetite for work was insatiable, but he was a tall, well-built man with a mental constitution that matched his physique, so that at ninety he was still producing a flow of original and carefully worked-out ideas. Like his superior, George Nicholls, Chadwick rarely relaxed and had little sense of humour, though he enjoyed a play on words. Like Nicholls, too, he had no nagging doubts about the importance of the task on which they were engaged. The well-planned, well-built, well-run workhouse was to be the solid memorial to his great master, Bentham, and the New Poor Law was, he wrote to Lord John Russell in 1838, like 'a cold bath—unpleasant in contemplation but invigorating in its effects'.

The Poor Law machine later gained a reputation for attracting poor quality, badly-paid staff, but in the early days able young men competed to work for the Commission, partly because it was, in 1834, the first modern government department, with far greater powers and independence, and more efficient direction than its predecessors.

Looking at the documents turned out by the Commission in its first year it is impossible not to be struck by the thoroughness and efficiency of the newly-created machine which produced them. Detailed account books listing every garment issued to a pauper, certificates for 'extras' prescribed for the sick, diet sheets, suggested salary scales for workhouse staff, these and hundreds of other documents poured out of Somerset House in a never-ending stream. Most important of all, since it was the foundation of the whole system, was the Admission Order book, consisting of perforated slips, with counterfoil, reading: 'Admit ... to the workhouse'.

But before the first Relieving Officer could tear out the first Admission Order, the confused, chaotic, administrative patchwork cobbled together over 250 years had to be ripped apart and reassembled into tidy new unions. To set these up was the first and most important task of a team of seventeen (later raised to nineteen) Assistant Commissioners—not to be confused with the investigators with the same title who had conducted the Poor Law enquiry of 1832-4, though one or two men did fill both positions. As with its office staff, the Poor Law Commission was lucky in its employees in the field. Even in a violently anti-workhouse novel, *Jessie Phillips* by Frances Trollope, published in the 1840s, the Assistant Commissioner is depicted as an attractive figure, superior in almost every respect to those he is advising, and George Nicholls, no mean judge of men, praised 'their intelligence and earnest devotion to the duties of their office'.

The first Assistant Commissioner to be appointed, in October 1834, was Francis, later Sir Francis, Head, a tough, extravert type, who had served in the Royal Engineers, managed a mining company in South America and written a travel book, *Rough Notes of Journeys in the Pampas and across the Andes*, also acquiring the nickname 'Galloping Head'. Later he became Lieutenant-Governor of Upper Canada where, having provoked a minor rebellion, he put it down so successfully that he was rewarded with a reprimand and a baronetcy. Lord Melbourne called him to his face 'a damned odd fellow', and his biographer described him candidly as 'a better writer of boys' books than a governor'. He really belonged to the pages of one himself.

Most of Head's colleagues were less colourful characters, the largest single group being barristers in their thirties or forties, though there was a sprinkling of country squires like Tom Stevens of Bradfield in Berkshire, who might have come straight out of a novel by Thomas

Hughes. Stevens's family had ruled their district for two hundred years and 'There was a homely wit and a rural dignity about him', wrote an admiring friend, 'that always recalled green fields, water-rights, timber-felling and harvest time. Classics and literature did not seem his line'. But this was no disqualification and, having successfully stamped out the abuse of out-relief in Bradfield—where he also founded a village school that blossomed into Bradfield College—he was soon, as an Assistant Commissioner, being called on 'whenever there was a bit of rough work to be done, a refractory Board of Guardians, or some old parliamentary [i.e. pre-1834] union obstinately persisting in its own line'.

To men like Stevens, of course, the salary of £700 a year, plus two guineas a day subsistence allowance, was unimportant, but most of the Assistant Commissioners depended on it and it was certainly not over-generous. The whole burden of creating the new unions rested on them, the ideal being a union covering a radius of about ten miles from some central market town. To achieve the desired aim of roughly 10,000 people in each union usually involved persuading thirty parishes to join, which meant obtaining the support of a two-thirds majority of the existing Guardians or ratepayers. Even more troublesome than parishes that insisted on remaining independent were the Gilbert incorporations, often formed only a few years before and understandably reluctant to undergo another upheaval, and for years after 1834 both groups formed 'lagoons' of separate rule in an otherwise neatly unionised landscape.

To manage each union the Act created an entirely new body, an elected Board of Guardians consisting of at least one representative from each parish plus, as ex-officio members, any magistrates who happened to live in the area. To set the electoral machinery in motion was the Assistant Commissioner's second duty. The Poor Law electorate was large, numbering about two million, three times as many as those with the parliamentary franchise, but voting was confined to ratepayers and property-owners, with additional votes on a sliding scale for the wealthier residents. Voting took place in private; the ballot papers were left at each elector's home and were collected the next day, when signed. Proxy voting was allowed and a keen elector could collect an impressive number of votes; one Chelsea man, in 1838, was authorised to cast no fewer than 83.

Fears that the humble electors might swamp the polls and elect candidates pledged to pamper the poor proved unfounded; the vast majority of candidates, especially in country districts, were from the first returned unopposed. Equally, the Commissioners' boast that 'members of the upper- and middle-classes act together as a body in the dispensation of relief' was rarely justified; members of the aristocracy, if they agreed to serve at all, inclined to be poor attenders and most rural Boards were dominated by farmers or clergy. In towns, service as a Guardian offered a successful tradesman the chance to make useful social and business contacts and contested elections were more common, but, neither in town nor country, was there any prospect of a working man becoming a Guardian, since no one occupying property worth less than £25 a year was eligible to stand.

The difficulties and successes which the Assistant Commissioners were likely to experience were rapidly discovered by Sir Francis Head, who was assigned to the highly-pauperised county of Kent. He spent the winter touring his new province, and then in the spring of 1835 began a whirlwind round of union-forming visits which led to ten, in East Kent alone, being created within a few weeks. His chief problem, like that of his colleagues elsewhere, was not with the independent parishes, where the overseers were often delighted to lay down the burden of their unpopular office, but with places like Eltham, where the Guardians of a 'Gilbert' union informed him that 'they were quite adequate to the management of their parochial affairs'. Head responded by calling a public meeting attended by 200 leading residents, where he made a long speech displaying in the opinion of one originally hostile listener, the Vice-Chairman of the Ashford Board of Guardians, 'great tact and cleverness'. He skilfully directed his 'pungent sarcasm, deteriorating ridicule and subjugating irony' at the opposing arguments, in 'a winning address, made more attractive by softness of voice, an agreeable smile and almost invariable attention to good breeding'. To one apparently telling charge, that it was wrong to separate husband and wife in the workhouse, Head had his answer pat:

> It was no greater hardship for these persons to be separated than for the officers and soldiers of Her Majesty's Army and Navy. We urged the one was a voluntary separation. 'No, no', replied the Assistant Commissioner. 'It is quite optional whether the parties you advocate go into the contemplated union house.'

When the chairman called for votes against joining the new union not a hand was raised, while at a later meeting Head 'caused the

Guardians very quickly to succumb' and to surrender in three hours the rights they had jealously exercised for years.

Other Assistant Commissioners proved equally forceful. At Sutton in Sussex a local clergyman stood up to oppose the suggestion that the existing 'Gilbert' union should be dissolved and merged in the new Westhampnett union. 'Before he could address the meeting', an eye-witness later told a parliamentary committee, 'Mr Pilkington (the Assistant Commissioner) got up and said "Hold your tongue, sir!" and... there was a burst of laughter... The moment the word was out of his mouth he said, "I beg your pardon, sir", but it completely unhinged Mr Eadle so that he could say nothing all day.'

Once the new unions had been approved by the Commissioners work could begin in earnest and the vice-chairman of the Ashford Guardians, whose high opinion of Sir Francis Head has already been quoted, found himself in the summer of 1835 attending long meetings every few days, as well as conferences, called by Head, of all the chairmen and vice-chairmen of Boards in his area. There were, too, regular visits to inspect progress on the new workhouse, after a local earl had public-spiritedly offered an excellent site on his land, for the modest annual rent of £3 6s. 8d., and the lowest tender, £4,000, had been accepted for erecting the building. Unfortunately, like so many people with a builder at their command, the Ashford Guardians could not resist frequent changes of mind. The main wards, it was decided, ought to have wood floors instead of the brick which had been budgeted for; walls, instead of mere partitions, should be built between the various yards, to make 'Classification' more effective, but, as an offsetting economy, the exercise yards were to be paved with gravel instead of stone and — a kindly afterthought — there was to be a fireplace in the wash-house. October 1835, the scheduled completion date, came and went with the building still unfinished. So did Christmas, and finally Lady Day, 25 March 1836, was fixed for the grand opening ceremony. Already, however, as the walls rose higher, the Guardians were getting a return for their money. The mere sight of the workhouse had caused applications for relief to fall off.

By 1836, with the workhouse open, the Ashford union was able to proceed to the attack on out-relief. Unlike many others it applied the law humanely, even continuing weekly allowances in some deserving cases, though sternly refusing to subsidise men in work. This was a typical meeting of the Ashford Guardians that year, as seen by their vice-chairman:

The chairman takes the relieving officer's notebook and proceeds thus:

Chairman: 'C.D. of Merstham, applies for assistance, he has a wife and six children. He is a man of good character, I think?'
Officer: 'Oh yes, sir, a very honest, industrious and sober man.'
Chairman: 'How happen it he applies?'
Officer: 'He has been laid up with an ague, sir, for four or five weeks, and his wife can do nothing now he is so ill; he also asks for a doctor.'
Guardian: 'I propose that he have 10*s*. and medical attendance.'
Second Guardian: 'I second it.'
Chairman: 'Any dissentient? None. Granted. 10*s*. and a doctor ... Who is this G.H?'
Officer: 'He is a single man, very subject to fits; but this is a longer bout than usual.'
Chairman: 'Can he be got into the hospital?'
Vice-Chairman: 'My brother is a subscriber, I will make enquiry; this man is a poor helpless unfortunate creature, I propose that he be taken into the house till an opportunity be found to get him into hospital.'
Chairman: 'Any amendment? None!—*adopted*. Man to be sent to the house.'

If all Boards had been as reasonable as that at Ashford the Poor Law Amendment Act might have been introduced everywhere, as it was in Kent, with little public opposition. But the men in charge of many unions, perhaps genuinely believing that only harshness could save the country from ruin, were so unfeeling that kinder citizens rapidly became outraged by what was being done in their name: 'To see the number of poor and aged persons brought from nearly twenty miles round every succeeding Wednesday, on account of their usual allowance having been stopped...was truly shocking to humanity', wrote Robert Blakey, the mayor of Morpeth in Northumberland, in 1837. 'Here the poor creatures were jammed into the staircase of the Town Hall, subjected to cold, piercing draughts of air, with very thin and scanty clothing upon them, sometimes for the space of seven hours together, before their cases could be decided'.

'Even the very steps of the building used for meetings of the Board', wrote a Bridgwater Guardian, John Bowen, in 1837, 'present more of misery and suffering than could be detailed in a volume. Worn-out creatures may there be seen who, having, after a life of labour, or an attack of disease, crawled many tedious miles to tell their tale of woe, are kept faint and shivering hour after hour, while the time which ought to be devoted to their relief is wasted ... in frivolous and irrelevant harangues.'

The full effects of the new system were seen at their clearest at Andover in Hampshire, a small market town serving a wholly rural hinterland. The Board was dominated by its chairman, a clerical magistrate, always the harshest type of Guardian, who made even applying for relief as burdensome as possible. Applications to the Relieving Officer for one's district could be made only on a Thursday and the Relieving Officer for the town itself, much the largest place in the union with its 6,000 inhabitants, lived four miles outside the town. The candidate then faced a further journey to the workhouse on the following Saturday morning, to wait outside the Boardroom while his case was considered. If, as was his right, he then asked 'to see the gentlemen' he was either told 'it is contrary to law' or ordered to go away and return the following week, since the Board tried to rattle through its business by one o'clock. But word soon spread that a personal appeal was fruitless, for those who did get inside the Boardroom, one Guardian admitted, 'were looked upon with suspicion. The treatment of the Guardians was not kind; they would even speak in this way to the sick. When the Relieving Officer returned them as suffering from debility or rheumatism, the chairman would often say, "Oh, debility or rheumatism, is it? The house is the finest place in the world for that; nothing like a change of air; come into the house, we shall soon cure you there!" ' It was not surprising, this observer felt, that 'I have heard them say that they would almost rather starve than apply again'.

At Andover the chairman had established a ruthless ascendancy over all his colleagues. With the Relieving Officer standing close beside him, ready to record his decisions, he would seize the latter's *Application and Report Book* and read from it at breakneck speed, announcing his decision all in the same breath—and the verdict was almost always the same:

Phoebe Watson, Abbotts Ann, idiot ... Workhouse!

John Goodall, Married, 3 children, New Street, Andover ... Workhouse!

Charles Davidge, Andover, has lost use of one side, paralysed, applies for relief, wife and 3 children ... Workhouse!

Thomas Chevis, wife and 7 children, applies for relief ... Workhouse!

Thomas Jones, labourer, 43, wife and children . . . Workhouse!

In this last case, another Guardian protested, 'I really think that man ought to have some relief, he is a very good labourer', but even while other members of the Board were agreeing with him the chairman was dealing with the next case but one, his only response being to repeat 'Workhouse!' more firmly than before. The presence on every Board of a Guardian from an applicant's home parish was supposed to ensure that at least one member knew his circumstances and could speak up for him, but at Andover this proved a doubtful advantage to the poor. When one man's request for relief was heard in his absence, because he was too ill to appear, the response of the Guardian from that area was to offer to investigate, which he did by riding over to the man's cottage and shouting for the sick man's wife to come out. When she appeared he replied to her account of her husband's illness with grim and callous humour: 'I must send him over to old Mac's; his physic is so strong that they cannot stand it'— 'old Mac's' being the workhouse.

Even the 'impotent poor', hitherto treated compassionately in most parishes, got short shrift at Andover. When John Holday of Kempton, 'About 70 . . . nearly blind', sought parish assistance 'they put him to wheeling stones and he is obliged to put his hat in one place, his coat in another, and his waistcoat in another, so that he may find his way to the gate'. Another applicant for relief was a 77 year-old labourer from the village of Woolhouse:

> He was a very old and infirm man. He was obliged to walk with a stick, completely double. He was required to go two and a half miles to work every day. The Guardian of the parish to which he belonged said he did not care whether he did any work or not, but he should show himself in the field or else he should not have any pay . . . Frequently he did not get above 1*s*. or 2*s*. in the week . . . He kept on at it till one evening he became so exhausted in getting back from his work that he fell into a hedge and was found by . . . a farmer in the neighbourhood almost dead . . . Of course he could not go afterwards. Within a short time he went to pick up a few sticks and was found dead.

Even where the old were not treated so callously the change from parish poorhouse to union workhouse was widely criticised, as in this 'before' and 'after' comparison by a correspondent of the *Daily Dispatch* in 1838. At Hellingley, near Eastbourne, there had formerly stood, he wrote, a 'neat, homely-looking house . . . surrounded by a nice garden, carefully cultivated... During the long summer evenings, on a bench outside the door, generally sat about sixteen old men and women, chatting over the events of bygone days, looking as healthy and cheerful as possible; after which one of them would read a chapter from the Scriptures; and then they would retire to bed.' Now this idyllic picture was seen no more, for the comfortable old building had been torn down and the site was occupied by 'the Bastille of the Hailsham union...surrounded with high walls...surmounted with cast-iron... The walls also enclose a yard, in which the inmates (about 300) take exercise', with, of course, no seats provided and the sexes rigidly separated.

The harsher treatment of unmarried mothers aroused far less public indignation. A woman who found herself pregnant with an illegitimate child no longer had any personal redress against the man concerned, and the parish could only obtain a maintenance order against him at Quarter Sessions, instead of, as in the past, from any two magistrates. More justifiably, the mother now had to provide corroborative evidence of her accusation, which was inevitably difficult. Even when an order was obtained the amount was usually only 1*s.* 6*d.* to 2*s.* a week and this did not benefit the mother, since the money went into union funds.

To anticipate later developments, in 1844 the law was changed again to allow any mother, whether a pauper or not, to seek an affiliation order against the alleged father, and the union lost its right to do so, though it regained it in 1868 for children in the workhouse. Whatever the reason, the proportion of illegitimate births in England and Wales, though not the actual number, did show a marked decline between 1845 and 1890, falling even more sharply thereafter as knowledge of birth control spread.*

But in the 1830s it was 'moral restraint', in the shape of chastity before marriage, and a small family thereafter, which the educated classes urged upon their inferiors. One of the first steps taken by most unions was to end all cash allowances to unmarried mothers, substituting for them at first an allowance of a 'gallon for a bastard', that is an 8lb or gallon loaf, to keep a child for a week. The next step was to withdraw this assistance and to 'offer the house', though here

---

*So deep an impression had Malthus's teaching made that at first birth control was known as 'neo-Malthusianism'. The pamphlet which Charles Bradlaugh was prosecuted in 1877 for publishing had an even more euphemistic title: *The Fruits of Philosophy*.

policy varied. Some Boards would accept the child without the mother, to allow her to re-establish herself outside and perhaps make a home for it, but many insisted that both must enter, or leave, the workhouse together. Among the rigorists was Squire Tom Stevens of Bradfield where the Guardians resolved in 1835 'that no bastard under the age of eight years will be received into the house without its mother, if she be living and unmarried'. Great success was claimed for this policy. 'The mothers of at least half the bastards in the union attended the Board . . . to apply for a continuance of out-relief. In every instance except one (where the mother of the child was blind and the child sickly) the order first made was adhered to [and] several . . . upon hearing the determination of the Board said that "they should continue to keep their children out of the house" ', which was, of course, the Board's real aim.

Some Boards at first made a distinction between the girl with one natural child and the woman who made a habit of acquiring them, but this was ruled to be contrary to Poor Law policy and the Commissioners in 1842 specifically forbade the Guardians in Easingwold, Yorkshire, to pay a shilling a week out-relief to an unmarried mother described as 'a deserving character'. The Guardians resigned in protest but were forced back into office with threats of being surcharged for any loss the union suffered in their absence.

The Commissioners themselves had, as usual, no doubts about the wisdom of their policy. In their *Second Annual Report* in 1836 they proudly pointed out that in the past year alone, as mothers refused the offer of the workhouse, the number of bastards chargeable to unions had decreased by 10,000. There were even signs, they believed, that the long decline in female virtue had been halted, for in the past year only 17,600 illegitimate children had been born in England and Wales compared to at least 20,000 in 1831, when the records were incomplete. According to some officials quoted in the *Report*, fear of the workhouse had produced remarkable results. 'In our parish', explained the assistant overseer of Llanasa in Flintshire, 'it seldom happened at the ceremony that the bride did not think it decent and requisite . . . to conceal her shape under a cloak. But in the eighteen marriages which we have had since last August all the ladies, except one, retained their virgin shape and appeared without their mantle'. The overseer of St. Giles parish, Oxford, put it more succinctly: 'Fear of the new law', he reported, 'makes the girls cautious.'

6 Offering the House

We proceeded to direct our chief attention
to the general introduction of the workhouse
system.—*First Annual Report of the Poor Law
Commissioners*, 1835

The New Poor Law was buckled down upon Southern England with
a speed and ease which confounded the pessimists. They had warned
that the withdrawal of out-relief would lead to disturbances like those
of 1830—'There is no petition like a blazing rick', wrote one farmer,
'for it can be read by half the country round'—and that attempts to
move labourers into the workhouse would be resisted by maddened
mobs, armed with pitchforks and turnip-knives.

None of these disasters occurred. Resistance to the changes was
slight, sporadic and soon overcome. By the end of 1836 the workhouses were going up all over the Southern counties, their plain,
squat, four-square shapes dotted about the landscape at intervals of
twenty miles or so, recalling the castles built by an invading army to
hold the population in subjection. There, however, the resemblance
ended. A generation later, the gentry and architects, faced with such
an opportunity, would probably have ornamented the bare walls with
turrets and battlements, even perhaps a drawbridge, but in 1834 the
age of Victorian Gothic was still to come. The workhouses of
the 1830s were mainly simple, solid and strictly functional. Grim
austerity was the keynote, discouragement—to inmates and potential
residents alike—the aim.

During those first few months even the weather seemed to smile
upon the Poor Law Commissioners. The harvest months of August
and September 1834 were fine and hot, the winter which followed
mild, and the only difficulty came from overseers who assumed that
they could abandon their duties when the new law came into effect.
A circular from Chadwick, instructing them to carry on for the present,
soon set them right, also explaining that the immediate policy was
to taper out-relief off gradually and, wherever possible, to start
paying at least half of it in kind.

Even this, according to Sir Francis Head in Kent, 'operated as a self-acting test of the validity of a claim', for many men claiming to be in desperate need showed little gratitude when given bread or a ticket for fuel. Some such applicants 'assembled in great numbers to attack . . . their own magistrates . . . . Armed with clubs they dragged the independent labourers from their work, forcibly obliging them to join their gang . . . [and] grossly insulted women who earnestly desired for the sake of their children, to accept the bread . . . . They [the rioters] declared to one or two of the Kentish yeomen that if they dared to interfere "they would hang them up by the heels to their own trees".' But no one was, in fact, hung up, by his heels or otherwise, and though the mob did 'cruelly beat two gentlemen of great worth and respectability', the only result was to convert other solid citizens into becoming eager supporters of the new law.

The substitution of bread for allowances of money also led to the rumour that it had been poisoned to reduce the population, reflecting no doubt a garbled version of Malthus's teaching. Since it was bought cheaply in bulk the bread did frequently have an unfamiliar taste or appearance and Assistant Commissioner Gilbert, busily forming unions in Devon, was assured 'that all the children beyond three in a family are to be killed; that all young children and women were to be spayed [i.e. sterilised] [and] that if they touched that bread they would instantly drop down dead . . . . I saw one poor person at North Molton look at a loaf with a strong expression of hunger and when it was offered to her, put her hands behind her and shrink back in fear'. In Bradford-on-Avon one clergyman was assured by a pauper 'that the bread was as black as my coat and that it was expected that the poor would die of it like sheep with the rot'. Undeterred, this curate tasted it and found it excellent. Another belief was that accepting the bread marked the recipients out as paupers 'and the Guardians would immediately seize them, kill their children and imprison their parents'. In Sussex, when the Archdeacon of Lewes, who had recently joined the Hurst-monceaux Board of Guardians, generously invited the school-children to a treat, it was whispered that they would be taken for a sail in Pevensey Bay and drowned.

A heavily ironic article in *Blackwood's Magazine* in April 1838 entitled 'New Scheme for maintaining the Poor', which pointed out the profits to be made by tanning the skins of dead paupers to bind the official registers, was no doubt taken seriously by some simple souls and even more alarm was caused by a pamphlet entitled *Marcus on*

Populousness, a title clearly chosen to invite confusion with Malthus's famous essay. This was circulated from 1838 onwards and existed in two versions: the more restrained merely argued in favour of compulsory limitation on the size of families but a more scurrilous one 'explained' how a pregnant woman could murder her unborn infant by swallowing poison gas. Some credulous people accused the Poor Law Commissioners of producing *Marcus* and though they issued an official denial, the rumours persisted. What more convenient place to liquidate unwanted paupers, it was whispered, than the workhouse, this sinister new building, with its high walls and guarded gates?*

The most serious disturbance which the Poor Law Commission faced in its first year occurred at Chesham in Buckinghamshire when the Guardians planned to move 'ten old men and one boy' from the local workhouse to a new institution at Amersham. The men concerned had all agreed to go but the local opponents of the new law realised that the move was the first step towards the closing down of all the small local workhouses and a howling mob gathered outside the workhouse gates on the Saturday morning in May 1835 when it was due to take place. The magistrates who tried to reason with the demonstrators were greeted with 'hootings and groanings' and 'stones thrown in showers' and finally read the Riot Act, which caused the crowd to allow the cart carrying the terrified paupers to set off. But, although escorted by a magistrate on horseback, it was repeatedly attacked and despite one of the occupants 'defending himself against the attempt...to pull him out of the wagon, with a knife', he and the other occupants were forcibly 'rescued'. Those injured by their liberators' stones were left to lie by the roadside and the rest were carried back in triumph to Chesham, while the escorting magistrate was chased by an angry crowd and finally cornered on Chesham Bois common, where he was abused, called a tyrant, pelted with dirt and stones and finally knocked down amid 'cries in the crowd of "Kill him! Smash his head!" etc'.

With the Guardians virtually besieged in the workhouse and the town in an uproar, the magistrates swore in special constables, dashed off urgent pleas for aid to Somerset House and the Assistant Commissioner at Aylesbury and also sent to London for a detachment of the

---

*Such credulity was nothing new. During the first cholera epidemic in 1831-3 mobs had 'rescued' patients being removed to hospital where, it was widely believed, they would be murdered to provide subjects for dissection.

metropolitan police — the only organised and disciplined civilian force available at this time. By eight o'clock that night the paupers were all back where they had started, while a jubilant mob, 500 strong, celebrated its victory in the streets outside and the anxious magistrates learned 'that messengers had been sent from the mob at Chesham to the neighbouring parishes and to the railroad to resist the intended apprehension of the rioters on the morrow'. An attempt on the Sunday to smuggle the paupers into Amersham — they were given a shilling 'for refreshments on the road' and told to make their own way there — proved a failure; after learning at *The Boot and Slipper* inn on the way that 'if they went to Amersham they would get killed, for there were above one hundred at the top of the hill waiting for them', they not unreasonably turned back. On Monday morning a crowd of howling women, labourers and navvies, some armed with sticks, confronted twenty London 'Peelers' in the market-place, while outside the town troops of armed yeomanry sent from High Wycombe and Aylesbury waited for orders to come in and clear the streets. In the end a blood-bath was avoided. The mob reluctantly acknowledged 'They are too strong for us, or we would have had a row', the ring-leaders in the disturbance were carried off to Aylesbury jail, escorted by troops, and, on the Tuesday, the paupers were quietly removed to Amersham after all.

The origin of the trouble, one Guardian later discovered, was the rumour that 'all the labourers' children, whether paupers or not, were to be taken from them', the flames being fanned by 'dissatisfaction amongst the bakers at the contract for bread being made with other than tradesmen of Chesham'.

Such rare incidents apart, the Poor Law Commissioners had good reason, in their *First Annual Report* in August 1835, to look back on the past year with satisfaction if not complacency. On appointment, they explained, 'We proceeded to direct our chief attention to the general introduction of the workhouse system', and the Assistant Commissioners had started work in the worst-affected areas of southern England, one even making his headquarters at Newbury, the birthplace of the Speenhamland system. All Berkshire, all Kent and Hertfordshire was 'unionised', along with most of Sussex, Hampshire, Cambridgeshire, Buckinghamshire, Essex and Bedfordshire, and parts of several other rural counties, like Wiltshire. Altogether 2,000 — nearly one in seven — of the country's parishes had now been merged into 112 unions, covering a population of 1,400,000, and the poor-rates were already down by a third in the most pauperised areas and by a sixth over the country as a whole. Everywhere, farmers reported, 'an extraordinary change is taking place in the conduct of their labourers, who appear...to be becoming more civil and apparently more anxious to secure constant employment'. Of 710 members of the gentry consulted by one Assistant Commissioner, 705 approved the change. One observer, in the Bradford union of Wiltshire, referred to 'the almost magical effect of the new measures', while at Hendon in Middlesex two of the four parish poorhouses were now locked-up and empty and in the whole union not a single able-bodied man remained on outdoor relief. Nassau Senior, chief author of the Act responsible for this transformation, was jubilant about its results. 'Our domestic revolution', he wrote at the end of 1835, 'is going on in the most peaceful and prosperous way'.

The Poor Law Commissioners' *Second Annual Report*, covering the year to August 1836, also had a success story to tell. 6,200,000 people from nearly 8,000 parishes, accounting for 45 per cent of the population and 65 per cent of all the poor-rates, had now been tidily assigned to 351 unions, and the results seemed to bear out all the optimism expressed a year earlier.

'Able-bodied pauperism will soon be but a name', predicted a union clerk, at Ware in Hertfordshire, while at Halstead in Essex 'Three families from one most pauperised parish, Ridgewell, accepted tickets for the house... One... a man and his wife, with eight children, submitted for only three weeks to the confinement and ten hours per day hard work at the mill...and I believe this example will have the best effect.' The clerk to the Bicester union in Oxfordshire, who not long ago had 'known in the Winter fifty or sixty able-bodied men standing in the street' also had an encouraging tale to tell:

> Since the formation of our union I do not think we have ever had more than three able-bodied labourers on relief . . . If any apply, the workhouse is offered them and very few indeed go in . . . A tailor in the union who had been on the parish invariably for the whole of the Winter was . . . refused relief and . . . ordered into the workhouse. On the relieving officer giving him his order he . . . said he would rather be tied to the top of the highest tree in the parish than go there and has never applied for relief since.

One farmer from the Cirencester union in Gloucestershire was equally enthusiastic. 'I have men working for me now', he claimed, 'who used to be always grumbling and insubordinate and good for very little as labourers; now they are contented and trustworthy and go whistling to their work as happy as birds.' The rector of Cranfield, Bedfordshire, himself a Guardian, believed that the workhouse might usher in a new golden age. 'I hope', he wrote, 'ere many years have passed away, that the English labourer will be restored to what he was before 1796, that bees and poultry may be attended by the wife, the cottage garden cultivated in surplus hours by the husband and we shall then have our places of worship filled with women dressed in red cloaks, the men in good coats with nose-gays in their buttonholes.'

places the working-class seemed ungrateful for the benefits being pressed upon them. They admitted that:

> Partial riots have occurred in many different counties, but by the aid of small parties of the metropolitan police . . . (who can now be sworn in and paid as special constables in any county of England and Wales), occasionally aided by the support of a military force, these disturbances have been put down without any consequent injury to property . . . Open and direct resistance on the part of the pauper has in no instance been permitted to prevail and we have the highest satisfaction in being able to state that no loss of life has occurred.

So promising did the situation seem that the number of Assistant Commissioners had been increased from 15 to 21 and 'We entertain a confident hope that, by assigning one to each district, we should be able by Midsummer next [i.e. 1837] to bring the Act into operation in every part of the country in which our exertions are not impeded by the existence of Gilbert's Act incorporations or by some local Act.'

Parliament had frustrated the original intention to end all out-relief to the able-bodied at a stroke and had insisted that any 'General Orders', applicable to all unions, must first be laid before the House. This difficulty was evaded by the Commissioners by withdrawing out-relief by means of 'Special Orders', addressed only to one or two named unions. By mid-August, 1836, out-relief, at least to able-bodied males, had already been banned in 94 unions and the Commissioners were hopeful that the same rule could steadily, if gradually, be extended to the whole country.

But not all Guardians were as optimistic. 'I think the people will submit to long and severe privation and may be induced to commit crime rather than accept the offer of the house', wrote the Chairman of the Basingstoke Board in Hampshire in an ópen *Letter to the Poor Law Commissioners* at this time. 'Banish from your minds the very idea of promulgating the much-dreaded edict prohibitory of outdoor relief... So you will carry on the system without exasperating the people and reform the habits of the labourers without producing a convulsion.'

But the policy of banning out-relief to the able-bodied continued to be applied in more and more unions, until in the autumn and winter of 1836, it faced its first real test. Hitherto fortune had smiled on the Commissioners. The weather had favoured them and the unexpected boom in railway construction had absorbed many surplus labourers, but now the reformers' luck began to change. The miserably wet autumn of 1836 was followed by an exceptionally hard winter when many farm labourers were laid off. The Board feared, and its enemies hoped, that the new workhouses would be swamped if all applied for relief together, but both were proved wrong.

At Cuckfield, in Sussex, in December 1836, with snow piled up on the fields and all outdoor work stopped, 149 men demanded relief. 118 were 'offered the house'; 6 accepted. Another 60 then applied and received the same dusty answer. This time 5 entered the work-house, but 3 left within a few hours of discovering what life there was like. What happened to the rest was not recorded; many, no doubt, shivered and starved in their unheated cottages and cursed the weather and the gentry. But so far as the Poor Law Commissioners' statistics were concerned, they were 'self-supporting'.

The Commissioners had been apprehensive about applying the new law to London, with the press and a few MPs eager to publicise complaints against it, but most of the metropolitan parishes already had a large, and often 'classified' workhouse of their own and the withdrawal of out-relief from able-bodied applicants from October 1835 onwards provoked little trouble. More opposition had been expected in industrial areas, where the working-classes were better organised, more independent minded and more politically conscious than in the countryside, but even here surprisingly little resistance was encountered at first. Stoke-on-Trent, in the heart of the Black Country, was the first manufacturing town to set up a Board of Guardians, in March 1836, when they almost immediately faced a major strike in the pottery trade, which threw 30,000 people out of work. The workhouse was soon overflowing and those left outside were given bread and fuel, but no money. At Nottingham, when a recession in the stocking trade presented similar problems, the new Board moved existing occupants, old people and children, out of the workhouse into hired premises, and squeezed 700 of the able-bodied applicants into the vacant wards. The remainder were accommodated in a temporary 'day' workhouse in wooden sheds, where meals were provided in return for labour. By the summer of 1837 trade was back to normal, the labourers were back in work, and the Guardians' authority was unshakable. But now came a far fiercer trial of strength, in the Industrial North. The working-class here, unlike the scattered shepherds, carters and cowmen of the softer southern counties, were tough, turbulent, well organised, and above all, well led, by middle-class sympathisers. In Huddersfield, in January 1837, the declaration of a union proved little more than an empty gesture. The first Board of Guardians to take office took one frightened look at the threatening scene around them and decided to adjourn. So did the next, encouraged by a threatening mob led by the popular orator, Richard Oastler, which broke into the Board room and contributed to their deliberations with shouts and missiles. It was not until nearly two years later, in September 1838, that the Guardians began to exercise their powers, but it was a long time before all resistance died down, as this report in *The Times* in April 1839 revealed:

> On Monday last Mr John Banks, the Relieving Officer of Kirkheaton, presented himself before the Guardians of the Huddersfield Union in a most deplorable plight, his clothes hanging in tatters and his head and face greatly disfigured. It appears that the deluded populace of his district had been on the look-out for him for three days, threatening his life if he durst commence his duties under the new law. However, on Monday he presented himself at the workhouse for the purpose of relieving the poor, when a large body of semi-barbarians surrounded the building, forced the officer out and chased him over hedge and ditch to a great distance, pelting him with mud and stones, amidst the most hideous and barbarous yells. He took refuge in a house . . . but the inmates unmercifully expelled him and drenched him with a can of water . . . The mob seized his bags and books and threw them into a pond. His coat was torn from his back, his hat trodden under foot and his person severely bruised. In this state, he proceeded as well as he could, followed by a brutal crew, until he took refuge in a house and thus made his way to Huddersfield.

Opposition at Bradford was at first almost equally violent. When the new Guardians met in October 1837, a determined attempt was made to overawe them and they moved from the court-house to a hotel, and then back again, while a magistrate pleaded, vainly, with the crowd to give the new system a fair trial. When the Assistant Commissioner, who was generally detested, left the building, he was violently attacked, while the local police looked on, and eventually the Guardians met behind serried ranks of cavalry, recalling the famous 'Peterloo' massacre eighteen years earlier. Happily this time, although the Riot Act was read, the troops charged, and shots were fired, no one was killed, but a large body of soldiers was quartered in the town until the unrest died down.

The place which put up the stoutest and longest fight against accepting a workhouse was the small town of Todmorden, twenty miles from Manchester, whose leading citizen and chief employer was the Radical MP and factory-reformer, John Fielden, a highly-enlightened mill-owner, who had been a pioneer critic of child labour. When, in January 1837, the Poor Law Commissioners proclaimed the formation of the Todmorden union, Todmorden and two other places boycotted the whole proceedings and refused to elect any Guardians. When the new Board none the less met, with Todmorden unrepresented, Fielden and Company instantly dismissed all their workpeople, several thousand strong, and announced that the works would stay closed until the Board resigned. A poor-rate was finally levied but Fielden and others refused to pay it and one Friday afternoon in November 1837, two luckless constables were sent with a horse and cart to seize £5 worth of goods to pay the resulting fine. On the officers' appearance the factory bell, which normally summoned the workers to their looms, called them instead to arms:

> From all sides hundreds of angry men and women hurried to the village. A terrible scene ensued. The horse and cart were thrown violently down, with one of the constables on the top. The cart was smashed and burned. The two constables were compelled by the mob to swear never to engage in the like business again. Being let go they raced along the road to Stoodley, pursued by an infuriated crowd who repeatedly assaulted them, until at last they found shelter in Eastwood. The following Wednesday a rumour spread through the district that the constables were coming with a company of soldiers. This false report led to a still more serious riot. Hundreds of men, armed with clubs, assembled . . . and then

proceeded to visit the homes of the Guardians or of prominent supporters of the new Act and to break windows, doors and furniture. At Todmorden Hall [where the chairman of the Board lived] damage to the extent of £100 was inflicted. Special constables were sworn in and soldiers, both horse and foot, were quartered in the town. A raid was made on the mills of Fielden brothers and about forty men were taken into custody.

Most of those detained were let off with a caution, though one of the ringleaders got nine months in jail, but Todmorden was far from tamed. The Guardians were forced to hire buildings as small poorhouses and it was not until 1877, long after Fielden's death, under a threat from the Poor Law Board to break up the union and divide it between Halifax and Rochdale, that the town at last relented and built its own workhouse—one of the last places in England to do so.

The industrial North remained an untidy anomaly in the neat new pattern of Poor Law administration. In April 1837 Lord John Russell had advised the Poor Law Commissioners to move slowly there and soon afterwards a highly effective device for creating new unions by stealth was discovered with the introduction of the compulsory registration of births, marriages and deaths. In many places in Lancashire and Yorkshire 'registration districts', coinciding in area with the new unions, were formed and gradually the Guardians responsible for them assumed all the usual powers. The Poor Law's opponents found themselves outmanoeuvred, as one indignant petition to Parliament complained, by 'low cunning and deceit'.

By the end of 1839 95 per cent of all the parishes in England, or nearly 14,000 with a population of 12 million, were applying the Poor Law Amendment Act, and only 2 million people, in 800 parishes enjoying special powers under local Acts, or isolated by indissoluble 'Gilbert' or 'parliamentary' unions all round them, were still unaffected by it.

In 1844, although the recalcitrant areas of the industrial North were tacitly excluded, it seemed safe to issue a General Order finally banning all out-relief to the able-bodied, a rule long in force in most unions. This had been the first, and greatest, aim of the reformers. To achieve it had taken just ten years.

7 The Pauper Palace

You may call your workhouse a palace, if you
please. He deems it a prison and nothing better.
Sir George Crewe, *A Word for the Poor and
against the New Poor Law* (1843)

In addition to building new workhouses, the new unions faced the
problem of making those already in existence, in the words of one
Assistant Commissioner, 'wholesomely repulsive'. In the palatial
East Anglian workhouses, built in the previous century, conditions
had become so lax that the most potent method of taming the recalcitrant was to threaten to give them their discharge. The Assistant
Commissioner, Dr James Kay, indignantly reported to London an
all too typical incident. An inmate of the Shipmeadow workhouse, in
the Wangford union of Suffolk, Elizabeth Stannard, having returned
from her usual Sunday outing, drunk and obstreperous, had been
searched, 'when the following articles were found upon her person:
three quarters of a pint of rum, two pounds of pork, half a pound
of sausages, six eggs, some apples, some bread, half a pound of cheese,
three packets of sweetmeats, two bunches of keys, £1 9s. 0d. in silver,
7¾d. in copper, and in her box £5 10s. 0d. in gold and many articles
of clothing'.

Elizabeth, Dr Kay discovered, had been happily established at
Shipmeadow for fifteen years, while at Blything, in the same county,
he found two families who had lived in the workhouse for three
generations. The son and grandson of one of the original arrivals had
both been born there and had brought their brides back to live within
its hospitable walls. In the same building another pauper was running
a licensed shop, well-patronised by the supposedly destitute paupers,
while the weekly market at Stowmarket was regularly enlivened by
the arrival of paupers laden with baskets of groceries for sale, con-
cealed beneath dirty linen. In the local workhouses, Dr Kay established, the rations amounted to 272 ounces of solid food a week,
against the 168 supplied to a soldier in the line, and the 122 which,
according to the 1832 Enquiry, the average labourer in work received.

But even this did not 'prevent butchers' meat, pies and sweetmeats and spirituous liquors being introduced and it was not infrequent for paupers to feast their friends within the walls, especially on Sundays and at christenings', the food and drink at the latter being traditionally 'on the house'.

While attempts were being made by the Poor Law Commissioners to ban drinking in workhouses and to stop the granting of extra food and drink to inmates who did the domestic chores of the house, all inmates in Suffolk were receiving 10 to 14 pints of beer a week, while washerwomen and other domestics were rewarded with up to an extra five pints *a day*.

These discoveries explained one mystery which had previously puzzled Dr Kay: the number of rooms in some workhouses locked or boarded up. They belonged, he learned, to long-term inmates who had gone away for a few weeks' holiday but wanted to reserve their usual accommodation for their return. Weekend excursions, like that of Elizabeth Stannard, were also a well-established tradition. At Heckingham in Suffolk two beerhouses near the workhouse were specially opened on Sundays to cater for the male paupers, while the female inmates 'had boxes in the neighbouring cottages, containing dresses, which...they exchanged for their workhouse garb and, thus attired in more attractive style, flaunted about the neighbourhood with young men'. As for the separation of the sexes, a long-suffering local landowner complained that his woods had become the groves of Isis, goddess of love, and that the workhouse seemed to be her temple.

This pleasant, well-fed, life was not disturbed by excessive labour. At Heckingham, a typical 'general mixed workhouse' of '450 paupers ...the aged, and infirm, and able-bodied men, women and children having common yards and dayrooms...some pretence of employment existed in a sacking manufactory...but the paupers were seldom kept at work'. Understandably they did not take kindly to the prospect of a new regime. 'On entering the yards—with the Rev. Stephen Clissold one day', Dr Kay reported, 'the able-bodied paupers, rushed out to stare at us in wild and disorderly groups... They had openly threatened to assault Sir Edward Perry (a local Guardian) upon his next visitation.' At the Cosford House of Industry, also in Suffolk, the chairman of the Guardians, a clerical magistrate, described to the Assistant Commissioner how the previous governor, 'a timid person', had 'been fairly frightened out', leaving his successor an appalling situation:

> The great evil is that there has been no employment and it has
> come about by the yielding of the late governor to successive
> claims as to privileges and rights that the paupers have become
> very unmanageable. There are now more than 200 of all ages
> within the house and the object of nearly all of them seems to be
> to intimidate the new governor ... The practice with the most
> disorderly among them is to do all the mischief they can, by
> breaking the windows, etc. Yesterday they threw some stones
> through a partition wall at the governor, and when he sent for one
> of the offenders he refused to attend the summons; and when the
> governor, with two others (who act as constables) went too fetch
> him out of the yard they were all attacked, thrown down, and the
> constables staves taken from them. Another magistrate and
> myself sent eight of the worst of them to gaol last night.

showed:

> Among the varieties of mischief practised by the inmates, one is
> to break to pieces all the chamber-pots which they can lay hold of;
> I am told they have lately demolished about forty of them.
> The governor refused to supply them with more, and sent them
> a pail instead, which they pitched out of the window, and made
> use of the corner of the room in preference. He afterwards
> furnished new ones . . . One of these was broken by being thrown
> at the door, as he was leaving their bedroom; but at this time the
> practice with the paupers in the . . . wards is to filthify the floor of
> their bedroom to the utmost. This morning, at my suggestion, the
> governor ordered two of the men to clean the room (two others
> having performed the task yesterday) and [on their refusing] I com-
> mitted them. All the rest have refused today. But I have recom-
> mended the governor to assign the task every morning to any two
> whom he may select, and I have determined to give them 21 days
> hard labour if they refuse, and to send them all to gaol by
> instalments.

With this backing, the new governor set about his reforming task,
according to the Assistant Commissioner, 'with equal firmness and
prudence', as the governor's own report showed:

> When I arrived at the workhouse . . . I found considerable breaches
> made in the walls of the main building, brick floors torn up,

fireplaces pulled out, chimney-breasts demolished, door-frames torn away and burned, and window frames removed and destroyed. The glass was broken in every direction. There was scarce a whole window in the house. The windows of the dining-hall were so much broken by the practice of throwing stones at the governor as he was passing through the hall, that the meals of the inmates could not be served, excepting by day-light, as no candle could be kept lighted in the room. The repairs of the breaches and damages in the house and out-buildings cannot have cost much less than £300. The insubordination of the inmates was so extreme, that if the governor attempted to correct any disorder, the whole of the paupers rose in a body to resist his authority, and more than once violently assaulted him, tearing his clothes and subjecting him to gross personal indignities. The chief object to which it appeared desirable that I should direct my attention . . . was to provide constant employment for the able-bodied inmates . . . and within three days of my arrival they were set to work . . . to level the ground surrounding the new workhouse, and afterwards to make new roads to the house and other improvements. In the first fortnight twenty of the inmates left the house . . . Very few of those who had, at the period of the formation of the union, apparently taken up their permanent abode in the house have remained inmates until this period.

The problem in Suffolk was large and rowdy workhouses; in Kent the difficulty often came from small and more peaceable, but equally indulgent, ones, as Sir Francis Head reported, following his whirlwind tour of his new province in 1834–5:

Throughout these receptacles the diet varies but little. Almost everywhere the Kentish pauper has what are called three meat-days a week, in many cases four meat-days and in some cases five; his bread is many degrees better than that given to our soldiers; he has vegetables at discretion and, especially in the large workhouses, it is declared with great pride that there is no stinting, but that 'We gives 'em as much victuals as ever they can eat'. It is very true that the ploughman in the workhouse receives as much as ever he can eat, provided always, says the unwritten code, that he clears his plate before he asks for more. In order, therefore, to obtain a third edition of meat he must previously manage to swallow greens and potatoes enough to choke a pig and as he is confined to the sty . . . the able-bodied pauper in the workhouse has the tight appearance of being overfed.

Some parishes had an even more generous diet, specifying that their paupers must be fed on 'bacon with green peas ... good mackerel ... fresh herrings', baked puddings and roast meat four times a week, and pea-soup made of 'beef, peas, potatoes, leeks, onions and Scotch barley', it being the duty of 'the assistant overseer to see that the ingredients are all put in'.

Head discovered on the walls of one workhouse a copy of the 'Conditions of contracts' awarded by the parish which called on tradesmen tendering to supply the workhouse to

> furnish warm, wholesome, sweet, clean, comfortable beds, bedding, blankets and sheets, and *good* sufficient shoes, hats, bonnets, caps and wearing apparel of all kinds, as well linen as woollen . . . good, sweet, wholesome, meat . . . to consist of good, fat beef, leg of mutton pieces and chuck of good ox beef . . . the beer to be good, sound, small beer, the flour to be best household flour . . . the bread to be the best second wheaten, the cheese to be good Gloucester cheese, the butter to be good and clean . . . All the other articles to be good of their respective kind.

Head was scathing about this particular workhouse, where the contractor was ordered 'to provide firing for warming and candles for lighting ... and good coal fires in the general room from 1st October until 1st of May'. The ultimate indulgence came in regulations 22 and 23, calling on the contractor 'to have the paupers' hair cut once in six weeks' and 'to provide wigs for such as wear them or require them'.

In this particular establishment the very name workhouse was a misnomer, for the published regulations required the contractors 'to provide as many servants as shall be necessary for cooking and serving up the victuals: for washing, cleaning and keeping in order the workhouse, and the poor therein, and attending on them when necessary'. It was not long, under Head's energetic direction, before such notices were everywhere being torn down.

Besides establishing a regime based on plain living and hard labour, the 1834 reformers had planned to get rid of the 'general mixed workhouse', but the cost of building a whole series of separate new institutions in each union—one for the sick, one for the healthy women, one for the able-bodied men, and so on—rapidly proved prohibitive and the temptation to retain old buildings was strong. The case 'for the adaptation of existing workhouses in different classes, instead of building new ones', was well, if pessimistically, put by a Kent magistrate to Sir Francis Head:

> In the first place, upon our system there is a great saving of expense; our homes have cost us under £300 . . . I dislike the appearance of these new houses all over the country . . . I fear the consequences. When we have eight workhouses there is hardly an inducement to pull down one only, and to pull them all down in next to impossible . . . Our system . . . eludes the grasp of insurrection. Besides this, how much more perfect is the classification. How secure are our separate schools from all contamination. How small are the masses of pauperism which we bring together, compared with the congestion of one vast House. With us, our Houses are not like prisons, for we require no high wall to separate the classes; eight or ten miles distance is far more effectual than the highest walls.

But the Poor Law Commissioners favoured 'one strong efficient building' as prison-like as possible, as Sir Francis Head explained:

> The very sight of a well-built efficient establishment would give confidence to the Board of Guardians; the sight and weekly assemblage of all servants of their Union would make them proud of their office . . . while the pauper would feel it was utterly impossible to contend against it. In visiting such a series of unions the Assistant Commissioner could with great facility perform his duty, whereas if he had eight establishments to search for in each union, it would be almost impracticable to attend to them.

Twenty years later, George Nicholls, looking back, was convinced that the 'big workhouse' party had been right. 'Using the old parish workhouses...and assigning one or two classes of the paupers belonging to the union to each house, was', he recalled in 1854, 'done in a few instances, but it rarely answered; it was found both more effective and more economical to provide a well-arranged and sufficient workhouse... In most cases an entirely new building was erected'. Some of the leading reformers never forgave this decision. Chadwick remained violently critical of it and Nassau Senior reminded a House of Commons Committee in 1862 that the 1832 Royal Commission had recommended separate buildings 'for the children . . . for the able-bodied males...for able-bodied females; and...for the sick. We supposed the use of...four distinct institutions...We never contemplated having the children under the same roof with the adults'.

'I was not ambitious', wrote the chairman of the Cranbrook Union in Kent, 'of immortalising my architectural taste in one of those unsightly structures by which the eye of the traveller is now so frequently offended', but most Boards entered eagerly into their share of one of the most grandiose building programmes of the century. During the first year of the Poor Law Commissioners' life everyone was preoccupied in forming the new unions and beginning the attack on out-relief, but during the second year, from 1835-6, the Commissioners approved the building of no fewer than 127 workhouses, covering almost every part of England except the North. Most of these were very large. Twenty-three unions felt that they needed from 400 to 500 beds, 46 expected an 'indoor pauper' population of 300 to 400 and only 58 felt they could manage with accommodation for fewer than 300, the cost ranging from £10,535 for the most expensive building on the list, at Bishop's Stortford in Hertfordshire, to no more than £1,050 at Catherington, Southampton, where only 80 inmates were expected.

Alterations and enlargements to existing buildings in 78 unions were also authorised on a vast scale. Some of the sums voted were modest, occasionally as little as £20 or £30, but often the reconstruction cost almost as much as a brand new establishment. In rural Sussex, for example, recognised as being in the front line in the fight against pauperism, no less than £6,531 was forthcoming to impress the recalcitrant peasantry around Midhurst, while another £4,000 was spent not far away at Westhampnett, near Chichester. Significantly, counties like Dorset which had insisted they could not afford to pay their labourers properly found little difficulty in raising vast sums to build capacious workhouses.

One reason why new workhouses were needed, and why existing buildings needed major structural alterations, was the determination of the Commissioners to introduce a thorough-going 'classification' of all inmates into seven distinct categories:

1   Men infirm through age or any other cause
2   Able-bodied males over fifteen
3   Boys between seven and fifteen
4   Women infirm through age or any other cause
5   Able-bodied females over fifteen
6   Girls between seven and fifteen
7   Children under seven

'This separation', insisted the Commissioners, 'must be entire and absolute between the sexes, who are to live, sleep and take their meals in totally distinct and separate parts of the building, with an enclosed yard for each.' The one concession made, that 'infants may be kept by the mothers until of age ... to be sent to school', was not in practice honoured, and the regulations made no mention of the types of inmate who were to prove most troublesome of all, such as the feeble-minded, people suffering from infectious diseases, tramps and prostitutes. As a matter of policy no distinction was made by Somerset House between the 'deserving' and the 'undeserving' applicant. The offence lay in being a pauper; the reason was irrelevant.

Although subject to central approval, each Board of Guardians could indulge its own tastes in designing its workhouse. The Commissioners issued model plans with their *First* and *Second Report*, prepared by a young and hitherto unknown architect, Sampson Kempthorne, who had only recently gone into practice in Carlton Chambers, Regent Street. In 1836 he completed, for £8,500, the first workhouse erected under the new law, and his services were soon in general demand, for in the next few years he had a flood of commissions, for churches, a country house, a City bank and some twenty government-financed schools. For reasons unknown, he emigrated to New Zealand around 1840, and died soon afterwards, while workhouses built to his plans were still springing up all over the English landscape.* Kempthorne's own taste, his other work suggests, was for the Gothic or Italianate style, but his workhouse plans are functional to the point of severity, the emphasis being on meeting the specifications at the lowest possible cost.

Three basic types of workhouse were envisaged. The most imaginative was hexagonal shaped, with each of the six sides about a hundred feet long, the space they enclosed being divided by a Y-shaped building. The spaces formed by the arms of the Y were sub-divided to provide for three yards each, on both the men's and women's sides, serving respectively the infirm, the able-bodied and children aged seven to fifteen. The centre blocks contained four day rooms, for infirm and able-bodied men and women respectively, a schoolroom for the children, and, at the junction of the Y, the master's parlour, where he could see what was happening in any part of the establishment. The blocks which formed the outside

*For a detailed account of workhouse architecture, see Appendix.

walls contained workrooms, washrooms, the 'refractory ward', the 'dead house', the bakehouses, and the receiving wards and wash-rooms where new arrivals were stripped and cleansed. On the first floor were situated the dormitories, with the master's bedrooms separating the two sexes, the dining hall, which also doubled as a chapel, and the Board Room, from the windows of which the Guardian could look down both on applicants at the gates and on the existing residents, busy in the yards. On the top floor were more bedrooms with the boys' and girls' bedrooms separated by the lying-in ward and the nursery.

As an economical method of accommodating several hundred people in a small compass, where they could easily be watched, these plans had much to commend them, but their defects were equally obvious. Any sick and infirm unable to negotiate the stairs from their first-floor dormitory would be virtual prisoners, while the mothers in the lying-in ward on the top floor would also have to drag themsel-ves and their babies down several flights of steps to obtain fresh air. The infants in the nursery and the older children in the bedrooms adjoining the lying-in ward would be exposed to the gruesome sounds of childbirth in that pre-anaesthetics age, while the women themsel-ves would be intolerably packed together. 'We have it determined', wrote one critic, 'that in the excruciating hour of labour, with all its inevitable and humiliating accompaniments, a crowd of poor women may be thrust into eight beds in a low narrow room sixteen feet long!'

This lack of space was typical of the whole workhouse. The same observer, who watched the official plans being put into operation in his native town of Bridgwater, pointed out that 'the space assigned to 300 persons by the Poor Law Commissioners would not accommo-date 45 on the scale of the London hospitals and not above 65 on the scale of the military hospitals . . . The same authorities have prescribed a room ten feet in length [it was, however, fifteen feet wide] as a nursery for ten children and their attendants. They have officially authorised all the Boards of Guardians in the kingdom to shut up 32 industrious, honest labourers in a low room twenty feet long.' He also drew attention to a major and far more serious omission:

Here is no infirmary, no provision for dangerous disease. The very dying must die jammed up in their allotted space by their less fortunate sufferers . . . Thus measles, ophthalmia, erysipelas, small-pox, dysentery, scarlet and typhus fever, and all the long train of infectious diseases, are to be indiscriminately scattered through these buildings and the virulence of infectious poison intensely heightened by the dense mass of living creatures, crammed into these murderous pesthouses contrived by the Poor Law Commissioners.

But this was not how the workhouse-builders viewed their designs at all. 'Instead of the dirty and indecent huddling together of offices and persons, as is the too frequent practice in labourers' dwellings, here each apartment has its distinct and appropriate use', one Assistant Commissioner told his masters. 'The rooms are more cleanly, airy and better built.' His only anxiety was that 'The quiet and excellent accommodation of the new workhouses is so congenial to the old that I fear lest they should become attractive, when experience has shown that they are not so comfortless as described. At present their prison-like appearance and the notion that they are intended to torment the poor inspires a salutary dread of them.'

The prison-like appearance was intentional; the softening influence of curves or decorations of any kind was rigidly eschewed and most workhouses seemed designed to cut the inmates off from even a glimpse of the world outside. The critic already quoted protested even before the local workhouse was built, in the summer of 1836, at 'the small size and gaol-like position of the windows', which were six feet from the ground, ensuring that 'the inmates...are...shut up in a gloomy cell, without the power of alleviating a tedious confinement by looking out of a window [and] denied the harmless indulgence of being able to withdraw their eyes from a dead wall, to look even into a narrow court'. Upstairs he discovered another refinement: the window sills sloped downwards to prevent the inmates using them as a seat or shelf.

In the recommended plans not even a chimney broke the bare lines of the roof, and although some heating was provided, it was never enough. One ward full of old women complained a few years later to a workhouse visitor of the appalling draughts which meant 'that after the fires were out at half past eight they dreaded to wake, for the cold draughts gave them so much pain'.

Although Kempthorne's hexagonal design was not widely adopted, many Boards opted for another of his plans in which the walls round the workhouse formed a square, divided up by two-storey blocks of buildings forming a plus (+) sign, and with an additional wing at the front, housing the waiting hall, the Board Room, and the porter's lodge. This became the most familiar style of workhouse, though some unions settled for a single slab-like rectangular block, like a Victorian barracks, surrounded by 'airing yards' instead of parade grounds.

In equipping their workhouses, few Boards erred on the side of extravagance. The basic item of furniture was the cheap, wooden bed, with a flock-filled mattress made of sacking and two or three blankets. Pillows were generally regarded as unnecessary and sheets, if provided, were of the coarsest kind. Few people enjoyed the luxury of a single-bed, and some beds, both single and double, were arranged in two tiers, like bunks in an army barrack room. Even in the sick wards, beds were often so tightly packed together that the occupants could only get in or out by climbing over the end and clothes had to be dumped on the bed, or under it. In the male workrooms no seats were provided, and in the dining rooms only the roughest wooden tables and backless benches; in the whole establishment there might not be a single chair with a back or arms and certainly none that were upholstered. The only decorations on the walls were the lists of regulations, enjoining instant obedience to the master, and the official diet tables, the pauper having the right to demand to see his rations weighed. There were no newspapers, no books except an occasional improving tract and, for the younger inmates, no games and no toys. The children, like their elders, fought, teased each other, threw stones or, most commonly, sat listlessly about, stupified with boredom and apathy.

The reality of workhouse life was thus even worse than the Poor Law Commissioners intended. According to their model timetable, later slightly amended, the workhouse rising bell rang out at 5 am from March to September, and at 7 am for the rest of the year. Break-fast, preceded by prayers, followed from 6 to 7 (7.30 or 8 in winter) and then work from 7 (8 in winter) until 12. After an hour for dinner everyone worked again until supper, from 6 to 7, followed by more prayers and then bed, by 8 at the latest. The routine was meant to be dull and the work which filled the day hard and disagreeable. The Poor Law Board recommended oakum-picking, sack-making or, best of all, the use of a corn-grinding mill, operated by a number of men trudging round in a circle and pushing the bars of a capstan hour after hour.* The Commissioners warned that a small, four-handed mill was better than the more impressive 16-bar machine since it might, if the workhouse were doing its deterrent job, be difficult to muster that

*These and other tasks are described in Chapter 20.

number of able-bodied paupers at any one time. Its optimism here was not misplaced. At Cuckfield in Sussex, the Assistant Commissioner found in 1835 that there had been 23 able-bodied paupers in the house, but on the introduction of a hand-mill the number had gradually dwindled away while 'in many of the other unions the mills have absolutely been rusting upon their stands for want of hands to turn them'. Another Assistant Commissioner proudly reported having seen a similar machine covered in cobwebs.

Immediately on his admission, a new inmate's clothes were removed and stored. After he had been searched, washed and had his hair cropped, he was required to put on workhouse dress, as a visible symbol of his new status. Each union was free to indulge its own sartorial taste and though the Poor Law Commissioners ruled in 1842 that 'the clothing worn by the paupers need not be uniform either in colour or materials', in practice it always was. One observer can remember seeing 'workhouse dress' being worn in Suffolk in the early 1930s, the women in shapeless, waistless frocks reaching to their ankles, with a pattern of broad, vertical stripes, in a rather washed-out blue, on a dingy white background, the men in shirts of a similar pattern, and ill-fitting trousers, tied with cord below the knee. Beneath such exterior garments, at least during the nineteenth century, the women wore under-drawers, a shift and long stockings, with a poke bonnet on their heads, the men thick vests, woollen drawers and socks, with a necker-chief around their throats and, in cold weather, a coarse jacket. As for the children's outfits, one kind-hearted woman visitor protested that 'the singularly ugly and disfiguring uniform, too often adopted, has brought real misery to the wearers, besides being hated as a badge of pauperism . . . The frock of the pauper girl is usually of stout woollen material, good for winter, but generally worn all the year round . . . The frocks are too often clumsily cut and ill-sewed . . . and the long skirts in which the little girls are apt to be attired (to allow for growth) impede their movements, adding to their awkward gait', made worse by 'hobnailed boots with iron tips' so that 'these unlucky children have a heavy walk peculiarly their own'.

Each union also enjoyed discretion over the food it provided but almost all adopted one of the six model diets recommended by the Poor Law Board, which supplied 137 to 182 ounces of solid food a week. Since this was more than the 122 ounces the average independent labourer received, 'less eligibility' required that workhouse meals should be as dull, predictable and tasteless as ingenuity and poor cooking could make them. The official No 3 diet, for the able-bodied, for example, recommended that a man's breakfast, throughout the week, should consist of one and a half pints of gruel, accompanied by eight ounces of bread. For dinner, on Sunday, Monday, Wednesday and Friday, he received seven ounces of bread with two of cheese; for supper, on every day, six ounces of bread and one and a half of cheese. The culinary highlights were on Tuesday—when he received eight ounces of cooked meat and three quarters of a pound of potatoes for dinner—Thursday, when there was a pint and a half of soup, with bread but no cheese, and Saturday, a truly festive occasion, when five ounces of bacon appeared with the potatoes. At all meals women received rather less bread or meat than men. The only drink, for both sexes, was water, beer being rigidly excluded, and tea, like butter and sugar, being confined, if provided at all, to those over sixty. Children over nine were treated for catering purposes as women, and younger ones were 'dieted at discretion', the Board suggesting smaller portions of the adult menu at dinner time, with bread and milk replacing gruel or bread and cheese at breakfast and supper.

Was the workhouse diet truly insufficient? The Poor Law Commissioners, understandably, were highly indignant at charges that they were subjecting the inmates (as one critical Guardian complained in *The Times* in 1842) to 'a slow process of starvation', and to reminders that the prison ration, of 292 ounces of solid food a week, was more than double that provided in the workhouse, they retorted that the prisoner had no option about remaining in jail while the pauper, if dissatisfied, could always leave. On the whole, it was the quality of workhouse food, rather than the amount, which came in for most criticism. The standard breakfast dish, gruel, a thin oatmeal porridge made with water and unflavoured with milk or sugar, was particularly hated, while the taste and appearance of the bread, often baked on the premises, was also constantly criticised.

Less defensible than the scale of workhouse rations was the practice of forcing the inmates to eat with their fingers. In many unions in the 1830s no cutlery was provided, so that bread and cheese had to be broken in the fingers, meat and vegetables were scooped up by hand and gruel was drunk from the bowl. Private attempts to improve conditions were forbidden. One Poor Law Board inspector actually went round an old folks' ward about 1860, collecting the tea-pots which they had somehow acquired and ceremonially smashing them.

In all workhouses the principle of separation—of men from women, mothers from children, husbands from wives—was rigidly enforced. One Hampshire labourer told an enquiry in 1846 that in ten weeks in the workhouse, including Christmas, he had seen his seven children only when they passed him on the way to chapel. A husband who crossed the dining hall to talk to his wife at dinner or supper was liable to be punished both for fraternising with the opposite sex and for speaking at meal times. The Poor Law Commissioners were adamant about the need for separation, arguing in their *First Annual Report* that to allow a man to enjoy his wife's company or vice versa, 'might have the effect of reconciling [them] to habitation in a workhouse'. Somewhat illogically, they pointed out that some married couples actually preferred to live apart, the best of reasons in a deterrent workhouse why they should have been kept together. Occasionally, however, a more convincing case was quoted, as at Eastbourne, where the first attempts at classification led to a riot. 'The ringleader in the disturbance...who was most clamorous against a separation from his wife', the Assistant Commissioner reported, 'was brought before me. He was also charged by the governor with constantly absenting himself from the Sunday service in the workhouse chapel.' The culprit's explanation came curiously from such a devoted husband: ' "I'm not going there to hear that fellow", meaning the chaplain. "I'm married, worse luck, it was he as spliced me and I ha'nt forgiven 'un for it yet." '

The authorities faced opposition from a different quarter in trying to enforce another rule, that no inmate could leave the workhouse, except permanently, even to attend church. As many Poor Law officials pointed out, nine out of ten paupers had never entered a church while they had the chance and one enthusiastic Assistant Commissioner recalled that the workhouse inmate's spiritual needs were better catered for than anyone's outside the universities.

Nonconformist ministers on the whole welcomed the policy of allowing the clergy into the workhouse, instead of letting the residents out, for it gave them, for the first time, equality with their Church of England brethren, but some well-meaning Anglican clergy petitioned the Poor Law Commissioners to change it. They refused, not unreasonably, for Sunday in the past had often been a disturbed, rowdy day in the workhouse as the 'church-goers' staggered noisily back. The Master of the parish workhouse of St Andrew and St George the Martyr, Holborn, wrote to the Commissioners in 1836: 'I do not remember one Sunday that has passed during the last twelve years

without some scence of drunkenness or disturbance, occasioned by
those paupers who have had leave to go out. They have been carried
home by the police drunk, or with their clothes torn, followed by trains
of vagabonds . . . One . . . old woman, about eighty years of age, has
never gone out on leave to the Catholic chapel but she has . . . returned
drunk.' It would be fatal, he believed, to allow the non-Anglicans out,
for 'If this liberty were given almost all the paupers would turn
Catholics and dissenters... to go out and beg and get the means of
getting liquor and indulging themselves in vice.'

Perhaps the fairest assessment of the 'reformed' workhouse was
made by the poet George Crabbe, whose description of a parish poor-
house in 1786 hs already been quoted.* In 1810, in *The Borough*, he
wrote an account of one of those then being set up, which were to serve
as a universal model a quarter of a century later:

> Your plan I love not. With a number you
> Have placed your poor, your pitiable few;
> There, in one house, throughout their lives to be,
> The pauper-palace which they hate to see:
> That giant-building, that high-bounding wall,
> Those bare-worn walks, that lofty thundering hall!
> That large loud clock, which tolls each dreaded hour,
> Those gates and locks and all those signs of power:
> It is a prison, with a milder name,
> Which few inhabit without dread or shame.

One must look to a poet, too, for an inmate's eye view of the
workhouse. James Withers Reynolds, an unsuccessful shoemaker
from a Cambridgshire village, spent some months in the Newmarket
workhouse with his wife and children in 1846. He was later 'discovered' and taken up by literary society as 'the workhouse poet'.
Eventually he fell on hard times, dying poor and forgotten, but leaving
behind several volumes of verse, including *Written from Newmarket
Union*, in 1846, a verse letter to his sister:

> Since I cannot, dear sister, with you hold communion,
> I'll give you a sketch of our life in the union.
> But how to begin I don't know, I declare:
> Let me see: well, the first is our grand bill of fare.
> We've skilly for breakfast; at night bread and cheese,

*See page 30.

And we eat it and then go to bed if you please.
Two days in the week we have puddings for dinner,
And two, we have broth, so like water but thinner;
Two, meat and potatoes, of this none to spare;
One day, bread and cheese—and this is our fare.

And now then my clothes I will try to portray;
They're made of coarse cloth and the colour is grey,
My jacket and waistcoat don't fit me at all;
My shirt is too short, or I am too tall;
My shoes are not pairs, though of course I have two,
They are down at the heel and my stockings are blue...
A sort of Scotch bonnet we wear on our heads,
And I sleep in a room where there are just fourteen beds.
Some are sleeping, some are snoring, some talking, some playing,
Some fighting, some swearing, but very few praying.

Here are nine at a time who work on the mill;
We take it in turns so it never stands still:
A half hour each gang, so 'tis not very hard,
And when we are off we can walk in the yard...

I sometimes look up to the bit of blue sky
High over my head, with a tear in my eye.
Surrounded by walls that are too high to climb,
Confined like a felon without any crime;
Not a field nor a house nor a hedge can I see—
Not a plant, not a flower, nor a bush nor a tree...
But I'm getting, I find, too pathetic by half,
And my object was only to cause you to laugh;
So my love to yourself, your husband and daughter,
I'll drink to your health in a tin of cold water:
Of course, we've no wine nor porter nor beer,
So you see that we all are teetotallers here.

8 Master and Matron

'The workhouse is a large household...It resembles a private family on an enlarged scale.'
Annual Report of the Poor Law Commissioners,
1846

Even before the new workhouses were opened, every Board of
Guardians faced the problem of staffing them. In the past such posts
had often been filled on a distinctly casual basis, the appointment of
workhouse master, for example, sometimes being given to a failed
local business man as a kind of 'outdoor' relief. Those who operated
the Poor Law had frequently been little higher up in the social scale
than those they supervised. Now all this would, it was hoped, change
and new and better qualified men would be selected to apply the new
methods.

The key official in any union was the clerk, and some Assistant
Commissioners, in their eagerness to show spectacular savings in the
poor rates, encouraged the Guardians to combine this post with the
other vital appointment, that of master of the workhouse. This was a
mistake, for the two jobs required quite different qualities and each
was enough to occupy an able man full-time. Often in the 1830s some
local candidate, displaced by the recent reorganisation, had an obvious
claim to become clerk, but some strange appointments were made,
both then and later. The medical officer to the Westminster workhouse, around 1870, discovered that the clerk to his Board of
Guardians, who always objected to his certifying lunatics, himself
carried eccentricity to remarkable lengths, sporting 'a sheet of more
or less crumpled whitey-brown paper' instead of a shirt, and wearing
'clothes as torn and ragged as those of the most poverty-stricken
casual, his shoes down at heel and the legs of his seedy-looking black
trousers hanging in rags'. (When he died he left an estate of several
thousand pounds, which convicted him of having suffered from
miserliness, if nothing more sinister.)

Peculation in various forms was, despite all the elaborate checks
devised by Chadwick and his colleagues, always difficult to prevent

and it proved hard for local officials brought up under the old regime to realise that their traditional perquisites were gone for ever. The Commissioners issued dire warnings to tradesmen against paying 'rewards' to union officials in return for contracts, and black-listed known offenders, but it was remarkable how often a man dismissed by one Board turned up soon afterwards on the payroll of another. Often, too, Guardians covered up their own mistakes by allowing offenders to resign, and even providing them with testimonials, thus helping to ensure that a few vicious individuals gave the whole Poor Law Service a bad name. Relieving Officers, responsible for disbursing money to those still on out-relief, were also subject to constant temptation. At Basingstoke, the Chairman of the Guardians informed the Poor Law Commissioners, 'One of our relieving officers carried on a system of fraud to a considerable extent . . . by producing forged vouchers . . . We suspended him from his office within half an hour . . . Our Clerk lost no time in applying to a magistrate for a warrant, but he has hitherto eluded the pursuit of the police and escaped.'

Once a clerk had been selected, the most urgent task was to appoint a medical officer for each of the three or four districts into which most unions were divided, to deal with the 'outdoor' sick, a separate arrangement usually being made for the workhouse inmates. Obsessed by the desire to save money, the Poor Law Commissioners, while recommending fixed salaries for other officers, favoured each union providing its medical services, like its soap or coal, by competitive tender. The successful applicant was usually required not merely to provide all the paupers in his district with domiciliary care but also to supply them at his own expense with medicines and bandages, the aim being to discourage him from pampering his patients with frequent visits or costly medicines, instead reminding 'the applicant for medical relief that in receiving it he is a pauper'.

Sometimes competition was so keen that a conscientious union medical officer was left out of pocket, the Commissioners suggesting that he should console himself with 'the credit of the appointment . . . the wider fields the appointment offers for the display of care and skill and for obtaining reputation to [obtain] a more profitable practice'. In other unions, when invited to undercut each other, the doctors agreed not to tender at all, though the Commissioners attempted to crush such resistance by advertising in other parts of the country for some ill-paid sawbones or apothecary to act as a 'blackleg'. Where the doctors did secure reasonable terms by agreeing among themselves on the minimum tender, these might be disallowed by Somerset House. At Basingstoke, the medical officer resigned when, on orders from London, his salary was cut overnight by half, and the only two local doctors who applied to take his place both refused the terms offered, leaving in the field only an unknown young man from another area. 'We were', wrote the Chairman of the Selection Committee, in 1836, 'rather startled at the sight of such an emaciated candidate and such wearing apparel as made it difficult to distinguish our candidate from the paupers applying for relief. However, his testimonial being satisfactory and his tender...the only one...we elected him... The first communication we had from our hero was an application for a loan or advance out of his wages...to procure board and lodging.'

Like so many acts of meanness by employers, the Poor Law authorities' refusal to pay the medical profession a fair salary was to prove a costly economy. Just as the clergy were from the first the chief defenders of the workhouse, so the doctors rapidly became its most constant critics, and were from henceforward always to the fore in publicising its defects.

The other non-resident official to whom the workhouse inmates looked for spiritual, if not physical, succour was the chaplain, who, except in the very largest workhouses, combined the post with a living, or more commonly a curacy, outside. Like the appointment of a medical officer it tended to attract the worst-off members of the profession and though, unlike the doctor, the chaplain was not positively encouraged by his terms of employment to skimp his duties, he usually had too little time to perform them properly. For a callow young country curate, used to conducting Sunday morning service in his own church amid the devout responses of the local gentry and their deferential tenants, celebrating Matins in a workhouse dining-room amid a hostile silence, interspersed with the babble of conversation or blasphemous interjections, must been a painful experience. The portrait of the chaplain in the anti-workhouse novel, *Jessie Phillips*, published in 1844, was probably not overdrawn, for he was shown as a harassed curate with six children to feed who had taken the post on solely for the £25 a year salary, and hurried in once a week to gabble through the service, anxious only to get away in time for Matins at his own church, seven miles away. When one distraught, respectable inmate seeks his aid, he brushes her aside.' "A quarter of an hour!", exclaimed Mr Sims, positively trembling with haste, eagerness and alarm... "Go away, good woman, go away!" '

£25 was not an outstandingly low fee for a chaplain. A survey in the same year revealed that one Yorkshire union paid £10 and the average over the whole country was only £37. It was hardly surprising, therefore, that at this time, ten years after the Poor Law Amendment Act, more than a hundred of the 587 unions now formed still had no chaplain. One of the earliest appointments admitted in his memoirs in 1847 that he had been the only candidate for the post in his union and had taken it on merely as a duty; when, after four years, he found it too onerous to continue, no replacement could be found. His honorarium, for looking after the spiritual welfare of 200 people, from infants to the very old, had been £30 a year, in return for which he had been required 'To read prayers, and preach once on Sundays, to visit the sick and catechise the children and give the usual lecture on Friday evenings'. Later, some unions appointed full-time chaplains but the work was still beyond the capacity of one man. At Marylebone workhouse, for example, the chaplain was responsible for 1,600 inmates, which meant he would be hard pressed to carry out the noble aim, in one chaplain's words, of acting 'as a friend to the wretch whom every friend forsakes'.

The person upon whom, more than anyone else, the pauper's day-to-day happiness depended, was the workhouse master. 'The workhouse is a large household', wrote the Poor Law Commissioners in 1846, surveying the 1,238 masters and matrons now established in 600 separate unions. 'It resembles a private family on an enlarged scale'. But this was a misleading comparison. Even in mid-Victorian times few heads of private families deliberately strove to make life so unpleasant that the members would be eager to leave home. A few Boards were lucky in their masters. At Ashford, in Kent, that admirably run union, a much decorated retired naval officer, bearing excellent testimonials, applied and was immediately appointed, but the commonest source of recruits were former policemen and army NCOs. (Probably the worst master in workhouse history was ex-sergeant-major Colin M'Dougal of Andover, as will be mentioned later. Men from this background were used to taking – and giving – orders and fitting into a disciplined organisation, but their quality was often poor. 'Such a collection of candidates as the advertisement produced [he] could not have imagined', the rector of Marylebone admitted in the 1850s. Inevitably, supervising a workhouse tended to attract the rootless couple with no home of their own—another reason why it often suited demobilised soldiers—the man often a badly educated bully, the wife a nagging shrew with pretensions to gentility, delighted to command an unlimited supply of free servants. The job was, however, far from being a sinecure. The volume of paper-work alone, much of it designed to keep a check on the master himself, was sufficient to daunt a man of little education; the first master of Cerne Abbas workhouse, in 1837, lasted only a fortnight, for keeping the official books proved beyond him, and the Guardians filled the vacancy by promoting the porter, whose wife, formerly the school mistress, now became the matron.

Such promotions were not uncommon and accounted for the appointment of George Catch of the Strand, the most notorious master of a metropolitan workhouse, as Colin M'Dougal was of a rural one. Catch's career is worth examining in some detail, since it illustrates so many of the faults of the New Poor Law, above all, the opportunity the doctrine of 'local independence' offered a plausible rogue, once he had secured his first appointment, to inflict misery on the helpless inmates of one workhouse after another.

Catch had started his working life as a policeman in a Central London market, where he proved so useful to a local butcher that, on the latter becoming chairman of the Strand Board of Guardians, Catch was, in 1853, rewarded with the post of porter at the workhouse. At that time, in the words of a frequent visitor to it, a 'good homely couple' ran the house, but when they retired, Catch was made master and 'his wife being equally unsuitable, a reign of terror began'. Three years later Dr Joseph Rogers, one of the most famous names in work-house history, as Catch is one of the most infamous, arrived at the Strand to take up his first post in the public service and between the two a constant guerilla warfare soon began. When the doctor ordered extra food for a nursing mother, Catch would put her back on 'house diet'. When a woman was confined, Catch would delay calling in the doctor until nine days later, when he no longer qualified for an extra 'childbirth' fee. When the doctor took a day off, Catch reported him to the Board for being absent, although he had in fact appointed a locum, while Catch himself had been a hundred miles away, enjoying the hospitality of the firm who had installed the workhouse boiler. Matters finally came to a head when the master refused to allow Rogers to see a desperately ill woman in the lying-in ward and, as soon as the medical officer had left, rushed into the hall crying jubilantly, 'I have caught that damned doctor at last!' But his complaint to the Board, alleging neglect of a patient, misfired and instead the Guardians invited Catch to resign, providing him with a testimonial praising his 'general conduct'. The inmates were less half-hearted. 'All those who could leave their beds', the victorious doctor recorded, 'rose in open rebellion and with old kettles, shovels, and penny trumpets celebrated their departure from the premises'.

But this was far from being the end of George Catch. He instantly found himself a new mastership, at Newington workhouse, where his callous behaviour, which included depriving a lame inmate of his crutches, led in 1866 to a new demand for his resignation. Catch again blamed everything that had gone wrong on the doctor, producing his *Master's Journal* to reveal an entry recording how he had caught this official *in flagrante delicto* with a pretty nurse. Happily the accused doctor, forewarned by Rogers, had an answer to the charge, while the nurse, even more conclusively, produced a signed certificate from the chief gynaecologist of Guy's Hospital, testifying that she was a virgin.

Catch was for the second time ordered to resign but, incredibly, after a brief and unsuccessful spell as a publican in Islington, bobbed up again, in 1868, as master of Lambeth workhouse, where the Guardians had needed a replacement urgently for a man dismissed for misconduct, though they told the Poor Law Board that he resigned on 'the ground that he is prostrated with grief'. Here Catch surpassed himself, recruiting as taskmaster, to replace a man sacked for selling the inmates' bedsteads, a sinister figure called Pascal who had been dismissed for misconduct from no fewer than three workhouses. Pascal was a sadistic brute who had special reason to hate one inmate, a seventeen-year-old girl. She had given evidence against him at a previous enquiry, and he ill-treated her so grossly that, after being hurled against a wall, having water thrown over her and then being 'locked up for ten hours in a small dark closet', she had died.

As usual, the subsequent official investigation was inconclusive— nobody wanted to share the dead girl's fate – but one weekend soon afterwards there was another fracas, at Saturday tea time, when one girl refused to hand back some butter given to her by mistake and another, who stood up for her, was 'dragged...by the hair of her head out of the hall', a common sight in this workhouse. The original offender, dreading Pascal's vengeance, disappeared, and Catch, having, without result, offered the handsome reward of five shillings to anyone who would betray her hiding place, decided she had taken refuge up the chimney of the women's ward. In the middle of Sunday afternoon he ordered the young and feeble medical officer to 'smoke her out', by pouring hydrochloric acid into a spittoon filled with chloride of lime in the fireplace. No Caroline appeared—she was hiding elsewhere—but sixteen pauper nurses collapsed from acute chlorine poisoning, causing a scandal that could not be hushed up.

Even now the Guardians were reluctant to dismiss this 'model' master. Some even called on the President of the Poor Law Board, the Radical Sir Charles Dilke, with 'an account of the number of pints of beer Mr Catch had saved the parish' and it was only on Dilke's insistence that the union at last got rid of him. With extraordinary effrontery, Catch now appealed for contributions from other workhouse masters to enable him to sue for libel a barrister who had published a pamphlet exposing him, and raised enough to brief the Attorney-General. Even more remarkably, he won his case and was awarded £600 damages, to the great disgust of the judge, who publicly declared that Catch was clearly unfit to hold any post in the Poor Law service. And this proved for Catch the end of the road, for thereafter he drifted rapidly downhill, finally throwing himself in front of a Great Western Railway train.

Such was George Catch, workhouse master, a bad, but far from unique specimen of the breed, especially in his capacity to pull the wool over his employers' eyes. Like other tyrants, equally evil, he was unmasked in the end, but the suffering he inflicted in the years of his despotism must have been incalculable. The Poor Law Commissioners had long ago admitted that 'it is impossible that any code of regulations, however well devised, or any workhouse inspection, however vigilant, should altogether prevent the occurrence of abuses', but it is hard not to feel that persistent offenders, at least, could have been weeded out earlier. Instead, as will be seen, even Assistant Commissioners were often deceived and sometimes recommended as the very man to pull a corrupt workhouse together an individual discharged for cruelty or dishonesty elsewhere. As for the enquiries into particular scandals with which the history of the Victorian workhouse abounds, it is clear that the witnesses were often afraid to speak the truth, or were bribed to commit perjury. Dr Rogers, when the Strand Union was eventually broken up, moved to another almost as bad, Westminster. Here, on his initiative, the inspector was called in to investigate a whole series of abuses, whereupon eight 'of the very worst characters in the house' were mustered by the matron 'to depose to her and the master's continuous kindness and consideration'. Later. in return for their perjury, they were, with the help of filched medical supplies, 'entertained by the matron in the store room, a hot supper and brandy-and-water being provided'. In this case the inspector did, in fact, find most of the charges proved, but the Guardians ignored the report and even suspended Rogers for this 'disloyalty', though by now he had powerful friends and at the next election the offending Board was swept from office. The newcomers dismissed the master and reinstated Rogers, but few of those who exposed abuses enjoyed so gratifying a revenge.

Workhouse matrons on the whole came in for less criticism than their husbands, their besetting fault being perhaps *folie de grandeur*. One of the earliest workhouse visitors was very scathing about the 'first lady' of one South London workhouse, whom she discovered one afternoon in the 1860s 'playing the piano in her smart sitting room... She conducted me through the wards in a gay hat and feathers and a sweeping velvet train'. It was, this critic found, often the master, not his wife, who accompanied the doctor on his rounds, while the few conscientious nurses regularly complained of lack of support from above. 'Let me get a few things I have set my heart on,' one of these rare women told her, 'a few men's shirts, handkerchiefs, etc., in my store, and I shall think I have scored something.'

Scattered about the country's workhouses there were a number of such individuals with a real sense of vocation. In some places the same man stayed in charge for twenty years or more and the inmates wept when he left or retired, and one occasionally found 'a well-educated, ladylike' matron whose influence was wholly for good. Porters, too, perhaps conscious of the narrow gulf which separated them socially from the sad-faced creatures knocking on the gate for admission, were often surprisingly kindly men, except to vagrants and casuals, whom they tended to despise. Overall, however, the Poor Law service did not attract men and women who were well-qualified, much less dedicated, largely because the rates of pay were from the first ridiculously low. A constant grievance was that, at every level, workhouse staff received less than their opposite numbers doing comparable work in prison. Thus, while a prison governor, with 900 convicts in his charge, mainly long-term, was paid £600 a year, the master and matron of a workhouse responsible for 600 inmates, frequently changing and including every conceivable type of person from the helpless new-born infant to the destructive senile lunatic, were paid only £80 between them, the highest salary on record being £150. Where the matron was separately employed she received in the prison £125, in the workhouse £50. A full-time chaplain received in prison £250, against at most £100 in any union, a salaried surgeon £220 against £78. Even the prison porter was better off. He got £70, compared to the £25 paid to the workhouse doorkeeper.

Apart from the low pay, the chief grievance of workhouse staff was their intolerably long hours. Little provision was made for time off or regular holidays, and they were tied to the workhouse even more securely than the inmates, who could always leave on giving a day's notice. This inability ever to feel off-duty pressed particularly hard on schoolmasters and mistresses, who, unlike those in a normal boarding school, had no vacations to look forward to, and several investigators in the 1860s and 1870s concluded that it was this perpetual confinement which caused so many promising recruits to leave the Poor Law service. 'It appears to me quite unreasonable,' commented one inspector, 'that a schoolmaster of thirty years of age should be compelled to be within the walls at nine o'clock or half past nine every night, or that he should on every occasion be obliged to ask leave of the master of the workhouse before he can go outside.' One teacher, who had wanted to attend a concert which did not begin until 8 pm, had been ordered to be back indoors by 9, so had to abandon the outing.

9 The Poor versus the Poor Law

On the one side are the helpless poor, on the other
the aggregate property of the kingdom. John
Bowen, *A Refutation of Some of the Charges
preferred against the Poor with some Account
of the New Poor Law in the Bridgwater Union,*
1837

As, in one part of the country after another, the workhouses opened
their doors, hostility to the new system became vocal and widespread.
The Whig government had never expected the change to be popular
among the poor but many life-long middle-class voters now repudiated
any responsibility for what ministers had done in their name. The
Mayor of Morpeth, in Northumberland, for example, advised his
fellow Liberals to forget 'that any attack upon the Bill is a direct
attack upon the present liberal administration. Give no votes to any
person...let his other political principles be what they may', he
urged, 'who will not pledge himself to the total repeal of this monstrous
Bill. As for the luckless Whig candidate, let him, if not ashamed of
his party's record, appear bearing a workhouse dress in one hand and
a basin of water gruel in the other'. Another disillusioned Whig, in
Kensington in 1836, wrote to his member, Joseph Hume, expressing
'deep concern and regret that you should have voted for that most
cruel, arbitrary and anti-Christian Bill . . . Your own liberal and
enlightened mind will point out the necessity of retracing your steps
and thus avert from your country the great loss it would suffer
by your invaluable services being withdrawn from the House of
Commons'. Hume responded courageously, declaring that 'The Act
for correcting the Poor Law was the very best measure passed by the
reforming ministers', but not all MPs could take so high-handed a
line, and many now found the anti-Tory vote split by a rival candidate,
standing on an anti-Poor-Law platform. At Huddersfield, the committee campaigning for Richard Oastler issued a pamphlet denounc-
ing that 'Cruel, disgusting atrocious law'. The official Whig
candidate's attempts to defend the reformed Poor Law were brushed

aside with irony: 'The deserving poor almost worship the Poor Law Commissioner and with tears in their eyes they thank him and treat him as their greatest benefactor.' On the whole, however, outright denunciation was more popular. During one election the walls of Southampton were covered with such emotive appeals as 'No more starvation union poor houses', 'No more Bastilles to imprison the aged', and 'No more flogging of little children because they are sick', while 'At an election in Worcester', one indignant observer protested in a pamphlet, 'I heard an orator declare to the mob that the opposing candidate had voted in Parliament that the aged poor should be killed.'

The unpopularity of the New Poor Law put the Conservatives in something of a quandary, which did not escape the shrewd eye of Charles Greville, Clerk to the Privy Council. 'In as much as the Tories are the largest landed proprietors they are the greatest gainers by the new system and if a Tory government should be in power at the... determination of the Act they will not hesitate to renew it' he noted in his journal in August 1837. 'Nevertheless, when they found some odium was excited in various parts of the country (during the recent General Election) against the new Poor Law...they did not scruple to foment the popular discontent... Peel has never said a word in favour of the system... The Duke of Wellington took part in the original measure very frankly but...last year, though appealed to, would not say a word.'

The Whigs themselves behaved little more courageously. Lord Chancellor Brougham, the Act's most energetic and outspoken champion, was dropped as soon as it was on the statute book. He was, wrote Disraeli perceptively, 'destined to be the scapegoat of Whiggism and to be hurried into the wilderness with all the curses of the nation and all the sins of his companions', and although he did not die until 1868 he never held office again. He consoled himself by dabbling in spiritualism under the guidance of a medium who promised to produce only 'superior spirits' and duly transmitted messages from the dead Duke of Kent, father of Queen Victoria.

The reason why, the workhouse survived, though abused on all sides, was plain. Manhood suffrage in the towns lay a whole generation away, and in the countryside, which was chiefly affected, two generations away, so, with no working-class MPs in the House, popular opposition to the law was grossly under-represented in Parliament. The anti-workhouse party formed, indeed, a strangely ill-matched group, including such incompatible characters as the mill-owner,

John Fielden, who genuinely cared about the poor, the rising young writer, Benjamin Disraeli, professing a romantic belief in the old parochial system, and Colonel Sibthorpe, arch-apostle of reaction, who opposed the New Poor Law's 'unconstitutional' centralising tendencies. The most respected member of the group, which never formally worked together, was probably John Walter MP, the proprietor of *The Times*, who in 1841 gave up his rural Berkshire seat to fight industrial Nottingham—successfully—as an anti-Poor Law candidate. His real importance to the movement lay, however, in his journalistic position, which ensured that the fullest coverage was given to every workhouse scandal, and as it was the custom of the time for newspapers to reprint colourful items from each other, a great deal of publicity, almost all of it bad, was given to the Poor Law Commission during its early years.

In Parliament the workhouse's most vocal and persistent critic was undoubtedly Thomas Wakley, a violent-tempered, somewhat eccentric Radical doctor who had founded the *Lancet* in 1823 to fight against the medical 'establishment'. By 1834, now aged thirty-nine, Wakley had become known as 'the member for medicine', and to this role he eagerly added that of 'member for the poor'. A Radical to the core, Wakley rapidly made his name after entering the House in 1835 as the most outspoken and persistent champion of the Tolpuddle martyrs and, until he retired in 1852, he was for ever attacking some abuse, from flogging in the Army to the stamp duties on newspapers, but the iniquities of the New Poor Law supplied his most regular theme.

One typical story, later exposed by Lord Brougham, concerned a labourer who gave notice to leave the workhouse with his wife and family, only to be told: 'You cannot take your wife out. We buried her three weeks ago.' An enquiry by the Poor Law Commissioners revealed that 'the Report was originally communicated to some friends of a gentleman at Huddersfield . . . by a person in Lapton . . . who being further questioned, said he heard it from his brother, who had it from a friend, to whom it had been related by a pauper, who said he had been in the same house, but whose name and abode he confessed he did not know'. The authenticity of many similar tales was equally suspect, but they were widely believed and often continued to circulate for years.

By 1837, hostility in the country to the New Poor Law was growing in strength rather than diminishing. During the 1837 parliamentary session, of 314 petitions on the subject, 107 prayed for its abolition, the rest raised particular grievances, and only 35 supported the 1834 Act. Yet when, in February 1838, a motion to repeal it was debated in the House of Commons, members defeated it by the overwhelming majority of 309 to 17. This division of opinion was reflected in a Select Committee on the working of the Law, set up in February 1837, which had been intended by Walter to discredit the new system. Instead it vindicated it and in its *Report*, in August 1838, the members expressed themselves 'convinced that the utmost benefit has resulted from the general adoption of this system of relief', and recommended giving the Poor Law Commissioners enlarged powers to dissolve existing incorporations. The Committee did, it was true, make some suggestions for ameliorating the effects of the Act, such as reminding Guardians of the desirability of relieving widows of good character with young children outside the workhouse and they also urged that unions should combine to move children out of the workhouse into separate schools, but, over-all, the Committee's recommendations came as a bitter disappointment to all the New Poor Law's opponents. The Poor Law Commission, due to expire in August 1838, instead had its existence prolonged, at first until 1842, by annual instalments and then for five years, until 1847.

Frustrated in Parliament, the enemies of the New Poor Law in the country became ever wilder and more extreme. The most outspoken of all was probably the Rev. Joseph Rayner Stephens, a combative North-country Methodist who thought nothing of delivering three open-air sermons, totalling seven hours, on a single Sunday. At one meeting Stephens publicly warned Lord John Russell 'that the Poor Law is the law of devils and that it ought to be, and will be, resisted to death... Let the man who dare...accept the office of Guardian; we are determined "an eye for an eye, a tooth for a tooth"... It shall be blood for blood, so help us God and our country'. This was too much for the Whig government, always ready to see revolution under every hay-rick, and Stephens was charged with incitement to sedition. He went to court in style, in a post-chaise, escorted by a reporter from the *Manchester Guardian*, and in court conducted his own defence, pointing out that equally extreme speeches had been made only a few years before in support of the Reform Bill and the Whigs had never objected to *them*. But he was sentenced to eighteen months in jail, the first martyr in the anti-workhouse cause.

Many other critics of the 1834 Act were hardly less violent in their language. Samuel Roberts, the Sheffield Radical, pointedly recalled in a pamphlet published in 1839 that 'the voluptuous profligacy of the higher orders in France, with their oppression of the poor . . . had drawn down the severe vengeance of Almighty God', and, with comparative mildness described the New Poor Law as 'the most . . . unjust, dastardly, God-defying Act that was ever resorted to by the government of any country in the world'. In *The Wickedness of the New Poor Law addressed to Serious Christians of all Denominations*, in the same year, Roberts predicted that 'The destruction of the church, of the higher classes of society, will be the inevitable consequence of the New Poor Law . . . The allotted period of the duration of this work of Satan is at hand.'

Like many Radical writers, Roberts used the conservative argument that the most objectionable feature of the 1834 Act was its novelty. 'Our divine old Poor Law', he wrote in one pamphlet, 'was a kind of sacred compact between the nation and Almighty God.' John Walter, MP, two years later, as reported in *The Times* of April 1841, complained similarly that 'the New Poor Law was "beating down" our Alfred-established parishes into detestable French *arrondissements* and communes . . . The old laws were to be overturned'. 'The legal right of the poor to relief', pointed out John Bowen of Bridgwater, 'is older than the right of four fifths of the landed proprietors of the country to their estates.'

Richard Oastler pleaded in a pamphlet addressed to the Duke of Wellington that the veterans of Waterloo had a special claim on their country's gratitude. 'Many of your victorious comrades in arms, whom war spared, have . . . sunk into despondency and died of despair suffering imprisonment in a union workhouse, separated from their wives . . . as a recompense for their bravery.' But the 'Iron Duke' remained unmoved.

About some anti-workhouse literature there was an engaging note of aristocratic eccentricity. Sir George Stephen of Princes Risborough neatly rode two private hobby horses together in *A Letter to the Rt. Hon. Lord John Russell on the probable increase of Rural Crime in Consequence of the Introduction of the New Poor Law and Railroad System*. The author warned that once the new railways were finished the country would be 'covered with straggling, able-bodied mendicants' (unemployed navvies making their way home) to whom 'the workhouse . . . as a refuge . . . is worse than purgatory'. At the same time 'the rapid desertion of our . . . roads will follow the introduction of railways', so the men concerned would support themselves by 'the old system of highway robbery', with 'footpads as plentiful as black-berries in October'. Stephen's remedy was recruiting paupers into the police force, thus providing 'a new field of exertion...to compensate them for that loss of parochial aid' and acquiring a body of stalwart 'Peelers' with 'an intimate acquaintance with the habits of the labouring class'.

Popular indignation against the workhouse was fostered by *Oliver Twist*, which appeared in book form in 1838, though it deals with conditions before 1834. But the most effective novel written specifically to attack the New Poor Law was Frances Trollope's *Jessie Phillips*, published in 1844. This describes the sad fate which overtakes Jessie, a beautiful village maiden, seduced by the squire's son, who ends up in 'that bare-faced monster of a union poorhouse, which seems to glare upon us from a hundred eyes from what used to be the prettiest meadow in the parish'. Here she meets various types of inmate, from 'the vilest and most thoroughly abandoned women' to the deserving mother of a decent family ruined by a fire who constantly pleads in vain 'For the love of God let me see my poor crippled husband..and child'. Jessie also encounters the workhouse dog, a vicious mastiff belonging to the matron, who boasts that with 'just one little sniff' Growler can identify a pauper and react accordingly, with 'front feet firmly set and tail erect'. Despite Growler's attentions, Jessie escapes from the workhouse and confronts her seducer, setting in train a whole series of misfortunes, in which he murders his own baby and is drowned, while she dies of shock after being acquitted of the crime. Even the Assistant Commissioner comes to a bad end, falling into disgrace for authorising the expenditure of £2 5s. 6d. to keep seven people out of the workhouse, and everyone, from the well-meaning squire, left without an heir, to Silly Sally, the village idiot, now incarcerated in the workhouse, is the worse for its introduction.

The workhouse prompted a good deal of verse, but most of it is poor stuff. *Poor-Law Sonnets*, which appeared in 1841, are only too typical:

> 'Poor Simon's sick.' 'Then for the doctor send.'
> 'The union doctor? He lives far away.
> Nor comes the doctor without order penned
> By the overseer — and this is market day.'

Although 'Nature was kind and Simon did not die', his recovery availed him little, for

> Then came the Union law. Drawn in a cart
> To a far-distant workhouse—there confined;
> No neighbour to drop in and cheer his heart;
> No village sunshine on his face—he pined—
> Without a crime, condemned—imprisoned—died.

Against emotional appeals of this kind, the defenders of the workhouse could make little headway and many of their efforts read like caricatures of the most unctuous type of sermon. Thus, the Rev. Herbert Smith. Chaplain to the New Forest Union workhouse, in 1838, unconvincingly addressing *My Dear Friends* in *A Letter to the Labouring Classes* could only counsel them unconvincingly 'fear God and honour the Queen and you may yet do well'. Equally valueless was the *Word or Two*—which ran to fourteen pages—*addressed to his Parishioners by a Beneficed Clergyman in Bucks,* which promised absurdly week or two less in the Winter in the workhouse'. In a 16-page pamphlet published in 1841, the Rev. Thomas Spencer, of a parish near Bath, a passionate convert to reform, trenchantly denounced *The Want of Fidelity in Ministers of Religion respecting the New Poor Law*. 'Satan's most successful metamorphosis in modern times', the writer declared, 'is into the character of the "Poor Man's Friend" . . . Some [ministers] have expressed a wish to see the poor comfortably provided for . . . Yet Christ himself, who was able to provide abundantly for all, suffered his disciples to hunger . . . The apostles themselves so distributed the funds placed at their disposal as to cause murmuring amongst certain widows; a class at the present time most covetous of parish pay and also the chief murmurers.' With supporters like this, the Poor Law hardly had need of critics.

For more effective in discrediting the workhouse than any of the numerous pamphlets attacking it were the factual accounts of workhouse atrocities which from 1836 onwards began to fill the columns of the newspapers. One of the earliest and worst cases, raised by John Walter in the House of Commons in February 1837, concerned the 'great neglect and inhumanity' shown to three small children in the Droxford Union, near Southampton. Here, the public learned, five-year-old Jonathan Cooke, 'weak in intellect' and suffering from a physical disability which made him incontinent and dirty, was constantly 'flogged for it' with a birch, by the workhouse master, or beaten with a special instrument expressively known as a 'spatter', similar punishments being inflicted on two children aged three and four. The schoolmistress had brought with her to the schoolhouse her own pair of stocks, which were set up in the middle of the school-room, and here the three infants were often imprisoned 'for the greater part of the day...They had stood from meal-time to meal-time, from about 10 to half past 12 standing all the time' and again all the afternoon.

When the unhappy trio were moved to another union 'the boys', the master of the receiving workhouse observed, 'were haggard and very pictures of distress and misery...none of them could walk, none even stand without assistance'. Jonathan, the worst treated, was removed to hospital, where he ultimately recovered and soon everyone concerned was trying to off-load the responsibility for what had happened. The Poor Law Commissioners blamed the Guardians. The Guardians blamed the workhouse master. The workhouse master blamed the schoolmistress, who made the classic excuse: 'I acted under orders.' Everyone blamed the medical officer, who resigned, while the Assistant Commissioner, whose job it was to prevent such abuses, assembled all the workhouse inmates and persuaded them to pass a resolution 'that they had no complaints to make whatever'. This was to be the pattern for many subsequent scandals and no one came out of it well except those who had all along urged that the workhouse was an intrinsically brutal institution.

The next outcry concerned the alleged neglect of an elderly woman, 66-year-old Honor Shawyer of Bishops Waltham, who complained one morning of feeling ill, was given an aperient by the union doctor, and soon afterwards died, a post mortem revealing a serious bowel condition. The target of criticism here was the workhouse matron, Rachel Privett, denounced by the local rector as 'a most unfit person to have the management of the sick...a notorious character in the parish . . . given to drinking'. At the subsequent inquest the jury attributed Honor Shawyer's death to neglect and called for the dismissal of Mrs Privett and her husband, the master, to which, a few weeks later, the local Guardians agreed.

Complaints that the workhouse was a death-trap were always good for several column-inches in the press and one union which provided these in abundance was Westhampnett in Sussex. Hardly had the new workhouse there opened its doors than the inmates began dying in rapid succession, due, it now seems clear, to the privy leaking into the well. The chairman of the Board, the Duke of Richmond, was a thorough-going champion of the new law and when, in January 1836, a local woman, Mrs Charlotte Legg of North Mundham, applied for relief for her three children, aged two to eight, her husband having been imprisoned for smuggling, the family was inevitably ordered into the workhouse. Almost at once, Mrs Legg later complained, the children's stomachs rebelled at being given 'nothing but gruel night and morning', but 'Master said we were to have that or nothing.' Within a week the three children were ill; within nine weeks two of them were dead. Mrs Legg begged for a cart to remove her sole surviving child, who was too ill to walk, but, according to her story, the Duke, who was visiting the workhouse, retorted that 'He would not let the living go without the dead', meaning that she could only leave if she paid for the burial of her two dead children. In the end the grief-stricken mother managed to do so by selling her sole valuable possession, her husband's watch, and getting herself a job on the land at 6s. 8d. a week. 'I would', she insisted, 'do anything and half-starve sooner than go into that place again', a sentiment the Poor Law Commissioners must have applauded.

Life in the new workhouse at Bridgwater, opened in August 1836, was also distinctly dangerous, according to one local Guardian, John Bowen, an uncompromising opponent of the new law. 'On the one side', he wrote in 1837, 'are the helpless poor, on the other the aggregate property of the kingdom' and within a few months there were in the new 'union' more than thirty cases of illness, with five or six diseased children or three adults sharing a bed, though many were suffering from diarrhoea. Bowen vividly described the sight, and smell, which greeted the members of the Visiting Committee that month. 'A number of persons of all ages were suffering intense agony; others apparently worn out by the operation of the disease; those . . . not yet affected bearing in their countenances the strongest marks of terror and apprehension; and all breathing and absorbing a heavy, foetid atmosphere, saturated with the poisonous effluvia of putrid excrement.' When the main body of Guardians insisted on sending more paupers into the house, Bowen carried out his threat to raise 'the cry of murder and appeal . . . to the public', publishing a list of dead paupers in *The Times* that July. Within ten days the Poor Law Commissioners had ordered an enquiry, although it finally, if unconvincingly, acquitted the Guardians of all blame.

There was a similar ending to another *cause celebre*, that of Mary Wilden, about whom Samuel Roberts of Sheffield published a 50-page pamphlet in 1839. Mary, an epileptic in her forties, had been removed from the workhouse at nearby Dinnington by her sister, who had been shocked at her condition, despite the warning that 'she would not have a farthing allowed her' for Mary's nursing and support. When her relations soaked off her chemise they 'found her covered with thousands of lice in the hair of her head, on her person and her clothes', while a neighbour, later testified on oath that 'She was black and blue all over. The skin was off her knees in pieces as big as a crown piece.' Mary blamed her condition on a nurse who had made 'a rod...for the children at the workhouse out of an old birch besom and...beat her with the thick end of it over the hips, thighs and shoulder...because she could not eat her porridge fast enough', but when, ten days after being 'rescued', she died, the coroner's jury finally accepted the official explanation that her injuries had been caused by falling out of bed. But neither Mary's family nor the public were satisfied, and the case continued to feature for years in anti-Poor Law literature.

Hardly had the echoes of this affair died away when, in the following year, John Stokes, porter of Kidderminster workhouse, was charged with ill-treating an eight-year-old boy who suffered from a disease of the bladder which caused bed-wetting. Stokes, the local paper reported, 'had often punished the boy for the involuntary effects of the complaint', until one morning 'groans were heard issuing from a sack hanging up from a beam, and on the governor of the workhouse cutting it down the child was found doubled up within the bag, in which state the porter had kept him suspended all the morning'.

Stokes was duly convicted, on the evidence of the workhouse master, but far harder to detect were cases where the master himself was at fault. Over Christmas that same year, 1840, the nation was shocked, or secretly titillated, by far worse revelations about events at Hoo, near Rochester. Here, *The Times* reported, the master, Miles, had mercilessly beaten the nine small children in the workhouse and regularly whipped the older girls, 'verging on womanhood', who were made 'to strip the upper parts of the person naked to allow him to scourge them with birch rods on their bare shoulders and waists'. One 13-year-old had been made to lie on a table, held down by the other teenagers, while he 'took her clothes off and beat her...until the blood came' and another girl, a year older, had had 'her chemise [pulled] off the upper part of her body' and 'her bosom . . . laid bare'. These facts were brought to light after a younger girl, ten-year-old Susan Barnes, who had been employed by Miles's wife as a domestic drudge and constantly beaten by both of them with a poker, had escaped from the workhouse through a window at 6 a m one Saturday 'because she broke a piece out of a milk jug and was told that she would have the rod the next morning'. Susan walked the eight miles to the house of the woman she called her 'grandmama', who had sheltered her when she became an orphan. Hardly had the neighbours 'examined her body and found that parts of it were turned green and yellow' than the workhouse master arrived on horseback, flourishing a whip like a villain in melodrama, and replying to her protectors' pleas for mercy, 'I will give her as much as I am able'. Soon the whole street had turned out to protect the terrified child and the result was a public outcry which led to Miles being dismissed, though the Poor Law Commissioners refused to prosecute him.

A few months later, in 1841, appeared a comprehensive anthology of every abuse ever attributed to the New Poor Law. Although weakened by incessant exclamation marks, underlinings, and puerile asides such as 'Fie! How naughty!', the thousands of press reports and quotations from speeches, sermons and private letters it contained added up to a striking indictment of the workhouse, even if only a small proportion of the quoted incidents was true. The author was G.R. Whythen Baxter of Hereford, otherwise unknown to history. He 'deemed there was need in our libraries of a ... standard history of anti-New Poor Law eloquence and benevolence and of pro-New Poor Law enormities and horrors...composed not only...to excite the abhorrence of future beings for an atrocious law...but...to show...that that there were not wanting men...who...dared be honest...dared be humane and oppose it.' Among this noble band Baxter undoubtedly included himself; he had, he told the reader, 'to the best of my pen, ink and lungs...excited the inhabitants of Herefordshire, Carmarthenshire, Glamorganshire, Pembrokeshire, etc. to prove restive under the constraints of Somerset House and...on one occasion last winter treated some chaps, with pints round, to hiss and groan at an Assistant Commissioner'.

The Book of the Bastilles began with a stage direction for a mock-dialogue: 'Scene: The outside of a new-built "union": Groans, weeping and gnashing of teeth and the agonising cries of innocents writhing under the lash heard from within' and the incidents and anecdotes which followed lived up to this promising introduction. Baxter's taste, like that of many Victorians, was for bold colours, basic emotions and simple stories, played out against a background of snow and moonlight. No novelist, surely, could have bettered the tale of poor Widow Deacon of Woburn, who, having honourably raised four children with the help of out-relief, after being told 'some time before Michaelmas, 1836...she was not to have relief except in the workhouse...came home in a very depressed state of mind...and on the night of Christmas Day' drowned herself, her 'son...stating that he had tracked his mother through the snow to the moat... which borders upon the rectory garden'.

Equally impressive were the cases of an 18-year-old girl discovered living in a haystack near Chester and eating 'the grass of an adjacent field [as] she feared being sent to the union', and a 12-year-old boy found 'cuddled up like a hedgehog under the wall' near Stockport, who had fled from Stowmarket workhouse, after he had discovered his sister 'fastened in a kind of stocks...They were cutting her hair off, and they were flogging her because she cried'.

The blind and dumb old man at Chester, refused a gift of snuff by order of the Assistant Commissioner, the old woman in Kent whose daughter was not allowed to take her a seedcake, 'the poor female cripple, hurled down headlong...upon rough stones', for refusing to surrender an ounce of tea—all were now recorded. So, too, was the parsimony of one Welsh union which, when a cripple on its books died, tried to reclaim his wooden leg on the grounds that it was parish property and merely on loan to him, though his widow wished it to be buried with him.

'So much', commented Baxter on a similar case of union meanness, 'for the means by which savings are achieved under the administration of the New Poor Law Amendment Act...I blush for its supporters and am proud to be numbered among its...most active opponents'.

10 Scandal at Andover

It has been proved before the Committee that...
instances occurred in which inmates of the workhouse...ate the gristle and marrow of the bones
which they were set to break. *Report of the Select
Committee on the Andover Union*, 1846

Despite the unceasing flow of abuse heaped upon them, the Poor
Law Commissioners had, by 1845, grounds for sober satisfaction.
Contrary to the forebodings expressed in 1834, they had not
provoked a revolution, but they had destroyed the Speenhamland
system and covered the country with a wholly new system of poor
relief, centred on the workhouse. 594 unions had been formed,
employing 8,000 paid officers and with a total payroll of £400,000 a
year, and all the earlier regulations concerning diet, classification,
punishment and rest, drafted by Civil Servants guided only by theory,
had been tested and perfected by hard experience, and consolidated
in a massive General Order in April 1842, which became the 'Bible'
of the workhouse master. In ten years, more than £3 million had been
spent, and scrupulously accounted for, in building new workhouses
or enlarging old ones. By now almost every union, except a few in
Wales and the intransigent areas of the industrial North, had a workhouse but, as the Commissioners liked to point out, contrary to
popular mythology, only a small proportion of those on relief were
actually forced inside it. In 1837 11 per cent of paupers had been
workhouse inmates; by 1844 the total was still no more than 15 per
cent. The occupants of Poor Law workhouses at that time numbered
about 180,000, compared to close on a million on out-relief, though
these figures masked great variations between unions, as some applied
the 'workhouse test' far more ruthlessly than others. In the course of
a year the numbers who received some form of relief, often free
medical treatment, were rather larger, totalling, in 1843, 239,000
people admitted to the workhouse and 1,300,000 given relief outside it, making a total of one and a half million in a population of
16 million.

Although the population of England and Wales had risen from less than 14 million in 1831 to more than 16½ million in 1845, the cost of poor relief had dropped steadily, from £6,300,000 in 1834 to £4,900,000 in 1844, so that the average expenditure per head of population had been cut from nearly 10*s*. to just over 6*s*. It was understandable that the Poor Law Commissioners felt indignant that their solid achievements had gone unrecognised by the public, which had preferred to condemn the New Poor Law on the strength of a few untypical abuses. As Nassau Senior, who believed that 'his' Act had done all that had been expected of it, wrote anonymously in a pamphlet published in 1847: 'Single cases of neglect or ill usage of the poor—such as must occur in every country and under every possible form of administration—have been selected with care, exhibited with ostentatious minuteness, heightened by exaggeration and represented as the natural fruits of the system.'

Certainly the Whig government had no doubts about the system it had introduced in 1834, for in July 1838, following a rapid tour of the whole of Ireland by George Nicholls in 1836, an Irish Poor Law had been introduced on the English model, though far more rapidly, and more drastically, than in England. Out-relief was almost totally abolished and within a year 130 brand-new workhouses built, on a common pattern. The Irish patriot, Daniel O'Connell, was highly critical of this achievement, alleging that Nicholls 'was whirled in a post-chaise at the public expense, from Dublin to Cork, from Cork to Sligo, from Sligo to Belfast...He calculated everything and was accurate in nothing'. In fact, until the disaster of the potato famine in 1845, the Irish Poor Law worked at least as well as its counterpart in England. Then, with the workhouses swamped, out-relief had reluctantly to be restored, but by 1853 the workhouse population had sunk back to its regular level, of fewer than 80,000, in a country of six million people, while in the whole of Ireland only 2,000 people were on out-relief.

Although morale at Somerset House should have been high, beneath the surface all was not happy, due to the intriguings and disloyalty of Edwin Chadwick, who had never reconciled himself to his subordinate role there as secretary. He claimed, absurdly, that no decision of the Commissioners was valid if taken in his absence and, when this demand was rejected or ignored, Chadwick felt himself entitled to use some of his superabundant energy in conspiring against the Commissioners and in trying to advance his status at their expense.

Between 1839 and 1842 Chadwick had been heavily preoccupied with conducting a vast investigation into working-class housing and its influence on destitution and disease, which culminated in the classic and immensely influential *Report on the Sanitary Condition of the Labouring Population*, which bore his name. His findings, however, did nothing to alter Chadwick's attitude to social reform. It was the untidiness, inefficiency and wastefulness of preventable illness and poverty which motivated Chadwick, rather than the suffering they involved; he was that relatively rare being, a reformer who fundamentally cared little for humanity. One critic of the New Poor Law protested in 1837 at 'the complex machinery with which mere pen-and-ink men presume to supersede the charities and other duties of life', but Chadwick would probably not have resented the description: pen and ink were less wayward instruments than emotions.

The first shadow of the approaching storm became visible in 1842 as 'the Hungry Forties' sent the number of applications for relief soaring. In June William Smith, an agricultural labourer of Wilmington in the often-criticised Eastbourne Union of Sussex, petitioned the House of Commons in protest against his 'oppressive and cruel treatment...there' by which 'his life was endangered'. He had, he complained, been locked with other men in a room only eight feet by fourteen for seven hours a day, pounding into dust, for use as fertiliser, bones collected from local butchers and private houses, though some consignments included human bones, which were disposed of 'down the privy hole'. 'If I had stopped two months longer in the bonehouse', Smith declared, 'I should not have come out alive.'

The Poor Law Commissioners' only response was to announce, wrongly, that they had no power to stop bone-crushing, but the Eastbourne case was widely publicised in a pamphlet, *The Murder Den and its Means of Destruction*, and shortly afterwards bone-crushing caused more trouble at Basingstoke, where it was blamed for an outbreak of fever. Assistant Commissioner Henry Parker, who investigated the circumstances, later gave evidence to a House of Commons Committee. There were, he explained, bones and bones: that is, 'bones of commerce', which were boiled to make soup or soap, before being dried and pulverised, and 'green bones', straight from slaughter-houses and kitchens, which still contained marrow and had fragments of meat clinging to them. The crushing of the latter sort of bones in workhouses should, he suggested, be banned, or else be done in an enclosed mill and not by hand.

This advice, it subsequently came out, was 'not popular at Somerset House', where bones were a sensitive subject. The Home Secretary, Sir James Graham, 'disapproved of that mode of employing the poor', but Commissioner George Nicholls was a great enthusiast for it, and had indeed introduced it into the workhouse at Southwell which had made his name. A second Commissioner, Sir George Cornewall Lewis, blew hot and cold, at one time wanting to forbid bone-crushing, at another agreeing to leave the decision to individual unions, and in the end nothing was done.

One union where bone-crushing was highly regarded was Andover, hitherto best known as a coaching stage on the main route to the West. From the Commissioners' point of view it was a model union and, as mentioned earlier, the Guardians had from the first followed the lead of their chairman, the Rev. Christopher Dodson, in sending every possible applicant to the workhouse. All out-relief to the able-bodied had stopped as soon as the workhouse was opened and Andover was one of the few unions not to relax this rule during the 'great freeze' of January 1838. It had, a week or two earlier, failed to provide the paupers in the workhouse with a Christmas dinner and, six months later, also decided against serving extra rations in honour of the Queen's coronation, when all the poor outside the workhouse were entertained to a dinner of roast beef and plum pudding in the market square, followed by games and dancing. The Board's ruthlessness shocked even the Rev. Thomas Mozeley, a convinced opponent of the old Poor Law, who before 1834 had helped his father to introduce a deterrent workhouse in the latter's parish in Derby and was now himself rector of Cholderton on Salisbury Plain. 'Some of my poor parishioners, in spite of my remonstrances', he complained, 'were hurried off to Andover union, there to rot and die', and on his journeys round the district he regularly passed carts en route for the workhouse laden with 'bones from Mr Assheton's dog-kennels'.

Within the grim red-brick walls of the house itself, the work was hard, the discipline strict, the diet scanty. At Andover no little indulgences had been allowed to creep in. There was no nonsense about supplying cutlery; children and adults alike ate with their fingers, while any man who tried to exchange a word with his wife at meal times soon found himself in the punishment cells. Even 'fallen women', usually the most troublesome group of inmates, were kept firmly in their place: all were identified by a yellow stripe on their dresses and any who answered the master or matron back had their hair cropped short like convicts and were forced to stand all through Sunday morning prayers.

The firm discipline which prevailed was due, the Guardians believed, to their happy choice as workhouse master of an ex-sergeant-major, Colin M'Dougal, a veteran of Waterloo. He arrived in 1837, at the age of 44, with a limp, a strong Scottish accent, first-class testimonials—his discharge papers described his character as 'exemplary' —and a wife, Mary Ann, whose grim manner qualified her well for the post of matron. The admiring chairman described 'Mrs Mac' as 'a violent lady, rather', and both M'Dougals rapidly took their cue from him. When the Visiting Committee toured the workhouse to hear complaints, 'Old Mac' was always at hand to discourage skrimshankers and he showed an equal determination to save the ratepayers' money. Thus, 16-year-old Ann Coleman and her 12-year-old brother, who had a settlement elsewhere, were turned out 'with a quart of bread and three or four ounces of cheese . . . with clothes in a very ragged state and without any money . . . to walk 34 or 36 miles before they reached their mother's house', being helped on their way with a blow from M'Dougal's fist. Thus, Louisa Barnes, only slightly older, was, on the onset of labour pains, 'ordered . . . to change her clothes and leave the house immediately', M'Dougal declaring that 'she belonged to Stockbridge', eight miles away and should ask assistance there.

The Guardians acknowledged that even this admirable couple had their little faults. Mrs M'Dougal's sharp tongue was sometimes publicly directed at her husband instead of its proper target, the paupers, while M'Dougal himself was often irritable due to the indigestion to which he was a martyr and was usually the worse for drink on the night his pension came. But that, the Board felt, was only to be expected of an old solider, and in securing his services for £80, plus board and lodging, and his wife's for another £40, the Guardians clearly believed they had obtained a bargain.

Most of them were, in any case, only too ready to leave the management of the union's affairs to their domineering chairman but their desire for a quiet life was constantly frustrated. One Guardian, Farmer Hugh Mundy, was frequently at odds with his colleagues whom he infuriated by paying his labourers ten shillings a week, two shillings more than the neighbouring landowners. Their other constant critic was one of the union surgeons, Dr Thomas Westlake, who, most of the Guardians considered, was for ever lavishly prescribing every imaginable luxury, from extra cheese to beef-tea. In fact, M'Dougal saw to it that such instructions were usually ignored, for having once served in a military hospital he fancied himself as a physician, and dealt with all complaints of illness by distributing 'salts and senna'.

In December 1844 Hugh Mundy laid a motion before the Board of Guardians to end bone-crushing in the workhouse, but it was promptly voted down by the chairman and his supporters. During the next few months, however, ugly rumours began to circulate in Andover of what went on in the bone-yard at the workhouse and in May 1845 Mundy formally warned his fellow Guardians of what was being said, as he later described:

> I had heard that men employed in crushing bones were in the habit of eating the marrow and gristle . . . The Guardians would not believe it . . . I succeeded in getting two or three to go with me and I desired M'Dougal to call ten or twelve men before us . . . They then told us that ten out of the twelve were in the habit of doing this daily. Two of them stated that they had not done so but had seen the others do it. They said that when they found . . . a fresh bone, one that appeared a little moist, that they were almost ready to fight over it, and that the man who was fortunate enough to get it was obliged to hide it that he might eat it when he was alone.

The men also produced for Mundy bones they had hidden which were 'all over ashes and in a decomposed state', and one of the group explained that the rotting meat from bones was an acquired taste, but 'once they had taken to eat them they preferred that employment to any other because they then get more food'. The Guardians decided to take no action, apart from suspending bone-crushing during hot weather, and eventually Mundy decided to make the whole business public. He turned to Thomas Wakley, who on Friday 1 August 1845 rose in the House of Commons to ask Sir James Graham about a complaint, sent by a Guardian to the Poor Law Commission, that the paupers at Andover were 'in the habit of quarrelling with each other about the bones, of extracting the marrow...and of gnawing the meat'. The Home Secretary replied that he 'could not believe in the existence of such an abuse', though he promised to 'institute an inquiry this very night', and on the following day Henry Parker, the Assistant Commissioner responsible for Andover, was ordered by Somerset House to establish the facts.

It cannot have been a welcome assignment, for, like all the Assistant Commissioners, Parker was already scandalously over-worked. The 21 Assistant Commissioners of 1839 had gradually been reduced to 9, as the work of setting up new unions diminished, so that Parker, an Assistant Secretary at headquarters from 1836 until 1839, had in his charge by 1845 the care of 1,20,000 people, scattered over 1,382 parishes and 86 unions. Another Commissioner estimated at this time that he paid 225 visits a year, and travelled 1,000 miles in three months, while Parker himself admitted that to inspect a single workhouse thoroughly took at least two days. As a result, he complained, he had had to work 'from nine in the morning till long past midnight' from Monday to Saturday, and often for much of Sunday as well. It was all very well for the Commissioners, in 1844, to issue a reminder that 'the utmost activity on the part of the Assistant Commissioner in visiting Boards of Guardians and work-houses is indispensable'. There were limits to what one man could do and at Andover, as elsewhere, they had long since been overreached.

But orders were orders and, no doubt privately cursing his superiors and the trouble-makers who had started what would almost certainly turn out to be another mare's nest, Henry Parker, ex-barrister, ex-colonial judge, a Civil Servant known by his superiors to be both energetic and conscientious, rode into Andover at nine o'clock on the morning of Monday 4 August 1845 to begin his enquiry. He began by taking statements from Farmer Hugh Mundy and from various former inmates of the workhouse, and by next day was able, reluctantly, to report back to London that the charges were true. 'Amongst the bones, supplied to the workhouse by the bone gatherers', he wrote, 'many are fresh from the kitchens of the gentry, and the inmates . . . acknowledge having picked out such bones and eaten the marrow from them...Two inmates...partook of horse flesh found on bones purchased from the dog-kennel and Green [one witness] avows that he has frequently eaten stale and stinking meat from beef and mutton bones.' He also discovered the equally unwelcome fact that all the inmates of the workhouse had apparently been kept short of bread.

On the 14 August Parker was instructed to investigate any alleged 'neglect or misconduct on the part of the Master or officers of the workhouse', it being 'most important that such an investigation . . . should be substantially fair and open,' though he was also ordered 'to bring the enquiry to a conclusion with as little delay as possible'. In the event his attempts to be both fast and thorough satisfied no one. When he tried to exclude irrelevant evidence, he was attacked in the press for planning to hush up injustice; when he granted a brief adjournment to allow more witnesses to be assembled, the Commissioners accused him of wasting time.

Events took a dramatic turn when, on 29 September (very wisely in view of revelations to come) M'Dougal announced his resignation. Parker, trying to be helpful, recommended an unemployed protégé of his, the former master of the Oxford workhouse, to take over from M'Dougal, until—a piquant touch, much appreciated by all enemies of the Poor Law—it came to light that this man, too, had been dismissed for misconduct. Parker was summoned back to London but when he suggested consulting the Commission's solicitors about prosecuting M'Dougal, the lawyers advised against it. The Commission was left with a hostile press, a critical Parliament, a seriously alarmed public opinion and no scapegoat.

From now on it is clear that the unlucky, overworked Assistant Commissioner was cast for this role. When he drafted a letter from the Board to the Andover Guardians he was accused of trying to throw the blame on the Commissioners, and to his protests that he could hardly be blamed for bones being crushed without his knowledge, the Board replied unsympathetically that he would have found 'the bonehouse fast enough if he had simply followed his nose'. On 16 October Parker was called on to resign and his only reward for years of devoted service was a suggestion that he should seek employment with one of the expanding railway companies.

The Poor Law Commissioners, by dismissing Parker, no doubt felt they had saved themselves; but they were wrong. The former Assistant Commissioner published a long pamphlet in his own defence which effectively indicted his recent superiors and his case was rapidly taken up by a group of anti-Poor Law MPs, along with that of another Assistant Commissioner, William Day, who had also been peremptorily ordered to resign after years of loyal service, nominally because he had been laid up for several weeks after falling down some steps. His real offence had been that, like Parker, he had been given an impossible task, namely, to introduce the New Poor Law into Wales against the determined opposition of several Boards of Guardians, who objected to the cost of building new workhouses. Like Parker he had been sacrificed to propitiate his employers' enemies.

The public unease produced by the dismissal of two Assistant Commissioners, one of whom he had personally recruited, provided Chadwick with too valuable an opportunity for trouble-making to be missed and he exploited it to the full, encouraging Members of Parliament to keep the issue alive, even though the condemnation of his employers also reflected on him. On 8 November 1845, the Poor Law Commissioners tacitly acknowledged the justice of the attacks made on bone crushing by issuing a General Order forbidding any pauper to be 'employed in pounding, grinding or otherwise breaking bones, or in preparing bone-dust', though George Nicholls formally recorded his dissent, and years later he remained unrepentant, blaming the trouble at Andover on 'the depraved appetite of the men', and attacking his colleagues for giving way to 'the excitement of the moment'. But in any case, the abolition of bone-crushing came too late. Public opinion was now seriously alarmed and the government bowed to it. On 5 March 1846 a Select Committee of the House of Commons was appointed 'to enquire into the administration of the Andover union and...the management of the union workhouse...the conduct of the Poor Law Commissioners and...all the circumstances under which the Poor Law Commissioners called upon Mr Parker to resign his Assistant Commissionership'.

The fifteen members of the 'Andover Committee'—they included three known opponents of the workhouse, John Fielden, Thomas Wakley and Benjamin Disraeli—began work only two weeks later. In the next three and a half months a motley procession of witnesses filed in front of them: George Nicholls, Edwin Chadwick and other officials from Somerset House, Farmer Mundy and Dr Westlake, who had set the whole ponderous process in motion; the Rev. Christopher Dodson, refusing to hear a word against his trusted M'Dougal; M'Dougal himself, insisting, in the face of all the evidence, that he had been wronged; Henry Parker, who truly had been; and, most important of all, sundry labourers, unmarried mothers and other paupers, brought up from Andover for an unexpected day out in the capital. The tale which, in their homely Hampshire accents, was daily unfolded in the sober surroundings of the Palace of Westminster, was reported at length in the newspapers. The committee room, everyone realised, had become a courtroom; it was the New Poor Law, the Whigs who had created it, and the gentry who had administered it, which were on trial.

The bones which had begun the affair soon receded into the background, though not before the Committee had learned, with patriotic pride, that British bones were best. Imported bones, one witness explained, are 'very old and of very little service'. The superior Hampshire bones were, it transpired, collected by the ton from Winchester and Salisbury and pounded to pieces at Andover in long open troughs, in a small room opening off the men's yard.

Bone crushing was useful as a punishment and the cry 'Keep him well to the bone-tub!' was often heard when any inmate seemed recalcitrant. One man had been sent to the bonehouse for speaking to his wife, the Committee heard, and a boy of thirteen had been sentenced to it for running away. Even children aged no more than eight or ten were forced to crush bones, although too small to lift the usual tool unaided or even to reach over the edge of the trough. 'Two boys', it was explained, 'used to be put to one rammer; they were obliged to stand upon the edge of the box'. Yet even for a fit man it was very hard work, for the rammer, of solid iron, weighed up to 28 pounds and, apart from the appalling smell, one's hands were soon blistered and one's back breaking, while the former porter to the workhouse, who had given up his job in disgust at the smell from the bonehouse, testified that he had 'seen men with dreadful faces in consequence of some particles of bone flying into their faces'.

But bone-crushing made a handsome profit. The going rate for old bones around Andover was only £1 a ton, while the resulting dust could be sold to farmers at 23s. to 24s. a quarter, though it emerged, embarrassingly, that the Guardians had auctioned it among themselves in the Board room, at 17s. to 19s. The rules were never bent, however, in favour of the paupers; a proposal to grant a beer ration to the men employed in bone-crushing had been overwhelmingly defeated.

Far more serious were subsequent revelations, for scraping meat from decayed bones soon proved to be only one of the many ways in which inmates of Andover workhouse had supplemented their inadequate rations. Several children had been slapped for eating raw potatoes meant for the pigs and Mrs M'Dougal had beaten others for picking the hens' oats off the ground.* 'I could eat it up'—i.e. the whole day's rations—'at one meal,' said one man bluntly, 'and not have a bellyfull then.'

The Andover Union back in 1836, had, it was now learned, adopted the lowest of all the suggested dietaries, even retaining it when it was withdrawn a few weeks later as inadequate, while much even of this scanty allowance had never reached the paupers. M'Dougal, various grocers testified, had ordered goods of superior quality for himself, telling them to recoup the cost by delivering short rations to the inmates. Thus, when they should have enjoyed four ounces of bacon they received only one and a half. A man slaving all day in the bonehouse received for his main meal only one ounce of poor quality cheese with his bread, while M'Dougal was boasting that 'Bridger's cheese is very capital', or only one and a half ounces of bacon, instead of four, while most of the meat and beer, tea and butter ordered for nursing mothers and invalids had gone the same way; one woman breast-feeding her baby, ordered extra rations for twenty-two weeks, had received them for three. Even the children's milk had not been spared, for M'Dougal had skimmed off the cream and diluted what remained with twice its volume of water.

The Visiting Guardians had, it was obvious, been criminally negligent. When the paupers had grumbled that their 'broth' was merely the water in which the previous day's meat had been boiled, M'Dougal had assured the Guardians it was 'beautiful soup' and none of them seem to have thought of sampling it. M'Dougal's method of distributing the paupers' food was rough and ready even by workhouse standards. 'He used', said one former occupant of the bonehouse, 'to come in and chuck it down and we used to snap it up.' Even the work-house pigs had done better than the paupers for, it emerged, they had been fattened up for sale on potatoes, while for seven weeks the inmates' regular 'meat dinner' had been served only with cabbage.

Although the Guardians had long known of M'Dougal's weakness for the bottle, they now learned for the first time that, to the delight of the paupers, he had more than once been drunk at prayers and sometimes read the Lord's Prayer twice over by mistake. His weekend

---

*Ex-Assistant Commissioner Parker was not impressed, however. 'Almost anything,' he wrote, 'will be consumed by certain classes of pauper.' He had known one man who had drunk a whole pot of paint.

excursions were notorious. 'Most Saturday evenings he reels round
the land tolerably groggy', admitted one witness, and when he failed
to return at all Mrs M'Dougal and the porter would set off to comb
the public houses in search of him, leaving the workhouse in the care
of M'Dougal's 22 year-old daughter. When found, his temper
tended to be violent and on at least one occasion, after his wife had
challenged him, with good reason, about what went on between him
and the cook while she was at church on Sunday mornings, there
had been a stand-up fight, only ended when the couple's children
woke two of the inmates to come and help them. They found both
combatants covered in blood and swearing violenty, but M'Dougal
had had the worst of the encounter, for his wife was seated on the
sofa while he was stretched out on the floor, 'His head was
bleeding', one of the paupers present later told the Enquiry, 'and
there was blood on the carpet and on the wainscot . . . I never saw
anybody look so dreadful in my life.'

The next morning, still suspicious, Mrs M'Dougal decided not to
go to church but sent for a rope and announced her intention of
hanging herself, though the threat was not carried out and M'Dougal
profited by this incident, since the inmates concerned were afraid to
tell his wife of his approaches for fear she really would kill herself.
Soon a regular procession of girls was obeying his summons to the
sickward or his bedroom — he and his wife had separate rooms — sometimes in return for a promise of extra 'victuals and some beer' — or
were enduring lesser intimacies as they went about their work. 'He
asked me to come and hold the window', explained one. 'I did that,
and he put his hand into my bosom; he said, "How beautiful and
soft!" ' 'He pulled me about and kissed me and tried to put his hand
up my clothes', another young woman told the Select Committee and,
incidentally, the whole country, since the newspapers avidly reported
every new revelation. M'Dougal's scapegrace son, Joseph, aged 17,
was shown to be a real chip off the old block, for after his father
had installed him on the union payroll as workhouse schoolmaster he
developed a little weakness for wandering off into the younger
women's dormitory at bedtime. About him, as about all the
M'Dougals, there is a distinct echo of the Squeers family immortalised
by Charles Dickens in *Nicholas Nickleby* a few years before. All of
them strode arrogantly about their small empire, issuing orders,
administering slaps and beatings, dispensing occasional favours and
smiles, and abusing all who crossed them, to quote Mrs M'Dougal's

favourite phrases, as 'ungrateful faggots' and 'good-for-nothing brutes'.

Even more perhaps than their treatment of the living, what finally destroyed the M'Dougals was their treatment of the pauper dead. When the records were scrutinised, the puzzling fact came to light that of fifty babies born in Andover workhouse since 1837 only six had been baptised, and that many who had died after three or four weeks had been described by M'Dougal as 'stillborn'. The reason, it now appeared, was that baptism cost a shilling—sixpence each for the officiating minister and the sexton—and the 'stillborn' description avoided awkward questions about infants dying unbaptised.

Another of M'Dougal's meannesses also sent a thrill of horror through the nation. When both an old man and an unbaptised child had lain in the 'deadhouse' he had remarked 'It will save a coffin to bury the child with old White', and brushing aside the widow's objections, had thrown the baby's body in beside the old man's.*

But of all the stories brought to light, none aroused more public indignation than the suffering of Hannah Joyce, an unmarried mother in her twenties, whom both the M'Dougals detested. They knew, as her fellow inmates did not, that Hannah had previously been charged with infanticide, though acquitted, and when, pregnant again, she arrived at Andover, they were immediately suspicious of her.

One Saturday evening, when her new baby Emma was five weeks old, it did indeed suddenly die, though Hannah's grief, as she cradled the dead baby in her arms, seems to have been genuine enough. When the other women rang the bell to attract the matron's attention, 'Mrs M'Dougal halloaed to them and said if they did not go down she would throw a bucket of water over them' and when she did reach the ward, greeted Hannah with the remark: 'You good-for-nothing brute, you will be hanged, for you have killed your child.' M'Dougal arrived soon afterwards, a little unsteady on his feet—it was, it will be remembered, a Saturday night—and called Hannah, already in tears, 'a good-for-nothing hussey...a whore and a faggot', ordering her to spend the night in the mortuary beside the body of her dead baby. Incarceration in the eerie, unlighted 'deadhouse' was a favourite punishment at Andover, but Hannah protested so violently that she was finally locked into the sick ward by herself, while a doctor was

*For the reactions of one nurse to the same mortuary a century later, see the *Foreword*.

sent for to examine the baby's body. Happily he was a friend of Dr Westlake, and ignoring Mrs M'Dougal's warning that 'That good-for-nothing nasty creature has murdered her child', he rapidly decided that the baby had died from 'stoppage of the lungs', a diagnosis upheld at the subsequent inquest.

The M'Dougals, disgusted at this verdict, determined to punish Hannah in their own way, and on the following Tuesday evening, while it was still light, presented her with her baby's coffin and ordered her to take it to the churchyard, a distance of about a mile, where poor unbaptised Emma was buried without a prayer said over her, or tear shed for her, except by her mother.

On the following Saturday Mrs M'Dougal told Hannah to leave and ordered the other women 'to rattle her out of the house', telling them that 'if they did not do it they were as bad as her'. Such 'rattlings', or 'skimmingtons', were a traditional way of showing disapproval and Hannah later described how, as she 'came down the steps a number of the women that were in the house came round the corner of the house with tin cups and spoons and plates and knives and fire irons and several other things, rattling and hallooing'.* They followed her into the street, telling her, 'We are ordered to go through the town with thee', but at this point the Guardian from Hannah's home parish of Chilbolton, who was attending the weekly Board meeting and watching from the Boardroom window, told the mob to go back inside, the chairman and his colleagues having merely watched the scene with amusement. This was hardly surprising, for in their eyes 'old Mac', as the reverend chairman called him, could do no wrong. He was, observed Dr Westlake, 'a general favourite with the Board'. He 'possessed extreme influence over the Guardians', considered another witness. The chairman, a man of the same age and equally insensitive, had, it was clear, been completely hoodwinked. 'I don't believe a word of it', he retorted as one new misdemeanour after another came to light, and, when the evidence was too great to be ignored, he suggested that 'the best thing would be for M'Dougal to resign, like other great men. He can say the duties are too arduous for him and that will prevent a great disclosure'.

---

*Readers of *The Mayor of Casterbridge* (published in 1886) will recall the skimmington of which Henchard and Lucetta were the victims. My mother, born in a Somerset village in 1887, witnessed a 'skimmity ride', as it was known locally, as a child, directed at a married man who was paying attention to a neighbour's wife.

In fact, although M'Dougal had already retreated to Dundee, where he survived until the age of seventy-one, the 'great disclosure' came, not merely in the *Evidence* heard by the Select Committee, which filled two enormous volumes totalling several thousand pages, but in its *Report*, published in August 1846, which contained a scathing indictment of everyone concerned.

The Hannah Joyce affair was described as 'an outrage', and M'Dougal and his wife were found to have shown 'utter unfitness for the situation of master and matron'. The members recorded their 'astonishment' at the influence M'Dougal had exercised over the Guardians, who had, it was found, failed in their duty to visit the workhouse, and applied the law in a way bound to cause 'serious individual hardship'. The diet, it was ruled, had been 'too low and... often further diminished by the dishonesty of the master... It has been proved before the Committee', Lord Courtenay and his colleagues agreed, 'that some of the inmates of the workhouse were in the habit of eating raw potatoes and grain and refuse food which had been thrown to the hogs and fowls . . . Instances occurred in which inmates of the workhouse, employed in bone-crushing, ate the gristle and marrow of the bones which they were set to break'. The Committee recommended that no labour of a 'penal or disgusting' nature should be adopted by Boards of Guardians.

Assistant Commissioner Parker was blamed for showing 'an unlimited confidence' in the Andover Board of Guardians, but the Committee agreed that he had carried out his ordinary duties with 'zeal and laboriousness' and conducted the first enquiry 'with ability and promptitude'. The dismissal of both Parker and William Day was 'irregular and arbitrary', involved 'cruel injustice' and was an obvious attempt 'to direct existing public dissatisfaction from the Poor Law Commissioners by concentrating it on Mr Parker and Mr Day'. The Commissioners' handling of the whole affair, the Select Committee crushingly concluded, had not been 'in accordance with the statute under which they exercise their functions and [was] such as to shake public confidence in their administration of the law'.

The Poor Law Commissioners themselves, not unnaturally, took a different view. They had, complained George Nicholls, been 'exposed to the insults of all the refuse of the House of Commons', having to tolerate as their 'chief opponent...the Secretary of the Board... without the power of dismissing him'. The government announced that it proposed to take no action on the *Report*, but it had privately decided that the Commission must go, partly to placate public opinion, but also because it had done its work. The poor rates had been cut; out-relief to the able-bodied had virtually ceased and almost the whole country had been unionised, with 643 unions now in existence, 595 of them formed since 1834, providing between them 707 workhouses, with room for 200,000 people. The time, it seemed, had come when the 'three kings of Somerset House', as the Poor Law Commissioners had been nicknamed by their critics, could safely be replaced by a body enjoying less dictatorial powers and directly responsible to Parliament.

When the Act which had extended the life of the Poor Law Commission ran out in 1847 it was not renewed and the Poor Law Board Act was passed in its place, setting up a new body, the Poor Law Board. The Board consisted in theory of four senior ministers, the Home Secretary, the Chancellor of the Exchequer, the Lord President of the Council and the Lord Privy Seal, but in practice, like the Board of Trade, it was a mere fiction, never intended to meet. The real power rested with its President, who was eligible to sit in Parliament, and his two Secretaries, one of whom could also be an MP. It had been expected that the President would sit in the House of Lords and his Parliamentary Secretary in the Commons, or vice versa, but in practice both ministers were usually MPs. The new Act, despite an eloquent attack by Disraeli, and a violent defence of Chadwick by Lord Brougham, passed easily into law, the new President, Charles Buller, taking up his post in December 1847. Buller was said to be 'a surpassingly brilliant man . . . created for the House of Commons', but he died a year later and few of his successors made any great name for themselves, though, parodoxically, one— G.J. (later Viscount) Goschen—is still remembered because he was forgotten by Lord Randolph Churchill.* The post of his deputy, the Parliamentary Secretary, also invariably went, according to the candid biographer of one holder of it, to one of 'the industrious, painstaking, eminently respectable and eminently dull persons who are chosen by every government for the smaller places in the official hierarchy'.

This policy was not an accident. Between 1834 and 1847 the Poor Law Commissioners had deliberately sought the headlines. Their

---

*In 1886 Lord Randolph resigned as Chancellor of the Exchequer, confident that there was no one to replace him. Instead he was succeeded by Goschen and never held office again, it being said ever afterwards that he had 'forgotten Goschen'.

Annual Reports were full of colourful anecdotes sent in by the Assistant Commissioners, and had a deliberately propagandist aim. Now the attempt to win over educated opinion was given up. Individual cases were no longer quoted and the Poor Law Board's *Reports* became, in the words of Sidney and Beatrice Webb, no mean judges of tedious writing, 'almost unspeakably dull'. The intention now was to avoid controversy, publicity and—as far as possible—change, which attracted both.

Some of the 'men of 1834' survived the upheaval of 1847, but only just. George Nicholls became permanent secretary of the new Board, at a much reduced salary, retiring three years later at the age of seventy, with a pension, a knighthood and a bad stomach, though he lived to be 83. Edwin Chadwick, too powerful to be passed over, was found a seat on the Board of Health, set up in 1848 to fight the coming cholera epidemic, but when in 1853 this body was replaced by another, modelled on the now well-established Poor Law Board, he was, he complained, 'turned off like a piece of lumber' at the age of 54. Though he lived to be 90 and finally got his knighthood, he never held office again.

The Poor Law Board was itself succeeded in 1871 by the Local Government Board, responsible for both health and poor relief. Its President, unlike the President of the Poor Law Board, was almost invariably a member of the Cabinet and the post was held by a succession of men of high calibre, including A. J. Balfour, a future Premier, John Burns, the first working-man Cabinet minister—though he proved a sad disappointment, once in office—and two extremely able Radicals, Sir Charles Dilke and Joseph Chamberlain, both 'future Prime Ministers' who never reached Downing Street. If not the graveyard of ministerial reputations, the department usually did little to enhance them: it was as though the shadow of Andover workhouse still hung over Somerset House, exacting a belated revenge for all the suffering to which its files bore witness.

11 Aged Inmates of Respectable Character

> 'It is a melancholy sight to see the aged collected
> from thirty or forty parishes like a heap of cast-
> off, worn-out tools, to be buried alive in the
> solitude of a workhouse.' Sir George Crewe,
> *A Word for the Poor and against the New Poor
> Law* (1843)

From the very start of the New Poor Law, uneasiness on the part of
the better-off about its treatment of the old, combined with the fear
among the poor of ending their own days in the hated 'house', was
responsible for much of the hostility which the workhouse aroused.
It would, for example, have been a hard-hearted reader who could
have remained unmoved by this account of an old woman's last night
in her own home, published in 1838:

> See her worn out, diseased frame, sitting solitary on that night by
> the last bit of fire she will ever call her own; see her surrounded
> with memorials of former times. There is the bridal bed—the bed
> on which her husband and her children died. There is the cradle
> in which the latter were rocked, and some of the little books in
> which she taught them to read of a God and a Saviour who cared
> for little children or widows, and for all the poor . . . Her spinning
> wheel, too, was there, then the widow's comfort and support...
> but her hand was to touch it no more. On all these she silently
> gazed as a solitary tear trickled down her furrowed cheek; but
> when her petted cat—her only companion, now to be forsaken,
> sprang upon her lap, and gazing in her face began his usual
> purring song, her heart seemed breaking and she sobbed aloud.

Against such appeals, reasoned arguments in defence of the policy
of sending old people to the workhouse could make little headway,
though some writers asserted that the old actually enjoyed life in the
workhouse, like the 'old sailor rough in his manner, but right in his
heart', whom one farmer claimed, in 1836, to have met in a
workhouse near London. ' "My old shattered hulk must sink at last" ',

he told his visitor. 'Never mind, I shall go down bravely in my own country, not like many of my old shipmates, buried in a foreign land . . . It is time for me to weigh my anchor and depart.' This model pauper was philosophic about the loss of his former pleasures. 'Poor Jack', he explained, 'is in too good a port to be lost for a drop of grog now.'

Other champions of the authorities pointed out that to be seventy was not the same as to be saintly. 'On no class', protested one Assistant Commissioner in the same year, 'does the public mind require enlightening so much. . . the characteristics of the aged pauper are dirty and intemperate habits, begging and stealing. . . Rather than be washed, shaved, have his hair cut and put on clean linen, many a pauper has gone away from the workhouse as he came in, a heap of filth and wretchedness.' The farmer, mentioned above, described one 84-year-old inmate of a London workhouse as 'equally unfit for this world or the next', confronting everything with a 'hollow eye . . . scowling brow . . . bitter sneer of his lip' and replying to all overtures with 'a sort of thankless murmur'.

Even those with the interests of the poor at heart sometimes favoured sending the very old into the house. 'Taking aged or infirm or sickly persons out of crowded and filthy places and putting them in places where they might be well attended', was, insisted Dr Westlake of Andover in 1846, 'a beneficial and humane course'. Humane or not, it was the method adopted. By 1867 the old and infirm formed the largest single group, 10,300, of the 28,000 occupants of forty London workhouses. But their special needs were rarely recognised, even though the 1834 Royal Commission had recommended that 'the old might enjoy their indulgences'. So indeed they might have done had separate workhouses, for different types of pauper, been set up. As it was they tended to be treated like other inmates, different from them chiefly in that only death would give them their discharge.

The New Poor Law, in fact, recognised only two types of adult 'indoor pauper', the able-bodied and the infirm and mere age was not usually interpreted as infirmity. This explained sights like that which greeted three former parish overseers who visited the Holborn workhouse during the 1830s and:

> . . . found forty females, of ages varying from forty to eighty, confined in a small room, seven feet nine inches in height, several feet below the surface of the earth, and built over a large sewer, the smell from which was very offensive. The room was . . . exceed-

ingly dark, and these aged females were confined eleven hours out of the twenty-four, at very severe work, pulling wool for mattresses.

Forty years later, conditions had changed little, as a book by a former workhouse employee, published in 1872, made plain:

Some are set to pick oakum, to sweep yards, peel potatoes, etc. whilst others congregate in the day rooms which are provided . . . These rooms are occasionally below ground, dark, damp and dismal . . . Out of five or six hundred, all who can totter resort there, some to rest upon forms, others to loiter about . . . The women lead a similar life . . . Night comes on, the old men and women retire to their wards . . . some of these are small and only contain two or three beds . . . whilst others, of one of which I had charge for six months, contained fifty beds and was more like an immense barn than anything else . . . Many of the occupants of this room were bedridden and, to shelter themselves from the cold winds, I have often seen them huddle themselves under the clothes; the variety of coughs was quite a study; not only were the sufferers kept awake, but from the incessant and various noises produced by the arthritic and bronchitic others were prevented from sleeping.

Although the Poor Law Commissioners had told the unions as early as 1842 that workhouse uniform was not compulsory so long as the inmates' own clothes were removed, few Boards, this man revealed, took advantage of the concession:

The poor old folk are as plainly branded by their dress and in many cases more ashamed of it than a felon would be . . . Even if they have decent clothes on entering, or should friends supply them, they are only permitted to wear parochial clothing and must walk about the streets labelled as paupers. I have known many refuse to avail themselves of the monthly holiday because they were ashamed to be seen so dressed . . . The garb varies with the taste of the Guardians. In some unions a dirty brown is the colour . . . with brass or bone buttons; in others a grey not unlike that worn in our prisons and convict settlements. The clothes of the women fulfil the same purpose, a grey shawl, a black or brown straw bonnet, with parochial trimming, a dress which in material is generally unfit for the season . . . with comfortless shoes with little regard to fit.

A variation on the convict theme was to provide shirts and dresses printed with broad vertical stripes in colour on a grey or dingy white background, and some Boards supplied a special outfit for Sundays. One rural union, in 1865, 'clothed all the inmates of the workhouse in a pronounced livery for their Sunday best, the men in white fustian and the women in blue serge, and expected them to go to church or chapel in procession'—a humiliating experience for all concerned.

Just as the old were expected to wear the same clothes as other inmates, so, too, few concessions were made over workhouse food. Here also the only distinction generally made was between the healthy, who received the standard 'house diet', and the sick, who could only receive extras prescribed by the doctor, no allowance being made for the failing digestions, crumbling teeth and fluctuating appetite of old age. Even medical advice was often ignored. In one workhouse an anti-workhouse meeting was told in 1839, 'the doctor ordered port-wine and sago' for an elderly inmate with a bowel complaint, but 'the port was considered too dear and gooseberry wine was given' instead. Soon afterwards the patient died.

The former workhouse employee, quoted earlier, described in 1872 a medical officer 'annoyed by the interference and petty insults of the Guardians and master if his diet contains half a dozen eggs or half a pint of wine more than usual'. Although old people needed frequent, small meals, 'The last meal of the day', he noted, 'takes place at 5 p.m. and until 8 the next morning the majority, many of them more than 80 years of age, have to go without any nourishment'.

One of the hardest-fought campaigns, waged on behalf of the inmates of what would now be called the geriatric wards, was over the right to possess 'dry tea' and sugar, to enable them to brew themselves a hot drink. One speaker at a Social Science conference—itself a sign of the changing times—in Birmingham in 1857 pointed out that water was the principal, or sole, workhouse drink, while in prison both tea and cocoa were served regularly. Many charitable people tried, openly or illicitly, to provide the old folk with tea, but even if the ingredients were available the necessary utensils usually were not. One woman, a regular visitor to her workhouse in Devon, described in 1857 how she had pleaded 'that there should be a cup and saucer and spoon allowed them, to take the place of the one tin, which looks more fit for my dog to drink its water from than for decent old folk to be reduced to use', but the crockery and spoons she had sent to the workhouse had been 'returned to me as against the rules of the Poor Law to receive them'. She discovered—what no male inspector had ever done—why workhouse tea, when supplied at all, was so often barely drinkable: the same container was used for it 'which has held gruel, suet pudding, meat or rice'.

But far worse than the lack of medical comforts or even tea was the poor quality of the food. A speaker at the 1857 conference already mentioned described seeing an old, bedridden woman pick up the potatoes on her plate and gnaw them by hand as there was no one to cut them up for her, while the broth consisted of little more than hot water with oatmeal floating in it. Four years later, in 1861, the medical officer of the Strand Union wrote to the Guardians reporting that 'large quantities of pudding and pea soup are left untouched, and subsequently thrown into the pig-tub' since 'very many of the aged and infirm' could not eat them. He suggested bread and mutton broth or 'leg of beef soup, pearl barley and rice', but his proposal fell on deaf ears.

As late as 1900 one Poor Law Inspector recalled a workhouse where, a visitor told him, 'They had two coppers so set that their tops were separated only by three inches. When I was there they were boiling clothes in one and soup in the other; and there were no lids on them. When the soup boiled over into the clothes I made no objection, but when the clothes boiled over into the soup, I would not stay to dinner.' It was only at about this date that a real improvement in workhouse diet began, partly because workhouse masters were for the first time given some discretion over their own menus. Previously official permission had been needed for a workhouse master to serve pork instead of beef, or to vary the quantity of currants in a suet pudding.

As with clothing and food, the authorities were loathe to make the old people's quarters more comfortable for fear that the idea of 'pampering the paupers' might spread through the establishment like an epidemic. One royal visitor, a titled pamphleteer protested in 1843, had offered to provide armchairs for the elderly women he had seen occupying hard benches, only to be told this would require special permission from the Poor Law Commissioners.

By 1851 one visitor to a West country workhouse observed that the old people's ward had 'a nice boarded floor, bright fire, neat beds (though only straw filling, for aching limbs)' but no more than 'two armchairs', so the woman she came to visit, 'used to sit on the foot of the bed or even on a tiny stool'. Six years later, the Birmingham conference heard of workhouses where there were still no seats at all in the wards and where, after working all day the old people had to sit in the yard or on the stairs. Other furniture was almost always lacking.

'None of these poor people', noted the West-country visitor already quoted, 'had even a box or drawer to call their own. Sally's bag was kept inside her bed. I have seen in it her hymn-book and spectacles, a piece of cake which I had brought her, a bit of black pudding, my letter to her, an old comb, a bit of sugar twisted up in a small piece of paper.'

Worse even than the absence of furniture was the lack of any occupation. Books and needlework given to the inmates were, in at least one workhouse in the 1850s, confiscated by the matron, and those patients able to get up, one speaker told the 1857 conference, 'sit round the walls, vacant and dreary', a description echoed by Mrs Emma Sheppard of Frome, a pioneer workhouse visitor:

> I can never forget my first impression when I sat down among the old and infirm . . . the listless look, the dull vacuity—the lack of all interest except for the petty details of tea versus gruel—potatoes versus rice, the only object from their windows of moving interest the parish hearse preparing to take away their former companions. There were several old women, all between 70 and 90, crouching round the fire, full of complainings of rheumatism-ache and that friends outside had forgotten them . . . In a bed in a corner lay a poor crippled woman who had been born and brought up in the country, had been in the house three years and who wept over a bunch of common hedgerow flowers I had gathered on my way up . . . She grasped them and all but kissed them.

This lack of contact with the outside world was partly due to the union system itself. Instead of being accommodated in the parish poor-house, the aged, as a pamphlet in 1843 pointed out, were now 'collected from thirty or forty parishes like a heap of cast-off, worn-out tools to be buried alive in the solitude of a workhouse'. 'In August last', wrote one Derbyshire clergyman in 1844, 'I found that excepting the very rare visits of the one clergyman no one . . . went near the sick and dying . . . An old woman one day said to me, "Why, sir, no one has been near us since Mr—was obliged to give up, and here we are, a parcel of old blind creatures, hard at death's door, and no one seems to think of us, or to care whether we go to heaven or hell".'

The opening up of the workhouses to visitors, which was to benefit every category of inmate, began in the 1850s. The decisive step was taken by a London woman, Louisa Twining, who belonged to that large and often derided group of Victorian spinsters who found in good works the fulfilment that motherhood provided for their married contemporaries. The Twinings were a comfortably-off family who owned the tea-importing business which still bears their name and Louisa, born in 1820, was the youngest of eight children. Her childhood was secure and happy but the children were taught to remember those less fortunate than themselves and Lousia's first experience of how the poor lived was gathered in cottage-visiting near Rugby, her brothers' school.

But some of the most wretched hovels in London were to be found in the mean streets off the Strand, near the family's former home, and by her late twenties she was regularly visiting families in the area. Her first personal contact with the workhouse came after an old woman she had befriended was forced to enter the Strand Union, which then had a kindly master, soon to be replaced by the intolerable George Catch, whose regime has already been described. Even before Catch's arrival, the local Guardians refused to allow regular visiting, but Miss Twining was not easily rebuffed and in the following year obtained an interview with the President of the Poor Law Board himself, who was courteous but unhelpful. He would, he said, allow workhouse visiting only if the local Board of Guardians raised no objection. But object they did, most emphatically, no doubt fearing that unwelcome publicity would inevitably follow. Louisa Twining did not give up. She continued to visit any workhouse which would let her in, wrote numerous pamphlets and letters to the press on the subject and eventually, in 1857, got it raised in Parliament, though the minister, a Liberal, characteristically refused to 'interfere'.

By now a number of others had taken up the cause. In West London a local lady mayoress formed her own Visiting Committee, and other women penetrated into the workhouse infirmaries with 'flower missions', allowed in on Sundays to decorate the sick-wards. Finally, in May 1859, largely on Louisa Twining's initiative, a committee of 63 highly respectable citizens, whom no one could accuse of wishing to 'pamper the poor', was formed to set up the Workhouse Visiting Society. The Committee included doctors, barristers, the wives of leading politicians, numerous parish clergy and four bishops, one of whom, the Bishop of Bath and Wells, was himself a former workhouse chaplain, and no fewer than twelve titled members of the aristocracy.

Louisa Twining became the secretary and driving force behind the new Society and during the next four years its *Journal*, a 32-page monthly magazine costing sixpence, became the spearhead of the campaign for workhouse improvement. The *Journal* was discontinued in 1865, its editor explaining that 'it has in some measure done the work which it was intended to accomplish' but the Society, and its influence, remained.

As for the Society's real founder, she had now discovered her true vocation. Louisa Twining became a full-time workhouse reformer and an acknowledged authority on the whole subject, pouring out a stream of pamphlets and letters to the press and visiting workhouses all over the country, to the alarm of idle masters and complacent officials. In middle age she was active in a whole range of good works, and when, in the 1880s, women became eligible for election to Boards of Guardians, she stood, was triumphantly elected and, though now in her mid-sixties, began to give five days a week to attending meetings and making far from cursory inspections of workhouses and Poor Law schools. At seventy she retired to Worthing, where she was soon busy organising a system of district nursing. She then moved to Tunbridge Wells where she started a children's nursery. In old age some of her earlier compassion weakened—she became, for example, a firm supporter of workhouse dress for all but children—but by her death at the end of the century few people had done more to help the pauper.

One of the chief sources of the New Poor Law's unpopularity had always been the separation of man and wife and a clause in the Act setting up the new Poor Law Board in 1847 laid down that every union must, if requested, provide any married couple over sixty with a separate bedroom. In practice little attempt was made to honour this clause as, a quarter of a century later, in 1872, one writer pointed out:

> With few exception, couples who have been married as many as forty years are for the last four or five years of their lives practically separated from one another . . . In a workhouse I know well, containing over a thousand aged inmates, there was only accommodation . . . for twelve couples. Their quarters are called rooms, but in fact are simply divisions . . . about the same size as those seen in common lodging houses, with partitions . . . By stretching out the hands it is almost possible to reach over to any part of the rooms without getting out of bed . . . It would be humorous, were it not pitiful, to see how eagerly, on the death of any occupant, these quarters are sought after . . .

Those not fortunate enough to secure such accommodation were still, as in 1834, confined strictly to their own wards and exercise yards:

> Between the two a wall is erected, at the doorway of which the husband or wife may often be seen looking about like some guilty wretch . . . to have a few minutes stolen interview with the partner of all their woes . . . Once a week they may meet for an hour to enjoy each other's society and perhaps fortify one another for next week's banishment.

In 1877 the separate bedroom concession was extended to any couple where one partner was over sixty or disabled, but eight years later in 1885, Arthur Balfour, the Conservative minister responsible, still found it necessary to remind all Boards of Guardians of their legal obligations. The cynics noted that, by a curious coincidence, his concern had only been aroused on the eve of the first election in which two million working-class people in rural areas had the right to vote, but the regulation continued in any case to be ignored. Ten years later only 200 married couples had their own rooms in the whole of England and Wales, the official explanation that the rest actually preferred sharing a large communal dormitory being manifestly untrue.

Despite this failure from the late 1850s onwards, the more progressive unions began to treat aged paupers less harshly than other inmates and by 1861 the Poor Law Board was urging one union to 'cheerfully supply all that their necessities and infirmities require'. Already the master of one Surrey workhouse was proudly describing in the press how far his establishment had moved from 'the principles of 1834' with its 'reading room with periodicals' and 100-volume library. 'If any inmate complains that he or she loathes the food supplied', claimed this official, 'a substitute of something more palatable is given', while the over-sixties all receive 'tea, sugar, butter and one pint of tea daily', possessed their own 'tea-can, tea-pot, soup-can, knife, fork and spoon' and, as a crowning luxury, were given 'a clean plate at each meal'.

Another sign of the times was a more tolerant attitude towards tobacco and snuff. At Worcester, in the 1830s, the workhouse master, on the Assistant Commissioner's orders, refused 'to allow one penny-worth of snuff to be received by a mother from her daughter', and was warned that he would be personally fined £5 if he allowed such contraband to reach a pauper. Although the Guardians resigned in protest, the rule remained in force. For many years the Poor Law Board Inspectors, who replaced the Assistant Commissioners, continued to try to root out the hated weed, but in 1880 it was reluctantly conceded that the workhouse doctor could prescribe tobacco on medical grounds. Five years later unions began to be allowed to issue tobacco to inmates, provided the recipients were not able-bodied and were 'employed upon work of a hazardous or specially disagreeable character'. The real victory—if victory it can be considered—came in 1892, when the authorities at Liverpool, after a hard fight by the city's MPs, were given the right to issue a small weekly ration of tobacco to all the elderly men in the workhouse and later that year all unions were authorised to make a similar allowance to the over-sixties of both sexes.

Other, more striking, changes in the old people's wards occurred in the 1890s, largely due to the work of Charles Booth and other investigators, which revealed that most extreme poverty was 'involuntary'. The discovery that at least one in three of all citizens reaching the age of seventy had to seek union assistance finally convinced most Guardians that it was not only the thriftless who became 'indoor paupers,' and the result was a marked and progressive softening of the workhouse regime. In 1893 the Local Government Board, now the ministry responsible for poor relief, advised unions that they could allow elderly inmates 'dry tea', with milk and sugar, to brew their own drinks, without having to seek special permission from the Board, coffee and cocoa being added later. In 1895 and 1896 there were more radical reforms. The policy of treating everyone in the workhouse alike was finally abandoned and the unions were instructed that the old folk should not be forced to have their meals, or get up and go to bed, at the times laid down for other inmates. More rooms should be provided for married couples, workhouse uniform should not be insisted on, and all but the most untrustworthy old people should be allowed to go out for walks. In 1898 the minister suggested that a Sunday outing alone was not enough, and that 'In the case of aged inmates of respectable character leave of absence might well be allowed on weekdays more frequently than is now the case'. An even greater innovation was the decision to treat inmates differently according to their character. Those who had 'previously led moral and respectable lives', urged the Local Government Board, should be provided with a separate day-room, apart from rowdier paupers with rougher backgrounds. The new century began with the unions being urged, in

1900, to make other concessions, such as allowing all those over sixty-five to get up and go to bed when they liked, and providing them with locked cupboards in which to keep their possessions. The ghost of segregation for the old was finally also laid; the day-rooms for the deserving elderly inmates 'might, if thought desirable', said the Local Government Board, 'be available for members of both sexes'.

One County Councillor described the changes recommended in these years as adding up to a whole new Poor Law, but he was wrong. In the 1830s many unions had had to be bullied and coaxed against their will into treating their old people harshly, but the lesson had been mastered too thoroughly to be unlearned without a struggle. In Essex, a typical county, one observer found that conditions and attitudes around the turn of the century were little different from those of sixty years before. At Chelmsford the old people were, after 1901, allowed to walk in the garden until 5 pm, but they still had to go to bed at 7 pm and the first garden seats were not provided until 1905. At Ongar, free access to the garden was not allowed until 1907. At Maldon, in 1901, an inspector found the old men still sitting 'bolt upright' on hard forms but the Guardians accepted his advice to buy some Windsor chairs, and even, in 1906, went to the lengths of installing some in the dormitory. £3 was spent on books for the library and two half-penny papers and a weekly local paper were ordered at the ruinous cost of one shilling and fourpence a month.

What could be done by a progressive authority was shown at Woolwich, where the old people were moved out of the workhouse into a separate building indistinguishable from an old folks' home, and at Bradford, where the aged paupers were provided with separate day-rooms equipped with armchairs, cushions, curtains, carpets, coloured table cloths and even pictures and ornaments. The Local Government Board now readily approved plans to spend union funds on such luxuries as a library subscription, or a harmonium, and a whole range of new items was added to the workhouse menu for the aged: butter, cocoa, seedcake, onions, lettuce, rhubarb, stewed fruit, semolina, and even 'a small allowance of milk pudding'. But one indulgence the Civil Servants—ironically, in view of Whitehall's own reputation— would not approve. The Board 'was not prepared', the union authorities of St George's, Hanover Square, were told in 1900 'to assent to the proposal of the Guardians for the infirm men and all men over the age of 65 years to have half a pint of tea daily at 3.30 pm between the midday and evening meals'.

The changing character of the institution was reflected in two poems by workhouse inmates. About 1860, 87-year-old John Bundy of Eaton Socon in Bedfordshire had taken a distinctly gloomy view of the fate in store for his contemporaries:

> A poor old man when he reaches four-score,
> And has done all he can, can do no more;
> To ask for relief, it makes him afraid,
> Since they took up with this body-snatching way,
> He must go and die in the union!

But a composition by Thirza Elizabeth Hardy, living in Cerne Abbas, Dorset, in 1913, though of no more literary merit, expresses very different sentiments:

> In the well-known county of Dorset
> In the ancient town of Cerne,
> Close by Baker's House a union you'll discover,
> A home for the old and helpless ones,
> A rest beside the way,
> For the weary traveller who seeks a shelter every day.

A Poor Law inspector, writing at about the same period, remarked on the transformation which had occurred during the past quarter of a century:

Workhouse is now a misnomer. In many of them labour has to be hired, even for washing or scrubbing. The aged and infirm enjoy a large amount of liberty, they are only set to such light tasks as are sufficient to occupy them pleasantly and in all material conditions of feeding, housing and clothing they are much better off than the aged poor outside. When one sees knots of the old men gossiping by the fire or basking in the sun, when one finds the bedridden old woman carefully nursed and fed . . . it is difficult to help contrasting their conditions with some of the village poor. I have often heard an aged inmate say that he had always declared that he would die rather than enter 'the house', but if he had known that it was so comfortable he would have come there long ago.

12 Death in the Workhouse

> The poor woman died in the night. Her motive
> for going into the house was to save expense to
> her family. *Journal of the Workhouse Visiting
> Society*, 1861

Of all the sad fates which overtook the unfortunate victims in Victorian drawing-room recitations, few were more tragic than dying in the workhouse and being carried to a pauper's grave. In many parishes before 1834 it had been the kindly custom to give the departed pauper a dignified send-off, but this was one of the first extravagances against which the Assistant Poor Law Commissioners waged determined war. 'Less eligibility' required that every parish funeral should demonstrate the public disgrace which resulted from failing to provide for one's own old age.

At Bridgwater, for example, the Guardians, on the advice of the Assistant Commissioner, agreed in May 1836 to cease to give a grant to bereaved families to make their own funeral arrangements, voting the entire management of pauper funerals into the union's hands. The poor were so affronted, however, at seeing their loved ones carried to the grave by parish bearers—usually workhouse inmates—in a plain coffin, uncovered by a pall and unaccompanied by the tolling of the passing bell—one chime for each year of the departed person's life— that within three months these traditional trappings had been restored. Cut-price funerals led to actual disorder in so many places that to avoid jeopardising all their work the Poor Law Commissioners reluctantly agreed that unions could incur expenditure on such items at their discretion.

But most Boards refused to restore pauper funerals to their former modest glory, provoking many complaints about the 'lack of decency' attending such functions. Penny-pinching over these occasions was featured at length in *The Book of the Bastilles*, in 1841, and in *Poor Law Sonnets* in the same year. One of these, *The Poor Man's Burial,* struck a note that was widely-echoed:

> Ho! Contract coffins for the parish poor,
> Eight shillings each, complete with shrouds and nails...

although this seems to have been an under-estimate; even Andover allowed fourteen shillings. Poetic licence, rather than union carpentry, seems to justify, too, the same writer's warning to the bearers to leave the coffin at the church door as it will fall to pieces if carried as far as the chancel, but the writer's other complaint

> "I hear no bell."
> "Your honour, the New Laws won't have it tolled".
> "What! Stint a poor man's soul a parting knell?"

was undoubtedly justified.

The authorities never seem to have understood how bitterly such economies were resented and feared. Louisa Twining, visiting a workhouse in mid-century, was asked by a respectable old woman to 'give her some old garment which she might have for her burial'. This belief that the body would be stripped after death was well-founded. A report on one union in 1878 described how 'The dead are laid in shells, the boards unplaned inside, upon a sprinkling of sawdust, perfectly naked, with a strip of calico over the body only.' The burial service, Louisa Twining learned, was often conducted 'in indecent haste' and was inevitably an occasion of melancholy. 'Not even the decent exterior of a pall covers the shell which enclosed the cold ashes', wrote one workhouse chaplain compassionately. 'A few rough planks joined together; the black initials, age and date; the bearers in the grey frieze dress of the union, the badge of their misfortunes, and who, forgetful of the occasion, seem glad of the opportunity of again mingling with their fellow creatures and breathing the air of freedom.'

The official regulations from the 1830s onwards specifically enjoined the workhouse master 'to take care that no pauper at the approach of death shall be left unattended, either during the day or night', but this humane rule was constantly broken, or interpreted to mean that, instead of being left alone to die in peace, frightened and suffering patients spent their last hours in a crowded ward, a painful experience for all concerned. A chaplain also told Louisa Twining of the boys in one workhouse who had shared a dormitory with a dying man and 'were dreadfully frightened all night by his cursing and swearing', while she witnessed for herself condition's on the women's side that were little better. After befriending one inmate, 'at one visit I found the woman in the bed close to her chair just dead. Presently she would be washed and laid out, all in full view, for there were neither curtains nor screens in these rooms'.

Far worse, however, were cases where the dying were treated with

callous indifference, like that which one contributor to the Workhouse Visiting Society *Journal* described in 1861:

> The only time I was ever in a London workhouse was when my
> sister and I made a most painful visit, about ten years ago, to the
> Union, to see an old servant whom we much respected, and who
> had chosen to move into the infirmary *to die.* We were ushered
> through many rooms and passages to the one where the poor
> woman was lying, —a large, high, airy apartment, with a good fire,
> all looking cheerful and comfortable, but for the dreadful inmates.
> About twenty women round the fire stared rudely at us, some with a
> fierce, wild look. We asked for Mrs E—, and were pointed to the bed
> where she was apparently asleep, when one of the women . . .
> caught her by the shoulder, and shook her. The poor thing, who
> was then *actually dying*, recovered her consciousness in dreadful
> agony, groaned, passed her hand over her face, repeating, 'It's
> dreadful! dreadful!' When she remembered us, she said, 'Water!'
> No one took the least notice, till a wretched woman burst into a
> hardened laugh, calling out, 'Water! why, she is dying!' I turned
> to them and said, 'Is there no one can fetch a cup of water?' when
> they began to growl, 'You go!' 'I shan't; can't you?' etc. I had to
> repeat the question, when one of them got a cupful, which she
> *thrust* on the dying woman. I took it in my hand, and gave it her.
> She looked up and said, 'What I suffer you can't tell; oh, why did I
> ever come in here?...' We asked for the *nurse,* but one and all
> seemed equally hardened, rough, and cruel. They talked among
> themselves, —'She'll be dead before night.' 'What should ladies come
> and see *her* for?' etc. Many particulars I have now forgotten; but
> we left with aching hearts, hoping the poor woman's sufferings
> might be mercifully shortened, and truly thankful were we to feel
> ourselves outside walls which seemed to us to encircle such misery.
> The poor woman died in the night. Her motive for going into the
> house was to save expense to her family, and in the hopes of being
> better nursed than she could be in her lodgings.

Who did suffer that much-feared fate of dying in the workhouse?
Probably the largest group in rural workhouses were former farm
labourers, like James Hammett, one of the Tolpuddle Martyrs, who
entered Dorchester workhouse when his sight failed rather than
become a burden on his family, and died there in 1891. In the towns
most elderly paupers were former domestic servants too old to work,

but there was usually a large rough element—ex-convicts, broken-down tramps, and—if the temperance writers were to be believed—people from all walks of life, degraded by drink.

Although in the workhouse every failed clerk claimed to have been a great tycoon and every prostitute a royal courtesan, dramatic changes of fortune were not uncommon in the Victorian age, and every workhouse contained a minority of inmates who had come down in the world. A collection of such case-histories was made by one workhouse chaplain in 1847. One of them concerned Charley, whom the chaplain graphically described as 'the last of the family' and who had been destined for the Bar. His father having died when he was seventeen, he had emigrated instead to the United States, made good in a firm of merchants and married. Then his wife had run off with one of his own junior clerks, and Charley, heartbroken, had return-ed to England, only to see his two children die, and to lose his life-savings from trade with the West Indies, £4,000, in a fraudulent business. Now, at 81, he was in the workhouse, although he was later found a place in an almshouse.

Another unfortunate was a 63-year-old man, admitted starving, whose long-lost daughter was summoned to see him by the chaplain, though they barely had time to exclaim 'My child!' and 'My father!' respectively before the latter died. He had, it appeared, begun life as a jeweller's apprentice but after rising to eminence in his trade had moved to a grander district, where his wife had pined and died. He had tried to marry his daughter to 'The Marquis of B., a young man of high principle and amiable disposition', only to discover that the price of the alliance was to settle his future son-in-law's gambling debts, which he refused to do; he himself had finally been ruined by rash specula-tion. Crushed by misfortune he had lost his wits and wandered away from home, next being heard of by his family when on his death bed.

The chaplain was even more affected by the arrival in his care of 'The Author...a miserable, emaciated and care-worn object' with 'nothing but the tattered clothes which he wore', who was carried in from the lodging where he had collapsed from starvation, his rent unpaid. He died three days later and beneath the mattress in his old lodgings his sole possession was discovered, a manuscript modestly, but accurately, entitled *The Ramblings of an Author*. This revealed that the author had turned to literature as a young man because he despised commerce and 'although the remuneration I received was infinitely below what I felt was my due'—a feeling not uncommon among writers—'yet I submitted . . . to the paltry exactions which were practised upon me by the publisher of my compositions . . .When avarice attempted to apply the screw beyond it due bounds . . . spurning the mean wretch whose selfishness for once outwitted him, I sought to find one who might less greedily press on the vitals of genius'. In other words, he decided to change his publisher, but unfortunately made such a bad choice that it needed only sundry other misfortunes and a disastrous lawsuit to bring him, 'a poor friendless outcast', as he sadly confided to his manuscript, to the workhouse.

In another of the chaplain's stories, *The Oath*, the central figure was an old man whose son had many years before sailed to the United States, and lost touch with his parents. One night their peaceful existence is shattered by a smuggler who forces his way in, taking refuge from the revenue men in hot pursuit outside. The intruder threatens the woman of the house that if she betrays him he will shoot her, and her husband enraged, cries out: 'God's curse rest on you, villain!' at which all three suddenly recognise each other as parents and child. At this dramatic moment the excise officers arrive and the returning prodigal is carried off the jail, transported, and dies on the voyage out. His father never recovers from having cursed his long-lost son and, a broken man, dies in the workhouse.

But of all the dying inmates this chaplain encountered, the one who made the deepest impression on him was 'the Atheist', who had already attracted his attention by pointedly paying no attention throughout the weekly service and smiling off-puttingly throughout every sermon. When challenged he revealed the awful truth. 'I can't see why I should be made to attend chapel,' he told the shocked chaplain. 'I think that . . . God exists only in fancy and don't believe that there is any life after this, but when a man dies there is an end of him.' Further enquiries established that this viper in the union nest was the son of a yeoman farmer who, after falling in with a group of freethinkers, had become involved in crime, settling down, after two years in jail, to a life of fraud, until at 67 he had drifted into the workhouse. His end was gratifying to the chaplain, if distressing, for on his death-bed 'his former surly look had settled down into an expression of perfect cowardice and alarm', after a fellow-inmate had helpfully sought to raise his spirits by reading him a tract on the dangers of hell-fire. The Atheist's final words might have been written for him by a Victorian tract-monger: 'Oh horrid, horrid, worse and worse. I'm raging now, the fire consuming me, the very devils are mocking me.' 'He expired,' the chaplain dutifully

recorded, 'in the most excruciating torments' – in fact from a rup-
tured blood-vessel—'and with groans that pierced the heart. If such
were his falling asleep, what must have been his fearful awakening!'

Union medical officers also saw many deaths, though they described
them with less relish. Among the cases that interested one workhouse
doctor, whose memoirs appeared forty years later in 1889, was that of
a woman aged 100 who claimed that earlier in life she had been 'under
the protection', that is the mistress of, someone connected with the
fashionable Drury Lane Theatre. She boasted that, socially or profes-
sionally, she had moved in the highest circles in the land, distributing
her favours impartially to all parties and both armed services, the
recipients, according to her, having included the Prince Regent,
Charles James Fox, William Pitt, Edmund Burke, the Duke of Wellington and Lord Nelson. Sustained by her memories she had lived
to the respectable age of 104. Indeed this workhouse seems to have encouraged longevity, for another inmate was a woman of 105, whose
great-grand-children had finally tired of looking after her, and another
resident, aged 95 on arrival, also lived for years. Her chief interest in
life was to send for the Roman Catholic priest and the doctor whenever
she felt that her end was imminent. The doctor took in good part being
called out to attend her yet again at 11.30 at night 'when the snow was
on the ground and it was blowing strongly from the North East',
while she achieved what was probably a world record for receiving the
last rites, having extreme unction administered to her no fewer than
nineteen times.

Not all the tales of past wealth and social standing told by elderly
paupers were untrue. One penniless patient claimed to have owned
large estates in Yorkshire and to have been a Master of Foxhounds, and
proved indeed to have been well-connected, for five separate firms of
solicitors requested a death certificate to help clear up his affairs,
which meant for the doctor an unexpected five guineas in fees. Nor
was it only in Victorian novels that professional men were ruined
by love. Among those who passed through a London workhouse was a
French doctor from Soho, a 'very gentlemanly looking person', whose
parents had been executed in the French Revolution. After beginning
his career as a regimental surgeon in Napoleon's army, he had started
a prosperous practice in London, only to become infatuated with a girl
who worked in a milliner's in Regent Street. Having made all his
money over to her, he discovered, when she died intestate, that he had
no legal claim to it and finally expired penniless in the workhouse at

the age of 95. He was, however, spared a pauper's burial for the work-house doctor appealed in *The Times* for funds to bury his professional colleague in style and raised £25.

As women lived longer than men they usually formed a majority of the occupants of the old people's wards and many came from respect-able backgrounds, and had gravitated to the workhouse via ill-paid outwork. Louisa Twining met a typical unfortunate of this kind in St. Giles's workhouse in Holborn, a 'dear old woman', a well-spoken elderly spinster, who had come from Plymouth with her sister many years before. They had established themselves in London as high-class shoe-makers, but were so ill-paid by the tradesmen who employed them that they could only afford to live in a single room and when one died the other had been forced to enter the 'union'. The East End, traditional home of the most sweated of trades, tailoring, produced many such cases. Needlewomen, described by the Medical Officer of the White-chapel Union, as 'the most ill-paid class of people and the most hard-working on earth', often ended their days in a workhouse bed, having for years previously 'earned from three to four shillings a week' after being 'compelled to work from three o'clock in the morning till ten at night'.

If many characters in the 'aged and infirm' wards could have stepped from the pages of the numerous reports on poverty and exploitation which appeared in the closing decades of the nineteenth century, some inmates seemed to belong to the world of contemporary fiction. There was, for instance, an echo of the famous lawsuit in *Bleak House* in the story of the 'poor old woman' one visitor befriended in the 1860s, 'who has found her way up from Devonshire hoping, so she says, to hear the end of a suit in Chancery begun 200 years ago'. Nor would Thomas Hardy have been ashamed to have invented Mary Ann Bull, 'a hawk-like creature with small, black roving eyes, tousled grey hair, her body clad in layers of petticoats', who, like Diggory Venn in *The Return of the Native*, followed the trade of reddle-merchant. Widow Bull toured the Wessex countryside in 'a two-wheeled cart, sleeping between the sacks draped below it' and earning her living by selling the dye used in marking sheep and silver sand for polishing harness. Her devoted dog went everywhere with her and did his best to 'protect' her from the union officials who arrived to remove her to Cerne Abbas workhouse, when she caught pneumonia while camping out. Life within four walls did not agree with her and she died soon afterwards, her cart, a familiar sight in Dorset for many years, being sold to meet the funeral expenses.

Even Thomas Hardy's gloomy indignation, however, could hardly have conjured up the bizarre fate suffered by another resident of Cerne workhouse, Inmate No 1299, Johnny Trott, who at the age of 71, was ringing the bell for breakfast, one morning in 1924, when it came away from the wall and struck him a fatal blow on the head, so that he was quite literally killed by the workhouse.

But not all workhouse stories ended so sadly and many old people, in the sheltered environment, managed to live to a ripe old age. This was especially true of the south west, where, claimed the local Poor Law Inspector, appointed in 1896, 'it is common to find old folk hale and hearty at an age when, in other parts of the country, they are long past work'. In his district, covering the sunny, agricultural counties of Somerset, Devon and Cornwall, 73 out of every 1,000 inhabitants were aged over 65, compared to only 33 in damp, industrial Lancashire. Perhaps due to the kindly climate, the old people in the workhouse seem to have been a cheerful lot, complaining of little except deafness. The inspector particularly warmed to an old sailor who recounted tales of 'chilly experiences' while searching for the lost explorer, Sir John Franklin, and an old poacher who kept his room-mates entertained with tales 'of bamboozled keepers and of captured pheasants'. One veteran of the same craft even sent a hamper of poached game to the governor of the prison where he usually spent the winter, but confinement in the workhouse did not suit him, and he died soon after his arrival, at the relatively early age of 83. His wife, equally game, to use the *mot juste*, when asked on her death bed if there was anything she fancied, begged for 'a slice of young pheasant'.

13 Fallen Women

The depraved women bring contamination with
them; the unwed mothers, who come to lie-in,
go out laughing, with a promise to come again.
Journal of the Workhouse Visiting Society,
1865

The policy adopted in 1834 of refusing out-relief to unsupported
women soon resulted in them forming the second largest group, out-
numbered only by the old, in nearly every workhouse. Some had been
abandoned by their husbands; some were domestic servants between
jobs; some were widows struggling to bring up a family. But a high
proportion from the first were women of, in the eyes of the authorities,
low moral character, ranging from tearful girls of seventeen or so
expecting their first baby, to bedraggled and brazen harridans with a
lifetime of prostitution behind them.

One of the first to face the challenge of these fallen women was the
Rev. Herbert Smith, who, on its formation in 1836, became chaplain of
the New Forest Union, where unmarried mothers and their children
immediately formed a quarter of the inmates. 'The able-bodied
women's department', he recorded in his diary, 'was the most
painful to inspect and the most difficult to manage.' The women had
'little appearance of a sense of shame and their general conduct [was]
such as must occasion the most painful feelings to those who are interested in the moral and religious welfare of the inmates.' But he bravely
did his best to reform them. 'To the women with illegitimate children
I point out that their situation is the consequence of their own sin and
that they ought to feel thankful that they have found such a refuge.'

Nor did he shirk his duty with individual sinners. 'Visited Catherine
Collins in the receiving ward' his diary for one September day in 1838
recorded, 'and conversed much with her on her past conduct and
present state...Catherine Collins has been living in a house of ill
fame at Southampton... For six weeks before she returned to the
workhouse she was in an awful state of disease.' As his contribution
to preventing such tragedies, Smith, an earnest, well-meaning young

man published his experiences in a twopenny tract 'for the benefit of the young and inexperienced among the female sex...that they should...learn a timely lesson of prudence and virtue'.

To remind them that they were moral outcasts, many unions put their unmarried mothers into a distinctive yellow uniform, the colour of a ship's plague flag, the wearers being nicknamed 'canary wards', but the practice was banned in 1839 as distinguishing between paupers on moral grounds. Some Boards were not to be so easily cheated of their pound of moral flesh, however, and at Andover the Guardians kept to the letter of the law by dressing their fallen women in an ordinary frock, but with a broad yellow stripe down it.

A few girls were as full of remorse as the sternest moralist could wish. One workhouse chaplain, writing in 1847, recounted the case-history of Eliza, whom he called 'the Penitent'. Eliza's parents had died when she was nine, leaving her to spend the next three years in the workhouse. At twelve she had been sent out as servant to a farmer but after five happy and useful years had taken a post at a 'fashionable watering place' where she succumbed to the first tempter she met. By eighteen she was back in the workhouse, with an illegitimate child and on her death-bed, at which point a mysterious stranger in his late fifties arrived to see her, confessing to the chaplain that he was Eliza's seducer. After a moving reconciliation with him, Eliza died happy, knowing that her baby would be brought up by its father in his comfortable home.

This particular child was lucky to survive when its mother died for until the great clean-up of the 1860s the lying-in wards in most workhouse infirmaries were appalling, even by the undemanding medical standards of the time. Dr Joseph Rogers, who became medical officer of the notorious Strand workhouse in 1856, discovered that 'the female insane ward...was situated...immediately beneath the lying-in ward. When we had a troublesome or noisy lunatic in the ward, it must have been anything but a comfort to the lying-in women above'. The nursery ward to which the new-born infants were moved, opposite the labour ward on the third floor, Rogers described as 'A wretchedly damp and miserable room nearly always overcrowded with young mothers and their infant children. That death relieved these young women of their illegitimate offspring was only what was to be expected and...frequently the mothers followed in the same direction...I used to dread to go into the ward, it was so depressing. Scores and scores of distinctly preventible deaths of both mother and children took place during my

continuance in office through their being located in this horrible den.'
Dr Rogers considered that the wards were 'an utter disgrace to the
Board', and 'altogether unsuitable for the reception of any human
being, however degraded'.

Often the doctor was the only outsider to visit such wards, for the
more timorous chaplains gave them a wide berth. One of the first and
most famous workhouse visitors, Mrs Emma Sheppard of Frome, was
told by a nurse, 'Oh no, ma'am, you must not go there. No lady or gentleman can go in; the smell of the room, the abuse which you would meet
with, is not fit for anyone.' But Mrs Sheppard persisted and

> found about ten wretched, degraded looking women crouching
> round the fire; several in bed, one especially, who hid her dis-
> figured, diseased face under the bedclothes from me...I went up
> to them, laid my hand on a shoulder and said, 'My poor women, is
> it true that if I offer to come in and see you now and then you would
> treat me with abuse and coldness? Can this be true of English wo-
> men to an English lady?' They rose, turned round, and with a re-
> spectful curtsy, said, 'Oh, do come to us; nobody seems to care for
> us.' I sat down among them, read to them of the woman who was a
> sinner, and they all knelt down reverently; the poor creature I had
> noticed before was convulsed with sobs.

Despite such gratifying signs of repentance, however, Mrs Sheppard
found that girls who had been cured and left the workhouse were for
ever coming back. 'When I found them returning again and again to
that loathsome ward,' she wrote, 'and sorrowfully reproached them,
the answer was,"What can we do? No one would give work to such as
we; we must either have died on a dunghill or gone back to sin" .'
Mrs Sheppard bravely passed on these observations to the readers of
The Times. 'What is there before them when they wish to leave?',
she demanded in a letter in 1857, 'Starvation or sin. I have seen dozens
of them, softened and brought to their senses by long seclusion in that
fearful ward and longing to lead a better life when they left. But who
would employ them?'

Sadly, few workhouses seem to have tried to build on the one
unselfish instinct that all but the most abandoned women possessed,
love of their children. One visitor in the 1850s was shocked to see a
mother trying to push food into her sleeping baby's mouth. 'If it did not
eat then, the mother explained, it would have nothing else till the next

1   Parish workhouse, St James's, London, before 1834. This was the luxurious type of 'unreformed' workhouse. The 1834 reformers objected to its air of ease and spaciousness as much as to the squalid overcrowding of some parish poor-houses in country villages.

2 The workhouse at Eversholt, Bedfordshire, in the early nineteenth century. The stocks were a useful reminder that the workhouse had a deterrent and punitive role as well as being a place of shelter.

3 Fulham and Hammersmith Union workhouse, London, 1849. This vast, well-planned establishment with walls strictly separating the various categories, represented the ideal at which 'the men of 1834' aimed, although the children's swing in the foreground represents an untypical concession to sentiment.

4 A small, rural workhouse built to the Poor Law Commissioner's design.

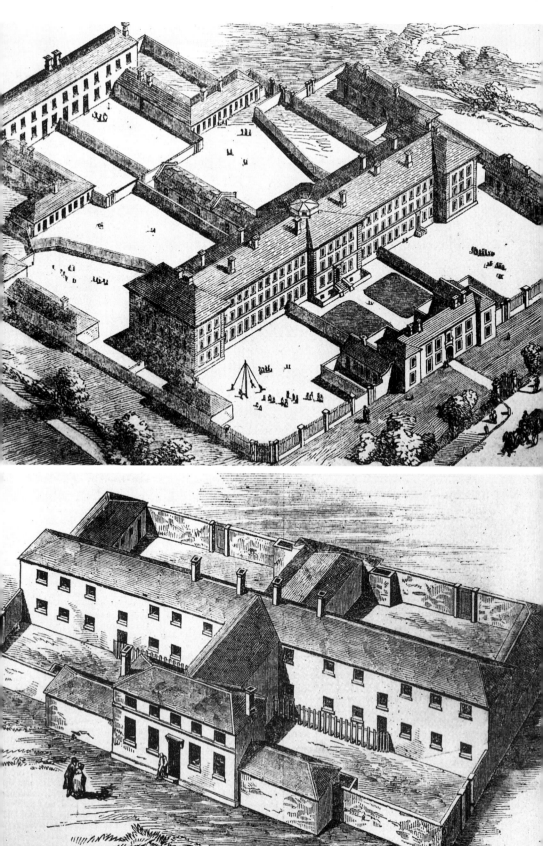

5 and 6 Anti-workhouse propaganda. Two drawings by John Leech from the propagandist novel, *Jessie Phillips, A Tale of the Present Day*, by Mrs Trollope (1844). The top one shows a women's ward with the crippled, the aged, and mental defectives thrown together. The other shows a Board of Guardians in session. One applicant, weak from hunger, has fainted at her harsh reception.

7 The women's yard of a union workhouse. The grotesque faces
are typical of drawings of the period—probably late 1830s or early
1840s. Note the workhouse uniform and the deaf old lady on the
left.

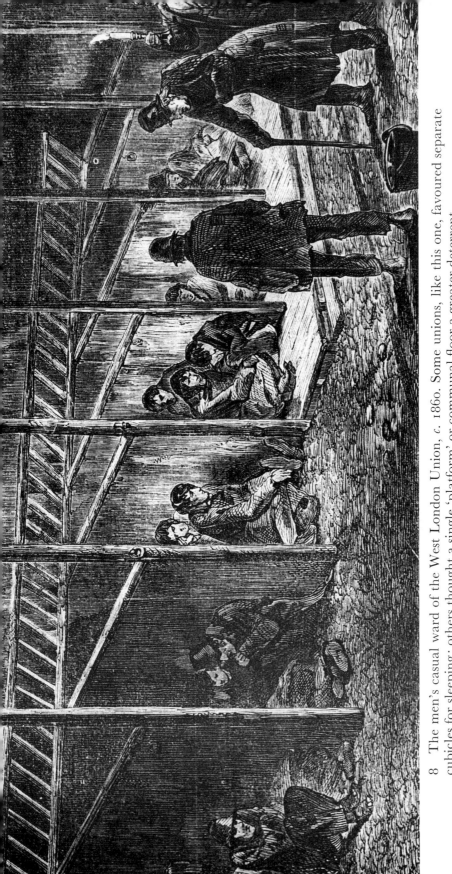

8   The men's casual ward of the West London Union, *c.* 1860. Some unions, like this one, favoured separate cubicles for sleeping; others thought a single 'platform' or communal floor a greater deterrent.

9   Refuge for the Destitute and Houseless Poor, Whitecross Street, London, 1843. The 'Houseless' was a short-stay workhouse: sleeping quarters were open spaces covered with straw.

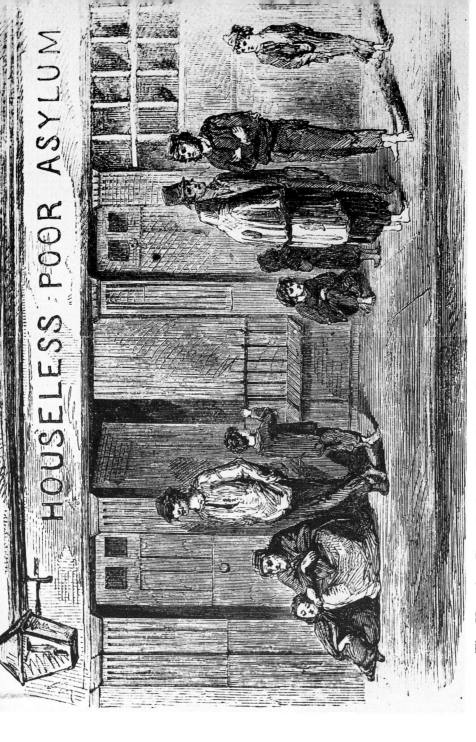

10   The Houseless Poor Asylum, Cripplegate, London, 1846. The people in the picture are probably waiting to ensure a place when the doors opened. In bad weather institutions like this tended to be crowded with applicants.

11 The Labour Yard, Bethnal Green, London, 1868. Labour Yards provided men with food in return for work but they slept elsewhere.

12 The Lord Mayor visits the women's casual ward of the West London Union, c. 1860. This shows the 'sleeping platform'.

13　Refuge for the destitute, 1843. The 'trough' type of sleeping accommodation on the right was also found in many men's wards.

14 A newly-opened casual ward at Marylebone workhouse, London, probably late nineteenth century. The ubiquitous texts are typical of the period.

15 The communal bath in a casual ward. The rule that all newly-admitted casuals must have a bath was strictly enforced for deterrent as well as hygienic reasons. This drawing by Gustave Doré is dated 1872.

16 and 17 The girls' dining-room and the boys' dormitory at Salford workhouse, Lancashire, in about 1890. The pictures on the walls and the fact that these photographs were taken, suggest better treatment than in many workhouses.

18 Dinner-time at St Pancras workhouse, London, 1900.

19 The dining-room at Cambridge workhouse, *c.* 1910. The scales on the table recall 1834, when the right of any inmate to have his rations weighed in front of him was first established.

20 and 21   The women's day-room and men's sick ward at Cambridge workhouse, *c.* 1910. A showpiece rather than a typical example of the 'improved' provision for old people introduced in the 1890s. The old ladies are, however, still in uniform and they have to sit upright on hard chairs.

meal came round... The pretty, fair babe, about eight months old, would probably wake up in an hour ravenous with hunger.'

What was particularly dismaying to all those who tried to help prostitutes was the realisation that it was often the workhouse itself which had converted 'poor sinful girls' into 'depraved and degraded women'. It was the lying-in ward, the nursery and the able-bodied women's day-room, which threw a basically decent, and perhaps tearfully repentant girl into the company of hardened older women, so that, as one speaker told a conference in 1857, they 'laugh at her simplicity and too often shame her out of her repentance'. A start was made in some workhouses, like Alverstoke in Hampshire, around 1860, by accommodating the girls under sixteen in a separate building, it being hopefully remarked that they 'will now be able to earn their living reputably', but once sent across to the adult wards, all this good might be undone. Sometimes a girl frankly told the workhouse master on leaving that she had no intention of going into service, having learned that no life could be worse than that of maid-of-all-work in a single-servant family.

Even the ladies of the workhouse Visiting Society, employers all, complained that 'many strong girls have utterly lost their health before they were twenty years of age from the effect of the cruel labour exacted from them... the time necessary for food and rest being too often denied'. A brothel, or back-street lodging with frequent 'gentleman callers', was often a haven of luxury compared to the average servant's basement kitchen or cheerless attic and a 'life of shame' could be far preferable to residence in the workhouse. Henry Mayhew, while researching into the life of the London poor in the early 1860s, met one widow 'on the game' who acknowledged that she would rather support her children in this way than be separated from them in the house. He also talked to a former servant who had been refused admission to the union for her small son, who was half-frozen and, having failed to support him by ill-paid sewing work, had been reluctantly driven back on to the streets.

The *Journal* quoted a complaint from the master of Greenwich workhouse in 1862 that 'by far the majority' of the girls formerly in his establishment 'had turned to prostitution'. 'The depraved women', protested a writer in the *Journal* three years later, 'bring contamination with them; the unwed mothers, who come to lie-in, go out laughing, with a promise to come again'. Twenty years later conditions had, if anything, deteriorated. Of eight girls who had left one workhouse, one

social worker reported in 1889, every one was now a prostitute. 'Many girls', complained a Guardian, 'discharge themselves in the afternoon for the purpose of prostitution and return later to the house.'

The best way to reclaim such women, most observers believed, was to get them out of the workhouse into 'Magdalen homes', which were essentially small, privately run reformatories, to teach them, to quote one chaplain, habits of 'good conduct and steady industry', and then, after three or four years, to place them in carefully selected homes as skilled cooks or housekeepers. When applied to hardened harlots such ventures were rarely successful. Many girls sold the outfit provided for them and returned to their old way of life, and the subsequent careers of girls brought up in the workhouse were little more encouraging. A conference of the newly-formed National Association for Social Science was told in 1862 that of 74 girls placed from one workhouse, only 13 had subsequently proved to be doing well. Of 160 put out to service in one union, after spending from three to sixteen years continuously in the workhouse, 58 had been back within its walls within three months. In another union, of 165 discharged in three years, 73 had soon returned and only 18 were known to be doing well.

Not everyone, however, who removed young women from the workhouse did so with good intentions. Dr Rogers encountered a curious case in the Strand workhouse when a 'gentlemanly looking person' called on the union authorities claiming to be a doctor and asked them to recommend a 'healthy young woman' as wet-nurse for a patient. As it happened there was in the workhouse the very person, a German-American girl who, on her way back to Chicago, had been seduced and abandoned in London by a Frenchman, and whose baby, born in the workhouse, had just died. When she arrived at the 'doctor's', however, she had found it was not a patient's baby who required her ministrations but he himself and when, after a struggle, she escaped, it transpired that he was an army officer who had already, through the same ruse, contacted and assaulted four girls from other workhouses. This time he went to jail, while the usual appeal by Dr Rogers in *The Times* raised £45 for the intended victim, more than enough to pay her fare home.

Despite the age's reputation for moral rectitude, many Victorians were reluctant to blame the ordinary unmarried mother for her condition. 'If we consult the experience of the clergy . . . or men . . . like the Brothers Mayhew . . . we find that female honour by no means holds [in practice] its theoretical position in public esteem', wrote Dr William

Acton, the great authority on mid-Victorian prostitution, in 1857. 'It cannot be denied by anyone acquainted with rural life, that the seduction of girls is a sport and habit with vast numbers of men, married and single, placed above the ranks of labour... The "keeping company" of the labouring classes, accompanied by illicit intercourse, as often as not leads to marriage; but not so that of the farmer's son, farmer, first or second or third class squire. The union house is now often enough the home of the deserted mother and the infant bastard.' Nor were conditions much better in the towns. 'In parts of the manufacturing and mining districts, where the infant labour produces an early addition to the parents' income', reported Acton, 'it is considered unthrifty and unnecessary to marry a woman who has not given evidence of fertility... To keep female domestics virtuous for any length of time' was, he advised, often impossible.

The God-fearing ladies of the Workhouse Visiting Society, although unlikely to have read Dr Acton's classic book, would certainly have echoed his sentiments. 'A very large number of young girls fall through causes one might almost say impossible to prevent', urged a writer in the Society's *Journal* in 1861, 'or at least there are so many extenuating circumstances that their fall should not be too harshly judged.' Such victims of society, they suggested, might be allowed to leave their first illegitimate child in the workhouse, although 'should they fall away again they should not have the same privilege'. In fact such multiple sinners were only too numerous. 'Four, five and six times have girls been known to come into the workhouse for the same purpose', admitted the Society, for domestic servants were corrupted, not merely by those around them but even by their employers, to a 'frightful extent'. Parliament, the Society pointed out, provided 'no legal protection for single women except an action at law for loss of service and even this is not available when the girl is an orphan, or where her master is the guilty party, just the very circumstances in which protection is needed... The only inconvenience the father of an illegitimate child can be made to suffer is the weekly payment of eighteen pence for its support, if it unfortunately lives. If it dies, he may go on his way rejoicing'.

Whatever the path which brought them there, the inmates of the able-bodied women's wards were traditionally the noisiest and worst-behaved part of the workhouse population. Every workhouse master dreaded above all sounds to hear, as he looked out from the parlour window over the exercise yards and worksheds of his small empire, the 'peculiarly ferocious scream, really worthy of wild beasts...commonly known as the workhouse howl'. This, according to the woman author of a series of *Workhouse Sketches* published in *Macmillan's Magazine* in 1861, usually meant that a fight or full-scale riot had broken out among the younger women. 'The Chaplain of a large union', she went on, 'once described to us a scene which has haunted us ever since—a ward full of these "unfortunates" locked up together through the whole blessed summer time, wrangling, cursing, talking of all unholy things, till, mad with sin and despair, they danced, and shouted their hideous songs in such utter shamelessness and fury that none dared to enter their den of agony.'

Reluctance to interfere in such cases was understandable, as an account by the matron of the infirmary at the vast Liverpool workhouse of what happened to one of her colleagues in 1866 made only too clear:

> On Saturday the women in the sheds attacked her, threw her down, tried to run hairpins into her eyes and when assistance arrived were pounding her all over. She had made herself un-popular and an active part she had taken in the seizure of a woman who had attacked her fellow officer the day before was the cause of this ... we are expecting the death of another female officer who was attacked by a girl, thrown down and scratched.

How were such violent spirits to be tamed? The authorities placed their faith in the twin virtues of pious exhortation and hard work. In one workhouse, a correspondent complained to the Workhouse Visiting Society, the chaplain had requested that poor profligate women might be 'kept out of his way' as 'they had shown themselves obstreperous and irreverent'. His attitude was understandable. At Kensington, around the turn of the century, one inmate behaved so outrageously while a missionary was reading aloud that she was sent to the refractory ward, whereupon 'forty women rose to the rescue, assaulted the officers and barricaded the ward. The police were called in and they had to break the door open and carry four of the girls to jail'.

Trouble-makers were often sent to jail but the prison authorities dreaded their arrival. 'We witnessed', wrote the governor of the Cold-bath Fields penitentiary, 'in the demeanour of young girls from fifteen years of age and upwards such revolting specimens of workhouse education, that the exhibition was at once frightening and disgusting. The inconceivable wickedness of these girls was absolutely appalling...

Their language, their violence and their indecency shocked every beholder.' The chaplain at Newgate found ex-workhouse inmates, 'by far the most saucy and impudent' prisoners, while another prison chaplain found that most women in the punishment cells had graduated from workhouse 'cages'.

Other methods having failed, the Workhouse Visiting Society propounded in 1860 the revolutionary notion of trying leniency instead: 'If kindness and mercy were shown to these unhappy creatures', commented the editor of the Society's *Journal*, 'they could be saved the degradation of walking to jail, bare-headed, in the company of policemen and spending a month in the company of thieves and prostitutes... The fact of their remaining in a workhouse shows that they have at least one virtue, that of chastity. They have preferred imprisonment in a workhouse to earning the wages of sin in the streets.' Although this charitable conclusion was probably misplaced, the Society's civilising influence was widely felt. In one West London workhouse, a notoriously rowdy establishment, which constantly suffered 'brawls so bad that the house was the pest of the neighbourhood', a new master, a sincere and kindly Christian, introduced a more liberal regime, treating the inmates as voluntary residents rather than dangerous prisoners. The results were striking. Within a short time, not a single able-bodied girl was to be found there instead of the former 30 or 40, while five or six unmarried couples had now married 'and were now living together honourably'. And even in the most old-fashioned workhouse, feminity managed to assert itself. One visitor, in 1889, heard of 'young women, set to pick oakum, secreting portions of it to make themselves tournures, and the poke bonnet... provided in a girl's outfit for service, being speedily cut up and made to resemble as nearly as possible the more fashionable hat'.*

By the end of the century, even that group singled out for harshness by the reformers of 1834, the unmarried mothers, was being treated with common humanity, though the suspicion that to do so was to reward sin died hard. Curiously enough, one of those most conscious of it was Louisa Twining, who had probably done more, especially in her thirties and forties to humanise the workhouse than any other person in the whole nineteenth century. Now, at 78, she was almost apologetic at having secured the building of a special separate and single-storey maternity block in one workhouse. 'One may perhaps',

*Tournures were hip pads worn to improve the look of the figure.

she wrote, 'be allowed to grudge the expenditure of £3,000 for the class of patients...we have to admit and care for in these wards, but whoever and whatever they may be we cannot and must not punish them by death.' The admission was made almost reluctantly, but made it was; something had clearly been gained since 1834.

14 Outcast Infants

No child under twelve years of age shall be
punished by confinement in a dark room or
during the night. *Article 136 of Poor Law
Board General Order*, 24 July 1847

Few fates were less enviable than that of the 'juvenile pauper'—the
infant, child or adolescent brought up in an institution designed for
the supposedly work-shy adult. Those given this depressing label
came from a wide variety of backgrounds. A few were foundlings,
abandoned in the street, like the small London girl discovered on Her
Majesty's birthday, who was christened Victoria Queen, and later
chose a husband—a carpenter in steady work—called Albert. Some,
especially in the early days, arrived as part of a family. One labourer
of Herne in Kent, in February 1838, 'finding his bodily health decreas-
ing and his wife and family in a state of starvation... procured a wheelbarrow, in which he placed three of his children and drove them to the
workhouse, a distance of eight miles, his wife carrying the infant and
the eldest child walking in the road'.

Within a few years, however, the old practice of relieving a family
by taking one child off the parents' hands was creeping back, and the
results were perhaps even more distressing. At a farm workers' rally
on a 'bleak Winter's night', in January 1846, 'in a cross road near
Goatacre', near Calne in Wiltshire, the audience of 'a thousand half-
clad and nearly wholly starving peasantry' was stirred to hear an eight-
shilling-a-week labourer describe how the relieving officer had offered
him an admission order to the house for *one* of his eight children. That
night as he looked round the wretchedly empty table at his ragged,
underfed offspring, each had pleaded piteously, 'Oh father, let it not
be me.'

But for every child from a loving, if desperately poor, home, there
were probably two for whom the workhouse was a real place of shelter.
Sometimes quite small children had struggled valiantly to keep a home
going. One London Relieving Officer was impressed in 1859 by ten-
year-old Biddy, who had sold watercress in the streets to support her

bed-ridden mother, only entering the workhouse when the mother died.

An analysis made in 1861 showed how various were the routes by which girls—no one ever showed the same interest in boys—had reached the workhouse. 'M.A.', for example, had stayed with an uncle when her blind father was forced to become an 'indoor pauper', until the age of fifteen, when the uncle could no longer support her. Others in the same survey included a fifteen-year-old girl, whose father was a sailor and whose mother, 'a needlewoman . . . could not afford to keep her when out of place'. After leaving the St. George's-in-the-East workhouse she had been placed 'at a lodging house for sailors but got no wages during the eight months she was there'.

In a surprising number of cases child inmates came from formerly prosperous families. One workhouse visitor in 1863 claimed to know several children whose fathers had been clerks and bailiffs or, in one case, a bookseller, while others had had fathers who were skilled crafts-men, including a carpenter, a tailor, a blacksmith and a shipwright. 'In providing these girls with a respectable home', this woman assured her readers, 'we are not in any way raising them above the position they would have filled had their parents been living.'

It was not until late in the nineteenth century that the proportion of children in the workhouse, who had up to that time formed from a fifth to a quarter of the whole 'indoor pauper' population, began to show any significant drop. A census as late as New Year's Day, 1889, revealed that of the 192,000 souls in the workhouse at that time no fewer than 54,000 were aged under sixteen.* Of these 54,000, 33,000 were classed as 'orphans and abandoned', who had little hope of leaving before they were grown up, 4,000 were 'sick and infirm', 7,000 were the illegitimate children of other inmates, and only the remaining 10,000 were likely to be short-term residents, since they belonged to able-bodied paupers, a term which by this time usually meant tramps or street traders.

The presence of children is the workhouse presented the Poor Law rigorists with a problem. 'A child cannot...be indigent as the consequence of his own want of industry, skill, frugality and forethought' conceded one Poor Law official in 1838. Yet it was re-cognised that children in the workhouse could hardly fail to be better

---

*The proportion of children on out-relief was approximately the same: 204,000 out of a total of 820,000.

fed and clothed than many of their 'independent' contemporaries outside, thus, it was feared, tempting the labourer to unload his own children on the parish.

The solution was found in subjecting the workhouse child to the same 'deterrent' regime as his supposedly idle elders, in defiance of the fact that, unlike them, he could not leave the workhouse at will, and indeed, if he did run away, would be forcibly brought back. One consequence of this policy was that many children rapidly became, to use a modern term, 'institutionalised'. One Local Government Board inspector, investigating in 1873 the case of a 15-year-old girl who had died in the workhouse, discovered that she had never set foot outside it. A woman who invited two girls, aged nine and thirteen, for Christmas, a little later, discovered that this was their first outing for five years. The girls begged shyly to be allowed to see the dinner being cooked as this was something they had never witnessed before. And change came slowly. A kindly visitor who asked a small boy idling listlessly about a workhouse yard in the 1880s what he hoped to do when he grew up, was astonished to learn that he was looking forward only to moving over 'to the men's side, where he could do as he liked'. He had never left the workhouse since entering it seven years before and 'Such a thing as being independent never struck me', he admitted.

This ignorance of any other way of life was largely due to the decision made in 1834 that children should normally be taught within the workhouse walls. Like other aspects of the new system it was at first claimed as a great success. 'Three months' education in a well-conducted workhouse', boasted one Assistant Commissioner in 1836, 'was worth to the children almost as many years of attending village schools.' The key phrase here was 'well conducted'; many workhouse schools, as will be seen, were abysmal. But, bad or good, their mere existence troubled some purists, who argued that as most labourers' children did not go to school, no workhouse child should do so, especially as it would give him a permanent advantage over them, though they acknowledged that the better a child's education, the less likely he was to become 'chargeable' in the future. To overcome this difficulty one Board of Guardians at Bedford, in 1836, proposed an ingenious compromise: they would teach the workhouse children to read but not to write. This, however, the Poor Law Commissioners would not permit, on the grounds that 'workhouse children should not be treated so as to fix upon them any permanent stigma, in that all other children who learnt to read also learn to write'

Behind the Bedford attitude lay, in fact, other motives than the desire to penalise the workhouse inmate. 'To teach a pauper child to write', wrote the great educational reformer, Sir James Kay-Shuttleworth, who had begun his public career, as Assistant Commissioner Dr James Philipps Kay, the year before:

> was regarded by some Boards as not merely preposterous but dangerous. It was to many of the Guardians like putting the torch of knowledge into the hands of rick-burners... What had the hedger and ditcher, the team-driver, the shepherd, the ploughman to do with letters except to read incendiary prints about Bastilles and the oppression of the New Poor Law?

In many workhouse schools at this time the pupils were, in any case, in little danger of learning anything, for often the Guardians economised by using others inmates as teachers. At Salisbury, in 1840, the school-master was an educated man who had come down in the world through drink and the schoolmistress could not write. At Southampton she could barely read, while her male colleagues was so old and deaf that the boys could communicate with him only by shouting. At Coventry the female pauper in charge, knowing her limitations, taught neither writing nor reading, while some small workhouses, like Shrewsbury, had no teacher at all. 'There is no class of officers', wrote one Assistant Commissioner to his employers, 'of whom such continual complaints are made .. I need not call to your recollection the numbers you have been obliged to dismiss for drunkenness or other immoralities.'

D.L. Cousins, author of *The Diary of a Workhouse Chaplain*, published in 1847, recalled the case of 'a man who, when schoolmaster, endeavoured to seduce several of the older girls in the school', while as late as 1868 a Poor Law Board inspector was writing that 'In numerous instances, I had to recommend the instant dismissal of teachers for gross inefficiency, cruelty or immorality.' One workhouse school at this time was in the charge of the governor's thirteen-year-old daughter, while a new master, arriving at Deptford workhouse, found that he replaced in the classroom two illiterate ex-seamen 'addicted to swearing, lying and drinking' and 'a lunatic who died soon afterwards of brain disease'.

The report of the inspector who visited one workhouse school in 1868 would have been true of many other places:

I attempted to examine them but the result was so absurd that I was obliged to give it up. A total ignorance of the Bible and of arithmetic, miscellaneous spelling and blunders of every conceivable sort characterised their examination papers ... In another, the children apparently read fluently, but on examining their books I found that many were held upside down. The children could not read at all, but had been taught to repeat certain sentences and to hold their books before them as if they were reading.

Often, of course, the classroom accommodation and general atmosphere combined to make the teacher's task difficult, as another inspector had pointed out in 1861:

Familiarity is insufficient to blunt the sense of prison-like confinement and want of spring and life created by the aspect of the place and its inmates. Most workhouse schools open into a court enclosed by a high wall... The schoolroom is generally twenty feet long by ten broad and ten or eleven feet high, imperfectly ventilated by means of openings under the ceiling and by perforated zinc tubes, which traverse the room from wall to wall. The windows are generally small and square and if they should happen to look on any of the adult yards, are darkened by whitewashing the glass. During the dark winter months the instruction of the children is much hindered by want of light, while their health and spirits are affected by the closeness occasioned by the lowness of the room. The girls are generally not unbecomingly dressed, but unnecessarily disfigured by cropping their hair, a practice which marks them out as workhouse girls when they are placed in service. Some Boards of Guardians have been considerate enough to allow their hair to grow to an ordinary length before they place them in situations. The boys, besides being hideously cropped, are disfigured and degraded by a dress which seems as if it had been specially designed to humble them and impress on their mind ... that they are paupers. The material of which it is composed has the further demerit of an intolerable and unwholesome smell until it has several times been washed.

A recurring complaint throughout the century was the cruelty which, in workhouse schools, often went undetected for years. This was the experience of one Somerset clergyman, a passionate believer in the New Poor Law, in the 1830s:

> At the commencement of the union, I went with a number of Guardians to Walcot workhouse, and on enquiring for the children we were conducted to a room in which about thirty little wretches stood in a class; and a man holding in his hand a large whip, standing in the midst. He was a pauper with only one eye. Seeing no books or slates, we at first doubted whether this was the schoolroom and the following dialogue was the result:
> 'Are you the schoolmaster?'
> 'Yes'.
> 'What do you teach the children?'
> 'Nothing'.
> 'How then are they employed?'
> 'They do nothing'.
> 'What then do you do?'
> 'I keep them quiet'.
> A gentleman who was formerly an overseer of that great parish, containing 26,000 inhabitants, informs me that it was the constant practice to flog the children: that he has frequently seen it, and has sometimes been requested to flog them himself.

The regulations about corporal punishment were later set out in a General Order in July 1847, which banned it altogether in the case of girls and older boys. Boys under fourteen could be beaten, but only by the schoolmaster or workhouse governor and 'with a rod or other instrument...approved of by the Guardians'. No rules were so often broken. 'I have reason to believe', admitted one Assistant Commissioner in the 1840s, 'that great cruelties have been practised upon the children which probably do not always come to light, as a schoolmaster has no difficulty in aweing an unhappy orphan, who probably has not a friend in the world. In one case...the schoolmaster was in the habit of tying up with a handkerchief the jaws of those boys whom he thought deserved punishment, to prevent their screams being heard.' 'Being ignorant of the art of controlling and disciplining children, the teachers sometimes resorted to cruel punishment to maintain their authority,' complained another inspector, in 1868, 'I remember that in one school the master said he could not keep the boys in order though he had broken several sticks on them.'

Mrs Emma Sheppard of Frome, the great champion of the workhouse children, as Louisa Twining was of the adult pauper, published in 1858 an account of 'a poor girl...so beaten...for not spelling a word right, that the skin of her back came off on her linen when it was removed'. A letter from a friend, quoted by Mrs Sheppard, revealed even worse maltreatment in another, unspecified, workhouse in the South of England:

> One day I saw a little girl with red eyes at our school (for they had no school-mistress at the workhouse) whose heart seemed bursting, and on enquiring the cause, she said: 'Missus has roped me'. Her back and arms were red and covered with great weals and marks of rope. The child told me that it was done for the merest trifle; and that all the union children told how it was the 'missus's' constant habit to beat them with a thick hair rope, made on purpose. It had two knots at the end and a loop for the hand. When the Guardians met to examine into the case the mistress denied that there was such a thing in the house, but...the chairman desired two Guardians to go with one of the girls to the spot mentioned and there, sure enough, it was! The Guardians to a man exclaimed with indignation. This master and mistress actually got testimonials from the chaplain and medical man; they resigned before the London Central Board had time to call on them to do so, and went to America, where he...is thriving upon the money he cheated the parish of.

Although Article 136 of the 1847 General Order already quoted specified that 'no child under twelve years of age shall be punished by confinement in a dark room or during the night', 'locking up' in a detention room was a favourite method of enforcing discipline and there were others almost as brutal. One newly-elected Guardian, visiting a workhouse school at Stapleton, near Bristol, in 1840, found that 'the master appeared much astonished', when he raised objections to 'the punishment of the trough', which involved forcing the children to kneel on the floor like animals and 'to take their meals from a trough, without knife or fork'.

Cruelty is the dominant theme in the sole account of life in a workhouse school which has survived, written by the most famous 'old boy' of such an establishment, the explorer Sir Henry Morton Stanley, who in 1871 achieved international fame when he 'presumed' to discover Dr Livingstone. Stanley, originally christened John Rowlands, was the illegitimate son of a Welsh girl who had run off to London, leaving him with her parents, who handed him over to another elderly couple, to whom his mother's brothers paid 2*s.* 6*d.* a week for his keep.* Then, having married again, they stopped the allowance and one Saturday morning in 1847 the 6-year-old John was taken for a walk by the grown-up son of his foster-parents, supposedly to visit an aunt:

> The way seemed interminable and tedious, but he did his best to relieve my fatigue with false cajolings and treacherous endearments. At last Dick set me down from his shoulders before an immense stone building and, passing through tall iron gates, he pulled at a bell, which I could hear clanging noisily in the distant interior. A sombre-faced stranger appeared at the door who, despite my remonstrances, seized me by the hand and drew me within, while Dick tried to soothe my fears with glib promises that he was only going to bring Aunt Mary to me. The door closed on him and, . . . I experienced for the first time the awful feeling of utter desolateness.

The small boy's fears were justified, for he had been, in fact, delivered up into the care of the St Asaph's Union, near Denbigh, and though he sobbed his heart out he soon learned 'the unimportance of tears in a workhouse'. Before long, numb with misery, he settled down into the deadening routine which never varied from day to day, from the clang of the rising bell at 6 a m until the click of the key in the dormitory lock at 8 in the evening. In between, in an 'uninteresting garb of squalid fustian, with hair mown close to the skull' the boys were kept busy 'sweeping the playground with brooms more suited to giants than little children... washing the slated floors when one was stiff from caning... hoeing... frost-bound ground, when every stroke on it caused the nerves to quiver, the thinly clad body all the while exposed to a searching wind'. The diet, carefully measured out, revolved round bread and gruel, rice and potatoes, as drab and depressing as the uniform.

But life was not wholly grim. 'We sometimes played hide-and-seek and excited ourselves by mild gambling with stones', John Rowlands later recalled. 'The older ones, through some mysterious connection with the outside boy-world, became acquainted with spring-tops, tip-cat, kite-flying, hop-scotch, and marbles, leap-frog and follow-my-leader.' Although John often saw his half-sister (product of another of

*John Rowlands later took the name Stanley as a compliment to his American benefactor.

his father's seductions), he was not allowed to speak to her, the thirty boys, aged five to fifteen, being kept separate from the girls, although he discovered that, like himself, she was described in the records as 'a deserted bastard'. It was not till he was twelve that he discovered that every child had a mother, when his own, now married to a later partner, visited him, to be greeted by her son with a puzzled stare.

The workhouse school was housed in two rooms, one for each sex, and—the future explorer recalled—there were no maps and no geography lessons, no arithmetic, nor even slates to write on. The work revolved round the Bible, the catechism and *Dr Mavor's Spelling Primer*, already fifty years out of date. The schoolmaster was a former collier who had lost one hand in a pit accident and was 'soured by misfortune, brutal of temper and callous of heart':

> No Greek helot or dark slave ever underwent such discipline as the Boys of St Asaph under the heavy masterful hand of James Francis. The ready back-slap in the face, the stunning clout over the ear, the strong blow with the open palm on alternate cheeks, which knocked out senses into confusion, were so frequent that it is a marvel we ever recovered them again. Whatever might be the nature of the offence, or merely because his irritable mood required vent, our poor heads were cuffed, and slapped, and pounded, until we lay speechless and streaming with blood . . . If, while . . . he was reading to us, he addressed a question to some boy, the slightest error in reply would either be followed by a stinging blow from the ruler or a thwack with his blackthorn. If a series of errors were discovered in our lessons, then a vindictive scourging of the offender followed, until he was exhausted, or our lacerated bodies could bear no more.

Half a century later Stanley could still remember two appalling floggings, one when he was only eight years old, for mispronouncing the word 'Joseph', the other, two years later, for eating some forbidden blackberries. One handsome boy, rumoured to be the illegitimate son of a lord, disappeared suddenly and his classmates found his body in the mortuary, covered with bruises and gashes—a crime that went unpunished.* Finally the day came when a workhouse table had been accidentally scratched and the sadistic Francis announced he would flog the class one by one. But John Rowlands, now a sturdy fifteen,

---

*This schoolmaster was, however, later certified insane and died in an asylum.

was very different from the docile, weeping six-year-old who had first
suffered in St Asaph workhouse, and on being thrown over a bench, he
kicked out at Francis, smashing his glasses and causing him to fall
over the bench so that 'the back of his head struck the stone floor...
I bounded to my feet and possessed myself of his blackthorn... rushed
at the prostrate form and struck him at random over his body'. Determined to 'die before submitting again', John Rowlands literally climbed
the workhouse walls, the start of a series of adventures that was to
carry him to rank, fortune and enduring fame.

Although the only inspector to visit St Asaph's concluded that the
children's white faces were due to their not being forced to work hard
enough, many were more discerning and the best made substantial
efforts from the very beginning to make the workhouse schools at
least the equal of those outside. As early as 1835 Dr James Kay
produced a highly influential report on the apprenticing of pauper
children and encouraged English unions to recruit young teachers
from Scotland, where public education was far in advance of that in
England. Among these was one 'enthusiastic Scotch youth', who 'was
a phenomenon in these small workhouse schools... Everything was
transformed when he appeared. When he left one workhouse to proceed
to another school... the master and the scholars alike had been
awakened from a torpor into which they could not at once sink back'.
But such paragons were rare and, however much they achieved, the
all-pervading workhouse atmosphere remained, so that Kay, like later
reformers, became eager to remove children from it into separate
boarding schools.

In 1834 there were already several privately-run schools near
London which accepted workhouse children for a fee of around 4s.
6d. a week and Kay found that 'The rooms were generally clean' and
the residents were 'decently but scantily clad'. What troubled him
however, 'was the pallor, the subdued mien and listless demeanour of
the children...I found children changed to logs of wood'. He set out
to improve matters with the co-operation of the proprietor of the best-
known of the schools, Aubin's at Norwood, persuading the Home
Office to contribute £500 a year for the purpose. 'Rough workshops',
Kay wrote, 'were built, the schoolroom was divided up by curtains...
desks, benches and apparatus were bought. Teachers were selected
from Scotland and skilled handicraftsmen were put in charge of the
workshops...The domestic training of the girls...included the
cleaning of the teachers' apartments, waiting on them at meals, plain

cooking, instruction in the washhouse and laundry, domestic hygiene, the care of infants and the rudiments of sick nursing.'

The results, he claimed, were striking. 'The children now at least display in their features evidence of happiness; they have confidence in the kindness of all by whom they are surrounded; their days pass in a cheerful succession of instruction, recreation, work and domestic and religious duties... Everything was done happily, some things even joyfully. The instruction of the school awakened their intelligence and fed their minds.' An official delegation, led by Lord John Russell, then Home Secretary, which visited the school in 1839, was equally impressed and for years, Aubin's school remained a showplace of public education. A two-man deputation from the Manchester Board of Guardians, inspecting it in 1841, produced a highly flattering report, which noted that corporal punishment was banned and 'a style of mild and winning address is uniformly adopted towards the pupils'. During a tour lasting several hours they saw only two of the 1,200 boarders in tears.

The other famous 'farm' school—to which the unions 'farmed out' their children—was Drouet's at Tooting, which the visitors from Lancashire praised equally warmly, but which seven years later became the scene of a famous scandal. In 1848 cholera burst upon the supposedly model establishment, killing 180 of the 1,400 children and its proprietor was charged, unsuccessfully, with manslaughter. Charles Dickens launched a violent attack upon it as 'a disgrace to a Christian community', and the whole conception of such schools, run by private citizens for profit, suffered a blow from which they never recovered.

By the 1860s the opening up of the workhouse to visitors, and the attendance of workhouse children at treats outside, had made many people aware of their disadvantages. One woman who had helped to provide tea for a contingent from her local workhouse described in a national magazine in 1861 how:

> The difference between their general bearing and that of ordinary National school children was very striking and sad.* By far the greater number had a depressed, downcast and spiritless look, almost as if they already felt themselves to belong to an inferior and

---

*A National school meant one provided, with the help of a government grant, by the National Society for Promoting the Education of the Poor in the Principles of the Established Church, i.e. a normal primary school of the time.

despised class and would never have energy to try to rise above it. Surely it would be well not to go on herding pauper children constantly together, but to let them attend some National school ... and so be mixed for some hours every day with non-pauper children?

This was a conclusion which many humane-minded people had already reached, and the use of outside schools increased rapidly after the Poor Law Board had given permission for union funds to be used to pay the fees incurred, usually twopence to ninepence a week. The old objection that there were 'independent' families which could not afford to send their children to school, ceased to be so effective after 1870, when education became compulsory in areas with adequate school places, and vanished altogether in 1880 when school attendance became obligatory everywhere, though fees were not finally abolished in elementary schools until 1891. By then, the use of the local state schools for workhouse children had become the general rule.

By 1897 only eighty workhouses still had their own schools and their quality had been altered out of all recognition, due largely to the improvement in teacher training initiated by Dr Kay.* One inspector described in 1889 how a schoolmistress at Dover workhouse 'had painted on the floor of the schoolroom and on the doorposts various diagrams showing the cardinal points of the compass ... and ... further decorated her walls with flowers of her own painting and with some of the pictures used as advertisements by the well-known firms of Pears, Nestlé, etc'. She had also, he noted approvingly, taken 'advantage of the country walks with her children by making them collect ... the various wild flowers of the district, whilst her window-sills are filled with growing plants and ferns of many kinds . . . This humanising process', he concluded, 'is rapidly raising the tone and intelligence of the children in a very marked degree.'

Another inspector remarked, on visiting a workhouse school for forty children in 1897, that its only resemblance to the old-style school was that both were approached through the workhouse gate:

The children can be visited once a month . . . and they have their toys and a small library. Boys and girls go out together for walks

*As Dr James Kay-Shuttleworth, Kay (who was subsequently Knighted) served as Secretary to the Committee of the Privy Council on Education, i.e. as the chief educational administrator, from 1839 until his retirement in 1849. He helped found the Battersea training college in 1839 and in 1846 secured the first parliamentary grants towards the cost of teachers in workhouse schools.

three times a week . . . The older boys have their allotments which . . . they can work on as they like. They play cricket in the workhouse fields. Both boys and girls go out to Sunday School and they are often sent out on errands . . . The children were at play as we walked up to the door, the boys at cricket and the girls with skipping-ropes and other amusements. Their voices sounded very merry.

By now, however, many Boards of Guardians had decided that neither better schools of their own, nor the use of local schools outside, were really satisfactory and that what was needed was to remove their children from the workhouse atmosphere altogether. The favoured solution now was not the 'farm' school, operated by contractors for profit, but the 'district school', run by salaried officials employed by all the unions making use of it. Combinations of unions for this purpose had been authorised as long ago as 1844, and the first, and most famous, district school serving London had been opened at Anerley in North Surrey in 1850.

Experience there was not at first encouraging. 'Their conduct outside the schoolroom', wrote one of the staff about the first intake of pupils—they eventually numbered 900—'was of a piece with their performance within. The slightest restraint exercised over them was immediately revenged by the destruction of property. During the first month nearly £100 worth of damage was wilfully done to the building in the demolition of windows, window sashes, tiles etc...Their habits were most filthy and revolting and their language of the same character.' But patience, mixed with kindness, produced a transformation. 'Their very appearance', the same observer noted five years later, 'is wonderfully altered for the better. They have lost the slouching gait and dogged, sullen look...Corporal punishment is becoming almost unknown among us...I believe we have succeeded in gaining their confidence and even affection. They no longer look upon labour as an irksome task but rather as an honourable and pleasurable employment.'

Many Boards, especially in rural areas, always distrusted District Schools and by 1856 only 3,000 pauper children in England and Wales were being educated in this way, compared to 40,000 still in the workhouse. A small but efficient workhouse school might well be a kinder place than a vast and impersonal 'barracks school', as their critics called them. Louisa Twining, that shrewd and indefatigable visitor, was not impressed by the large Poor Law boarding school, with 1,100 pupils and 70 staff, which she visited near London in 1859, or by its superintendent:

> In the dining-hall, he said 'We must overlook them all; they will pilfer or barter anything.' One boy broke into the store room and was seen carrying away loaves. For punishment he had to carry them about on his head, walking up and down . . . It was touching to see the poor things frequently beg for a bit from the superintendent's dinner, asking to have it upon his plate, their own being plain white ones. What a longing of the childish heart for change and beauty does this show! One room was filled with girls at work. They do not learn to cut out—'it would be too wasteful, it would cost threepence a head more if they did'. It is said that the superintendent is making . . . a fortune. He and his party certainly seem to live upon the fat of the land; he talks of his 'soufflets', in speaking of his dinner and of their parties with bits of fowl and so on.

Most Guardians regarded their periodic visits of inspection to see that all was well with the union children at a district school, as merely an agreeable day out, centring on a bibulous lunch at the ratepayers' expense, and there was often competition to become one of the favoured delegation, but there were honourable exceptions. One was George Lansbury, the future Labour leader, who became a Guardian for the desperately poor East London borough of Poplar in 1892 and soon afterwards visited the school which the union shared with Whitechapel:

> The buildings were in Forest Lane, Stratford, and were built on the barrack system—that is, long dormitories for scores of children to sleep in, with very little accommodation for recreation, and at the time I first saw it the children were dressed in the old, hideous, Poor Law garb, corduroy and hard blue serge, and the girls with their hair almost shaved off, with nothing at all to make them look attractive. The food was quite coarse . . . After our first committee meeting we were taken downstairs, where a seven course dinner was to be served. It was this which made me very disgusted with the middle-class men and women who controlled the institution; they could let little girls who they knew must be starved, stand and wait on them while they ate chicken, nice soups, sweets, etc, all at the expense of the rates . . . When, later on, we bought out

Whitechapel and took over the school all this sort of thing was abolished ... we appointed a new superintendent and matron and ... they have proved themselves most splendid officials ... although neither of them were Socialists.

While, in 1894, Lansbury was still struggling to reform the Poplar school, one of the worst workhouse scandals of the century broke over a similar establishment, at Brentwood in Essex, to which the Hackney Union, serving a poor area of north-east London, sent its children. The case revolved round the figure of Nurse Elizabeth Gillespie, aged 54, who had then been in charge of the children's dormitories for seven years. According to her letter of application she was an 'early riser, fond of children', but once installed, she carried everywhere a short stick, with which she dealt out 'handers' of up to twelve strokes on each palm. More serious misdemeanours were punished by knocking children, aged from five to thirteen, to the floor, forcing them to kneel on hot pipes covered in wire netting or beating them on their bare backs with stinging nettles, while the children were kept so short of water that they were forced to drink from the water closets or lap like dogs from puddles in the playground. But the torture which really captured the public imagination was 'basket drill', when, one witness explained, the children 'were compelled to walk round the dormitory in their night clothes, in their bare feet, and with a basket on their head containing their day clothes ... after being dragged out of bed', sometimes at four in the morning.

Retribution finally overtook Nurse Gillespie when she killed a girl by pushing her downstairs, for the victim, unlike most of her schoolmates, was not an orphan and though the Guardians were satisfied, the dead child's mother was not. The police were called in and though, to public regret, there was insufficient evidence to convict Gillespie of murder, she pleaded guilty to charges of cruelty and was sentenced to five years' hard labour. The subsequent enquiry by the Chief Inspector of the Local Government Board proved to be for the child pauper what the Andover investigation half a century earlier had been for the adult. During July 1894 thirty-four adult witnesses and thirty children testified to the way in which, at Brentwood, the state, in the shape of the Hackney Guardians, had failed to care for its infant poor, until, as one resident complained at a meeting in September, 'They were tired of seeing on the newspaper placards "Another Hackney scandal".'

It soon became clear that the whole establishment had been pervaded by an atmosphere of violence. The headmistress gave the girls black eyes and constantly hit out with a ruler; the masters on duty at night carried canes round the dormitories; the games master even took one on to the cricket field, so that, as the Inspector remarked, 'From the time the boys get up in the morning until they go to bed at night, they are never out of sight of a cane.' The whole staff had connived at Gillespie's cruelties, including the doctor, who had constantly treated, without protest, children who had been badly and even dangerously knocked about. The matron and her husband, who had assured the Guardians she was 'the best officer we have', actually raised a fund for her defence. As for the Guardians, it transpired that their surprise visits, specifically designed to uncover such abuses, were a farce: valuing their comfort, they had invariably sent ahead for a carriage to meet them at the station and had even ordered the usual lavish lunch beforehand.

The Inspector's report was scathing about the general management of the school. 'There has', he wrote, 'been a system of constant repression emphasised by "strokes", "clips", "tips" and "taps" from morning to night.' But he ended on a more cheerful note. 'When in the course of our enquiry we visited the dining-hall at dinner time we were much pleased to find, by the bright and cheery faces of the infants and their confiding manners as they pressed forward to catch hold of our hands after the usual manner of small children in workhouses, that the bitter past must already have...faded from their memories.'

The Guardians proved equally forgiving for, though dismissing the superintendent and his wife, they proposed to give them a pension. This was too much for the citizens of Hackney, who raised such an outcry at a crowded public meeting that the Guardians had second thoughts and the guilty couple, now 'on the verge of starvation', vanished, unpensioned, from Poor Law history.

The policy of using district schools survived the Gillespie case and by 1898, four years later, London alone made use of twenty, some of them lavishly equipped. The best were like that built in Surrey by Kensington and Chelsea, which had cost £90,000 and which one visitor in that year found 'gives the impression of a well-designed model village, delightfully placed amid country surroundings of woodland and down'. The children here lived in small houses, in groups of about 25, and the older girls took it in turn to act as 'house mothers'. But more important than the accommodation was the general atmosphere.

Many visitors had been struck in the past by the dejected and repressed air of workhouse children, but two visitors to the Strand Union school at Edmonton in the same year—the subject of a violently critical pamphlet earlier in the century—had no such complaints. 'The infants school is a cheering sight', they wrote. 'Be he never so small no child appears to have any doubt as to his own individuality.'

Queen Mary, wife of George V, had an even more striking demonstration of the lack of inhibition of Poor Law children when she visited the spacious school at Shenfield in Essex, opened by the Poplar Guardians, under George Lansbury's influence, to replace the institution that had so disgusted him. Lansbury was by now chairman of the school managers, but instead of regarding him with awe the children treated him like a favourite uncle. When he appeared on this occasion the children forgot all about the royal visitor, abandoned the patriotic song they were supposed to sing in her honour, and rushed forward to surround her companion, with shouts of 'Good old George!'

15 Friendless Girls and Boys

> While she is in the workhouse she does not
> comprehend her isolated position in the world
> but when she is sent out to work then her
> friendlessness is realised. *Journal of the Work-
> house Visiting Society*, 1861

Even after the improvements in workhouse education had begun,
the workhouse as a home, rather than as a school, remained a
wretched place. One Relieving Officer described in 1859 how 'sometimes on a Summer afternoon may be seen long rows of wretched-
looking children, clad sometimes in brown, but oftener in prison-grey
short jackets, and fustian trousers, mostly ill-fitting. Their countenances wear a vacant grin, intended for a smile, their gait and general
aspect indicate a tendency to premature age and their whole appearance
verges on the repulsive'.

A description of the young inmates of a Dublin workhouse,
published in the same year, was equally depressing. 'Stunted little
creatures, neither child-like nor human-like', wrote a compassionate
visitor, 'they are *at play*, sitting close-packed against the wall, or
gathered into knots, dull and stupified on their nursery floors; no ghost
of a ball, or hoop or pegging top to remind them of a child's nature;
pauper children must be taught to do without these things.'

A woman writing in *Macmillan's Magazine* in 1861 had a similar
experience:

> Rarely have we beheld so dismal a sight, for the ugly yard miscalled
> by that pleasant name was three inches deep in coarse gravel,
> through which walking was difficult and running impossible, even
> had not each poor little creature been weighed down like a galley-
> slave by a pair of iron-shoes as heavy as lead. The poor babes stood
> huddled in a corner, scared and motionless, when bidden by the
> matron in an unctuous manner to 'play as usual, my dears!' We tried
> to play ourselves, but were utterly foiled by those sad childish
> looks ... of ... the poor little ones, to whom life had not yet
> brought such wonders as a skipping-rope!

The meanness of some Boards was extraordinary, even in an age which applauded private extravagance while distrusting even the most essential public expenditure. Often it extended to such essential items as providing workhouse children with new shoes. 'How many a heart pang', one contributor to the Workhouse Visiting Society *Journal* remarked in 1861, 'would be spared to orphan children if kind considerate ladies would take upon them to see that their little feet were not punished by wearing shoes which they had grown out of.' The provision of recreational equipment for workhouse children was rarely even considered. In one union, an inspector noted at this time, 'one of the Guardians, having offered to erect a pole and circular swing at his own cost, if the Board would find the ropes, etc, they refused', for fear that 'more bodily exercise' would give the children healthier appetites and 'an apprehension lest there be a greater wear and tear of clothes and shoes'.

As late as 1884 an inspector of the Local Government Board was protesting that 'It is a lamentable thing to see children perfectly idle and listless within the four square walls of a court...and, in my opinion, a false economy when the children are not allowed the use of a circular swing on the ground that it makes them wear out their boots rapidly.' Grudgingly, the Board in that year at last agreed that bats, stumps and balls could be provided 'as the Board are advised that the practice of cricket would have a tendency to promote the healthy development of the workhouse children'.

The fight to provide toys took even longer to win. In one workhouse, a woman visitor found in 1859, 'the sole amusement for fifteen children under five years old was found to be the trunk of one doll' and there were 'thirty or forty infants under five in the nursery without any playthings'. When the Guardians were willing to provide such items they were discouraged by higher authority. In 1890 a zealous auditor at the Local Government Board disallowed the expenditure of 3s. 6d. on toys by the Wisberch Union, even though the Guardians promised that only sick children would be allowed to play with them. Another more humane official thereupon committed the unpardonable Civil Service crime of attacking his own department's policy anonymously in the *Morning Post*, so causing a question in the House of Commons. The result, in January 1891, was an official circular authorising—though not, alas, ordering—the purchase of both indoor toys and 'a reasonable amount of skipping-ropes and battledores and shuttlecocks', to which some unions even added that symbol of Victorian childhood, the hoop.

From 1842 walks outside the walls became officially permitted for
workhouse inmates under the age of fifteen, though only at the master's
discretion, and these outings brought the participants something
more valuable even than fresh air — contact with the local population.
Mrs Emma Sheppard of Frome in Somerset described in her often
reprinted pamphlet, *Sunshine in the Workhouse*, first published in
1858, how to put such excursions to good use:

> Do you never meet when out walking those long lines of dejected-
> looking children from the union? The thin print dresses, and
> washed and worn half-square turn-over handkerchiefs their only
> protection against the cold; the tiny ones, boys and girls, indis-
> criminately dressed in feminine costume, without fitting or looking
> tidy... Next time you meet the mournful looking workhouse
> schools, call them round you, see if you have a sixpence or a shilling
> in your pocket, ask 'Is there any head boy or girl here whom we can
> trust?' and entrust to him the few pence for apples or lollypops at
> the next shop they come to; then watch... as they walk on with
> a joy on their faces not seen before; see them even attempt a hop,
> skip and jump at the thought of this little variety in a dull day...
> And then, when any cheap panorama . . . comes to your town, and
> other little ones are crowing eagerly to give their pence and go
> remember the workhouse lads and lasses and let them enjoy it
> as well.

Always ready to practise what she preached, Mrs Sheppard soon
became the idol of every workhouse child in Frome. 'I hear the loud
whisper of joy run electrically through the line when they catch sight
of me... in the street,' she told her readers. Often she invited groups
of workhouse children in to sample scraps of cake and fruit from her
pantry and to play riotous games in her garden. Finally she asked twelve
girls from the workhouse to join her Sunday school at their next
annual party:

> When our eighty children came tumbling in, the pauper girls
> huddled apart, as if they dared not join them; but we soon reassured
> them and scattered them among the others and then I saw them
> chatting away and really looking happy at times... When the
> baskets and trays of huge hunks of cake were handed among the
> ranks of young ones, the workhouse girls let the same pass several
> times without helping themselves as others were doing and when

I said, 'Why don't you take a piece, my girls?' the under-whispered reply was, 'We did not know *we* were to have any'; the same when the ginger-wine came round... These girls felt they were not on a par with the village children and dared not presume to come forward and claim what others were taking as their due.

The *Journal* of the Workhouse Visiting Society was soon advancing other ideas to brighten the lives of workhouse children. Members, it was suggested, should appeal in the local press for old toys, picture books and prints suitable for colouring from the *Illustrated London News*, which would 'serve to wile away many a dull hour for the poor children in the workhouse'. Many now began, for the first time, to enjoy some of the normal pleasures of childhood. The newly-founded Workhouse Visiting Society at Wigan, in 1861 took the local work- house children to Southport, to enjoy donkey rides on the beach. At Bradford similar benefactors treated the children, most of whom had never been on a train, to a railway journey into the country, and then entertained them to tea on a farm, where they feasted on 'bread well covered with preserved fruit'. This the writer found 'so acceptable to the children that I would recommend its substitution for the established currant bun'.

An even more important result of the new interest in workhouse children was that in the 1860s, more attention began to be paid to what happened when they left the house. Most studies and charitable ventures were concerned solely with girls— since it was no doubt felt that girls who failed in their first jobs would be driven to prostitution, whereas boys could look after themselves.

The sole occupation for which workhouse girls were prepared was that of domestic service, and while the boys were at their lessons, an inspector noted in 1859, the girls were busy on 'bed-making, scrubbing, washing...needlework' and various unskilled jobs in the kitchen. Yet, despite all these chores, the workhouse was not a good training ground for servants, as many disillusioned mistresses, expecting to find it a source of unlimited cheap and docile labour, complained. The workhouse girl was often sulky and rebellious, so that she fell out with her fellow-servants, or employers, and, never having had any possessions, had no idea of the meaning of private property. The everyday domestic routine of a family was utterly strange to her. She had probably never mended a fire or laid a dinner table, and being used to the wooden platters, tin plates and tough earthenware mugs of the workhouse,tended to wreak havoc on the crockery and ornaments of the average private household. 'The use of knives and forks was unknown to them. The mat seldom failed to trip them up,' complained one writer in the Workhouse Visiting Society *Journal*, describing ex-workhouse girls aged from fifteen to eighteen. 'It required practice to enable them to get up and down stairs without falling.'

Some workhouse schools did try to break girl inmates in to a life of domestic drudgery. Those aged seven to nine attended school daily. At nine they began to spend alternate days in the needlework room and classroom and at eleven the range of chores was extended, so that 'Their muscular powers are brought thoroughly into action as they have to make all the beds and keep clean and in order sixteen large dormitories, the chapel...as well as the infirmary where they assist in waiting on their sick school-fellows.' At fourteen the girls entered the 'servants class', which meant ten hours a day hard labour in the laundry or kitchen or cleaning the staff quarters and waiting at table, their evenings being spent in repairing their own clothing and on such schoolwork as they still had time and energy for. The woman who described this exacting routine claimed that 'It is very rarely indeed that a mistress complains that a girl does not know her duties.' She was, however, concerned that well-meaning Boards of Guardians might 'economise labour by the introduction of washing machines, wringing machines, drying closets and other contrivances', which left the girls 'utterly incapable of going through the necessary processes in an ordinary house'; some, having seen catering only in bulk, could not even boil a potato.

Even when carefully prepared for their future life, the failure rate of workhouse girls in outside employment was high. A study of 80 from one union, made in 1860, showed that, apart from 18 discharged to the care of families or friends, all had become servants, but only 38 were still, some years later, in service, the rest having walked out, been dismissed, or made other careers as adult paupers (5), wives (5) and prostitutes (2). What had led the rest to throw up their jobs is not on record, but the basic reason was almost certainly overwork. 'We are apt to forget that all the households in the land have not each a cook and housemaid at least, and a nursemaid when there are children', one contributor to the Workhouse Visiting Society *Journal* reminded her readers in 1860, when there were estimated to be 400,000 single-servant households in the country. The unfortunate 'general servant, as the maid of all work is now genteely called', was,

however, unlikely to forget, for a sixteen-hour-day seven days a week
was not unknown for a wage of £5 to £6 a year. 'In the course of the
last ten years many strong girls have utterly lost their health before
they were twenty years of age, from the effect of the cruel labour
exacted from them', protested one member of the Workhouse
Visiting Society in 1864, the worst offenders in her view being
schools and lodging-houses, especially those 'in watering places
during the season'.

Many of the Society's supporters were already trying to bridge the
gap between the workhouse and the world outside, by offering a home
to girls after they had left the workhouse. 'While she is in the workhouse she does not comprehend her isolated position in the world',
the Society's *Journal* pointed out in 1861, 'but when she is sent out
to work then her friendlessness is realised.'

The Industrial Home for Young Women, occupying a large house
in Great Ormond Street in central London, opened in 1861, provided
training in the domestic arts for girls carefully selected from the
current crop of workhouse leavers, found them their first job, with a
supposedly kindly mistress, and provided them with a home to return
to if they failed to settle down. In its first two years' existence the
Industrial Home placed 152 girls, from fourteen unions, but the
results were not encouraging. The organisers lost touch with 36,
'of whom we fear about ten have gone utterly wrong', ten had been
sent to the colonies, where their prospects of marriage were good, but
nearly half had been re-admitted to the home, and over-all only
about a third appeared to have been placed satisfactorily.

Following the 1834 Act, the evil old practice of 'apprenticing'
boys by paying up to £10 to any employer who would take them off the
parish's hands had been officially forbidden. In Stepney, for example,
the result of the premium system had been, 'to induce the worst master
of the lowest description of fishing smack to apply for the boys, who
were often so ill-treated that they were forced to abscond', while in
Grimsby one could see queues of other reluctant 'sailors' waiting
outside the magistrates' court to be sentenced for having, 'jumped
ship', or refused to sail. Now there was actually some effort in the best
unions to train boys for employment outside, the show place being
Aubin's School at Norwood. As early as 1841, due to Dr James Kay's
efforts, the school employed 'competent paid instructors...in...
tin-plate working, joinering and iron and brass work', while 'all the
clothes, for both males and females, and also the shoes are made by

themselves...A large class of...youths intended for sea-faring occupations', the same visitor noted, 'are placed under the direction of a veteran tar, at whose command they perform all the evolutions peculiar to seamanship, and man and rig the model of a perfect ship of war, 240 feet long, with all its sails and tacklings'. So valuable was such training that most 'Old Aubinians', if the term may be allowed, were offered a job by the age of twelve.* The workhouse was, indeed, often said to provide an ideal preparation for the Royal Navy, since in both 'everything is so neat, clean and orderly' and a merchant captain reported that such recruits 'ran aloft without fear and were prompt in obeying orders'. At Stepney the boys, unusually for the time, learned to swim and slept in hammocks, with the result, it was said, they became 'three parts seamen without leaving dry land'.

In inland unions the Army was an equally common choice of career. A survey of 125 workhouse 'graduates' in 1860 showed that the largest single group, twenty-three, had 'gone for a soldier' and many school superintendents claimed that, apart from its vocational value, military drill was beneficial to all their boys. 'Instead of the dull, listless, unintelligent air of the boys, with a careless attention to their person, mixed with the coarsest and rudest of manners,' wrote the master of Wolverhampton workhouse school in 1861, there was now 'an unmistakable intelligence, a quick, sharp eye and ear, a smartness and pride in the boys' personal appearance... Their whole nature seemed changed ... Their marching in their weekly walks was the pride and talk of the town...It became easy to teach them.' The Guardians here were so impressed that they 'changed the workhouse garb to military blue tunics, trousers, cap, belt and stick', while a public subscription raised the cost of rifles and musical instruments. Many workhouses now echoed to the incongruous and uncertain sound of scales and simple exercises on the trumpet or trombone. 'Musical instruction on wind instruments,' one inspector explained in 1860, 'has been introduced into some of the large pauper schools with a view of preparing the children for enlistment in military bands', which soon became the most typical destination for workhouse boys. Already six Poor Law schools were, between them, turning out 200 potential bandsmen a year,

---

*It was not until 1893 that a universal minimum school-leaving age was laid down:—11, raised to 12 in 1899 and 14 in 1918.

a total which could easily be raised to 1,000, provided there were sufficient boys able 'to distinguish time and tune'.

Apart from the armed forces, most workhouses prepared their young male inmates for semi-skilled manual occupations requiring little capital, especially shoe-making. In the 1860 survey of 125 workhouse leavers already mentioned, the second largest group of boys, thirteen, had entered this trade, which could readily be taught in the workhouse, and another popular choice was tailoring. One critic in 1863 warned unions, however, that instructors were easy to find only because both trades were overcrowded. He suggested providing training in painting, glazing and baking, as under-manned 'though not particularly healthy' trades, and, if the workhouse had facilities to teach them properly, carpentry and engineering. Gardening, which many boys liked, was not be encouraged, since, though useful in the workhouse, it was little in demand outside.

Although nothing on the scale of the Industrial Home for girls was set up to help boys, that excellent woman, Mrs Emma Sheppard, clearly had a soft spot for them and in 1859 equipped at her own expense a hostel for eight boys from the local workhouse, run by an old solider. Within three months all eight had been found work, in factories, in stables or as errand boys, and they soon became partly self-supporting, for when their weekly earnings reached three shillings, they had to contribute a shilling towards their board and lodging. Some earned as much as 6*s*. 6*d*. and bought their own clothes, as far removed as possible from workhouse uniform. 'One fine fellow', wrote Mrs Sheppard proudly, 'came out last Sunday in a new top coat...a pin in his neck scarf, another with black hat and umbrella...I now have fourteen lads there, as fine a set as could be met with, losing gradually all the marks of pauperism.'

Already some enlightened people realised that the ideal way to care for unwanted children was in a normal home and as early as 1859 one writer described in the Workhouse Visiting Society *Journal* the change which life in an ordinary family could bring about:

The four little girls I have are very different in character, though the workhouse training has made them in outward appearance very much alike. They have a downcast, frightened look; like little machines, they are always falling into line and putting their hands behind them, as if to put themselves out of the way as much as possible... They seem so anxious and take everything as a

serious affair, even a play in the hayfield or gathering wild flowers
… But already there is a change… They begin to look as though
there was a place for them in the world and take delight… in using
the house implements, which they had never seen before or known
the name of.

Curiously enough, although boarding-out had long been common in
Scotland, many ingenious arguments were advanced to 'prove' that
it could not possibly succeed in England. Scotland, it was argued, was
unique in possessing a class of small occupiers of land, with room to
accommodate an extra child, but not so well off as to give a child ideas
above his station. The Poor Law Board feared that 'The Guardians
would be unable to exercise the necessary control and supervision of
the children', the same argument that had been used against district
schools, and that children would be cared for by 'those whose main
object would be to make a profit out of… their maintenance'—an
echo of the old 'farm schools' scandal of twenty years before.

But pressure from social workers—a term now just coming into
use—continued and in 1868, not without misgivings, the Poor Law
Board began to approve applications from unions to board out their
children. Inevitably criticisms were voiced that the state was favouring
the pauper, since the allowance paid, of from three to five shillings a
week, was far more than many working men could afford to spend on
feeding and clothing their children, but even this appeal to the sacred
principles of 1834 went unanswered. Ironically, one of those who most
wholeheartedly rejected it was Mrs Nassau Senior, daughter-in-law
of the economist who had drafted the Poor Law Amendment Act. She
had recently become the first woman Poor Law inspector and in 1874
produced a highly influential report, of which more will be heard,
favouring boarding-out wherever possible. By 1885 other lady inspectors were being appointed to inspect foster-homes with strict instructions to undress the children, if need be, in search of signs of
neglect.

In 1889 new regulations were issued allowing the placing of children
outside the union area, but its opponents were still not convinced. One
critic warned that removing children from an institution meant a
lowering of standards of physical care: 'Two children may not be
washed in the same water in a Poor Law school, but we are told that
boarded-out children need never be washed at all because it is not the
custom of working people to wash their own'. Most people now realised,
however, that for a child love and security were even more important

than cleanliness, and though some unions did abandon boarding-out after unsuccessful and short-lived attempts, the over-all failure rate, under 10 per cent, was remarkably low. The fear that boarded-out children might be ill-treated continued, however. One London Board, hearing rumours of this kind, decided to reclaim all its children, but the official sent to fetch them had a hard time. The allegedly ill-treated boys, guessing his mission, vanished as soon as he appeared and, when rounded up, tried to escape during the night by a rope of sheets from the bedroom window. In another case, in 1889, the mere sight of a visitor believed to be from the union 'has filled a little foster-child with dread, turning it pale and sick with fear; while more adventurous ones have fled to neighbouring coverts or in one instance spent two days and nights in the wood in order not to return till the supposed danger was past'.

There were many stories of how workhouse children had shown their longing to give affection and to be accepted as normal. 'Little Dicky was a queer little chap when he first came...' a foster-mother told an investigator, 'running in and telling all the neighbours what we'd got on for dinner and shouting out when my husband came home that he'd got a father now. Anyone could see he hadn't been brought up like other children but he was all right in a year or two'. And it would have been a hardhearted mother who did not warm to the story, recounted by Louisa Twining in 1898, of the small girl whose foster-parent was away for a week, and who remarked 'What a lot of kisses father will want when he comes home'.

By now nearly half the unions in the country had become converted to boarding-out and 8,000 orphans and abandoned children were as a result enjoying a near-normal home life. Institutional care was, however, necessary for the majority and Mrs Senior urged in her *Report* in 1874, that for children in need of long-term care for whom no foster homes existed, 'schools of a more home-like character, each house containing no more than twenty to thirty children [were] desirable'. Thereafter many 'cottage homes' of this type, each under its own house-mother and -father, were set up, though the sexes were segregated into different homes which, if placed together on a single campus, with its own church and school, might have little contact with the world outside. For this reason some progressive unions favoured 'scattered homes', with small communities of no more than a dozen children of both sexes, living in a house in a residential district and using the local school and other amenities, like those from normal homes. Some unions also made use, on a fee-paying basis, of 'certified houses' run by private, often strongly religious organisations like that founded by Dr Barnado in 1867, though these tended to cater mainly for children sent to them direct.

But despite all the improvements in child care, there remained hard core of children for whom there was no real alternative to the workhouse. They belonged mainly to those troublesome families known to Poor Law officials as 'ins and outs' or 'revolvers', who swung, largely according to the climate, between the security of the workhouse and the freedom of the streets, coming and going, according to one social worker, 'like buckets on a dredging machine'. One Marylebone family, in just over a year from October 1893, discharged itself and was readmitted 62 times, while another shiftless parent took himself and his children in and out of the workhouse on 43 occasions. One habitual drunkard regularly removed his children from Greenwich workhouse, with professions of parental love, in the morning, dumped them somewhere while he got drunk, and then brought them back, extremely hungry, at night. Parents who removed their children, whether from affection or as an aid to begging, whenever the authorities were about to send them away to school—for few workhouses now had a school of their own—were also highly troublesome.

A survey made in the 1890s of 700 children from one group of Poor Law schools, showed that only four had stayed for the full nine years of a normal school career, and 525 had left within a year, 70 for employment, the rest to return to parents who were in varying degrees inadequate. By 1906, however, the number of children aged under sixteen still in the workhouse had been reduced to 16,000, the vast majority of children in union care now being accommodated in district schools, 'cottage homes' or foster-homes.

But, despite all the improvements, the old spirit of 'less eligibility' had not wholly disappeared. The Local Government Board Inspector for the South and West, appointed in 1896, found that modern ideas had made little impact on many rural Guardians. One Board, to his horror, proposed to train their child inmates as beggars, sending them out into the street during the school holidays to turn cartwheels to 'attract the pence of tourists', while the farmer-chairman of another Board put up a staunch fight against 'the provision of nightshirts for the workhouse children... "I puts on a clean shirt" ', he affirmed stoutly, ' "on Sunday morning and I never takes 'un off till I puts on another the next Sunday. What's good enough for me is good enough for these 'ere children in the workhouse, and I'm agin all this cosseting." ' It was a cry from the heart, uttered a hundred times in different unions during the previous sixty years, but 'nevertheless the Guardians, to his great disgust, granted the nightshirts'.

16 The Lame and the Blind

> In the different wards, male and female, there were about a hundred patients, the greater portion advanced in years, some stricken by the infirmities of age and nature, some lame and some blind. *The Vision of an Overseer (Now in Office)*, 1851

Most impartial observers—few though these were in the fiercely controversial years after 1834—agree that the Poor Law Amendment Act did, over the country as a whole, improve the provision society made for the medical care of the very poor. The unions, unlike the voluntary hospitals, financed by charity, had a legal obligation to provide medical attention of a kind, and in-patient facilities if necessary, to all who were both destitute and in need of them and there was now, for the first time, a hospital, of a sort, in every area. The workhouse infirmary, with all its defects, became the poor man's hospital and the sick and infirm wards, at first provided mainly as an afterthought, to provide a service to the other inmates, were soon the busiest in the whole establishment.

Inevitably, and perhaps justly, many of the earliest accounts of the treatment they provided were hostile. Thus the *Book of the Bastilles* in 1841 recounted as typical the case of a girl who being 'afflicted with fits...fell and broke her leg' but was refused a doctor to set it, since, the master explained, 'she had no use for it, for she worked none'. In another workhouse, Baxter claimed, a desperately ill man fell out of bed and lay unaided on the floor until he died, but 'a man in the same ward who heard him fall and cried out for a light and help was sharply reproved for making such a noise and fuss'. Some abuses undoubtedly did occur, but the best workhouse infirmaries achieved a very high standard from the first. At Manchester in 1841 the retiring Board of Guardians described with justifiable pride the 'ample and convenient' sick wards they had provided, which included separate accommodation for surgical and medical cases, a lying-in ward, an 'itch ward', and a 'boys' and girls' sore head ward' with its own dayroom and exercise yard. The elderly sick had their own quarters, in 'dry, comfortable cellars and kitchen' while the staff included 'a resident surgeon', and 'an honorary consulting physician' with a 'commodious and conveniently situated' surgery, which also served other occupants of the workhouse. The history of workhouse medicine is really the story of attempts to raise the vast majority of establishments to the standard of the few. All too typical were the experiences of one overseer, writing in 1851, who described an infirmary which housed 'about 100 patients, the greater portion advanced in years, some striken by the infirmities of age and nature, some lame and some blind', in a very hot and ill-ventilated room at the top of the building. The windows could not be opened, and 'not one of the helpers', he complained, 'appeared to know the value and efficacy of fresh air. I mentioned the matter to several of the Guardians . . . but I was . . . generally laughed at for a fool for troubling myself about it'.

In achieving the transformation which in fact occurred, no one man did more than Dr Joseph Rogers, who as a young general practitioner arrived to take up his first appointment as a Poor Law medical officer, around the middle of the century:

> The Strand workhouse in the year 1856 was a square four-storied building...with two wings of similar elevation projecting eastwards from each corner. Across the irregularly paved yard in the rear was a two-storied lean-to building, with windows in the front only, used as a day and night ward for infirm women... On each side of the main building was a badly paved yard, which led down to the back entrance from Charlotte Street; on each side of this back entrance there was first a carpenter's shop and a dead-house and secondly, opposite to it, a tinker's shop, with a forge and unceilinged roof. This latter communicated with a ward with two beds in it, used for fever and foul cases, only a lath and plaster partition about eight feet high separating it from the tinker's shop ... Just outside the male wards of the house . . . were two upright posts and a cross bar. On the bar were suspended the carpets taken in to beat by so-called able-bodied inmates, from whose labour the Guardians derived a clear income of £400 a year... The noise was so great that it effectively deprived the sick of all chance of sleep, whilst the dust was so thick that to open the windows was entirely out of the question.

Rural workhouses, though newly built, were equally uncomfortable. As a woman workhouse visitor from Bristol in 1861 pointed out:

> In new country workhouses the walls are commonly of stone,
> not plastered but constantly whitewashed—and the floor not
> seldom of stone or brick also and without carpets. Conceive a
> Winter spent in such a prison; no shutter or curtains...to the
> windows, or shelter to the beds, where some dozen sufferers lie
> writhing in rheumatism and ten or fifteen more coughing away
> the last chances of life and recovery. The infirmary is an accident
> of the house...not its main object... The wards are hardly ever
> constructed for such a purpose as those of a regular hospital would
> be... In some cases their position entails all sorts of miseries on
> the patients—as for example the terrible sounds from the wards
> of the insane. In another court a blacksmith's shed had been erected
> close under the windows of the infirmary, and the smoke enters
> when they are opened, while the noise is so violent as to be quite
> bewildering to a visitor... The same rough beds (generally made
> with one thin mattress laid on iron bars) which are allotted to the
> rude able-bodied paupers are given to the poor, emaciated bed-
> ridden patient, whose frame is probably sore all over and whose
> aching head must remain, for want of pillows, in nearly a hori-
> zontal position for months together. Hardly in any workhouse is
> there a chair on which the sufferers in asthma or dropsy, or those
> fading away slowly into a decline, could...sit for a few hours,
> instead of on the edge of their beds, gasping and fainting from
> weariness. Arrangements for washing the sick and for cleanliness
> generally are most imperfect.

Few workhouses made any attempt to make the infirmary any more
welcoming than the rest of the house. 'The room, by its very first
impression', wrote one workhouse chaplain in the 1860s, 'makes you
feel cold almost to shivering. Blank, whitewashed walls meet the eye
in every direction, the only furniture massive beds and a few chairs;
the prospects from the small-pane windows either a gloomy look
against the high dead walls of the union grounds or the very position
of the new window precluding any view whatever.'

Louisa Twining's eyes were first opened to such conditions when she
entered St Giles Workhouse in 1856 to visit 'a poor old crossing
sweeper who had met and swept for years in Bloomsbury Square and
was well known to us':

He was in the basement yard, nearly dark and with a stone floor; beds, sheets and shirts were all equally grey with dirt. To get in... I had to wait with a crowd at the office door to obtain a ticket, visitors being allowed only for one hour once a week. The sick in the so-called infirmary, a miserable building...were indeed a sad sight, with their wretched pauper nurses in black caps and workhouse dress. One poor young man there, who had lain on a miserable flock bed for fourteen years with a spine complaint, was blind; and his case would have moved a heart of stone; yet no alleviation of food or comforts was ever granted him, his sole consolation being the visits of a good woman, an inmate, who attended upon him daily, reading to him to wile away the dreary hours.

The Workhouse Visiting Society's *Journal* drew attention to the way in which such long-stay patients were neglected, although becoming increasingly numerous. 'It is no uncommon thing to find persons who have spent eight, nine or eleven years in one ward or in one bed', it pointed out in 1860. 'We have hardly yet begun to look upon the workhouse as a home and last resting-place for those who cannot be kept in hospitals...and if they have no homes where they can be nursed ...must end their days in the wards of the workhouse infirmary.' A survey made in 1861 showed that more than a fifth of the adult inmates of workhouses in England and Wales, numbering 14,000, had been there at least five years. Of these, 6,000 were classed as 'old and infirm' and 5,000 as sufferers from mental diseases. By 1863 the forty-six London workhouses alone were handling between them 50,000 sick people a year, and a detailed analysis of the occupants of one showed how it had become a dumping-ground for every type of unfortunate, only the able-bodied, for whom it had primarily been created, being almost totally absent. Of the 586 inmates the largest group, 152, were aged sixty to seventy, and the second largest, 147, between seventy and eighty, 43 were aged eighty to ninety, and two were even older, while 33 inmates were aged under sixteen, too young to be self-supporting. The adult paupers, aged sixteen to fifty-nine, numbered 209 people, but when the majority of these had been excluded for reasons such as 'idiocy', incapable of earning their own living due 'to bad habits', being blind or deaf and dumb, or a nursing mother, only 48 were left: that is, less than one in ten of all inmates could be considered able-bodied.

One of the commonest causes which brought people to the workhouse infirmary was tuberculosis, or consumption, as in the case of
the twenty-two-year-old widow of a sailor, whom one visitor found
in an East End workhouse in 1863. Her own recently born baby
had died and—horrifyingly, in view of her condition—she had supported herself as a wet-nurse until her health finally gave way, for
'in appearance she was like a shadow'. Another group for whom
society made no provision was the blind and they, too, often gravitated to the workhouse. One visitor encountered in 1861 an almost
blind woman, paralysed with rheumatism, who, after half-starving
herself on out-relief of a shilling a week, had reluctantly entered
the house. 'Her crippled fingers', the visitor found, 'can no longer
hold a pen' but no one was able, or willing, to write a letter for her
to her son in the Navy. In another workhouse a blind man was never
read to; the rest of his ward were illiterate. In a Dublin workhouse
lay the former editor of a provincial newspaper, aged sixty-seven,
now blind and deaf, whose only means of communicating with the
outside world was by 'reading' messages placed in raised letters upon
his tongue.* But the commonest reason of all for being in the workhouse infirmary was simply old age. One visitor described in 1865
'a workhouse ward containing twenty-two beds; twenty-one were
filled with poor decrepit old women in the last stages of existence...
In the twenty-second bed was a young person of better habits... there
because she had no home to go to'.

Few workhouses made adequate provision for sick children. 'In
the infirmary', wrote one woman who visited a workhouse school in
1859, 'were some in bed, some sitting round the fire, miserable
diseased objects; one with dreadful eyes, who could scarcely see.
I asked what would become of him when turned out at sixteen.
He would probably be sent to "the house" and remain there for life.'

The 'dreadful eyes' were the trademark of workhouse children,
being caused by ophthalmia, a painful and disabling inflammation of
the eye, which if neglected could permanently harm the sight.†
But sometimes, in the hope of helping others to be sent to the comparative comfort of the infirmary, 'those with sore eyes rubbed their
infected rags well into the eyes of those who had hitherto

*The Braille system, first published in 1829, was not yet in common use.
†An outbreak of ophthalmia, which led to two boys at a private school in
  Yorkshire going blind, resulted in the court case which inspired *Nicholas
  Nickleby*.

escaped'. The disease was finally beaten by a doctor from the London Hospital, later a leading eye surgeon, who arranged for 300 children with the disease to be sent from the Anerley district school to 'an unused workhouse in Bow...a gaunt building, standing in a playground of small stones'. The methods pioneered here cleared Anerley of the infection, and in 1894 a specialist ophthalmic hospital, serving all the workhouses in London, was set up, which finally stamped out the disease.

Much of the early criticism of the workhouse infirmaries concerned their lack of elementary comforts, a natural consequence of treating their inmates—like the children in the juvenile wards—as ordinary paupers who could be 'deterred' from remaining there. Some of the first visitors allowed in during the 1850s and early 1860s, suggested such modest improvements as 'allowing benches with backs, or chairs' and 'the provision of lockers for patients' possessions instead of dirty bags'. Later writers went further, advocating rocking-chairs and hot-water bottles, a proposal received with incredulous scorn by most Boards of Guardians. The Workhouse Visiting Society, whose aims included 'the instruction and comfort of the sick and afflicted' suggested other inexpensive practical ideas. 'The gift of a few coloured pictures of sacred objects,' wrote a correspondent in the first issue of its *Journal*, 'has been permitted in some instances in the sick and infirm wards and it has been cheering to hear the remarks of wonder and admiration bestowed upon them by those who probably have not looked upon anything but bare or brown walls for months or years'. To help the weary hours pass the Society suggested 'cutting up cloth into strips for making rugs...making patchwork counterpanes', and, especially for the blind, 'tearing up paper for making pillows for the poor', a less depressing job than that found for one bedridden patient 'who is a good needlewoman and is constantly employed in making shrouds'. Another suggestion was the provision of caged birds which, it was noted, were always tended 'with great care and affection'. One old woman, bedridden for sixteen years, remarked that her canary was 'always happy, gay-like, and it does me good to listen to him'.

In many infirmaries books were automatically whipped away as 'contrary to the regulations', though the rules only prohibited those 'of an improper tendency or likely to produce insubordination', a definition interpreted to include everything except the Bible and the most nauseatingly unctuous tracts. Even the newspapers, which paid lip-service to the prevailing piety, felt that this policy went too far. 'That religious works should form a prominent feature is essential', the *City Press* told its readers in 1860, 'but we must deal with human nature as we find it and the truth is that books of doctrinal religion are not attractive to the general assembly of workhouse inmates. The best of books is but waste paper while it remains unthumbed and uncared for.' The Workhouse Visiting Society *Journal* went farther. 'We do not mean to advise that reading upon weekdays should always be on solemn and strictly religious subjects', it told its readers, 'though for the sick such may generally be more desirable; but entertaining and instructive books will help to cheer and enliven many a dull and vacant hour.'

A 300-page anthology of *Readings for Visitors to Workhouses and Hospitals*, prepared by Louisa Twining, failed to follow this advice, however, consisting largely of sermons on such themes as 'Sickness God's chastisement' and 'The Christian's desire to depart'. The hymns were also designed to help the inmates to accept their wretched lot. One, for example, was reassuring about both the Almighty and the workhouse doctor:

> Whatever my God ordains is right:
> He taketh thought for me;
> The cup that my physician gives
> No poisoned draught can be.

Another promised better times beyond the grave:

> Ye who suffer, sigh and moan
> Fresh and glorious there shall reign

the paupers were comfortingly told.

This was the message, too, of the lecturer invited to address the inmates of one workhouse, 'all taken from the agricultural labourer class', in 1862. 'Though their lot was now in the shadows of life', he assured them, 'there was a happy home where for ever they might join in the music and cheerful melodies of the blessed.' To prepare them for this pleasant future, his speech was illustrated by hymns sung by an invited choir.

Such entertainments, though common later in the century, were still the exception and the workhouse authorities in many places reacted with hostility to every suggestion for making life more comfortable and interesting, even for the incurably ill or the very old. A speaker at a social science conference in 1867 described one infirmary matron who had confiscated needlework given to a young bedridden girl, had taken away flannel underclothes provided for an old man of eighty, and even snatched away a shawl, supplied by a visitor, from the shoulders of a dying woman. It was only when a whole new generation of nurses had entered the workhouses that such excesses ceased.

Of all the criticisms made of the workhouse infirmaries in this period, by far the most serious and persistent were of the poor quality of the nursing. 'In an immensely large proportion of the houses', wrote one woman visitor, 'the sick are attended by male and female paupers, who are placed in such office without having had the smallest instruction or experience and who often have the reverse of friendly feelings towards their helpless patients. As payment, they usually receive allowances of beer or gin, which aid their too common propensity to intoxication.' Dr Rogers, when he joined the Strand workhouse in 1856, found that the nurses began the day drunk, as their liquor ration was issued at 7 a m and that they 'only in exceptional instances paid any attention to what I said'. He suffered particularly at the hands of one called Charlotte who 'invariably treated me with supreme indifference, not unmingled with supreme contempt'. When the Board finally agreed to his requests for linseed to treat patients with respiratory diseases, Charlotte's reaction was 'My God! Linseed tea in a workhouse!' Rogers only got rid of her when she died from alcoholism, due to over-indulgence in the brandy and wine stolen from patients.

It was axiomatic in many workhouses for the staff to defy the doctor —Dr Rogers's battle with the master at the Strand, George Catch, has been described earlier—and the mere term 'pauper nurse' almost guaranteed that her patients would be neglected. Louisa Twining discovered in 1861 'a poor woman…making piteous signs for something to drink, and the nurse objected to giving it because of the trouble which would ensue. On my insisting and giving her a mug of wretched cold workhouse tea the poor creature drank it like a man dying in the desert, with eagerness perfectly appalling'. To report such nurses only made matters worse. A public meeting was told a few years later of an old bedridden woman who dared not let a visitor cut her grotesquely long finger-nails because she would be punished by the nurse for 'telling tales'.

The Workhouse Visiting Society *Journal* in 1865 contained an account that was clearly not exaggerated:

In a great and well-ordered workhouse, I visited sixteen wards, in each were from fifteen to twenty-five sick, bedridden or, as in some cases, idle and helpless poor. In each ward all the assistance given and all the supervision were in the hands of one 'nurse' and a helper, both chosen from among the pauper women . . . The age of the nurses might be from sixty-five to eighty . . . I recollect seeing in a provincial workhouse a ward in which were ten old women all helpless and bedridden; to nurse them was a decrepit old woman of seventy, lame and withered and feeble and her assistant was a girl with one eye, and scarcely able to see with the other. In a ward where I found eight paralysed old women, the nurses being equally aged, the helper was a girl who had lost the use of one hand. Only the other day I saw a pauper nurse in a sick ward who had a wooden leg. I remember no cheerful faces; when the features and deportment were not debased by drunkenness or stupidity or ill-humours they were melancholy or sullen or bloated or harsh.

One matron frankly admitted that the withdrawal of the former shilling a week paid to nurses had robbed her of all control over them. 'They all drink,' she said resignedly. 'Whenever it is their turn to go out for a few hours they come back intoxicated and have to be put to bed.'

Some nurses virtually blackmailed their patients : 'I know that in one workhouse a poor woman could get no help but by bribery', wrote a correspondent in the Workhouse Society *Journal*:

Any little extra allowance of tea or sugar left by pitying friends went in this manner. The friends and relations, themselves poor, who came to visit some bed-ridden parent, or maimed husband, or idiotic child, generally brought some trifle to bribe the nurses; and I have heard of a nurse in one of the great London workhouses who made five shillings a week by thus fleecing the poor inmates and their friends in pennies and sixpences. Those who would not pay this tax were neglected and implored in vain to be turned in their beds.

But until a better class of nurse was recruited, the best advice the writer could offer her readers was to bribe the nurses themselves, provided they treated their patients properly. Yet there was something to be said in the pauper nurse's defence, as Louisa Twining pointed out in an open *Letter to the President of the Poor Law Board on Workhouse Infirmaries* in 1866:

She may be said to be at work almost equally during the twenty-four hours ... The nurse sleeps in [the ward] whether the patients are men or women ... She receives only the house diet, perhaps a meat dinner daily, and an allowance of beer and gin; in many cases not even dry tea, but that which is boiled in the general cauldron ... If a good and decent woman is ... found to fill the office she will not remain in it, for to be the lowest scrubber in any hospital is esteemed a higher post than to be nurse with the sole charge of a workhouse ward.

At this time a paid nurse in a workhouse was a rarity. In the 1850s there were only seventy in the whole of London, compared with 500 pauper nurses, of whom half were over fifty, a quarter over sixty, many over seventy and some over eighty. Up to this time, an adequate supply of trained nurses had simply not existed and the reformers at first aimed only to secure one or two in each workhouse to supervise the rest. They became more ambitious after the foundation in 1860 of the Nightingale School for Nurses at St Thomas's Hospital and while the first 'nightingales' were beginning to appear in the voluntary hospitals, two major scandals focused attention on the workhouse infirmaries. On Christmas Eve, 1864, a letter headlined 'Horrible Case of Union Treatment' appeared in *The Times* describing the sufferings of a man called Timothy Daly 'a well-made muscular man, aged 28 years', whose life had been endangered due to the appalling neglect he had experienced in Holborn workhouse and who, in fact, died that day from the effect of untreated sores.

The resulting public enquiry revealed that at Holborn some patients went unexamined for days and nurses often put food down out of their reach, though the inspector finally decided that there was no evidence that Daly had been 'ill-treated and neglected'. Only two weeks later, however, another suspicious death occurred at St Giles's workhouse, after a man called Richard (George) Gibson had smuggled out a message appealing for help from the Bow Street magistrates. When Gibson died an inquest was ordered, at which an outside surgeon testified that he had suffered from a 'horrible state of neglect'. The coroner suggested that those responsible 'could be guilty of manslaughter', while the jury, *The Times* reported on 31 March 1865, found that Gibson's death 'was greatly accelerated by the neglect...received at the hands of the whole of the officials connected with St Giles's workhouse'. The rider they added to their verdict was even more explicit:

The jury . . . desire to call the attention of the Poor Law Board to
Ward 47 . . . They think the said ward very deficient in light, ventila-
tion and proper accommodation for patients and ought to be closed.
They also think that the dietary . . . is deficient and that the patients
ought not to go from 4 o'clock p m to 8 o'clock a m without food.
They also think that more paid nurses should be appointed.

These scandals, the latest in a long series, brought the *Lancet* back
into the field. Its founder, Thomas Wakley the first, that great opponent
of the workhouse, was now dead, but his son, Thomas Wakley the
second, had inherited his father's crusading zeal, and in April 1865
announced the setting up of the *Lancet* 'Sanitary Commission for
Investigating the State of the Infirmaries of Workhouses'. Although
the three-man Commission had, of course, no official status, refusal
to admit it would have aroused suspicion and eventually 38 out of the
39 metropolitan unions agreed to the inspection, the exception being
St Margaret's, Westminster, though the *Lancet* promised that, 'on a
future occasion we shall probably honour St Margaret's with a special
report.'* The *Lancet* Commission published its findings week by week
and they were finally reprinted as a pamphlet. The three doctors system-
atically scrutinised every aspect of the workhouse infirmaries, from
their lumpy mattresses to their death rates. Sometimes it was the site
of a workhouse that was condemned, as at St George-the-Martyr,
Southwark, 'surrounded by bone-boilers, grease and catgut manu-
factories'. Sometimes it was the accommodation, like the 'straggling,
ill-built' wards of St Leonard's, Shoreditch, with their 'narrow staircases, low-raftered ceilings, stinking ill-trapped drains, abominable
closets', sometimes the equipment, as at Lewisham, where 'the beds
are nearly all eighteen inches shorter than the six foot bedsteads';
sometimes the diet, as at the Strand, where 'the beef which is supplied
. . . consists of those tough and leathery morsels technically known
as "clods and stickings"—an unpleasant name for a very unpleasant
and indigestible thing'. The investigating doctors were not easily
deceived. Despite the 'air of bescrubbedness' and the 'powerful odour

*This threat was duly carried out. Not merely did the *Lancet* reveal that in the
St Margaret's workhouse the patients were locked in at night with no heating,
no hot water, no bells to summon help, and only a tub for sanitation, but it
resurrected a famous scandal of some years before. This had led to the dismissal,
for dishonesty and immorality, of the union solicitor, matron and surgeon, and
the resignation of the Guardian who had appointed them.

of soap and water' in one infirmary, they soon discovered that all 'the bedridden patients habitually washed their hands and faces in their chamber utensils'. 'The female itch-ward', in another, was dismissed as 'the nastiest place altogether that our eyes ever looked upon'. In a third they found 'but one round-towel a week for the use of the eight inmates', suffering from syphilis.

'No properly trained nurse', they commented, 'would have tolerated such abominations as we witnessed.' Only eleven of the thirty-nine infirmaries had more than one paid nurse while fourteen others had one each and the rest had none at all, managing instead with pauper nurses who were 'aged and feeble and past work and have strong tendencies to drink'. The few paid nurses who were employed faced an almost hopeless task. The two at Bethnal Green, for example, struggled to supervise forty paupers 'whose tendencies to drink cannot be controlled', while at Shoreditch 'bandages seemed to be unknown' and only £50 a year was spent on drugs, which were 'administered with shameful irregularity...One nurse plainly avowed that she gave medicines three times a day to those who were very ill and twice a day as they improved'.

The *Lancet* team finally concluded that six workhouses were 'entirely improper as residences either for the sick or even for the able-bodied', and should be demolished, ten required major structural alterations and the rest could more easily be made satisfactory, if properly equipped. They also pointed out that the capital's workhouses now provided its chief system of medical care. Lambeth workhouse contained as many patients as Guy's Hospital, and St Pancras handled far more cases than St George's though both had a far smaller medical and nursing staff. Taking all the 39 workhouses together, the *Lancet* investigators found that 22,700 of the 31,000 inmates were officially sick, infirm or insane, and 6,000 more, though nominally fit, were crippled or diseased in some way. The infirmary, intended as a minor part of the workhouses, catering mainly for normally healthy inmates, was now by far its most important department and the chief reason why people became 'indoor paupers'. 'The state hospitals', the *Lancet* summed up, 'are in workhouse wards.'

The *Lancet*'s revelations produced an immediate response. Many provincial newspapers, as in Manchester, carried out enquiries of their own; an Association for the Improvement of Workhouse Infirmaries was founded; Charles Dickens weighed in with an indignant letter to the press; there were angry debates in Parliament; an archbishop led a high-powered deputation to see the President of the Poor Law Board; and the Board itself, attacked and harried on all sides, badgered the Treasury—successfully—to be allowed to appoint its first-ever Medical Officer, who was hastily dispatched on a tour of inspection of all the London workhouses. The *Lancet* claimed that as 'a result of the *Lancet* disclosures', by the time he arrived the worst abuses had already been removed. Paid nurses had been engaged almost everywhere, even—an unheard of luxury—night-nurses—while 'baths, towels and hair-brushes have multiplied'. It was, one observer claimed, the criticism of workhouse infirmaries which 'awoke the Poor Law Board from its long sleep'. For the first time, the sacred principles of 1834 were publicly repudiated. 'The evils complained of have mainly arisen from the workhouse management which must to a great extent be of a deterrent character, having been applied to the sick, who are not proper objects for such a system', the President of the Board told an almost incredulous House of Commons in 1867. 'We must peremptorily insist on...the treatment of the sick in workhouses being conducted on an entirely different system...'

Progress outside London was far slower than in the capital, since the problem there was less acute. In London even official statistics conceded that the proportion of workhouse inmates classified as sick reached nearly 50 per cent—though the actual figure was far higher. In the provinces it ranged from 14 per cent to 39 per cent. The interest aroused in the late 1860s proved short-lived and a *Report on the Nursing and Administration of Provincial Workhouses and Infirmaries*, commissioned by the *British Medical Journal* in 1894, revealed conditions not vastly dissimilar from those the *Lancet* had uncovered in London a generation earlier. 'There was only one paid nurse ...', protested the inspector responsible for Billericay workhouse, in mid-Essex, in 1896. 'There were no proper lavatories for aged men and women ... The supply of hot and cold water was not sufficiently provided for.' But not every Essex Guardian shared the offical faith in cleanliness. 'What do we want with a bathroom?', grumbled one at Ongar in 1899, in response to the latest official circular.

In 1867 the Metropolitan Poor Act gave the London unions power alone, or in combination, to set up separate infirmaries detached from the workhouse, and a new body, the Metropolitan Asylums Board, was set up to provide fever hospitals for patients with infectious diseases. By 1875 the new hospitals were admitting some patients not on poor relief at all, and although the Local Government Board insisted two years later that 'The hospitals...are essentially intended to meet the requirements of the destitute class and...the admission...of persons not in need of poor relief is altogether exceptional', it was fighting a losing battle. Thereafter the Poor Law Infirmaries and the Asylums Board institutions increasingly became ordinary hospitals in all but name, sometimes superior in accommodation and equipment, though not in the quality of the staff, to the old voluntary hospitals.

'The disinclination of the independent poor to enter the hospitals of the Metropolitan Asylum Board, which was considerable at first, has now practically vanished', wrote a Poor Law Board inspector in 1899, 'and I do not see why there should not be the same change of feeling with regard to Poor Law infirmaries in the country...I wish it were possible to get rid of the name of workhouse...for...it is to the associations of the name rather than to the institution itself, that prejudice attaches.' In 1897 the Local Government Board had officially banned all pauper nurses, though, under the title of 'helpers', they survived in the more backward workhouses for at least another ten years. The transformation achieved, in attitudes as well as physical conditions, between 1860 and 1900 could not have taken place but for a number of dedicated individuals within the Poor Law Service— nurses, doctors and inspectors. The 'Florence Nightingale' of the workhouse infirmaries was Agnes Elizabeth Jones, the daughter of an Army officer. Like Florence Nightingale she had worked in a hospital of the charitable institution at Kaiserwerth in Germany, but was not, to her great disappointment, sent to the Crimea because she was untrained. In 1862 she enrolled as a 'Nightingale Probationer' at St Thomas's hospital, where she 'almost worshipped' its famous founder, and in 1865 her own Scutari beckoned, in the shape of the vast workhouse infirmary at Liverpool. A local philanthropist had offered to pay the cost of introducing trained nurses there and Agnes Jones, now aged thirty-two, was appointed matron, being joined soon afterwards by a dozen newly-qualified nurses from St Thomas's, and seven probationers, chosen by Miss Nightingale.

Agnes Jones had in her charge nearly 1,300 patients and 60 nurses, of varying degrees of reliability, with another 150 'scourers' and 'carriers', and her task would have crushed a lesser woman. 'A hospital is sad enough, but a workhouse!', she wrote home. 'It almost seems as if over so many of those beds "no hope" must be written... There are many poor blacks here...severe colds are so fatal to them. There are many idiots and old people in their dotage; one keeps a birch rod under his pillow, which he daily presents to me with a long speech.' For many she could do little except comfort them as they lay dying. 'I had a bright death-bed today to cheer me', she wrote of one such vigil. Her most striking achievement, however, which made her name famous, was the spirit of kindness she infused into the whole workhouse. 'I think I am in heaven when she comes', one patient said of her, and she was often referred to simply as 'the lady'. When she died, in 1868, at the tragically early age of thirty-five, of typhus caught on duty, the huge attendance at her funeral showed how much she had been loved. 'The whole district seemed to be there', wrote one eye-witness, 'but the hush of solemn silence was so great that they could hear the fall of the violets on the coffin.'

One of the great lessons of the reforms which Agnes Jones had demonstrated at Liverpool was that decent young women would only be attracted into workhouse nursing if they were properly paid. Ten years earlier £8 to £10 a year had been common, but by about 1870 this had increased to £20 to £30, all found, for a trained nurse, rising to £50 for a ward sister and up to £100 for a matron. Accommodation and food, too, had greatly improved, and did so still more after the first women Guardians were elected in the 1880s. Louisa Twining, for example, when she joined the twenty men on the Board at Kensington in 1884, proved more than a match for them and, on discovering that the nurses had nowhere to spend their off-duty time except their bed-rooms, took over the sacred Board Room as a common-room, equipped it with armchairs, pictures, books and a piano, and also demanded and—despite the matron's opposition, got—immense improvements in their everyday diet.

The *Lancet* investigators had spoken highly of the workhouse doctors, concluding that 'Taken as a body, the medical officers . . . apply themselves with a zeal and an amount of success to their dispropor-tionate tasks which are surprising; and they . . . have in most cases . . . to fight the battle of the poor, with terrible earnestness, against the prejudices and the gross material interests of the worst members of their Boards of Guardians.' The man whom the *British Medical Journal* described in 1897 as 'the hero of workhouse reform', was Dr Joseph Rogers, who, as already mentioned, had begun his own career at the Strand workhouse in 1856 and remained in the Poor Law Service until shortly before his premature death from heart disease in 1889. Rogers was constantly at odds, throughout his life, with successive workhouse masters and Boards of Guardians, and even some of his professional colleagues who, he discovered, sometimes wanted only a quiet life.

He fearlessly exposed abuses and campaigned for improvements in every post he held, but his greatest achievement was to improve out of all recognition the status and conditions of service of the work-house doctor. A major landmark was the official decision, in 1867, acknowledged by the Minister concerned to owe much to Rogers's campaign, that drugs should henceforward be paid for by the union, not by the doctor. Rogers also helped to found and later lead the Poor Law Medical Officers Association, which served both as a professional trade union and as a pressure group on behalf of the sick poor. Its effectiveness could be seen in the salary scales for workhouse doctors, who had sometimes earned as little as £50 in mid century and were earning as much as £350 by its end. Rogers himself calculated that the £18,000 a year which had been added to the pay of Poor Law doctors in London alone had saved at least ten times as much in lives prolonged and ailments cured.

From the late 1860s onwards the reforming efforts of men like Dr Rogers were reinforced by pressure from Whitehall, in the person of Dr Henry Bridges, who in 1869 was appointed by the Poor Law Board as its medical inspector. Bridges was the son of a country vicar and had been head boy at Rugby and an undergraduate at Oxford, before becoming, in his biographer's words, 'a scholar physician'. As a medical officer at the Bradford infirmary and as a factory inspector in Yorkshire, he witnessed at first hand 'the brutality and insolence of relieving officers' and concluded that 'the Poor Law...as at present worked is a gross insult to the people'. Under his direction, commented Dr Rogers, 'an absolute epidemic took place as regards the building of asylum hospitals, district hospitals for fever and infectious diseases, asylums for epileptics, idiots and imbeciles...etc.', and though he had the reputation of being cold and reserved 'against wrong-doing, neglect or cruelty', claimed his biographer, 'his anger would be white hot'. He was famous for his searching eye. 'Matron', he would ask icily after a single glance round an infirmary ward, 'is it customary to leave the key in the medicine cupboard?' It was said that 'A Guardian was heard to exclaim, "May God deliver us from Dr Bridges"'. When retirement did deliver the unions from his dreaded inspections—he resigned in 1892 and died in 1906—Bridges left behind him a workhouse medical service that would have been barely recognisable to the Poor Law doctors of 1834.

17 Moping Idiots

The imbeciles are still in the workhouses.
Herbert Preston-Thomas, *The Work and Play
of a Government Inspector*, 1907

The village idiot was a familiar figure in the nineteenth century.
'Fifty years ago', wrote one mental specialist in 1870, 'one felt scandalised by seeing a wretched idiot or paralytic, clothed in rags and
scrambling through the streets amid the jeers of schoolboys. There
was not a village or a street where some object of pity to all right-
minded people could not have been seen, scavenging the road or hunting the gutters for a meal.' No attempt was made to distinguish between
the feeble-minded and the insane but both counted as sick and were
thus exempt from the ban on out-relief imposed after 1834, though
they suffered from the general scaling down of allowances. For those
already in care the changes made by the Poor Law Commissioners
were sometimes beneficial. This was how one unfortunate lunatic
had been cared for by the parish workhouse of St Philip and St Jacob,
Bristol, until it was visited by the Assistant Commissioner for the
South West during his first tour of inspection in 1835:

> ... I discovered a most dismal, filthy-looking room, which ...
> presented such a sombre, wretched appearance that curiosity
> prompted me to explore it. Judging from the appearance of the
> room I should think that water must have been excluded from it
> for years ... It reminded me of a coal cellar ... rather than the
> habitation of a human being. The sole tenant of this miserable
> abode was a poor, distressed lunatic. His appearance was pitiable
> in the extreme, his clothing was extremely ragged; his flesh
> literally as dirty as the floor; his head and face were much bruised,
> apparently from repeated falls. Shoes he had been furnished with
> ... had done their duty and his feet protruded through them.
> He sat listless and alone without any human being to attend upon
> ... him, staring vacantly around, insensible even to the calls of
> nature, and apparently unmindful of anything which was passing

in the room. He was endeavouring to avail himself of the only comfort allowed him from the few embers which were yet burning in the grate, for he had thrust his arms through an iron grating which was placed before the fire, intended doubtless to prevent the poor creature from burning himself . . . I endeavoured to arouse this poor pitiable fellow-creature, but the attempt was useless . . . To the very great shame of the parish officers I found he had been in this disgusting state for years.

Parliament had already made several attempts to get lunatics removed to county asylums. In 1828 the Lunacy Act laid down the procedure for certifying pauper patients—it needed the signature of a doctor and one other responsible person, such as a magistrate— but in 1845, when the 1828 statute was re-enacted, a proposal to compel every county to provide its own asylum failed. The Poor Law Board, having no alternative, reluctantly agreed that lunatics could be kept in the workhouse, provided the union medical officer agreed that this was safe. Most medical officers would, in fact, have been only too happy to be rid of them, but Boards of Guardians were often unwilling to agree, partly from the usual dislike of surrendering control over 'their' paupers, but mainly on grounds of cost. To keep a lunatic in the workhouse cost only 3*s*. 6*d*. to 4*s*. 0*d*. a week. Private madhouses charged from six shillings a week upwards, the best demanding at least fourteen, while the scale in public asylums, run by counties or by 'districts' of unions grouped together, varied from 10*s*. at the great mental hospital at Hanwell in Middlesex, to as much as £1.

One reason for such fees was that the Lunacy Commissioners, who were responsible for protecting everyone certified as of unsound mind, set far higher standards than the Poor Law Commissioners. 'Less eligibility' meant nothing to them and they reluctantly accepted the workhouses as 'registered houses', legally permitted to accommodate the insane, though their inspectors constantly harried the Poor Law Board and individual unions to improve conditions. They complained in 1847 of workhouse 'rooms' for lunatics which were mere cupboards, seven feet by three; they protested in 1857 at the inadequate care taken in transporting insane inmates; they demanded, in 1863 and 1867, a better diet, and urged that they 'should have the opportunity of taking exercise' and pleaded for the appointment of 'a competent paid nurse...for the lunatic ward'. But the Poor Law Board, while passing these requests on to the unions, did not insist on their being met, and violent maniacs, bewildered depressives and weak-witted mental defectives continued to be housed, inadequately, in the work-house, to their own detriment and to everyone's discomfort.

The Poor Law Authorities always refused to admit that 'mental infirmity' covered a whole multitude of different conditions and ruled in 1849 that every inmate was either a lunatic, who should be certified, or sane, in which case he must be treated as an ordinary pauper. The truth was, as every workhouse master and doctor knew, it was those who did not fall into either category who caused the trouble, especially the feeble-minded, who could be seen wandering vacantly about the wards and yards of every rural workhouse, and for whom treatment was useless and physical restraint merely cruel. It was not till late in the century that the Local Government Board adopted a more realistic approach. In 1879 London set up a separate school for educationally sub-normal children and in 1899 Parliament authorised the provision of such schools on a national scale. So far as adults were concerned the existence of the weak-minded, as distinct from the mad, was not really acknowledged until the passing of the 'Idiots Act' in 1886, followed in 1913 by the Mental Deficiency Act, which accurately defined the various types of mental handicap for the first time.

For most of the nineteenth century, however, terms like 'imbecile' and 'lunatic' tended to be used indiscriminately. 'Imbeciles and those afflicted with fits are to be found in every workhouse', warned one workhouse visitor in 1858, estimating the total for the whole country at around 30,000, or about one in six of all 'indoor paupers'. One London workhouse in 1863 classified 32 of its 586 inmates as 'subject to fits' and seventeen more as 'idiots'. Dr Joseph Rogers, arriving at the Strand workhouse in 1856, found that the ward for women mental patients was always full. A *Plea in Favour of the Insane Poor* published in 1859 by a doctor with many years experience of the problem, protested that complaints about overcrowding and inadequate care were met with the retort, 'What? They are only paupers.' This 'system of sordid but mistaken economy', he believed, was 'daily multiplying the sum of human misery' and discouraging people from seeking help until it was too late.

The *Lancet* enquiry in 1867 was highly critical of the conditions under which mental patients were accommodated and treated in London workhouses. In one they found a woman 'wandering up and down in a state of mingled frenzy and exhaustion. She had been admitted four days previously and had had no sleep since'. She had also gone almost wholly unfed, for she qualified only for the standard

'house diet' and 'practically none of this coarse food had been consumed'. At Chelsea, the investigators found that 'about thirty chronic
insane patients wander in a melancholy, objectless manner about the
house and the yards'. At St Leonard's, Shoreditch:

> The general aspect of the wards is one of extreme cheerlessness
> and desolation . . . especially lamentable in the case of the
> lunatics and imbeciles. Moping about in herds, without any
> occupation whatever, neither classified, nor amused, nor
> employed—congregated in a miserable day-room where they sit
> and stare at each other and at the bare walls, and where the
> monotony is only broken by the occasional excitement due to an
> epileptic or the gibbering and fitful laughter of some more
> excitable lunatic. It is quite an oasis in a desert when as at
> Marylebone, Newington and some other houses we find a garden
> with swings, bird-cages and rabbit hutches, for the amusement
> of these poor creatures and a number of pretty pictures pasted
> upon the walls of their day-room.

Although everyone, except some Guardians, agreed that even a
well-managed workhouse was no place for the insane, the number of
such inmates rose during the 1860s, partly due to the creation of the
Medical Register in 1858, which made certification easier, since any
two doctors on the register, whether mental specialists or not, could
sign a committal order. In 1862 Parliament, to relieve pressure on the
overcrowded country asylums, agreed that in future chronic, i.e. long-
term, lunatics, could be kept permanently in the workhouse, though
the Poor Law Board despondently admitted that it was not 'aware of
any workhouse in which any such arrangements could conveniently
be made'. In the following year, of 31,400 people in the London workhouses, nearly 1,700 were classed as insane; by 1870 the number had
risen to 2,000. Over the country as a whole the trend was the same. In
1859 there had been fewer than 8,000 workhouse inmates classified
as 'idiots' and 'lunatics'; by 1870 it was more than 11,000.*

The real problem was the desperate shortage of mental hospital
places. The famous asylum at Colney Hatch, opened solely for pauper
patients, had already by 1867 turned down 3,800 applications, due to
lack of vacant beds. 'It has', wrote the Medical Officer for Poplar,

---

*The number in these categories on out-relief had also increased, from 4,100
in 1859 to 6,000 in 1870.

'become a perfectly hopeless matter to obtain admission for a pauper ...
in any lunatic asylum in Middlesex.' 'There is scarcely a borough or
county asylum which, if not very recently enlarged, is not overfull',
complained the mental specialist Dr Stallard, in 1870. at Westminster workhouse, he pointed out, an urgent case had waited
eight weeks for removal—while another, twice certified, was still
there. Another dangerous lunatic had been kept in Whitechapel
workhouse for three months, and Fulham contained a potentially
violent epileptic. At Kennington the best that could be done for a
woman with acute mania was to tie her to a bedstead, and at St
George's, Hanover Square another who had threatened the two
frightened paupers who cared for her, was merely placed in a straight
jacket, a device already disliked by the more enlightened doctors.
In the circumstances, the offer to unions in 1876 of a four-shillings-
a-week Treasury grant for every lunatic sent to the county asylum
was little more than an empty gesture.

For many insane and mentally defective paupers the workhouse
remained their home and the workhouse medical officer the only
specialist they ever saw. Such doctors rapidly acquired a wide experience of mental cases and often devoted a good deal of time to them,
for a healthy lunatic provided an interesting change in the usual dreary
round of consumptives, unmarried mothers and geriatrics. Treating
the insane, acknowledged Dr Joseph Rogers, who served in two London
workhouses between 1856 and 1886, provided 'an agreeable episode in
my daily routine of all but thankless work'. Where, apart from the poor
food and accommodation, the mental patient in the workhouse did
suffer was in the lack of skilled supervision. Dr Rogers had much
trouble with one epileptic who:

when a seizure occurred, sprang up and then dashed himself to
the ground ... He contrived by these means to smash his nose,
make dreadfully disfiguring wounds on his forehead and face, and,
from a good-looking became a perfectly repulsive-looking person
... I got him away at last but I had two or three years of him, during
which time I had a very extensive surgical experience from his case
alone [for] I was constantly stitching up his wounds.

The mental patients who arrived at the workhouse came from an
even wider variety of backgrounds than the sane inmates, and had not
infrequently come down in the world. A survey published in the *Edinburgh Review* in 1859 revealed that the largest single group in the

female insane wards were former governesses, worn out by the struggle
to keep up appearances in their unhappy social half-world, while the
second largest group, more predictably, were maids-of-all-work. The
reason, the writer suggested, was that 'the single servant has no prospect but of toiling on till she drops, having from that moment no
other prospect than the workhouse. With this thought chafing at her
heart, her brain confused by her rising at five, after going to bed an
hour or two past midnight, she may easily pass into the asylum some
years before she need have entered the workhouse'.

Many of the patients treated by Dr Rogers at the Strand and Westminster workhouses had, however, formerly been self-employed.
Among them was a Welsh journeyman tailor who was suffering from
the delusion that he was about to be married and had bought a large
quantity of underclothing for his future bride, plus two dozen pairs of
kid gloves. When detained in the insane ward at the workhouse he
generously invited all the other inmates to attend his wedding, but
instead of church, he went to Hanwell, from where he was sent back
to an asylum in his native town, the trousseau of his imaginary
bride-to-be being sold to pay for his support. Even more tragic was
the case of a grammar schoolmaster, charged with murdering his
wife, who, thanks to Rogers's evidence, was reprieved after being
sentenced to death. He showed little gratitude, arguing that his
past services to youth should have prevented his being charged in
the first place, while there were attacks in the press on Rogers for
having enabled a murderer to escape the gallows.

Another 'homicidal lunatic', correctly diagnosed as such by
Dr Rogers, was a young man found wandering the streets before being
taken to the workhouse, but the Guardians criticised Rogers for
wishing to see a 'sane man' locked up and allowed the patient to leave.
'The day he was discharged', Rogers discovered, 'he came home and
sat down to his dinner; after the meal was over, the father resumed his
work, which was shoe mending, when his son, without saying a word,
struck him a severe blow on the head with a hammer. With the help
of neighbours and police and after a desparate struggle, he was over-
powered.' The man concerned was sent back to St Marylebone workhouse and, safely certified at last, to the great asylum at Hanwell, the
final home of so many pauper lunatics. In another similar case, in
1867, the Guardians insisted that a man whom Rogers had sent to
Hanwell was sane. Rogers complained to the Commissioners in Lunacy,
who returned the man to Hanwell, but a few months later he gained his

discharge. His wife, knowing him better than anyone, begged the authorities to send him back inside, but periodically he managed to talk his way out again, and Rogers always knew when he was at liberty for the madman celebrated his release by ringing Rogers's door-bell at 2 o'clock in the morning.

A somewhat similar case concerned a middle-aged married woman whom Rogers had certified without hesitation, only to have the order for her removal to Hanwell cancelled by the union clerk. Her unfortunate husband managed to get her into another workhouse but when he died she obtained her discharge and set about spending the £1,500 he had left her. She accomplished this in nine months, buying £24 worth of potted plants, £300 worth of clothing and even a 60-guinea piano, though she could not play a note, all these goods being delivered to her filthy lodging by shopkeepers who could see for themselves that she was insane. Penniless and turned out by her landlady because of her 'highly objectionable habits' she ended up in Rogers's care in the workhouse, but the local magistrate five times refused to send her to an asylum, and Rogers only secured her committal at his sixth attempt when the usual occupant of the bench was away on holiday.

Although the incarceration of a sane person in a lunatic asylum was a popular theme in Victorian fiction, every Poor Law doctor knew that the real problem was the very reverse. Dr Rogers suffered a great deal from his own Board of Guardians, which, like many others, rejected its doctor's advice almost on principle for, he suspected, highly questionable reasons. 'I have frequently noticed', he remarked, 'on the part of eccentric people this disbelief in and morbid sympathy with lunatics, and believe it to arise from a fear least they should also be incarcerated.' The Guardians, for their part, may have been prompted by fears, absurd though they seem now, that an underpaid workhouse doctor might certify a sane but troublesome inmate merely to collect the guinea fee. Dr Rogers, when first appointed, found that an outside doctor was always called in to sign the comittal certificate (which a magistrate had then to endorse), only being given the right to do so when his salary was raised from £50 to £75 a year— the extra £25 apparently being assumed to reduce the temptation to earn extra guineas in this way.*

Rarely dangerous, but wasting everyone's time, were patients suffering from what is now called 'Munchhausen's syndrome', after the

*Such suspicions persisted into the twentieth century. An Essex alderman publicly accused doctors in 1907 of having, because of the associated fee, 'an unconscious bias' in favour of certification.

fictional German teller of tall stories. Dr Rogers was proud of unmasking one such fraud, a man who had spent five or six years in the infirm ward. He had 'his knees drawn up and constantly asserted that he could not stand nor walk, nor put his legs down', so that under the Laws of Settlement, he could not be sent back to his own parish. He was finally caught taking 'his constitutional walk about the wards between 2 and 4 a m', while the night-nurse was, as usual, fast asleep.

Another fraudulent inmate was Maria Hall, an epileptic, who 'professed an inability to talk except unintelligible gibberish. She was very artful...claimed to be a deeply religious character and contrived to take in the benevolent lady visitor...She...would ask me to share with her the grapes, cakes and sweetmeats sent her by her dupes'. Eventually Rogers ordered her removal to the insane ward, whereupon 'she threw off the mask she had worn for twenty years and cursed as distinctly and clearly as any healthy person'.

Despite the popular dread of the asylum, the condition of the pauper lunatic in the workhouse was often worse. Dr Stallard, writing in 1870, was highly impressed by the case of 'D.W...a most sprightly and intelligent Irishwoman', whose last husband, her third, had died in the Crimea. Life in the workhouse, into which she drifted as an unsupported widow, finally unhinged her, due to 'the contumely and ill-treatment of the pauper-helpers who...despised her habits of cleanliness and decency':

> Removed to the lunatic ward ... she became really violent and abusive, both to the medical officer and the Guardians, and was in consequence certified insane and sent to Colney Hatch. She has now been there some years. The medical officer states that he has not a better conducted patient in the house. The little domitory is a picture of comfort and cleanliness ... She is kind, helpful to other poor patients. But why ... is she not discharged? Simply because she swears she will never again enter the workhouse. She has now neither home nor friends ... The very thought ... of going to the workhouse excites her wrath. It is that which drove her mad.

Colney Hatch, near Barnet, although much referred to in popular jokes, seems to have been an exceptionally well-run and progressive establishment.* Dr Stallard attended the annual fête there:

---

* Its name remained famous for years. I can remember, in Berkshire in the early 1930s, hearing one child tell another: 'You ought to be in Colney Hatch'.

In a meadow there had been erected several tents at which beer, tobacco, tea, coffee and other refreshments were freely sold . . . There was also a band of music, a group of nigger musicians, beside conjurors, acrobats, Punch and Judy etc. Kiss-in-the-ring and other games were carried on and so long as the action and harangues of the insane were confined within moderate limits there was no interference whatever with the discourses addressed to various audiences by the more loquacious of the patients.

Although such an environment was obviously better on every count for the seriously deranged, the number of places in county asylums remained inadequate. In 1890 a new Lunacy Act had been passed, authorising the removal to an approved institution of mentally-ill people who needed to be detained for their own or the public safety. The initial order, for three days, could be extended, if a magistrate agreed, to two weeks and then, with due safeguards, indefinitely. The workhouse was accepted under the Act as a suitable residence for such cases and the country would have been hard put to it to accommodate its insane citizens without it. The Essex county asylum at Brentwood, for example, built in 1853, was by 1897 crammed with more than 1,800 patients, of whom almost 100 were sleeping on the floor.

The overcrowding in the asylums helped to explain why the Essex workhouses at this time sheltered a variety of inmates who clearly needed psychiatric treatment. They included a pauper at Billericay who suffered from delirium tremens and during an attack needed six men to hold him down, another at Ongar, who 'sat in the yard with a shirt and a bit of carpet on', and several at Chelmsford who regularly made 'a terrible din', plus one rather more rational 'who only shrieked occasionally'.

The county's workhouses also suffered much at the hands of muddle-headed eccentrics who registered their dissatisfaction by breaking windows. The record seems to belong to a 30-year-old mentally-ill ex-convict at Braintree, in 1904, who, having knocked down the old man put in charge of him, smashed 96 panes of glass in rapid succession and climbed the sixteen-foot-high workhouse wall to embark on a career of vandalism, during which he badly damaged, with denominational impartiality, both an Anglican church and a nonconformist chapel, before, incongruously disguised in a cassock, he was recaptured by the workhouse master, who had pursued him by bicycle.

Where new asylums had been built, the excellence of the facilities they provided caused many Guardians and Poor Law officials to distrust them. Inspector Preston-Thomas believed that 'the extraordinary expense incurred by county and borough councils has doubtless frightened people' and he was scandalised by one Sussex asylum where even the pigsties were luxurious, it having cost £50 to house each pig. Building theatres and tennis courts for mental patients seemed to him indefensible. All but the most enlightened Guardians would have agreed with him. In 1895 the chairman of the Braintree Board, which still had thirty mental cases in its workhouse, refused to sign a removal certificate for one imbecile pauper, on the grounds that he 'could be kept at the union house for less than half the cost at the asylum'.

The real reason why many unions were unwilling to send their able-bodied but weak-minded paupers into special institutions was that, to quote Preston-Thomas, 'a good many are often found useful in the laundry and other domestic work of the institution' and many workhouses would have had difficulty in getting the household chores done without such help.

The feeble-minded women, claimed a Guardian at Braintree, 'did the work of the house and were very happy'. At Maldon, happy or not, the value of their work, it was admitted, 'exceeded the cost of their keep'. Some of the Essex unions seem, however, to have carried this policy rather far. At Ongar, in 1897, one 75-year-old was employed fifteen hours a day stoking the workhouse boiler. In 1914 the same job was being done by a stripling of 73, despite the twin handicaps of a wooden leg and a tendency to fits.

Despite all the disadvantages of keeping the insane or feeble-minded in workhouses— and Inspector Preston-Thomas investigated a workhouse at Kingsbridge in Devon in 1896 where one mad old man had made such a nuisance of himself that he had been beaten up and killed by his room-mates —improvements were slow in coming.* 'In all but a half dozen of the workhouse unions' in his area, complained Preston-Thomas to the Local Government Board in 1901:

> . . . the sane and insane still continue to be mixed up indiscrimi-
> nately . . . It is often said that the imbeciles live happily in work-
> house and that they are miserable shut up in an asylum [but]

---

*The jury at the subsequent request, however, decided, against all the evidence, that he had injured himself by falling on a bed-post.

surely regard should be had to the comfort of the other inmates . . .
Requiring sane persons to associate, by day and night, with gibber-
ing idiots . . . may almost be characterised as cruelty . . . In some
instances . . . they sleep in the sick wards . . . under the supervision of the nurses, and they frequently disturb other patients
at night. By day they are a source of much irritation and
annoyance . . . It is in the country workhouses, sometimes with
only a dozen imbeciles or less, divided among the sexes, that the
chief difficulty arises . . . I am much afraid that the question will be
postponed indefinitely and six or eight years hence the idiots will
still be worrying the sane inmates of workhouses.

This prediction proved only too accurate. In 1906 there were still
11,500 inmates officially of 'unsound mind' in the workhouses, an
average of about 19 per workhouse, and as late as 1914 the four
mid-Essex unions alone contained 400 certified lunatics between
them. But the Guardians and others, in authority remained loathe to
get rid of their mentally-ill inmates. 'It was very unpleasant for those
who had all their faculties to have to live with people of filthy habits',
admitted a Billericay Guardian, 'but he hoped they would not send these
poor people to the asylum', while at a county council meeting an alderman opposed 'branding those poor old people as lunatics'. And on one
subject all Poor Law doctors and inspectors agreed: despite all those
flesh-creeping novels, there were in the state lunatic asylums no
penniless but sane inmates, delivered up by heartless relatives into
life-long captivity. Inspector Preston-Thomas, writing in 1909, quoted
one example of an asylum inmate, highly plausible, as so many were
in their lucid intervals, who almost succeeded in persuading a visiting
magistrate that his wife had unjustly had him locked up. The effect
he had achieved was spoiled, however, when as the visitor turned to
go, he received a violent kick, accompanied by the remark, 'And that
will make you certain to remember me!' Another case, the inspector
felt, proved that insanity was not incompatible with common sense. A
colleague, visiting an asylum, had asked one 'strong hulking fellow'
working in the grounds why he 'insisted on wheeling his barrow upside
down'. The madman looked pityingly at his new acquaintance and
advised him to do the same, since 'If you wheel the barrow the right
way up they will put bricks in it and then it will be twice as heavy.'

18 Only at Christmas

In 1889 we gained a glorious victory against
beer on Christmas Day. Louisa Twining, *Workhouses and Pauperism*, 1898

Nothing did more to harm the public image of the workhouse than
the way in which the Poor Law Commissioners treated Christmas.
Before 1834 the day had been a traditional treat; the caterer serving
St Martin's-in-the-Fields poor-house, in Central London, for example,
had been enjoined in 1828 to supply 'roast beef, plum pudding and
one pint of porter' to each inmate, as well as 'buns on Good Friday. . .
one pint of porter on New Year's day and plumcake on Holy
Thursday'. After 1834 such concessions ceased. On Christmas Eve,
1836, the *Dorset County Chronicle* acknowledged its 'regret to learn
that the annual dinner of roast-beef and plum pudding, usually
allowed on Christmas-day to the paupers in the Bridgwater union has
been, by order of the Poor Law Commissioners, for the first time in
the memory of the oldest inhabitant, discontinued'. By the following
year even private charity was banned. The Guardians at Bath were
forbidden to accept funds from a public subscription to provide the
paupers with their customary Christmas dinner.

In fact, in some places the rule was broken. The paupers of Cerne
Abbas in Dorset, for example, celebrated their first Christmas in
their brand-new workhouse in 1837 with 'plum pudding and strong
beer', which at 2s. a quart must have been of truly ferocious potency.
The Board also ordered cider, the staple drink of the area, at 3d.
a quart, brandy (4s. 6d. a quart) and rum (3s. 0d.), though these were
probably destined for the officers and Guardians. Before long the most
miserly places were recognising Christmas in some way, and even
Andover, meanest of unions, served bread and cheese on the previous
'meat day' to save the ration of roast beef for Christmas morning,
following it by what one pauper grudgingly described as 'plum pudding without any plums in it' and 'a little drop of small beer'.

By 1840 the Poor Law Commissioners had accepted defeat, to the
extent of allowing extras to be provided from private sources, for that

year, following the Queen's marriage to Prince Albert, the Victorians really discovered Christmas. The Prince introduced into England such long-established German customs as Christmas presents and Christmas trees, a process encouraged by *A Christmas Carol*, in 1843, and Christmas soon became everywhere a sacred rite. Even the Poor Law Board, on taking office in 1847, overcame their Scrooge-like tendencies and authorised all Guardians to provide Christmas 'extras' for workhouse inmates out of the rates, though there was no compulsion to do so.

Christmas by mid century was being celebrated at many workhouses as an Open Day on which leading local residents paid a formal visit to the paupers in their care. A local newspaper described a typical ceremony at Bedford workhouse in 1859, where on Boxing Day 'the mayor, Mr Alderman Hurst and other gentlemen and ladies were present' and all 218 inmates 'dined together in the spacious and lofty hall, which was very tastefully decorated with evergreens'. Although the mayor 'addressed them' at 'considerable length' and was followed by the alderman...

> ... the greatest order and decorum prevailed ... The greatest attention was paid to the speakers, and perfect silence was observed, except when they could not refrain from giving expression to their feelings by clapping their hands ... One of the inmates then rose, and in a short and neat speech, proposed a vote of thanks to the Board of Guardians and the master and matron, for their kindness to them. The Mayor and Mr Alderman Hurst then drank the health of the whole company, wishing them a merry Christmas and a happy new year ... The visitors having retired amidst the hearty applause of the inmates, the men and women returned to their own rooms to encircle a cheerful fire, and the children to their school-rooms, where they were supplied with oranges and nuts. At six o'clock the whole company re-assembled to take tea together, after which they sang several hymns and then retired to rest, highly gratified with the pleasures of the day.

Before long even the most troublesome of groups, the able-bodied and refractory young women, were benefiting from the new spirit. One correspondent described in the Workhouse Visiting Society *Journal* a civilised, if excessively pious interlude in a London workhouse in 1860:

> On going to the oakum ward, on Monday the 26th December ...

I found that the nurse had provided a plentiful supply of boiling water — had placed the mugs in order for the nine girls, with a cup and saucer for me. I had taken a large teapot and we soon procured the refreshing beverage and buttered the cakes . . . After taking a cup of tea to appear sociable I read Christmas carols while they enjoyed their meal . . . When tea was over . . . I read to them the five chapters of *Revelation* and talked to them simply and earnestly . . . When we knelt to pray, I heard quiet sobs.

By 1864 even the much-criticised Strand Union was sharing in the fun, with tea parties in the wards, after which 'stories were read, or picture-books shown' and 'the married couples were put together'. At Brighton 'glees, ballads, etc.' enlivened the serving of 'tea, coffee and plum cakes' and the governor made a distinctly condescending speech. 'Our object', he explained, 'is to give the aged something to talk of, and to the younger ones present an opportunity of judging how much more real pleasure is to be obtained from rational amusement than from vicious indulgences'.

It was against such scenes as this that George R. Sims, in the 1870s, raised his powerful voice. Sims's name is now largely forgotten but, as he told an interviewer in 1897, he did not want to go down to posterity, only 'to go down well with people who buy papers, see plays and read books at the present day'. This he unquestionably did. After a false start in the family cabinet-making business he found his true vocation as a campaigning journalist, one series of articles on poverty and bad housing, *How the Poor Live*, causing a sensation. He began to write his own modern-style 'column'in the newly-founded *Sunday Referee*. A regular feature was a rhyming ballad, telling a strong and moving story in simple language. Reprinted as a sixpenny pamphlet, the *Ballads* sold 100,000 copies within two years, and recitations from them became a regular feature of charity matinées and of village concerts. As the *Daily Telegraph* commented, 'It is apparently the literary mission of Mr Sims to do in verse what Dickens did in prose, and to bind all classes of his fellow-citizens together with the bonds of sympathy'.

In 1877, when *In the Workhouse: Christmas Day* first appeared, Sims, at thirty, had not yet reached the height of his fame, which before his death, in 1922, was to result in his pets endorsing advertisements for patent dog cakes, and his picture appearing on bottles of 'Tatcho, the George R.Sims Hair Restorer'. Later, its opening line, somewhat inaccurately rendered, became a national catch-phrase and humorous and bawdy versions of the poem are still in circulation today, but when first published it was considered anything but humorous:

> It is Christmas Day in the Workhouse,
> And the cold bare walls are bright
> With garlands of green and holly.
> And the place is a pleasant sight:
> For with clean-washed hands and faces,
> In a long and hungry line
> The paupers sit at the tables,
> For this is the hour they dine.
>
> And the Guardians and their ladies,
> Although the wind is east,
> Have come in their furs and wrappers,
> To watch their charges feast;
> To smile and be condescending,
> Put pudding on pauper plates,
> To be hosts at the workhouse banquet
> They've paid for — with the rates.
>
> Oh, the paupers are meek and lowly
> With their 'thank'ee kindly, mums's';
> So long as they fill their stomachs,
> What matters it whence it comes?
> But one of the old men mutters,
> And pushes his plate aside;
> 'Great God!' he cries 'but it chokes me!
> For this is the day *she* died.'
>
> The Guardians gazed in horror,
> The master's face went white;
> 'Did a pauper refuse their pudding?'
> 'Could their ears believe aright?'
> Then the ladies clutched their husbands.
> Thinking the man would die,
> Struck by a bolt, or something,
> By the outraged One on high.

This strong opening (despite the lapse, typical of Sims, in the penultimate line) is maintained through seventeen more stanzas in which the rebellious pauper, John, denounces the Guardians ('the villains whose hands are foul and red') for having refused his wife, Nance, out-relief the previous Christmas Eve, when she was unwilling to enter the workhouse and be separated from him. Poor Nance dead of starvation, John enters the workhouse himself and is a model inmate until his memories prove too much for him. The poem ends with a few sharp remarks addressed to the assembled Guardians:

> There, get ye gone to your dinners;
> Don't mind me in the least;
> Think of the happy paupers
> Eating your Christmas feast;
> And when you recount their blessings
> In your smug parochial way,
> Say what you did for *me*, too,
> Only last Christmas Day.

Admire as one may the sincerity of Sims's feelings, it is hard not to feel a certain scepticism about this moving tale. Even the famous opening line is suspect, for most such visits took place on 26 December, but 'It is Boxing Day in the Workhouse' clearly lacks the sentimental appeal of the original. Nance was wrong in believing that she and John could, legally at least, have been separated, for as both were over sixty ('Bread for the woman who'd loved me, through fifty years of life'), they were clearly, in theory, entitled to a room of their own. The couple's plight, too, ('Give me a crust, I'm famished': 'Food for a dying woman'), seems to have been a case of 'sudden and urgent necessity', obliging any Relieving Officer to provide immediate assistance. But if any apologist for the Local Government Board advanced such arguments, his voice was soon drowned in the applause, mingled with sobs, with which the poem was everywhere received and, however dubious the details, it still has the ring of truth.

In Sims's ballad, the workhouse master's instant reaction to the old man's outburst had been to cry 'He's drunk', and beer for most of the century was considered an indispensable part of a workhouse Christmas in all but the strictest unions. By the 1870s, however, temperance had become a power in the land and there was even a misleadingly-named Workhouse Drink Reform League founded solely to agitate for the banning of all alcohol in workhouses. So successful was the anti-drink campaign that the Local Government Board, in 1884, finally gave way to it and ruled that no alcohol should be supplied in any workhouse except on medical advice.

The 'dry' workhouse policy, which was, of course, only a reversal to that adopted in 1834 but eroded by successive indulgences over the years, faced its first great test in 1887, with Queen Victoria's Jubilee. Although one patriot published a pamphlet suggesting that the Queen's health could be drunk in water, an attempt to prevent porter being served at Kensington workhouse failed. 'All I could gain', complained Louisa Twining, the veteran workhouse visitor who now led the temperance party on the Board of Guardians, 'was that the quantity should be reduced to half a pint.' But she had her revenge two years later. 'In 1889', she later wrote, 'we gained a glorious victory against beer on Christmas Day, by a majority of two ... No one complained and the master, with twenty years' experience, came before us to express his satisfaction, declaring that they had never passed so happy and quiet a time.'

But the tradition of Christmas beer died hard. At Braintree, in 1895, one old man, pressed to ask for an alternative to ale, decided after judicial reflection that 'If allowed his choice, he would prefer stout' and in the following year, the hospitality was sufficiently lavish for one handicapped woman to take off her wooden leg to enliven the festivities and find herself unable to put it on again. Beer for the able-bodied at Christmas was finally banned in this union in 1900, but the older members of the workhouse community continued to enjoy their festive glass; one, aged over eighty, danced an Irish jig, while another, over ninety, recited, though not, presumably, *In the Workhouse: Christmas Day.*

For many years, while their elders enjoyed their Christmas beer, nothing at all was done for the children in the workhouse. When, in 1837, the chairman of the Petworth Guardians had been asked before a Parliamentary Committee: 'Supposing any charitable lady in the neighbourhood were desirous of giving the children a dinner on Christmas Day, could you, as the chairman of the Board, allow a thing of that sort to be done?' he had been forced, sheepishly, to reply, 'No, I could not.' It was left to that warm-hearted Somerset woman, Mrs Emma Sheppard of Frome, to breach this heartless convention. In 1854 one of her children while 'we were looking forward to a happy Christmas . . . said, "Will anybody think of the

little sick children at the union?" '. She described what followed in
an article in a Bristol newspaper:

Well, I must tell you of what my dear ones began to devise for
the desolate little ones in the House. Shillings, lately given to
them, were brought to me with, 'Take it for them, we do not want
the money.' We wrote to our friends in the country town near,
to ask for contributions, saying that headless horses, eyeless dolls,
wheel-less wagons, and nursery rubbish would be acceptable.
We spent ten shillings on dolls, marbles, tops, penny boxes of
toys; begged at our draper's for scraps and patterns; at our bookseller's for old prints, etc... The next day boxes and baskets-
full reached us from the nurseries around, just what we wanted.
It was December 22nd; we set to work, dressed some dozen of
the penny dolls, divided our treasures into four packages, viz,
girls' school, boys' school, babies' nursery, and sick children.
Never were my young ones so happy. All was finished at last, and
on Christmas-eve we drove up to the Pauper Palace, the servants
as much interested as ourselves in carrying the baskets... The
girls' school first—spiritless, cowed, sad-looking girls, from three
to sixteen years old. We set our basket down, and collecting them
in a circle, tried to draw forth a smile. 'Now, then, look, what is
going to jump out? take care, here it comes,' producing one of the
monkeys on a stick, tumbling over and over, which did provoke a
quiet smile all round. But I must not weary you; we gladdened
every little heart of the sixty girls by some trifle, given into their
own hands... Then into the boys' school. I was all but pushed
over with the eagerness of the fine lads. 'A top for *me*, ma'am.'
'Marbles for Bill and me please'; and, dear boys, one liked to see
their joy in the present, forgetful for the time of pauper clothing,
pauper food, and pauper imprisonment. To the baby nursery
next, where every crib was made happy by a hairless, legless horse
or stump of a doll—something to cuddle and love... On, on,
through the long cold stone passages, clean and cold, and weary,
to the hospital, and first to the sick children's ward. Two were
in bed, their flushed faces gazing at the strangers with added
brilliance of feverish excitement, some on the floor, tiny things,
with the sharp stick... on the mantel-shelf; a sad scene—a
shadow indeed, on young hearts that should be gay and happy;

no mothers near them—many of them parentless. Into each bed
we slipped a full dressed doll. Oh! that every English mother and
child had seen the out-stretched arms for it—the quite silent
acknowledgement of companionship now granted; how the little
weary eyes closed as the arms enfolded the future companion of
its solitude; no more dreary nights, 'dolly would be there;' no more
dreary days, 'dolly would be talked to.' An orange and figs put by
the side of the bed were unregarded . . . The tiny ones on the
floor hugged a legless horse to their hearts, and grasped their
orange with small fingers . . . Mothers, children, nurses, shopkeepers, look out your 'rubbish', and if you can find a few shillings
for new and cheap toys, go and find at Christmas the sick, the
desolate, and the sorrowfull, in the Union near you.

Mrs Sheppard's article, reprinted under increasingly sentimental
titles such as *Sunshine in a Shady Place,* became a best-selling
pamphlet. Soon other middle-class mothers were visiting the
children's wards at Christmas and publishing accounts of their experiences, like this one, describing events some years earlier, which
appeared in *Macmillan's Magazine* in 1861:

The first time I made acquaintance with the children of C—
Workhouse School I went . . . to see them receive presents of
toys, sugar-plums, etc., collected . . . by some kind-hearted ladies.
We began with the nursery, where the babies and children under
three years old are kept. It was a cheerless sight enough, though
the room was large and airy, and clean as whitewash could make
it, and the babies—there were about twenty altogether—showed
no sign of ill-usage or neglect. Most of them looked healthy and
well fed, and all scrupulously neat and tidy. But it was the un-
natural stillness of the little things that affected me painfully.
They sat on benches hardly raised from the floor, except a few
who were lying on a bed in a corner of the room. All remained
perfectly grave and noiseless, even when the basket of toys was
brought in and placed in the midst of the circle. There was no
jumping up, no shouting, no eager demand for some particularly
noise or gaudy plaything. They held out their tiny hands, and
took them when they were bid, just looked at them listlessly for a
minute, and then relapsed into quiet dullness again, equally
regardless of the ladies' simulated expressions of delight and surprise made for their imitation, or the good clergyman's exhorta-

tion to them 'to be good children, and deserve all the pretty things the kind ladies gave them.' I saw only two children who looked really pleased, and understood how to play with the toys given them; and they, I was told, had only been in the house a few days.

This woman discovered in the babies' nursery what being an orphan in a mid-Victorian workhouse really meant. The children were not, she insisted, harshly treated, but the first object of the 'two nurses...both old women, one paralytic' who looked after them was 'to hush their charges into the state of stupid joyless inactivity, which gives them the least fatigue and trouble. "Goodness" and dull quiet are with them synonymous terms':

Leaving the nursery, strewed with neglected rattles, rag-dolls, etc., we passed on to the large school-room, where all the children girls, boys, and infants, were to be regaled with tea and plum-cake. The room was, like the other, spotlessly clean and tidy, as were also the children, who stood in long hushed rows before the tables, waiting to sing their grace before they began. The children of the infant school were as still and solemn as the babies; not a smile among them. A little fellow, half hidden by a huge round plum-cake, which stood on the table before him, attracted my attention by his woe-begone face, and piteous efforts to repress an occasional sob. He was one of the healthiest-looking of all the children there, with a brown rosy face, sturdy brown legs, and fat, dimpled arms—a great contrast to some of his poor, pallid, stunted companions. I lingered behind the rest of the party to ask what ailed him. The sobs came louder as he faltered out 'Mammy!' I enlarged on the glories of the coming Christmas tree, hoping to direct his mind from his grief for a little; but my eloquence was quite wasted; he only looked up and wailed out, 'Mammy! Mammy!' The sugar-plum I gave him was disdainfully thrown on the floor, as he begged, in passionate, broken accents, to be taken to 'mammy.' I was quite at a loss; but the mistress came up to us, and quieted him with the often repeated and often broken promise that, if Jemmy would be a good boy and leave off crying, she would take him very soon to see his mammy. The poor little fellow manfully choked down his sobs, and sat with eager black eyes fixed on the mistress, evidently trying hard to show her how good he was, in hopes of earning the promised reward. In answer to my questions, the mistress told me that

Jemmy had only been in the house two days. He was brought in with his mother, a respectable woman from the country, who had been forced by adverse circumstances to seek shelter in the workhouse. She further said it was hard work getting mother and child apart. 'He was her only one, and they had never been separated for so much as a day before, and, though he was three years old, he clung like a baby to her, and she, poor soul, was fretting worse for Jemmy than Jemmy was for her.'... The perfect indifference with which the matron, a good-natured looking woman, talked of both mother and boy's distress, showed she was too well used to such scenes.

Gradually, more frequent treats and excursions and the kindly interest of visitors like this one, succeeded in breaking down the listlessness and apathy which had so long marked out the pauper child. At the Kirkdale Industrial School, near Liverpool, which housed 1,000 pupils, mainly orphans, who never received a letter or a visitor, Christmas 1859 seems to have been a cheerful affair:

We arrived at the school shortly after 3 o'clock... We entered the girls' yard and were nearly deafened by the sounds of uproarious merriment proceeding from the little creatures... Immediately after supper, the whole school was marshalled into the hall, in the centre of which was the Christmas tree, and took their seats in the gallery. The tree was then lighted by means of innumerable wax tapers attached to the branches and on completion of the process the children gave an uproarious hurrah... Then commenced the distribution of the presents. First the boys and then the girls passed in single file under the Christmas tree and [each] after receiving his or her present at the hands of the lady managers from amongst the piles of toys, whips, dolls, etc. heaped up on the benches and tables surrounding the tree, passed out of the room through lines formed among the spectators. We retired thinking we had never seen a more successful merrymaking.

Although so many gifts were now arriving in the workhouses for such occasions that the total cost was often only a few shillings, even this remained too much for the Poor Law Board and for years no contribution was forthcoming from official funds. The idea that toys and private possessions might actually be necessary to a child's development had not yet percolated through the higher reaches of

Whitehall, but the sensible ladies of the Workhouse Visiting Society realised it clearly enough, as this report from Cork, on Christmas 1862, revealed:

> The lady visitors were in attendance, arranging to the best advantage on tables an endless variety of toys, including dolls of all sizes and every style of dress for the girls, toys and whips or musical instruments of every shape and sound for the boys, boxes of bonbons and comfits for both sexes ... To the eyes of those trained in a poor-house, accustomed to nought save a view of the gloomy, monotonous pile of buildings staring [at] them whichever way they looked, these toys were indeed magnificent, positively enchanting ... The moment each boy or girl was assured of its possession he clasped it as firmly as if he feared a breath of wind would deprive him of it or that, on leaving the hall, some rude playmate, in his anxiety to examine the present, would, by even a look, spoil its appearance if not do it some irreparable injury. It is not easy to forget the inward delight which each face betrayed as the little ones moved pompously from the table along the length of the hall.

Within a few years all but the most backward unions were acknowledging the existence of Christmas. Agnes Jones, matron of the workhouse infirmary at Liverpool, noted in her diary in December 1867 that 'Christmas preparations for 1,400 keep me busy. Seventy wards to adorn with evergreens. Two Christmas trees.' At Liverpool no one was overlooked. There were oranges, apples and cakes for the humble 'scourers' who scrubbed the wards and a Christmas tree and magic lantern show for the unmarried nursing mothers. Beer was as yet still flowing freely in this workhouse. 'One female patient and some scourers', Miss Jones noted, 'were rather the worse for the liberal ale allowance; but for 1,277 patients, 130 scourers, 60 nurses and 20 carriers to give no trouble was a great triumph'. And she felt well-rewarded when one helpless woman, taken on a stretcher to look at the Christmas tree, remarked: 'To think I should have lived so many years and not seen the like.'

19 Tramps and Vagrants

> The nightly occupants of the Vagrant Ward interfere with the regular inmates, harass the officers and . . . render it impossible to . . . carry out the ordinary regulations of the establishment. *Poor Law Board Circular* 30 November 1857

If the men who framed and operated the New Poor Law felt little sympathy for the ordinary unemployed labourer, they had no time at all for those whom the Elizabethans described as 'sturdy beggars' and the Victorians labelled 'casuals' or 'vagrants'. The Act of 1834 made no reference to them, but in 1837 the Poor Law Commissioners were forced to acknowledge the existence of 'wayfarers' or 'persons in a state of destitution . . . who . . . belonged to distant parishes' and recommended that they should be granted shelter and a meal in return for a task of work, being treated in other respects like ordinary inmates of the workhouse. Some unions took this advice, some provided a separate casual ward, but within a year or two the vagrant was becoming a nuisance almost everywhere. Two unions, at Lambeth and Colchester, pointedly asked the Commissioners in 1841 'whether the workhouse is to be a lodging house and to be inundated with these trampers'. The Commissioners reacted by advocating what was to become the standard policy throughout the century, namely to make the vagrant's life so disagreeable that he would hesitate to come back. A separate vagrant ward was to be provided wherever numbers justified it, but the bedding had to be worse than that of ordinary inmates. The room was to be unheated; each arrival was to be forced to bathe; and smoking and card-playing were to be prohibited. Some places tried at first to go even further and provide shelter without food, but this practice was officially condemned in 1841 after a starving but unfed casual at Newcastle-under-Lyme had, most inconsiderately, died during the night. The buildings appropriated to tramps, wrote one observer in the 1840s

... are generally brick buildings of one storey ... attached to the back part of the yard. In general they have brick floors and guard-room beds, with loose straw and rugs for the males and iron bedsteads with straw ties for the females. They are generally badly ventilated and unprovided with any means of producing warmth. All holes for ventilation in reach of the occupants are sure to be stuffed with rags and straws; so that the effluvia of these places is at best most disgustingly offensive.

At Andover, until the great scandal broke in 1845, up to sixteen 'wayfarers' were herded into a room only fifteen feet by five, furnished with straw palliasses but no bedding, and locked up from 8 p m to 8 a m. The rules about classification, so strictly enforced elsewhere in the workhouse, were here deliberately ignored, the matron, the fearsome Mrs M'Dougal, having ruled that 'They must all pig in together' so that the more brazen girls used to joke on leaving in the morning that 'If they should turn out to be in the family way they should swear it to the Andover union.' Conditions of this kind rarely drove away the incorrigible idler but they did nauseate decent couples. At least one at Andover refused to spend the night there and were given sixpence by the porter, who felt sorry for them, to find a bed else-where. Even genuine tramps occasionally protested at the quarters offered them. 'One evening, and this happened several times', wrote the master of a workhouse near Shrewsbury, a little later in the century, 'there came a vagrant. He was shown into the vagrant wards. He said, "Is this the place where I am going to sleep?". The porter said "Yes." He said, "Then go to hell and sleep there yourself", and so left.'

It was a firm article of belief among Poor Law officials that any suggestion of work would cause every tramp to give the workhouse concerned a wide berth. The virtuous unemployed man, it was con-versely assumed, would not object to performing 'a task' to obtain a bed. In 1842, therefore, Boards of Guardians were given legal powers to compel anyone receiving overnight shelter to perform a specified amount of work, though, even if he had not completed it, he could not be detained more than four hours after breakfast. The new Act was not successful. Few unions made use of it, and by preventing an early start, it also penalised genuine travellers. Ordinary tramps, by con-trast, were usually in no hurry to get away, and when they did leave, said an official of a Derbyshire union, 'it frequently takes them some time to decide whether they shall travel towards the North or towards the South'.

Almost as fiercely resented was the right given to workhouse authorities in 1843 to search vagrants before admission. The aim was partly to prevent them taking contraband like tobacco, or dangerous articles like knives, into their sleeping quarters, but much more to discover if they had on them any money, or any readily saleable article, which disqualified them from being destitute. Many tramps showed considerable ingenuity in evading this regulation. When travelling in a gang, one inspector noted, they 'appoint a banker to lodge out of the workhouse, or deposit [their possessions] at a small hucksters' shop and marine store shops', while solitary wayfarers made private arrangements. The master of Eton workhouse found a stone near his workhouse under which tramps regularly hid their coppers, while another, at Stafford, discovered that some of his casuals had 'almost pulled down a hedge near the workhouse by hiding money in it'. When a thorough search did take place it often revealed not only cash but poaching snares, picklocks, dice and thimbles, this last-named belonging to a 'thimble-rig' operator who practised on gullible gamblers a kind of 'find the lady' trick with three thimbles and a pea.

In 1844 the Poor Law Board decided to set up a number of 'asylums for the temporary relief . . . of destitute houseless poor', separate from the workhouse, but run on similar lines, though offering only short-term shelter. The asylums were designed to serve groups of unions in built-up areas with a large number of homeless people, namely London, Liverpool, Manchester, Leeds, Birmingham and Bristol, and one 'houseless' alone, Shoreditch in East London, had 9,000 applicants in its first year. Ultimately, however, this attempt to provide an alternative to the casual ward proved a failure, and the supply of beds was never adequate to the need.

Throughout the nineteenth century the fear was expressed that the new workhouses, so repellent to law-abiding citizens, were positively attractive to tramps. Some, it was said improbably, referred to the new 'union houses' as 'Queen's Mansions', thoughtfully provided for their benefit an easy day's march apart. One Welsh Chief of Police complained in the 1840s of the annual summer influx of tramps from Somerset, Wiltshire and London 'who told me they had heard of the accommodation and had come down to see the country'. 'The generality of tramps', complained a senior police officer at Bath, 'go from union to union, calling at Bath on their way, and watching the ladies in their walks, soliciting alms, which are afforded to get rid of their importunity. These characters generally come and go with

the fashionable visitors, whose ... charity affords great encouragement to them.' And some tramps were not above demanding money
with menaces. 'They stroll in bodies through the country places',
wrote one union official, 'terrifying the inmates of lone farmhouses
and cottages into giving them money. Since the establishment of a
more effective police in the large towns, an additional number of them
appear to have been driven into the country.'

The new workhouses had only been in existence a few years when
the trade depression of the 'hungry forties' led to a sharp rise in the
number of unemployed on the roads. St Martin's-in-the-Fields workhouse, in the heart of London, which had admitted only 367 casuals
in 1839—many no doubt, the same people returning time after time
—had to accommodate 1,376 in 1840, and in the middle of the decade
the potato famine in Ireland drove tens of thousands of desperate
Irishmen and their families to make the crossing to England as 'living
ballast' at 2s.6d.a head. The Irish influx swamped many workhouses,
especially in Lancashire and North Wales, for almost all landed
at either Liverpool or Holyhead. At Warrington, near Liverpool, no
fewer than 17,322 vagrants were relieved in 1847-8, of whom more
than 12,000 were Irish. St Martin's, in London, had in 1846 to
cope with a demand for 6,308 beds and in 1847 for almost 11,600.
The problem rapidly affected the whole country. Between April and
September 1846, 18,535 casuals had been admitted to workhouses
in England and Wales. In the corresponding period of 1847 the total
was 45,000.

Already much parliamentary and public interest had been displayed
in the whole subject of vagrancy. Perhaps because revelations of sharp
practice gave them a good excuse for ignoring the poverty that was
all about them, perhaps because they chafed secretly against their own
convention-ridden lives, many middle-class Victorians seem to have
had an almost insatiable appetite for details of the life and methods
of the tramps and beggars they so often encountered in the streets.
Although there were far more important aspects of working-class life,
such as bad housing and illiteracy, crying out for MPs' attention,
the House of Commons had in 1846 set up a Select Committee on
Vagrancy, at which the star witness was William Read, a crossing-
sweeper and former barman, who obligingly passed on to MPs some
helpful tips on effective begging. 'The best dress for a beggar to wear
in the streets of London' was a smock-frock which instantly 'excited
compassion', he advised, creating the impression of a poor rustic

seeking the wherewithal to get back to his native village. On the other hand, a 'townee' appearance and a Cockney accent were not assets in the country, since they instantly aroused suspicions of being cheated. Read also confirmed that conditions in many casual wards were even worse than the authorities intended:

> He applied at Newington about the beginning of this year . . . was given half a pound of bread and a rug to cover him. He was then put into a very filthy place; and the moment he got inside the door the bread was snatched away out of his hand and the rug too. He expostulated a little concerning it, and they heaved a pail of water over him and two or three began attacking him because he did not belong to the gang.

Read threw a new light on the policy of removing a vagrant's private possessions before he was admitted. This was, he pointed out, actually in the interests of an honest man since if 'he had anything about him such as a handkerchief or a knife, they would have it in the course of the night'.

Nor was it only the other occupants of the casual ward who suffered from the presence of this rowdy element; the remaining inmates of the workhouse, and even the staff, dreaded their arrival. The clerk of the Thirsk Union in Yorkshire reported about this time that fifteen vagrants had been sent to prison there 'for breaking windows or destroying their clothes', but these stern measures had not produced any lasting improvement. 'The vagrant ward window frames', he admitted, 'have been entirely pulled out and destroyed; as well as the forms for sitting on . . . The yelling, shouting and disorder in the ward has occasionally been such as to prevent the inmates from getting any rest and the officers of the workhouse have been wholly unable to quell the disorder.'

The Select Committee failed to make any effective recommendations, but the new Poor Law Board, on taking office, wrote rather despairingly to all unions in 1848 in response to 'representations from every part of England and Wales respecting the continual and rapid increase of vagrancy . . . which they ascribed to the 'regular provision of food and lodging at the public expense'. Clearly, the Board concluded, 'the roughness of the lodging and coarseness of the fare provided' were not sufficient to deter 'the dishonest vagrant', while 'the task of work . . . has, from its being only occasionally enforced, exercised no general influence as a test'. Although 'the Board are

unable to suggest any additional test or punishment that shall prevent
the abuse of relief', they did advise a greater effort to discriminate between the genuine seeker after work and 'the thief, the mendicant and
the prostitute', perhaps by employing an experienced police officer
as an Assistant Relieving Officer, a device which proved ineffective
in practice and was later abandoned.

In 1884 the Metropolitan Poor Act compelled all London unions
to provide a reception ward for casuals, to be open from at least 6 p m
to 8 a m in the winter and from 8 p m in the summer, and that year and
in the following one, the Board also issued circulars to all unions
throughout the country, designed to establish common standards of
discomfort. Only one large ward, they advised, should be provided
for each sex, and instead of separate beds there should be a
'sleeping platform' down each side, divided into compartments by
planks, with only coarse 'straw or cocoa fibre in a loose tick' between
the occupant and the bare boards. A rug 'sufficient for warmth' was
to be supplied but the food was to be strictly bread and gruel.

Many vagrants, however, did not take kindly to the loss of
other accustomed comforts. The master of Wem workhouse, near
Shrewsbury, described a typical encounter in the 1860s:

> A young woman was put into the vagrant ward. A short time af-
> ter came a young man; he enquired if a young woman had been
> put up; the porter said 'yes'. He said 'Where is she?' The porter
> replied 'Upstairs'. He said, 'I am going to sleep with her'. The porter
> said, 'I am sure you are not'. He said, 'I shall' and was very
> impertinent, and the master was fetched, who ... told him he could
> not allow anything of the kind. The young man was very abusive
> and said he would have his threepence, as he gave the young woman
> threepence before she came in, to sleep with her. The master sent
> for the policeman, but he left before the policeman came.

But other forms of misbehaviour were less easily dealt with and
most tramps, according to many workhouse masters, caused nothing
but trouble. If they came early, complained the master of Great
Boughton workhouse in Cheshire, they filled in the evening 'singing
obscene songs, cursing and swearing or relating some begging adven-
ture'. 'Tramps sometimes obtain orders from the relieving officer
between six and seven o'clock,' complained the master of Shiffnal
workhouse in Shropshire in 1866, 'get them countersigned by
the police-constable and then stop at public-houses in the town

till between eleven and twelve, when they come to the workhouse and disturb the inmates by violently shouting and kicking at the outer doors. The early part of the night in the ward is spent in giving each other an account of the previous day's route, frauds and success'.

'Almost all tramps are filthy, dirty and covered with vermin', wrote another workhouse master. 'They get so dirty that they cannot wear their clothing any longer, so go into the tramp wards, and in the course of the night tear up their clothing; this has occurred many times'. A 'tear up', in which not merely clothes but bedding was ripped into ribbons, was also the traditional way in which the tramp protested against poor conditions and a common cause of his being sent to prison.

Despite all the Poor Law Board's efforts, the number of vagrants seemed to increase remorselessly. In 1862 the average number of casuals relieved in a single night had dropped as low as 2,000; by 1868 it was four times as high. The number of tramps accommodated in the course of a year was, of course, far larger. Whitechapel, for example, in a poor area of East London, handled 20,000 admissions during 1867, though many of them were accounted for by the same individuals returning again and again.

By now the realisation was beginning to dawn that mere severity would not cure the problem and that many tramps were, in fact, physically or mentally ill. The members of the Workhouse Visiting Society, to their great credit, were among the first to point out that beneath the off-putting and evil-smelling rags and dirt there was, after all, a fellow human being. 'Follow an unhappy wanderer in London, stricken with disease without a sou in the world', suggested a writer in its *Journal* in 1860:

> You may watch such an unhappy sufferer tumble up the hospital steps and after some waiting, obtain an audience of the dresser or house surgeon. He has no letter and cannot be relieved without such an official recommendation of a governor . . . He is merely given a bottle of medicine and with this in his pocket he wanders forth again into the street, and tossed about from relieving officer to workhouse porter fails even here to find a harbour of rest . . . Unless the miserable applicant can establish some legal claim by residence or birth he is apt to be driven again into the streets; and there he may die.

Even the Poor Law Board inspectors were beginning to acknowledge that the causes of vagrancy might lie deeper than mere idleness. 'Many tramps', wrote one inspector to the Board in 1866, 'could not, if they would, take any effective steps to escape from their condition. Outcasts from society by their crime or vices, or unpleasant ways, or unbearable temper, they would seek in vain for employment.'

One item of never-failing interest for the middle-class Victorian was the 'bush telegraph' by which news spread from one end of the country to the other. The Chief Constable of Chester declared himself astonished, about 1865, at 'the perfect system of communication among tramps . . . I have tested it and find that about three days are sufficient to promulgate a new regulation among the fraternity'. Within two days of his starting to search each new arrival for pipes and tobacco, not one newcomer arrived in possession of either. A Relieving Officer remarked on the 'telegraphic despatch' with which 'whole corps of tramps become acquainted with any altered circumstances bearing upon . . . particular unions'. When the supply of oakum ran out at one workhouse, so that tramps had to be excused the usual task, the number of admissions rose in a fortnight from 20 to 45 and then soared to 75. As soon as a new consignment of oakum arrived the rate of applications dropped back at once to its former level.

One way in which tramps communicated with each other was by scribbling messages on the workhouse walls, like these, transcribed in 1865. 'If ragtailed Soph stays here, come on to Stafford... Saucy Harry and his moll will be at Chester to get their Christmas dinner, when they hope Saucer and the rest of the fraternity will meet them at the union ... ' Another establishment had earned three stars in the tramps' private guide-book: 'A stunning workhouse for a good supper and breakfast; Much Wenlock, lads, that's the place.'

'The poet laureate of cadgers, who', it was said, 'had embellished the vagrant wards throughout the country with scraps of poetry, written in a beautiful hand', was a tramp known as 'Bow Street'. He was highly critical of one union where no bread was provided:

> It's an ill dog that don't deserve a crust,
> Is a maxim true and just . . .
> It's very unkind, nay further, cruel,
> To give here merely a drop of thin gruel.

The Trysull Union, near Wolverhampton in Staffordshire, erred, he complained, in the opposite direction:

Dry bread in the morning, ditto at night,
Keep up your pecker and make it all right..
I would as soon lodge here as in Piccadilly,
If along with the bread they gave a drop of skilly.

The sole recorded contribution of 'Yankee Ben', shows far more poetic power, but may have been cribbed from a printed source:

A little power, a little sway,
A sunbeam on a Winter's day,
Is all the rich and mighty have
Between the cradle and the grave.

The use of nicknames was typical of tramps, many of whom gave a different, sometimes blatantly false, name at every workhouse they used. Three visitors to Ellesmere workhouse during a race meeting at Chester in 1865, claimed to be respectively George Fordham, Jemmy Grimshaw and Luke Snowdon, all famous jockeys of the day.

The use of false names made it difficult to 'ration' any tramp to so many nights in a particular area, while written documents could easily be forged, for nearly every casual ward contained a specialist in this art.* One writer suggested that every vagrant admitted to a workhouse should have his hair 'cut close in a circular patch and that by arrangement a particular spot should be appropriated to each union after the manner of a phrenological chart', though as one commentator pointed out in 1868, this would still leave the problem of the tramp who was bald.

The casual ward is the one part of the workhouse of which detailed first-hand accounts by the occupants exist, for from the 1860s onwards there was a vogue for 'exposure' journalism in which respectable reporters disguised themselves as tramps. One of the first discoveries rapidly made was that it was far from easy to play such a part convincingly and one well-meaning and highly respectable member of a Workhouse Ladies Visiting Society found herself vehemently accused by a genuine 'casual' of being a social worker in disguise, a charge her accuser clearly regarded as far worse than calling her a prostitute.

The first step was to don an effective disguise, like James Greenwood of the *Pall Mall Gazette*, who dressed in a 'snuff brown

*He was known as a 'gag-maker' and charged from 3d. to 2s. according to the complexity of the documents required.

coat...altogether too small..a "birds" eye [i.e. polka dotted] pocket handkerchief of cotton' and a 'battered billy cock hat, with dissolute drooping brain, managed one cold January night to gain admission to Lambeth workhouse as 'Joshua Mason, engraver, slept last night at Hammersmith' and after a compulsory bath in 'a liquid . . . disgustingly like weak mutton broth' found himself in 'the shed':

Imagine a space of about thirty feet by thirty enclosed on three sides by a dingy white-washed wall, and roofed with naked tiles which were furred with the damp and filth that reeked within. As for the fourth side of the shed, it was boarded in for [say] a third of its breadth; the remaining space being hung with flimsy canvas, in which was a gap two feet wide at the top, widening to at least four feet at bottom. This far too airy shed was paved with stone, the flags so thickly encrusted with filth that I mistook it at first for a foot of natural earth. Extending from one end of my bedroom to the other, in three rows, were certain iron 'cranks' (of which I subsequently learned the use), with their many arms raised in various attitudes, as the stiffened arms of men are on a battle-field. My bed-fellows lay amongst the cranks, distributed over the flagstones in a double row, on narrow bags scantily stuffed with hay. At one glance my appalled vision took in thirty of them—thirty men and boys stretched upon shallow pallets which put only six inches of comfortable hay between them and the stony floor. These beds were placed close together, every occupant being provided with a rug...In not a few cases two gentlemen had clubbed beds and rugs and slept together. In one case . . . four gentlemen had so clubbed together . . . The practised and well-seasoned casual seems to have a peculiar way of putting himself to bed. He rolls himself in his rug, tucking himself in, head and feet, so that he is completely enveloped; and, lying quite still on his pallet, he looks precisely like a corpse covered because of its hideousness. Some were stretched out at full length; some lay nose and knees together; some with an arm or a leg showing crooked through the coverlet. It was like the result of a railway accident.

Greenwood found those of his companions who were awake even more repellent, though one, in return for being given a drink from 'a horse-pail three parts full of water standing by a post in the middle of the shed', did helpfully advise him on how to make a bed with one rug on a straw palliasse and point out the side of the shed most sheltered from the wind:

Towzled, dirty, villainous, they squatted up in their beds, and smoked foul pipes, and sang snatches of horrible songs, and bandied jokes so obscene as to be absolutely appalling. Eight or ten were so enjoying themselves — the majority with the check shirt on and the frowsy rug pulled about their legs; but two or three wore no shirts at all, squatting naked to the waist, their bodies fully exposed in the light of the single flaring jet of gas fixed high up on the wall.

The men amused themselves by, illegally, smoking, spitting at a crank 'distant a few inches from my head', and telling 'little auto-biographical anecdotes, so abominable that three or four decent men who lay at the further end of the shed were so provoked that they threatened, unless the talk abated in filthiness, to get up and stop it by main force... For several minutes... a storm of oaths, threats and taunts... a deluge of foul words raged in the room'. When the uproar died down members of the noisier party contributed stories of past and future thefts, and a bawdy song, with most of those present join-ing in the chorus. But the highlight of the evening's entertainment was 'a swearing club', a traditional tramps' amusement:

The principle of the game seemed to rest on the impossibility of either of the young gentlemen making half a dozen observations without introducing a blasphemous or obscene word ... The penalty for swearing was a punch on any part of the body, except a few which the club rules protected. The game was highly suc-cessful. Warming with the sport, and indifferent to the punches, the members vyed with each other in audacity and in a few minutes Bedlam in its prime could scarcely have produced such a spectacle ... One rule of the club was that any word to be found in the Bible might be used with impunity, and if one member punched another for using such a word the error was to be visited upon him with a double punching all round. This naturally led to much argument; for in vindicating the Bible as his authority a member became sometimes so much heated as to launch into a flood of real swear-ing which brought the fists of the club upon his naked carcass ...

About midnight the noise died down, and Greenwood then had to endure 'the snoring and the horrible, indescribable sound of impatient hands scratching skin that itched', varied by the arrival in the small hours of ten 'great hulking ruffians', who carved out ample room for themselves at the expense of those already sleeping and snatched away the author's 'birds eye' handkerchief, which he had been using as a night-cap. The night was also disturbed by the constant clinking of the water cup as thirsty men sought a drink, and, worst of all, incessant coughing:

> As for the coughing, to lie on flagstones in what was nothing better than an open shed and listen to that, hour after hour, chilled the heart with pity. Every variety of cough . . . was to be heard there; the hollow cough; the short cough; the hysterical cough; the bark that comes at regular intervals, like the quarter chime of a clock, as if to mark the progress of decay; coughing from vast hollow chests, coughing from little narrow ones—now one, now another, now two or three together, and then a minute's interval of silence in which to think of it all, and wonder who would begin next.

To Greenwood the over-all effect was that of several men chopping wood or, in this case, 'chopping their way to a pauper's graveyard'.

After being awakened at six and ordered to wash, without soap or towel, from a single bucket in the yard, the men received a slice of bread and 'a weak decoction of oatmeal and water, bitter, and without even a pinch of salt to flavour it', though this gruel, detested by most workhouse inmates, was received by the tramps with 'a loud "hooray" and highly relished', merely because it was hot. Other researchers found that even warm water was valued for the same reason.

Once breakfast was over, the set 'task' of corn-grinding—to be described in the next chapter—had to be completed and release finally came at 11 a m.

In the same year that James Greenwood was posing as a 'casual', another workhouse reformer, Dr James Stallard, already mentioned, hired an intelligent but hard-up working-class woman to make a surreptitious survey of the female casual wards. She, too, found some difficulty in looking the part. 'I put on a blue velvet bonnet', she wrote, 'very old and dirty: a grey skirt, much torn . . . and a cloth check shawl and worn-out boots. I purposely went as dirty as I could but I . . . was regarded by the officials in every case with great suspicion . . . and they only let me through when they had seen my boots. . . which appeared to satisfy their standard of distress.' Once inside, her experiences were similar to those of James Greenwood, except that as it was now July, she was 'dreadfully hot' instead of bitterly cold all night and the dormitory was much smaller, being only 13 feet by 7 feet 8 inches, under a sloping roof:

There was a gas jet at one end and only a narrow passage between the beds and the wall. There were nine beds arranged in wooden troughs, with sides a foot high, so that when you lie down it is impossible to see the person in the next bed. The beds are made of straw in canvas ticks, with a straw bolster, both being very hard. There were two thick rugs to each bed: they were like horsehair and both doubled to the width of the bed. One was placed underneath and the other was used to cover and as the beds were so narrow the whole weight of the upper rug was thrown upon you if it was used at all . . . My trouble was increased by finding that the place was alive with vermin and that scores of bugs were running about the bed.

'Ellen Stanley' discovered that, while male tramps were 'deterred' by being forced to have a bath, female ones, on asking for water, were told 'You may have as much as you wish to drink, but none to wash.' This helped to explain the 'terrific stench' surrounding one gypsy-like woman, who 'had not had a wash for three weeks'.

Four days later the same investigator made a further visit, this time to the Lambeth workhouse in Kennington Lane, where James Greenwood had called seven months before. The eight women already there proved sceptical of her claim to be Jane Wood, an embroidery hawker from Greenwich, and 'asked me if I was married and how many children I had, or if I was an old maid. "Old maid be—", said one.' Although the writer admitted that 'it was necessary to soften down much of the language which was too gross for publication,' conversation seems on the whole to have been less coarse that in the men's ward, turning on the merits of various workhouses, and the demerits of different types of vermin. 'One woman said "She didn't care how many lice she had, but that she couldn't abide the Pharaoh flight [fleas]"; and she sat for twenty minutes catching them with great industry and cracking them between her nails.'

Beside marauding insects, the night was disturbed by a middle-aged woman, the wife of an occupant of the male ward, who jumped up and 'roaring with madness, stripped herself entirely naked, retaining only her bonnet and a small shawl. The clothes she took off . . . she tore into rags.' Although the writer felt 'in my whole life I have never seen so pitiable an object', the assistant matron threatened the culprit with imprisonment on bread and water, and having given her some old, ill-fitting clothes, turned her out as soon as her task was completed.

This researcher found 'in the next bed to me . . . a stoutish woman of about thirty-seven years of age, with her face drawn to one side by a fit . . . well known to them all as Cranky Sal' and at another workhouse, St George's-in-the-East, near the docks, where Dr Stallard's researcher made a subsequent visit, Sal turned up again with a black eye. She had been given it, she explained, ' "because I would not let a man do as he liked with me", upon which all the rest set up a loud laugh'. Soon afterwards the true story came out: a man she had met in the New Cut on Saturday night had bought her a pennyworth of whelks and a twopenny pie, and had then offered her a shilling to sleep with him and when she refused had hit her. Sal, indignant, had called the police but, she complained, 'they only laughed at me and said that the man must have a strong stomach to fancy such as me'.

In spite of the generally harsh way in which they were treated, the number of people on the roads continued to increase—or so it seemed to contemporaries. By the late 1860s a number of local associations had been formed for stamping out vagrancy in their districts, a lead being taken by members of the aristocracy. The fourth Earl of Carnarvon, for example, a notable workhouse reformer, seems to have regarded the phenomenal growth in the number of vagrants in Hampshire from 3,000 in 1860 to 26,000 in 1870 as almost a personal insult. From the casual ward, he told the National Association for the Promotion of Social Science, of which he was president, in 1868, 'after some ghastly revel during the night, or some brawl in the morning . . . they . . . start upon their circuits, with as much regularity as the judges who may have to sentence them, selecting those unions where the discipline is slack or the diet generous'. Some casuals, he complained, had visited the same workhouse 150, 170 or even, in one case, 208 times, and as a magistrate, he now set about driving these recurrent visitors out of the area to such good effect that in nine months the number of vagrants admitted to Hampshire workhouses fell by more than 60 per cent.

One of Lord Carnarvon's methods, copied in the 1870s and 1880s in several other counties, was the Way Ticket system, under which everyone using the casual ward was issued with a form of passport, stating the holder's destination. This entitled him to a half-pound loaf of bread at 'bread-stations', usually policemen's houses, at intervals of every five miles or so, provided he kept to the specified route. Way Tickets were said at first to have cut the number of tramps in some counties by almost half, but before long the plausible beggar realised that a Way Ticket was almost a certificate of respectability and armed with one he became more troublesome than ever, until the system was abandoned.

Private initiative having failed, the authorities tried again. The attempt to distinguish between the deserving wayfarer and the undeserving tramp was abandoned. Under the Pauper Inmates Discharge and Regulation Act, passed in 1871, no 'casual' was to be allowed to leave until at least 11 a m on the day after he arrived, and then only after completing his task, while a second visit within a month meant a full day's hard labour and detention until 9 a m on the third day. Accommodation, the newly-appointed Local Government Board reminded unions, must be clean but rough, food scanty and coarse, and all the regulations designed to make life unpleasant must be strictly enforced.

In 1882 the law was tightened up again. Now everyone admitted to the casual ward had to do one full day's work, leaving at 9 a m on the third day, on his first visit in the month, and two days' work, staying until the fourth day, on his second. The new rules, however, penalised the minority eager to find work and in 1885 Boards were advised, though not ordered, to allow paupers who had finished their task the night before to leave early—usually 5.30 a m in summer and 6 a m in winter—a concession extended in 1892 to anyone claiming to be 'desirous of seeking work', however improbably.

Although alarmist estimates of the allegedly soaring number of tramps were always being quoted in Parliament, the average number of 'trampers' on the roads was probably about 30,000, rising in periods of trade depression like the 1840s and 1860s as high as 80,000. Of these the casual wards never contained at any one time more than 2,000 to 10,000. How many of these were decent people down on their luck was much disputed. Sceptical fellow-tramps, when consulted, tended to put the figure no higher than 10 per cent, while optimistic social workers suggested it might be as high as 30 per cent.

The ordinary citizen tended to assume that all users of the casual wards were work-shy tramps but in fact they came from a variety of backgrounds. One large group were discharged soldiers who had lost the habit of sleeping under an ordinary roof, a few were skilled craftsmen equipped with a 'travelling card' which entitled them to help from fellow members of their trade union and many were young men in their twenties, who had taken to the roads to escape from some private problem: a girl in trouble, a nagging wife, a squire asking questions about poached game.

A survey of the occupants of the casual ward at Gloucester, made one night in 1886, found 111 people enjoying the union's hospitality: 87 men, 4 women and 20 children. Of these only 53 lived entirely by tramping. Over-all, of those whom the interrogator believed to be telling the truth, there were 56 who had been labourers, 2 carpenters, 4 seamen, and one or two each bricklayers, tailors, painters and plasterers. All four adult females had been charwomen and some of the older girls laundresses. The men included one 'white-collar worker', a clerk. On the same night in Gloucester the common lodging houses held 600 people and the social mix here was more varied, including an actor, a photographer, a nurse and an artist. The truth was, as the chief historian of tramping pointed out in 1887, it was not the genuine 'casuals' who turned first to the casual ward. 'When they are flush of funds, or whenever they wish for a debauch with their paramours, they frequent the lodging house. Vagrants frequent the casual wards as a matter of economy.'

A high proportion of the users of the casual ward were professional beggars, though some, when desperate, did earn their living honestly, like the pedlars who (partly to protect themselves from being arrested for begging) carried lace and ribbons with them, or the travelling umbrella repairers, known as 'mushroom fakers'. More numerous, however, were the petty tricksters who had sometimes spent a lifetime perfecting their particular swindle or 'lurk'. Among recognised branches of the trade was the 'fire lurk', practised by those 'ruined' when their home or business had burned down, the 'shipwrecked lurk', the 'sick lurk', the 'colliery lurk', pretended unemployment after a pit disaster, and the 'bereavement lurk', needing the aid of borrowed, or hired, children. This last had its hazards, as one tramp complained in 1871, for having slapped his twelve-year-old 'daughter' in the street she loudly 'called me "rogue, rascal and imposter"', and revealed that 'I had paid her mother half a crown for herself and her sister for the evening and that her mother was getting drunk with the money.'

But everyone with a first-hand knowledge of the casual ward agreed that at least a minority of those on the roads were basically decent, deserving people. In 1887 a young writer, James Craven, posing as an unemployed mechanic, who stayed at the Keighley Union in Yorkshire, found that his companions included 'a tailor, aged 67, decently dressed, a compositor, also respectably attired, and a band-maker', while most of the contingent, far from boasting of their skill as beggars, passed the time discussing their prospects of finding work at 'the new waterworks at Barrowford and Colne'. The food and accommodation, however, had not improved. Men clearly ill were denied a doctor, the bedding was alive with vermin, and one man claimed to have seen 'in Skipton workhouse the night previous ... his bread ... carried away by a ravenous rat as big as a cat'. This observer concluded that 'the general treatment of vagrants is ... a disgrace to any civilised country ... The lowest of mankind deserve better treatment than that accorded to pigs, dogs and other animals of creation'. It was, he felt, understandable, that the verses he found inscribed on one newly-whitewashed wall should have taken a pessimistic view:

> Dirty days hath September,
> April, June, and November;
> From January up to May,
> The rain it raineth every day;
> From May again until July,
> There's not a dry cloud in the sky;
> All the rest have thirty-one
> Without a blessed ray of sun;
> And if any of them had two-and-thirty,
> They'd be just as wet and quite as dirty.

The secretary of the Ladies Committee of Oldham workhouse, Mrs Mary Higgs, who in 1904, and again in 1906, disguised herself as a tramp and with a friend spent a number of nights in North-country workhouses, also rapidly discarded 'the prevailing idea in my class of society ... that tramps as a class were so incorrigible that ... the only thing was to severely penalise vagrancy'. She was shocked by the conditions she and her companion encountered, the accommodation, whether clinically clean or vermin-ridden, being uniformly cheerless and prison-like and the food even worse: saltless, or appallingly over-salted, gruel, dry bread and cheese, with no water allowed except at meal-times. Hot tea, the supreme luxury to all casual ward users, was never forthcoming. Everything possible seemed to be done to degrade women vagrants who were given no facilities to dry damp clothes and were strictly forbidden—even if put to work in the laundry —to wash their own dirty garments.

Mrs Higgs bravely declared that she would 'ever regard . . . with affection and respect' those she had met in the casual wards. They included 'a married woman whom I would gladly own for my own relation... She was the "black sheep of the family" and had drifted, probably through marriage...into destitute circumstances'. She and her 'old man', who was in the men's ward—'I know him by his cough', she said—had walked seventy miles to attend a sister's funeral, and though 'very, very weary with the long tramp' she still had 'a cheerful face, and an eye for others' sorrows'. Another new acquaintance, also married, 'was still better dressed, a shapely woman, with a face almost handsome', who had been 'waitress in a hotel . . . I knew well', and whose misfortunes had only begun 'when her husband's particular branch of trade failed'. Only two women were of 'a coarser kind': 'Pollie who . . . complained bitterly that the men were let out so long before the women... as her husband, one fine day, being let out of the tramp ward before her, left her behind . . . She knew the workhouses far and wide . . . She had thrown her bread and cheese at a matron . . . had been in prison for "lip" . . . was, in fact, a tramp proper, and with a little drink and boon companions, probably foul-mouthed and violent'; and seventy-year-old 'Grannie' who had 'brought up a family of five sons and daughters'. Only when her husband died and the son who had supported her lost his job, had she taken to the roads. Considering all her troubles, Mrs Higgs felt, 'she did not after all groan so very much'.

Beside having to endure the same discomforts as the men, women using the casual wards were also exposed to other dangers. When Mary Higgs and her companion arrived at one workhouse they found that the entrance lodge was an isolated building manned by a male pauper who 'finding I was a married woman . . . said, "Just the right age for a bit of funning; come down to me later in the evening"'. When her companion's turn came to be interviewed the same man 'tried to kiss her as she gave him the things . . . She joined me, very indignant'. At their next port of call Mrs Higgs once again found herself confronting a male porter, who 'looked more respectable than the other one', but 'began to talk in a familiar and most disagreeable manner. He asked me where my husband was and . . . said a married woman needed to "sleep warm". He . . . . said if there was [only] one woman [in the casual ward] "he often shared his breakfast with her". He produced a screw of salt and gave it to us as a favour'. But Mrs Higgs's virtue, needless to say, was not to be bought with salt, and she and her friend escaped unscathed.

In 1904, when the number of occupants of casual wards reached an all-time record, the government set up a committee of enquiry into vagrancy, but after two years' work it achieved nothing, beyond confirming that a third, or even two-thirds, of those on the roads could probably be resettled in normal life. No attempt to do so was ever made, however, and in the closing years before the first world war, severity and still more severity remained the rule, as he confirmed. Yet another campaigning journalist, Everard Wyvall, who posed as an out-of-work clerk walking from London to Portsmouth, in 1909. In one 'spike', as the casual ward was now nicknamed, he found himself locked in a small cell with barred windows and then, after a wretched day stone-breaking, which left him 'with hands almost raw' and 'aching and sore in every limb', spending a second night in a communal ward, where he was shut up for thirteen hours in an unlighted room with ten other men, with only seven hammocks between them.

Wyvall had, as a soldier, slept out in the rain behind enemy lines, but 'nothing' he wrote with a reminiscent shudder, 'will ever compare with that horrible night . . . Even now I find myself shivering at the thought of that dreadful experience'. At dawn, the door was unlocked and their breakfast, dry bread, was brought in and thrown on the floor as though they were animals. Soon afterwards they were allowed to leave. A fitting postscript to the episode was provided by a lame old man who had been worked without mercy on the previous day and as he passed the taskmaster, turned on him and said, 'Look 'ere mister, if ever I gets you outside this 'ere place I'll do for yer!'

Such was the casual ward under the enlightened Liberal government. Mr Asquith was now Prime Minister, but it could well have been Lord Melbourne.

20 Stones and Oakum

We'll hang up the miller on a sour apple tree,
And then go grinding on. *Song of workhouse
inmates grinding corn*, 1866

The 'task' was an essential part of the workhouse regime. Back in the
1830s the Poor Law Board had enthusiastically recommended unions
to purchase a multi-handle corn-grinding machine as a sovereign way
of making paupers anxious to leave the 'house'. By the 1860s, the
'able-bodied' wards stood largely empty, but the same methods and
even the same machines were now in use to 'deter' the occupants
of the casual wards. The experiences of the journalist, James
Greenwood, at Lambeth in 1866, were typical. After a wretched night
in the workhouse, described in the previous chapter, the following
morning he made the acquaintance of the taskmaster, who set them
to work and then left them to the care of the miller, who 'once or twice
. . . came in and said mildly, "Now then, my men, why don't you stick
to it?" and so went out again':

> The labour was to be 'crank' labour. The 'cranks' are a series of iron
> bars extending across the width of the shed, penetrating through
> the wall, and working a flour mill on the other side. Turning the
> crank is like turning a windlass . . . Close up by the ceiling hangs
> a bell connected with the machinery and as each measure is ground
> the bell rings . . . But the grinders are as lazy as obscene . . . At
> least one half of the gang kept their hands from the crank whenever
> the miller was absent . . . Some sprawled upon the beds and
> smoked . . . one turned hair-cutter . . . There were three tailors;
> two of them on the beds mending their own coats, and the other
> operating on a recumbent friend in the rearward part of his
> clothing . . . For thread they used a strand of the oakum . . . which
> the boys were picking in the corners. Other loungers strolled
> about with their hands in their pockets, discussing the topics of the
> day, and playing practical jokes on the industrious few; a favourite
> joke being to take a bit of rag, anoint it with grease from the crank

axles, and clap it unexpectedly over somebody's eye. The consequence of all this was that the cranks went round at a very slow rate and now and then stopped altogether. Then the miller came in; the loungers rose from their couches, the tailors ceased stitching, the smokers dropped their pipes, and every fellow was at his post. The cranks spun round furiously again, amidst a shout of 'Slap bang, here we are again!', or this extemporised chorus,

> We'll hang up the miller on a sour apple tree,
> We'll hang up the miller on a sour apple tree,
> We'll hang up the miller on a sour apple tree,
>   And then go grinding on.
>   Glory, Glory Hallelujah.. and then go grinding on.

Twenty years later corn-grinding was still in use in many casual wards, as James Craven, the 28-year-old writer mentioned earlier posing as 'Charles Burrell, on the road from Bradford to Burnley, trade: mechanic', discovered at the Keighley Union in Yorkshire:

Protruding from the wall, were six wheels with handles attached, and ... after being ordered to grind away at these, we were locked in. Some of the machines were dreadfully hard to turn . . . One of the vagrants, who had been at the game before, had made the calculation that to grind the requisite four bushels of corn, it was necessary to make 8,800 turns at the wheel. He adopted the process of counting the revolutions, and every time he reached 100 he made a note of it on the wall with a pencil, and then rested himself on the wheel handle before commencing the next century.

One frequently imposed task was stone-breaking, experienced by another investigator, already described, who posed as a pauper, Everard Wyvall. Wyvall first made the acquaintance of

. . . the taskmaster . . . a sour-looking man with the face of a bully and a coward, one who knew he had the whip hand. The thin lips denoted meanness and an uncontrollable temper. The eyes were sleek, cunning and watchful . . . Having called the roll, the taskmaster folded the paper and placed it in his pocket. 'Thomas Brown, you are to scrub out the ward and the cells, and move your lazy bones a bit. If I catch you skulking, I'll stop your dinner... You six men will saw timber—a pleasant little job, much too good for the likes of you. You four—follow me' ... We ... slunk behind him ...

and soon found ourselves in front of a strongly-built corrugated iron shed. The small windows were heavily barred . . . but some of the panes in the window were broken, and through these apertures the snow blew in clouds. Flinging open the door of the shed the task-master pointed first to a number of piles of stones which lay on the ground inside, then to a close-meshed sieve. 'Each man will break a pile of stones—two hundredweight—and pass them through that sieve.' We literally gasped as the enormity and almost impossibility of the task dawned upon us. The mesh of the sieve was less than a quarter of an inch; some of the stones were at least twelve inches in diameter* . . . 'When you've finished', added the tyrant, 'you can go' . . . He knew the task was well-nigh impossible. 'If you don't break them, I'll "run you".' In tramp language to be 'run' is to be handed over to the police. With loud protests one of the men started forward: 'I'm an ex-soldier; I've four medals. I've served my country, and curse me if I'll do it.' With a snarl the taskmaster turned upon him. 'Get on with it, or it'll be the worse for you.' . . . One . . . poor old man . . . now began to plead: 'I'm lame in one foot, and can scarcely stand. I'm aching in every limb. I want to see the doctor . . .' 'Can't see the doctor, he's gone.' 'I've a sore arm,' said one of the other men, pulling up his tattered coat sleeve showing a long raw scar . . . But the door slammed in his face, and the bolts shot on the outside . . . Pounding is carried out with long heavy bars of iron having square ends, the length of the bars being about four feet. They are of such a weight that only men in good health can use them properly. By the side of each pounder was a wooden box with an iron bottom. The stones were placed inside of the latter. Then, grasping the pounder with both hands, it was lifted about a foot above the stones and brought down with all the force at one's disposal. Nothing was given to us to protect our eyes, and one sieve had to do service for four. For half an hour I tried my best to pound those stones, but I seemed to make little or no impression upon them. Then I began to feel a peculiar tingling in the palms of my hands, and my fingers became so sore that it was most painful to grasp the pounder. Finally,

---

*Stone-breaking, with a hammer, was technically a different task from stone-pounding, but, in Wyvall's experience, even harder. A week later, at another workhouse, he was ordered to break a half-ton block of granite, but though 'I smote with all my strength . . . I made no impression whatever.' He expected to be sent to prison but was let off 'to give him a chance'.

blisters put in an appearance, and these breaking, the chafings gave way to blood, which soon began to trickle down my fingers ... I do not think my hands were particularly tender, because the hands of the other men were affected in much the same way. The lame man worked like one demented—smashing, sifting, and piling up the fragments ... In his eyes I noticed something suspiciously like a tear, and he often cried out that his back ached ... He ... refused dinner, and ... worked all the time. The fear of being 'run', and for ever branded as a jail-bird, had taken hold of him ... The lame man was nearest the door; he was judged first. 'Humph! you've nearly done, you can go in.' The poor fellow nearly took to his heels. 'You two men who haven't finished can stay out here till it's dark.' He referred to the man with the sore arm and myself. 'You'—to the ex-soldier—'you've refused to do your task, you're one of the lazy ones.' He stepped to the door and beckoned to someone who had hitherto remained out of sight. A blue-uniformed figure stood in the doorway. 'Arrest that man. He is charged with refusing to do the work laid down by the Local Government Board in exchange for "relief".' 'Relief! you—' almost screamed the poor fellow. 'Come quietly, mate,' whispered the man in blue. 'You'll be better in chokey than in this 'ere'ole. Chokey's all right compared with this.'

Probably the commonest of all tasks was picking oakum, which could be undertaken by both sexes and all age groups. In the 1830s and 1840s both small children and the very old had been kept occupied in this way, and nearly a century later oakum-picking was still a common form of employment in the casual ward for the elderly. In 1904 Mrs Mary Higgs of Oldham posed as a penniless casual at an unnamed North-country workhouse:

Three of us were set to pick oakum...We...sat on a bench in a cold room and three pounds of oakum each was solemnly weighed out to us. Do you know what oakum is? A number of old ropes, some of them tarred, some knotted, are cut into lengths; you have to twist and unravel them inch by inch. We were all 'prentice hands. One woman had once done a little; we had never done any. After two hours I had perhaps done a quarter of a pound, and my fingers were getting sore, while the pile before me seemed to diminish little. Then I was asked if I could clean and gladly escaped to a more congenial task. One woman picked oakum all day . . . She had never done it before and did not nearly finish her quota.

Domestic work, to which Mrs Higgs had been transferred, was the other task regularly demanded of all women in the workhouse, whether 'casuals' or ordinary inmates, and she left behind a vivid account of what it meant when, with a friend, she bravely set out on a similar expedition two years later, first in Lancashire and then in London. Here the two women had the ill-luck to encounter a taskmistress who was 'one of those women to whom . . . work is a joy in itself, and the utmost scrupulosity of finicking cleanliness a thing to be exacted as a matter of course . . . Nine hours' solid work (five in the morning, four in the afternoon)—that was what the law exacted and she got it'.

Seven o'clock . . . We began cheerfully . . . The ward was apparently clean, but the whole must be scrubbed. My portion was to do four cells and a long, long passage leading past eighteen cells (nine on a side, and two bathrooms and a lavatory with two WCs). Cloths, bucket and soda were provided, no aprons till later. I had a kneeling pad, my friend none . . . My friend was accustomed to wash for a family of nine . . . but never, never in all her working days, had she worked so hard. She cleaned the bathrooms and a whole flight of stairs, and then was put on the private sitting-room, to be done most particularly . . . Four bucketsful of water—one for each cell—seven for the long passage, two for lavatory and WCs, brasses to clean, paint to dust. It seemed a Sisyphean task, no sooner ended than a new one was exacted . . . At dinner-time, twelve o'clock, we stopped for an hour. I could not touch food. My friend . . . managed to eat a small portion of bread and cheese, washed down by cold water . . . Tired! That is no word for it! We had already done a charwoman's day's work. My friend could hardly speak, and I had no strength save to lay my head on the table and wonder how I should survive the afternoon.

One o'clock and hard labour. My friend, on finishing two bedrooms, was put to clean the storeroom . . . Meanwhile, the 'old tramp' (myself) must do the dayroom—it only served her right for the way she 'tickled the boards!'

Five long and very ornamental forms and two long tables, to be scrubbed on every inch of surface to immaculate whiteness with soap and water. The floor to be scrubbed and every place dusted. Kneeling had become such torture that the straining of the body up to scrub the undersurface of the forms almost produced faintness . . .

At last—five o'clock and respite. We both were more dead than alive . . . Every limb ached; my poor friend was no better; her knees were too sore to touch.

First-hand knowledge rapidly convinced Mary Higgs that society was guilty of far greater crimes against the workhouse inmate than the pauper had committed against society. The grim conditions and appallingly hard work made her wholly sympathetic to those who, lacking her advantages, turned to vice or crime. Was it any wonder that for her recent companions 'anything is preferable. Prison? It has lost its terrors—it cannot be harder. Sin? What's the odds? It may pay for a decent bed and food. The river? That is best of all, if one could manage to face it.'

As for the task, that cornerstone of the deterrent system, Mary Higgs believed that it was merely one more cruel burden on those whose lives had already been made intolerable. What use was it, for example, to demand work from 'Grannie . . . a poor old body of seventy, much plagued by rheumatics? Each leg was swathed in bandages, her feet wrapped in old stocking legs and bandaged, and men's boots put over all…She could hardly stand, had a cough and looked feverish…The one effect her wandering had produced in her was a deadly hatred of workhouse officials…"I can't help it", she said, "if it keeps me out of heaven. I hate 'em—I hate 'em all!"… She felt sure she would meet many of these her tormentors in hell, and then, she said, "I'll heave bricks at 'em".'

21 Turning the Clock Back

The workhouse system, where fairly and fully
tried, has not failed in a single instance. *Note
circulated by the Local Government Board,*
1872

The workhouse system, born in 1834 with astonishingly little
difficulty, and grown to maturity with remarkable speed, was to
be a long time a-dying. The initial severity was followed in the 1850s
and 1860s by a reaction in which out-relief, even to the able-bodied,
began to creep back, but an economic depression in 1866 and 1867
sent the numbers of unemployed soaring and in 1869 the Poor Law
Inspector for the metropolitan area called a series of conferences of
East End Guardians to warn them against over-generous relief. The
best way to discourage applicants, he urged, was to apply the old
panacea of 'offering the house', not merely to the able-bodied, but
to widows, who should have their usual six months of out-relief cut
down to three, and to deserted wives, who should be given only two
or three weeks, at most, to find themselves a new job, or a new
partner.

Almost the last act of the dying Poor Law Board was to call for a
report on out-relief from its inspectors, who duly reported that
'the workhouse test . . . should be offered more frequently'. The local
Government Board, taking over in 1871, sent out a circular in
December calling for greater strictness, including the total refusal
of relief, except in the workhouse, to able-bodied single men and
women, as well as to unmarried mothers, deserted wives and widows
with only one child. 'The aim of the English Poor Law,' all Boards
of Guardians were reminded in 1873, 'is to combine the maximum
of efficiency in the relief of destitute applicants with the minimum
of incentive to improvidence . . . The end thus proposed . . . can be
fully reached only by that system of administration which is commonly known as the workhouse system . . . . The workhouse system,
where fairly and fully tried, has not failed in a single instance.'

During the 1870s no General Order banning out-relief was

issued, but one MP, a leading figure in the newly-formed Charity Organisation Society, in 1876 moved a resolution totally condemning all forms of out-relief, though ministers, and his fellow-members, prudently stayed away, and the House was counted out. In the following year, however, although he had turned down a similar demand made by a deputation led by the same MP, the minister responsible did publicly express 'great satisfaction at observing the . . . more rigid and discriminating system of outdoor relief' which had now been introduced.

That unjustified faith in local independence which had already done so much harm was now once more used against the poor, and during the next twenty years, contrary to the whole intention of the Poor Law, how an applicant was treated depended very much upon where he lived. The detailed regulations varied from union to union, but almost everywhere any able-bodied man who could not convince the Relieving Officer that he had always been sober and provident was immediately whisked off to the workhouse. When out-relief *was* granted the amount was often related to the applicant's place on some locally-evolved scale of virtue. In Sheffield Class 'A' paupers, for example, the most respectable, merited 5s. a week, while Class D had to struggle along on *2s. 6d.*

Many Boards of Guardians automatically refused relief to people of 'immoral habits' or 'indolent habits'. One union sent all widows to the workhouse, but most spared those with more than one or two children. When out-relief was provided it was often cut off after a certain period, the line being variously drawn in different unions at one month, two months and six months, or when an only child had reached one year old, or eighteen months, or school age. Most places agreed that 'any person who may have given birth to an illegitimate child' was disqualified and deserted wives also came in for a hard time. Some Boards refused even to consider relief in such cases, for fear the husband's departure might be a put-up job and frequently relief was not paid until a wife had been abandoned for a specified period, from six months to five years.

Where such tests failed, there were often others to trip up the unwary, like living in a house rented above the average rent of the neighbourhood, keeping a dog or gun—the poacher's stock in trade—possessing an allotment or having a child at home over thirteen years of age capable of earning a living. Some unions also refused out-relief to any bereaved family where the funeral insurance had been 'lavishly or improperly expended'.

But the main attack was on the granting of out-relief to the able-bodied. Increasingly from the 1860s onwards many unions, especially in the cities, where the main struggle against pauperism was now being fought, made use of a device tried earlier on a small scale, the opening of Labour Yards or Stone-yards, either in the workhouse or on separate premises. Here, in return for their weekly allowance, applicants for relief had to attend every day to carry out a prescribed task, becoming 'semi-inmates' of the workhouse, living in their own homes but subject during the day to workhouse labour and workhouse discipline.

The qualifications for admission to the Labour Yard, or its female equivalent, varied and some unions restricted admission to single men, while others took only married ones, or men with more than one child, or men aged over sixty. To single women often no choice except the workhouse was offered, except occasionally for 'virtuous widows'. The rates of out-relief, where it was given, also differed from union to union, though almost always it was partly given in kind. At Poplar, in 1870, for example, a married couple received only five pence a day, plus a four pound loaf. Some unions offered as much as fourteen shilling a week to a man with a wife and four children, others as little as nine.

The tasks demanded were similar to those in the casual wards, described earlier, including stone-breaking, oakum-picking and wood-chopping, which seemed at first sight, more useful, though production tended to outstrip demand. One London workhouse which required 200 bundles of wood a week, soon found itself stocked up with sufficient kindling to light all its fires for many years ahead. Some women applicants for relief were put to sorting bristles for brushes, while other London workhouses required them to attend for several hours a day at needle-rooms or laundry-rooms.

In theory the 'semi-inmate' on out-relief was worked as hard as the indoor pauper in the workhouse but, *The Times* complained in 1888, the normal working week in London was 52½ hours, while the men in the stone-yard worked only 45 hours and sometimes as little as 32. 'Moreover', added *The Times*, 'carpenters or engineers have to be at work by seven o'clock even in the coldest weather; the stone-yard never opens its gates till 8 a m and . . .

one union last winter only commenced operations at 10 a m. The theory is excellent, namely that the men would have time to go round and seek employment before coming in; in practice, however, [some] applicants...preferred to lie in bed till their wives got their breakfast ready'.

The superintendent of the Leeds Labour Yard reported to the Guardians in 1906: 'When I am called away, nearly every man ceases work until my return . . . time after time I have looked from the Test Yard door and seen them gossiping in groups of four or five, some smoking pipes or cigarettes, others sitting on the barrows; one acts as a "crow" to warn the Yard when I return'.

The Labour Yard experiment also demonstrated once again, like innumerable experiments over the previous three centuries, that pauper labour was intrinsically uneconomic. At St Olave's, Southwark, in South East London, in 1895, a new and progressive Board of Guardians offered trade union rates of pay, though half was to be in kind, to all able-bodied applicants at the stone-yard, but the stone broken there proved to cost the ratepayers £7 a ton, against the normal commercial rate of five shillings. In its last week of operations, before it closed down after running up a wages bill of £17,000 in three months, 2,814 men sought work at the Labour Yard. The following week, when only 'the house' was available, the number of supposedly destitute applicants slumped suddenly to 74. There was clearly much justification for the belief that out-relief of any kind, however sparingly dispensed, would always attract the undeserving, though one inspector who publicly declared around 1900 that any 'outdoor' allowance was 'like the first taste of blood to a tiger', found himself widely denounced as 'un-Christian, inhuman, brutish and un-English' and the phrase became briefly notorious. Curiously enough, when he reworded his comment in more homely terms as 'like the first taste of jam to a schoolboy', his critics were content.

The campaign against out-relief was in fact remarkably successful. Between 1871 and 1876 expenditure was cut by nearly a quarter and the number of those on the union pay-rolls dropped sharply, from 881,000 to 606,000. It remained around this level for the rest of the century, dropping briefly to 596,000 in 1886 and to 558,000—its lowest point—in 1892.

Along with the new restrictions on out-relief went an attempt to revive another principle of 1834, which had gone unimplemented then: the provision of separate workhouses for different types of inmate. At Poplar, in 1871, the sick were sent off to a new infirmary, the children moved out to a Poor Law school, and the aged decanted into the workhouse belonging to neighbouring Stepney, leaving the Poplar workhouse to become a 'deterrent' establishment—or Able-Bodied Test Workhouse—for the able-bodied poor from all over London. Any who applied for relief in the twenty-five metropolitan unions now received merely an 'Order for Poplar', and on arrival were put to granite breaking or oakum picking, the amounts required, one relieving officer admitted, being 'very severe'.

The results came close to achieving the original ideal of the Poor Law Commissioners; a well-run, deterrent workhouse that stood almost permanently empty. Many inmates, boasted the Local Government Board in 1872, 'have almost immediately taken their discharge' while the average stay was under three weeks and 600 of the 800 beds were never occupied. Similar experiments were tried, with comparable results, at various other places, but in the end all the Test Workhouses failed, because no Board of Guardians could afford to keep one large, fully-staffed building standing almost empty, while its other institutions were overflowing. By 1882 even Poplar had again become an ordinary mixed workhouse in all but name.

In 1884 working men in the country constituencies—the very class at whom the Poor Law Amendment Act had been aimed—received the vote, raising the number of working-class electors from a third of the electorate to three-fifths. 'The centre of power has been shifted', the Radical Minister, Joseph Chamberlain, told a working-class audience, in 1885. 'You are in the position of men who have suddenly come into a fortune.' In fact, as Birmingham was in the grip of a trade depression, all that most of his hearers had inherited was the workhouse—and many of them were skilled craftsmen, like jewellers, whose sensitive hands might be ruined for life if put to breaking stones or picking oakum. The Birmingham Guardians refused, however, to grant out-relief to the afflicted families, despite Chamberlain advancing the revolutionary doctrine that 'The law exists for securing the assistance of the community at large in aid of their destitute members' but in the following year, 1886, he had a spectacular revenge for he became President of the Local Government Board and overlord of the whole Poor Law system. The Circular which he issued during his short spell in office marked a revolution in policy. The workhouse could still, he agreed, be used for vagrants and for 'ins and outs', but men unemployed through no fault of their own should be spared 'the stigma of pauperism' and be found jobs in large-scale public works organised by public authorities.

Chamberlain's Circular of 1886 acknowledged for the first time that to be workless was not the same as to be work-shy, and later bore belated fruit in many places. At the time, however, the results were disappointing. At Salford, late in the nineteenth century, men admitted to the workhouse were still sent out to labour in the streets with a large 'P' for 'Pauper' emblazoned across the seat of their trousers— a sight which would not have seemed out of place a hundred years earlier.

22 Hang the Rates!

From the first moment I determined to fight for
one policy only, and that was decent treatment
for the poor people, and hang the rates! George
Lansbury on his election as a Guardian, 1892

As the number of those on out-relief fell, following the policy of
severity introduced around 1870, admissions to the workhouse increased. After a brief drop in the number of inmates, from 156,000
in 1871 to 143,000 in 1876, a steep and permanent rise began, which
carried the total to 186,000 in 1886, 214,000 in 1896 and 216,000
in 1898, representing about seven in every 1,000 inhabitants of
England and Wales. These figures revealed only the number of people
in the workhouse on the day the census was taken. The total who
passed through it in the course of a year, if only as overnight
'casuals', was much larger, being estimated at from two to three
and a half times the average number of inmates. Thus, in a population
in 1901 of 33 millions, between half and three-quarters of a million
were likely to have had recent personal experience of the workhouse.

How they were treated ultimately depended upon the Poor Law
department of the Local Government Board which had a low reputation, even among the abler members of its own staff. Dr Henry
Bridges, whose work as the Board's first Medical Inspector has
already been described, was scathing about his colleagues. 'The Office
blunders on in the same dull, groping way', he complained in 1876.
'It is degrading to be connected with these shufflers', he wrote in
1887. 'There is a mixture of slipperiness, vacillation [and] popularity
hunting...about the whole matter that is utterly revolting to me.'
Competitive entry to the whole Civil Service had only begun in 1870
and where it had existed before had sometimes been only a formality.

The young Herbert Preston-Thomas, whose later career has already been mentioned, found on arriving fresh from Marlborough in
1859 to compete for a place in the Privy Council Office, that the only
other candidates were two dim-witted young men known as 'the
Treasury idiots'; the regulations required a minimum entry of three,

so this amiable pair were regularly put up to let the favoured candidate in. The creation in 1871 of the Local Government Board brought no immediate change. 'Its nucleus', he wrote, 'was the old Poor Law Board, which had been among the worst paid of government departments, had a low standard of entrance examination and had contained a very small proportion of men of liberal education.' Real reform did not come until 1884, when '8 clerkships of the higher division'—later known as the Administrative Class—were opened to competition. All were promptly filled by able Oxford and Cambridge graduates, whose influence, as they rose in the service, probably contributed to the reforms introduced a decade later.

But even with better quality men beginning to make their mark at the centre, another obstacle to reform remained, in the Boards of Guardians. Especially in the country, elections for most of the century were not contested and the same people, virtually self-appointed, tended to remain in office year after year. Their personal integrity was usually high, but many were inspired by a determination to keep the farm labourer's nose firmly to the agricultural grindstone. In the towns even integrity was often lacking. Dr Joseph Rogers, who served Boards of Guardians in Central London between 1856 and 1886, observed that places on the Board tended to be sought by profit-hungry tradesmen and contractors, 'the most dangerous members of the body politic'. The chairman of the Strand Union in the 1850s, 'would often come to the house on Sunday morning, dressed in the dirty, greasy jacket in which he had been serving à-la-mode beef the night before. . . Unshaven and unshorn, he would go into the chapel with the pauper inmates and afterwards go to the Board Room and have breakfast with the master and matron. . . Between the three there was an excellent understanding.' The chief interest of his successor, a wholesale fruit-dealer from Covent Garden, lay in getting pauper labour free and one former stonemason was employed for weeks in installing marble decorations in the chairman's house, never receiving even a meal in return. The work ended abruptly when the exploited pauper drowned himself, and the chairman died suddenly of heart disease, 'the only evidence', according to Rogers, 'that he possessed one'. Another Guardian, who had been a tax-collector in Soho, turned out to have embezzled £300 of public money, and a third, an almost illiterate ex-milkman, had risen in the world by buying up and letting slum property. Such landlords often became Guardians in poor areas, and one, who owned three hundred houses, was to Rogers's satisfaction, actually fined for keeping them in an insanitary condition.

In the 1890s Herbert Preston-Thomas, arriving as a Local Government Board Inspector in East Anglia, found himself having to cope, not with middle-class corruption, but aristocratic eccentricity, as displayed by the Earl of Kimberley, chairman of a Norfolk Board of Guardians:

> The Earl . . . despotically enforced his own opinion, however much it disagreed with the teachings of modern science . . . It chanced that I had to ask the Guardians to spend some money in improving the bathing and sanitary arrangements at their workhouse, which were of the most primitive description. But he gave me no chance of success. He actually objected to baths as dangerous to health, and assured me that when Foreign Secretary he had observed that the era of widespread epidemics of typhoid fever in Italy had begun with the introduction of modern sanitation in houses. It was useless for me to point out that since the general reform in such matters in England, not only typhoid fever but other 'filth diseases' had been diminishing steadily year by year. Lord Kimberley would not pay attention to anything outside his Italian precedent . . . the Wymondham Workhouse had to wait.

One of the charges made against the old village Overseers of the Poor in the 1830s had been their lack of education, but at the end of the century there were still, Preston-Thomas discovered, many Guardians with a very limited vocabulary. One spoke against giving a man an honorarium: 'If he had one he could not play on it. I am for giving him hard cash.' And several assumed that a candid certificate from their medical officer testifying of one applicant that 'he suffers from chronic inertia' referred to some rare disease. Worse, however, than ignorant Guardians were disorderly or humorous ones, as the same Inspector observed:

> One of my earliest visits was paid to the meeting of the Workhouse Committee of a large town; and here, notwithstanding the presence of a stranger, the Guardians squabbled till they almost came to blows; hid away under the chair-cushions each other's notes for speeches; played a practical joke on one of their number, who happened to be a teetotaller, by concealing a sample bottle of brandy (sent with a tender) in his coat-tail pocket; and were

altogether childish. The Chairman alternately called people
loudly to order without the least effect, and accepted the most
foolish and irrelevant proposals . . . I wondered whether this
was an average sample of the management of Poor Law business.

Self-appointed 'funny' Guardians were a menace everywhere and
often a real obstacle to progress. Proposals for providing newspapers
and magazines for the elderly inmates in one London workhouse in
the 1860s provoked only jocular remarks about giving the paupers
a billiard room as well, and at Maldon, in 1895, another humorist
responded to a proposal to instal garden seats with backs for the old
men, by sarcastically suggesting awnings to keep off the sun. Some
Guardians were troublesome in other ways. Preston-Thomas discovered one who 'from eccentricity or love of notoriety' regularly held
up the proceedings and eventually had to be removed by the police.
At another meeting of the same Board, one member launched a
violent verbal attack on another and then 'when his victim rose
to reply, he not only went to sleep but snored like a foghorn. The
Board was small, so was the room and these tremendous blasts over-
powered everything'.

But the greatest weakness of the Board of Guardians system was
that, when vacancies were contested at all, the same people tended to
get elected year after year. 'At some of the Board meetings which I
first attended', wrote Inspector Preston-Thomas, 'it was impossible
to help seeing that the demons of precedent, of routine and of dullness
held sway, and that an infusion of new blood and new methods was
desirable. Here and there the chairmen were obstacles to reform.
They had perhaps occupied their posts for many years, having been
elected again and again, even when age had enfeebled them.' When
the chairman of the Maldon Board of Guardians, in mid-Essex, retired in 1901, he could look back on twenty-six years in office, while
the vice-chairman of a nearby Board, Chelmsford, had, in 1899, been
a Guardian for forty years. Such long-serving members of a Board,
however conscientious, were rarely the stuff of which reformers were
made and many would have echoed the heartfelt response of one Essex
Guardian around 1899 to a demand from the Local Government
Board for information about proposed improvements: 'It is safer to
say nothing.'

Although some unions, like these, were to remain largely unaffected, two changes began during the 1890s which in other areas had a

profound influence on the composition, and ultimately the policy, of the Boards of Guardians. The first was the election as Guardians of an appreciable number of women. Women had, in theory, been eligible to stand ever since 1834, provided they owned property of the required value, but when, in 1850, one woman did attempt to become a Guardian, the Poor Law Board rejected her application, on the grounds that 'the objections to the appointment of a female... are so manifest' that the question was not 'of practical importance'. It was not until 1875 that the first woman Guardian was elected, at Kensington, this time without the Local Government Board being consulted, and by 1885 fifty had been appointed. One of them was Louisa Twining, elected, as already mentioned, in the previous year, and when, in 1893, she retired to Tonbridge, which had never had an election, she speedily got herself on to the Board there, too. She found that, though the workhouse was basically well run, improvements were never considered and the inspecting Guardians invariably wrote in the official record book 'two lines...remarking that "everything was satisfactory and in good order"'. Louisa Twining contributed instead 'two pages of suggestions on the infirmary, schools, etc., referred to a sub-committee for consideration' which led to such useful expenditure as providing a separate brush and comb for each child and the installation of a stove in the girls' bath-room. After 1894, when as will be explained, it became easier to become a Guardian, the number of women on the Boards rose within a year to more than 800. In the West of England, never the most progressive of areas, there were by 1900 fifty women Guardians, out of a total of 2,000, but Inspector Preston-Thomas had mixed feelings about them, conceding that while some feminine influence on a Board could be valuable, 'The wrong sort of woman has sometimes a terrible capacity for adding acrimony to debate by inflicting pinpricks.' All but a few stalwart anti-feminists agreed, however, that female Guardians did much to humanise the Poor Law, and the number went on increasing, to 1,100 by 1907 and nearly 1,300 by 1909.

The other decisive event which was to leave its mark on the whole Poor Law was the election of the first working-class Guardians and of others, both working-class and middle-class, of avowedly Radical, or Socialist, ideas. The elections for Guardians were chosen battleground for the members of the Fabian Society, founded in 1883, and after half a century of rarely being contested, many elections for Guardians in the cities were now not merely fought, but fought on party lines. Until 1892, when the Liberals reduced it to £5, the usual minimum qualification for service as a Guardian had been renting property worth £40 a year, which ruled out all but the better off. In 1894 almost all remaining restrictions were abolished, so that anyone who had lived in a union for a year could stand for election and anyone enjoying the parliamentary franchise—that is almost all males over twenty-one—had the right to vote. In rural areas the separate election of Guardians was abolished and rural district councillors, elected on a democratic franchise, now became ex-officio Guardians for their parishes. At the same time, magistrates in both town and country ceased to be ex-officio Guardians and the rules about co-option were changed, each Board being entitled to co-opt up to four members, including its chairman, from outside.

In the countryside the changes in the law had little practical effect; electorally speaking, the population continued to touch its forelock to the squire. In the towns, however, within a few years, working-men Guardians ceased to be a novelty, and in a few places the composition and attitude of the Boards was transformed. In these areas, for the first time in their history, the 'Guardians of the Poor' really came to merit that proud title and instead of being the eager practitioners of 'severity' and 'deterrence' became their most implacable opponents.

Of nowhere was this to prove more true than of the so-called 'capital of poverty', the East London borough of Poplar which, like the other parts of dockland, sheltered a mass of casual labour, improvident, insecure, and even in prosperous times, dependent on the vagaries of wind and weather. In 1892 Poplar had elected to its Board of Guardians the only former workhouse inmate known to have served on such a body. William ('Will') Crooks was the son of a ship's stoker who had become unemployed after losing an arm in an industrial accident, and his mother struggled to support the family by out-work on oil-skin coats, often slaving away all night. Will's earliest memories – he had been born, one of six children, in 1852 – were of sleeping in an orange-box, as they could not afford a cot, and of being hungry. As one of the three oldest children he was allowed three slices of bread at each meal; the younger ones got only two and a half. When, in 1860, Mrs Crooks applied to the Guardians for out-relief, it was refused and the family were ordered into 'the big poor-house by Millwall Docks', where as a 'workhouse brat' Will tasted for himself the watery 'skilly' served at breakfast.

Eventually the family discharged themselves to a single room in Poplar High Street, from which, although illiterate, Mrs Crooks insisted on sending her children to school. Will left at thirteen to earn five shillings a week as a blacksmith's mate. Later he was apprenticed to a barrel-maker and after being sacked as an 'agitator' finally found work as a trade union official. In 1892 he became the first Labour member of the new London County Council and, as already mentioned, was elected to the Poplar Board of Guardians, serving as its chairman from 1898 to 1906. In 1901 he became mayor of Poplar and from 1903-1910 was a Labour MP. He died in 1921 at the age of sixty-nine.

Crooks's partner and successor in attacking the Poor Law was George Lansbury, the son of a railway timekeeper, who had also been brought up close to the East End waterfront. His family had, briefly and disastrously, emigrated to Australia, but he had then settled down to work in Whitechapel, in a relation's sawmill, of which he ultimately became the owner. Lansbury, formerly a Liberal, became in 1892 'a Socialist pure and simple'. At the age of thirty-three, he was elected to the Poplar Board of Guardians, along with Will Crooks and, like him, became in turn a member of the LCC, mayor of Poplar and a Labour MP. In 1931 he was elected leader of the Party in succession to Ramsay MacDonald, but due to his pacifist views he was forced to resign in 1935. He died in May 1940, the congregation at his cremation breaking into *The Red Flag* as his coffin vanished from sight.

Crooks and Lansbury had both qualified for election as Guardians before the law was changed but they soon demonstrated that a passive majority was no match for a determined minority. As Lansbury later explained:

> From the first moment I determined to fight for one policy only, and that was decent treatment for the poor people, and hang the rates!...I took as my policy that no widow or orphan, no sick, infirm or aged person, should lack proper provision of the needs of life, and able-bodied persons should get work or maintenance... I never could see any difference between outdoor relief and a state pension, or between the pension of a widowed queen and outdoor relief for the wife and mother of a worker. The nonsense about the disgrace of the Poor Law I fought against till, at least in London, we killed it for good and all.

The Poplar reformers' first target in 1892 was their own badly-run workhouses, as Lansbury later described;

My first visit to a workhouse was a memorable one. Going down the narrow lane, ringing the bell, waiting while an official with a not too pleasant face looked through a grating to see who was there, and hearing his unpleasant voice—of course, he did not know me—made it easy for me to understand why the poor dreaded and hated these places, and made me in a flash realise how all these prison or Bastille sort of surroundings were organised for the purpose of making self-respecting, decent people endure any suffering rather than enter . . . Officials, receiving-ward, hard forms, whitewashed walls, keys dangling at the waist of those who spoke to you, huge books for name, history, etc., searching, and then being stripped and bathed in a communal tub, and the final crowning indignity of being dressed in clothes which had been worn by lots of other people, hideous to look at, ill-fitting and coarse—everything possible was done to inflict mental and moral degradation. The place was clean: brass knobs and floors were polished, but of goodwill, kindliness there was none . . .

The mixed workhouse at Poplar was for me Dante's Inferno. Sick and aged, mentally deficient, lunatics, babies and children, able-bodied and tramps all herded together in one huge range of buildings. Officers, both men and women, looked upon these people as a nuisance, and treated them accordingly . . . Clothing was of the usual workhouse type, plenty of corduroy and blue cloth. No undergarments for either men or women, no sanitary clothes of any sort or kind for women of any age, boots were worn till they fell off . . .

On one visit I inspected the supper of oatmeal porridge . . . served up with pieces of black stuff floating around. On examination we discovered it to be rat and mice manure. I called for the chief officer, who immediately argued against me, saying the porridge was good and wholesome. 'Very good, madam', said I, taking up a basinful and spoon, 'here you are, eat one mouthful and I will acknowledge I am wrong.' 'Oh, dear no', said the fine lady, 'the food is not for me, and is good and wholesome enough for those who want it.' I stamped and shouted around till both doctor and master arrived, both of whom pleaded it was all a mistake, and promptly served both cocoa and bread and margarine.

After this Lansbury and his Labour colleagues 'visited the work-house early morning and late at night, discovering many gross irregularities' and eventually in 1894 persuaded the Local Government Board to hold an enquiry into the way it was run, as a result of which the offending officials were dismissed and a kinder regime instituted.

But it was not only in Poplar that change was in the air. Charles Booth's massive survey of the *Life and Labour of the People of London*, published between 1889 and 1903, had demonstrated that most poverty was 'involuntary', that is, not the fault of its victims, and that at least one in three old people reaching the age of seventy had to seek help from the state. A Royal Commission on the Aged Poor was set up and by 1895 the Liberal President of the Local Government Board was recommending unions not to intimidate old people to whom they granted out-relief by making them collect it from the workhouse. In the following year the Guardians were ordered, by his Conservative successor, to discriminate between 'the respectable aged who became destitute and those whose destitution is distinctly the consequence of their own misconduct', the former being offered out-relief as a matter of course, a change which should 'be generally made known to the poor in order that those really in need may not be discouraged from applying'. Four years later, in 1900, the same Minister reaffirmed that deserving elderly people 'should not be urged to enter the workhouse at all', unless their home circumstances made this inevitable, and reminded Boards that out-relief should be adequate to support an applicant. But this was too much for most Guardians and very few unions raised the allowance to 5s. a week, the minimum needed to live, from the more usual 1s. or 1s. 6d.

Between 1893 and 1900 various changes were recommended to make life more tolerable for those who did still enter the workhouse, as already, described.* Many Boards of Guardians either ignored such suggestions, or accepted them reluctantly, but in Poplar and a few other places, every concession was eagerly applied. Here both the workhouse and the Labour Yard were rejected as a solution to the problem of the unemployed—'able-bodied paupers', as the traditionalists in Whitehall thought of them—and when, in the winter of 1904-5, unemployment in the borough reached the appalling level of one wage-earner in four, the Guardians began to

*See Chapter 11

grant out-relief with a readiness unknown anywhere since 1834. Relieving Officers, instead of bearing censure for being excessively 'soft', found cases sent back with instructions to substitute a weekly allowance instead of an admission order for the workhouse, so that the cost of out-relief multiplied three-fold in a few weeks. Two 'farm colonies' for the unemployed were also set up on waste land in Essex, the men, to the great indignation of all Poor Law rigorists, actually being given pocket-money. Several similar projects were launched elsewhere, often by local authorities, from growing potatoes in Croydon to attempting to reclaim part of Chat Moss, the vast Lancashire swamp that three generations earlier had nearly defeated the railway engineers. This was a period when many parks were built and many roads improved, a timely development as the first ungainly motor vehicles began to chug along the streets and lanes, and in 1905 the Conservative government carried through the Unemployed Workmen Act to encourage all these ventures, though it was hedged round with restrictions. Experience also proved once again that artificially created work was always uneconomic, costing up to ten times the normal amount and there were, too, the inevitable, and not always unjustified, complaints about 'idlers', taking things easy at the council's expense.

But the worst stories of extravagance and indiscipline concerned the two 'farm colonies' established by the Poplar Board of Guardians at Laindon and Hollesley Bay in Essex, and there were also wild rumours of waste and corruption in the workhouse itself. These became so serious that in 1906, for the second time in twelve years, there was a Local Government Board enquiry into the union's affairs. This time, however, Lansbury and his supporters were not the accusers but the defendants, for the inspector conducting the investigation was a sworn enemy of out-relief to the able-bodied and anxious to discredit 'Poplarism'. The proceedings also provided the press, deeply suspicious of all Socialists, with a field day. When wild stories were told of Guardians becoming drunk in the workhouse cellar Will Crooks predicted that 'We shall have all this in the *Daily Mail* in the morning', and there, sure enough, it all was. One paper even printed a cartoon showing Crooks and Lansbury smoking cigars and calling for a fresh barrel of beer from the workhouse stores, though both were lifelong non-smokers and teetotallers. Other evidence involved such intriguing questions as whether one Guardian had been offered jellied eels by the workhouse master and if another's rolling gait resulted from too much union beer. (It was demonstrated in court that it was his natural walk, the result of years spent on shipboard.) However the inspector's Report, though critical of some other Guardians, specifically vindicated Crooks and Lansbury as having 'derived no personal profit' from such abuses as had occurred.

Lansbury was by now deeply involved in a far more important enquiry, for the Conservative government had set up, in December 1905, a Royal Commission on the Poor Law and the Unemployed on which he had been invited to serve. Another member of the Commission was Mrs Beatrice Webb, who was deeply suspicious of the Local Government Board's motives. 'They were going to use us to get certain radical reforms of structure', she wrote in her diary on 2 December, 'but we were also to recommend reversion to the principles of 1834 . . . To stem the tide of philanthropic impulse that was sweeping away the old embankment of deterrent tests to the receipt of relief.'

The Royal Commission, under the chairmanship of Lord George Hamilton, a Conservative ex-Cabinet Minister, included five former Guardians, several Poor Law officials, two economists, several clergy and a strong contingent from the Charity Organisation Society, which firmly opposed indiscriminate relief.

It carried out in the next four years the most thorough investigation into the whole Poor Law system since 1834. It held 200 meetings, questioned 1,300 witnesses, sent its special investigators into every corner of the country and itself visited and scrutinised many workhouses, including some which seemed to have changed little, as Beatrice Webb described:

> We have ourselves witnessed terrible sights. We have seen feeble-minded boys growing up in the workhouse, year after year, untaught and untrained, alternately neglected and tormented by the other inmates . . . We have . . . seen idiots who are physically offensive or mischievous, or so noisy as to create a disturbance by day and by night . . . living in the ordinary wards, to the perpetual annoyance and disgust of the other inmates. We have seen imbeciles annoying the sane, and the sane tormenting the imbeciles. We have seen half-witted women nursing the sick, feeble-minded women in charge of the babies, and imbecile old men put to look after the boys out of school hours. We have seen

expectant mothers, who have come in for their confinements . . . working, eating and sleeping in close companionship with idiots and imbeciles of revolting habits and hideous appearance.

Disappointingly, after a prodigious amount of labour, the Commission's members failed to agree. Fourteen signed a *Majority Report*, filling 654 large pages and containing 239 recommendations; the *Minority Report*, with four signatures, including those of Lansbury and Mrs Webb, was not far behind, amounting to 500 pages, with 53 detailed proposals for changes. The *Majority Report* condemned the Boards of Guardians as 'generally unsatisfactory' and recommended the creation of a new Poor Law authority in each county or county borough. Existing workhouses, said the *Report*, were 'often ill-administered and normally demoralising', and should be replaced by new and separate institutions for the different categories of inmate. The *Minority Report* went even further, advising that the Poor Law should be broken up, and that the care of the various groups covered by it — the children, the old, the insane and the unemployed — should be transferred to separate authorities, with a national Registrar of Public Assistance to co-ordinate out-relief, and a new Ministry of Labour to deal with unemployment.

In 1834 the recommendations of the Royal Commission on the Poor Law had been hurried into law with almost indecent haste; in 1909 neither Report produced any result at all. The Prime Minister, Mr Asquith, prophesied that 'You will find that Boards of Guardians will die hard', and his reforming Liberal Government remained preoccupied with other matters, including 'Lloyd George's Ambulance Wagon', that vast programme of social reform which might eventually make the Poor Law unnecessary. In 1908 the Children's Act had given local authorities new powers to keep under-privileged children out of the workhouse; on New Year's Day, 1909, old age pensions were introduced; in the same year a national network of labour exchanges was set up, to help anyone without work to find a job. Unemployment insurance, at first confined to men in only five trades, began in 1911, as did health insurance for lower-paid employees, though not for their families. Of all these reforms, the one which had the greatest long-term effect was the introduction of old age pensions at 7s. 6d. a week for a married couple and 5s. for a single person, though anyone with an income of more than £31 a year, or who had received poor relief during the previous twenty years, was excluded. This latter rule was abolished in 1911 but few of those already in the workhouse managed to leave it, having long since lost touch with friends and relations. But the effect of the 'Lloyd George', as the pension was sometimes known, on the rate of new admissions, was immediate. By 1913 it was being remarked in Essex that 'only helpless old people come in now'. A man whose parents, when he was a boy, kept a corner shop in a poor part of Salford where the workhouse, known locally as the 'grubber', towered over the area, recalled how formerly 'Some of our neighbours went there, honourable men and women after a lifetime's work.' Now such tragedies were fewer and 'old folk, spending their allowance at the shop would bless the name of Lloyd George as if he were a saint from heaven'.

Inside the Poor Law system, too, there were many improvements. By 1909 every part of London was provided with spacious new hospitals, technically for the destitute, which were not really workhouses at all, even in name, although they were scarce in the rest of the country. Many unions now found themselves, individually or in combination with others, responsible for such diverse institutions as asylums for the mentally ill, sanatoria for consumptives, homes for the blind, and nurseries and boarding schools for abandoned children. It was this trend, rather than any recurrence of the policy of 'deterrence', which accounted for the steady increase in the number of 'indoor paupers' from 190,000 in 1899 to 238,00 in 1908 and an all-time peak, 280,000, in 1912. Thereafter old age pensions, health insurance and the other measures already described brought the numbers down.

In 1911 the term 'able-bodied' had officially been dropped from the workhouse statistics and in 1913 an even more significant change occurred when the name 'workhouse' ceased to be used in official documents, which henceforward referred to 'poor law institutions'. The alteration reflected a change of attitude, as well as the twentieth-century preference for euphemism. But the establishment itself still survived.

23 The End of the Workhouse

At midnight tonight a page of English local
history will be turned over. *The Times*,
31 March 1930

The first world war, despite all the suffering it caused, produced
a dramatic improvement in the numbers on poor relief. The number
of 'indoor paupers' dropped between 1914 and 1919 by nearly
100,000 to 183,000, while the number on out-relief slumped to
285,000, the lowest figure for two centuries. Even the casual ward
felt the influence of events. The cynics had often said that nothing
would persuade a tramp to settle down but the war proved them
wrong: 7,800 people had spent the night of 1 January, 1914, in the
casual ward. By New Year's Day, 1919, it sheltered only 1,100
occupants, another all time low.*

The war had brought other changes, too. The Poor Law infirmaries, pressed into service to receive the floods of casualties from
France, had enhanced their reputation still further, and there were
now two new ministries concerned with social welfare, the Ministry
of Labour, carved out of the Board of Trade in 1917, and the Ministry
of Health, which in 1919 had replaced the Local Government Board.
Only the Poor Law itself had survived. The 600 unions, designed to
serve the needs of an agricultural, uneducated and unenfranchised
population of 14½ million, had lived on into the industrial age, in
which every adult male, and every female over 30, in a population of
38 million, had the vote. It was little wonder that a committee on post-
war reconstruction, under Sir Donald Maclean, agreed in 1918 that
the whole Poor Law system had outlived its usefulness.

By now the effect of old age pensions was being felt; in 1919 the
average age of the eleven inmates admitted to one Essex workhouse

---

*Another unexpected effect of the war was a sharp reduction in the number of
certified lunatics, from 140,000 on 1 January 1915 to 117,000 in 1919, after
which the former upward trend was resumed, to 141,000 in 1929. Only a small
proportion of these were, of course, detained in workhouses.

was 89. But, in general, post-war conditions brought a rapid and dramatic change for the worse as a wave of unemployment of unheard-of dimensions swept across the country, so that by the end of 1926 there were 2½ million people on out-relief and 226,000 more in institutions. The worst effects of unemployment fell on about 200 unions, which between them contained nearly half the population. Among them was George Lansbury's Poplar, where in 1921 thirty borough councillors, including several Guardians, were sent to jail for refusing to pay what they considered an unfair share of the cost of poor relief in London. After an event unique in British history, a council meeting held in jail, the government gave way and the released prisoners were carried back in triumph to East London.

Five years later, in 1926, the government at last took powers, under the Board of Guardians (Default) Act, to take over the management of any union which the Ministry of Health considered was not being properly run, and before long three Boards had peremptorily been ordered out of office to make way for men appointed from Whitehall. One was at West Ham, in East London, where one in ten of the 740,000 inhabitants was on relief. Another was Chester-le-Street, in Durham, which had defied Ministry orders not to pay relief to healthy out-of-work miners. The third, also a mining area, was Bedwelly in South Wales, where the union had by 1927 run up debts of a million pounds. Even though some Guardians were clearly eager to have a fight with a government they hated, the Poor Law system, despite unemployment insurance bearing some of the burden, seemed to be foundering under a weight of out-relief it had never been designed to bear.

The end for the Boards of Guardians and the unions came finally in sight on 27 November 1928 when Neville Chamberlain, as Minister of Health, moved the second reading of the Local Government Bill which, with its 155 clauses and twelve long schedules he rightly described as 'among the greatest measures... presented to Parliament for many years. The trouble with the Poor Law', explained Chamberlain, 'is the same today as it was in 1834... The charges for poor relief, which fluctuate violently from time to time... fall upon areas so small that the burden is apt to become suddenly completely crushing'. The incidence of poor rates was also unfair; in depressed Gateshead the inhabitants contributed 10s. 5d. in the pound to support the poor; the citizens of prosperous Blackpool had to find no more than 5d. At the same time, as other authorities increasingly shared with the Guardians the responsibility of caring for special groups like lunatics, a network of overlapping institutions had come into being, some overflowing with cases, some half-empty, while that old enemy of every reformer, the general mixed workhouse, still survived. One 'Poor Law Institution' on one night that month had contained 55 infirm and senile inmates, 18 certified mental defectives and 9 uncertified, 7 acutely sick patients, 6 epileptics and—no doubt a pleasant relief for the hard-pressed staff—1 able-bodied male and 3 healthy infants.

The solution to all these problems, the government believed, was to abolish the Boards of Guardians and the unions and to hand over all their old powers to the county councils and county boroughs, which would handle each type of case—the sick, the aged, the insane, the children, the destitute, the able-bodied—through 'a number of special authorities, each dealing with different ailments'. Responsibility for the destitute would pass to a new Public Assistance Committee, two-thirds of whose members would be elected members of the Council, the remaining third, who must include some women, being co-opted. A number of local Assistance Committees would be set up to examine applications for relief and advise the county committee on how to deal with them. As each would roughly cover a former union area, it might, suggested Chamberlain, be called 'The Guardians Committee ... a concession to sentiment, but after all sentiment is a very powerful factor in human affairs'.

Few laws had been more criticised than the Poor Law Amendment Act, but the Government's plan to repeal it had a cool reception. Backbenchers on both sides were indignant at the loss of Private Members' time to accommodate the Local Government Bill and many Conservatives disliked the changes in rating procedure which it involved. The Labour Party, dedicated since 1909 to abolishing the Poor Law and the Boards of Guardians, felt that the over-riding need in 1928 was to deal with even greater issues, such as unemployment and disarmament, and that in any case Chamberlain's proposals fell far short of the root-and-branch reform that was needed. Chamberlain's 'concession to sentiment'—a somewhat suspect one, considering his reputation as the most hard-hearted Poor Law minister for many generations, provoked particular scorn from the Labour spokesman, Arthur Greenwood. 'He calls his committee "Guardians" ', Greenwood reminded the House. 'He is going to use the Guardians, the Guardians whom he has steadily taught during the last four years to reduce their scales of relief and to refuse out-relief to able-bodied poor ... It is still a deterrent system which discourages people in their trouble from going to the Poor Law authorities. . . It does not want to see them. It wants to be rid of them.' Greenwood moved the rejection of the Bill on the grounds that it 'perpetuates the evils of the Poor Law system. . . makes no provision for the prevention of destitution and fails to make unemployment a national responsibility'.

Then it was the turn of the Liberals, whose parliamentary forebears had created the New Poor Law, but this once-mighty party had now shrunk to a divided, opportunist rump. Its spokesman refused to say whether his followers supported the Bill or not and eventually they split and marched into opposing lobbies. The second reading was finally carried by 344 votes to 165 and, after various concessions to the dissident Conservative back-benchers, the third reading was comfortably achieved, by 292 votes to 113. In the Lords the third reading was carried on 20 March 1929 by 70 to 11 and on 27 March 1929 the Local Government Bill received the Royal assent.

Two months later, before the new Act had come into force, the government was defeated in a general election which led, in June, to the second Labour Government and Arthur Greenwood, so recently the Bill's chief critic, now as Minister of Health, became its principal defender, even praising those same Guardians whom Labour had for so long attacked. 'The Guardians were not', he told a farewell gathering of Guardians from all over the country 'handing over a bankrupt concern, but a valuable institution, consisting of, besides bricks and mortar, an organisation . . . and traditions which must be utilised by the new authorities.' This was typical of the views expressed during these closing months of the unions' existence. The 1834 Poor Law vanished, if not in a blaze of glory, then at least in a welter of nostalgia. During March 1930 *The Times*, which had so often carried stories of Guardians' oppression, reported the melancholy consequences of their impending dissolution. The Brentford Board, it revealed, were presenting their chairman with a portrait of himself and their clerk with a grandfather clock; Southwark, much criticised in the past, was sadly surrendering to a museum its prized snuff boxes, used at meetings for ninety-six years, after a ceremony in which 'the mayor will be invited to take a final pinch from each of the snuff boxes and he will then pass them to the Guardians'. The Epsom Board, *The Times* reported, were to hold a farewell lunch at the 'institution', as the workhouse was now

known, on Monday 31 March 1930, the final day of their legal existence. The guest of honour was to be a man of ninety-four who
had retired only the previous year after sixty-two years' service. 'At
midnight tonight', wrote an anonymous author in *The Times* that
day, 'a page of English local history will be turned over... the
Guardians of the Poor will cease to hold office. . . The Poor Law becomes "public assistance".'

No public ceremony marked the end of the workhouse. No bonfires
blazed, no fireworks soared skywards, no processions marched in
triumph along the roads down which wretched, ragged families had
once stumbled into separation and near-captivity. The country was
settling down into the miseries of another great depression and if any
ghosts walked at midnight that Monday they went unobserved. Even
at Andover no eerie noise of breaking bones and squalling paupers
was reported from the former workhouse buildings (today part of
St John's Hospital for the aged), no phantom clatter of pots and pans
came from the steps where Hannah Joyce had been hurried on her
way by Mrs M'Dougal's 'skimmington'. If the phantom of Colin
M'Dougal swayed back down Andover High Street from *The Globe*
(still a pleasant hostelry), or Edwin Chadwick rose in protest from his
grave seventy miles away in Mortlake churchyard, they did so unseen.
The union system, born in bitterness and tumult, died not merely un-
lamented, but almost unremarked.

For many years after the institution had officially been abolished,
the name 'workhouse' remained in everyday use. One man, Walter
Barrett, now in his eighties, who had left school at eleven to work as
a farmer's boy in a fenland village and became Assistant Master of
a rural workhouse in Norfolk in the early 1940s, found that the
abolition of the former union had made little difference. 'The old staff,
trained in Poor Law ways, knew one prayer only: God save the
ratepayers and bless the relieving officer who keeps us supplied with
replacements, so we can sit tight in our jobs till the day of superannua-
tion comes.' This 'Poor Law Institution' was still a 'general mixed
workhouse' in all but name, sheltering within its walls a handful of
able-bodied males, a large contingent of old people, many of them ill,
a number of mental defectives, some unmarried mothers and a
nursery full of infants, still bluntly described in the Admission Book
as 'bastards'.

The chaplain, like the harassed curates of a century before, arrived
at 10.30 on Sunday morning and left sharp at 10.55 to get back to

his own church and according to one witness, never administered Communion, so as not 'to waste wine on paupers'. The partly co-opted 'Guardians' Committee' still consisted largely of farmers and gentry, while the few Labour members of the 'House Committee' tended to look down on the paupers, a term still in daily, though unofficial, use. Nor did the proceedings at meetings seem to have changed very much:

> A lot of time was spent patting the master and matron on the back for keeping expenses down in spite of rising costs, and bemoaning the soaring price of shrouds, which were the only things not supplied by tender. The undertaker . . . had cut his price to £6 out of which he had to supply a hearse costing 30s., four bearers at 5s. each, petrol for a journey of six miles to measure and another to bring the coffin, and finally the burial. It was my job to see that the coffin conformed to the standard laid down by the Public Assistance Committee.

Barrett was shocked at the scant ceremony which still attended a pauper's funeral and his protests about the use of the cheapest sort of coffin, made of unplaned deal, echo almost word for word those heard in the 1830s. On one occasion, 'knowing that one of the oldest inmates would not have a single mourner I put on my bowler hat and followed her coffin; there was a quick run into the church and a quicker, gabbled committal. I told the parson afterwards he did not waste a lot of time on it. "Why should I?," he said. "Do you know what fee I get, after waiting a couple of months for it?" '

Another nineteenth-century practice, the employment of mental defectives as cheap labour, was still prevalent in the 1940s, as the inmates were reminded on the cook's day off, when the weak-minded inmates made the meals. An annual inspection by a Home Office inspector failed in its object for the Poor Law 'grapevine' invariably gave prior warning of her arrival and, when she left the staff would see if her car turned left or right, and then telephone the next workhouse in that direction that ' "the old cow" from the Home Office was heading their way. Then all the mental defectives there would be taken off whatever task they were doing, be given a pep talk and told to wash and tidy themselves. When they were eventually asked by the inspector "Are you happy here?" none were so daft as to say "No", as they knew what a hell of a life they would have if they did'.

This cynicism, deserved or not—and it seems hard to believe an experienced inspector was quite so easily deceived—was apparently shared by the inmates, for the same observer found written under the chapel reading desk what is probably the last workhouse poem to have survived :

> God bless the squire and his relations
> And keep me in my proper station.
> God made bees, the bees make honey,
> The paupers do the work
> And the Guardians get the money.
> Now I am compelled to sit and hear
> What the parson says while standing here;
> He tells us we are miserable sinners—
> He'd be the same on workhouse dinners.
> But he is fat like well-fed pork,
> He eats and drinks but does no work.
> We hear him promise that when we die
> There'll be great big helpings
> Of pie in the sky.
> Then he shuts his book
> And slings his hook. Amen.

The night-nurse in this institution was also cast in the traditional mould. 'That old nurse had held the post . . . for over forty years . . . She was so fat that she waddled around and . . . slept nearly all day and most of the night.' One night when this Assistant Master had to tour the building after midnight, following an air raid warning—it was, of course, wartime—he found 'the night-nurse . . . reclining in a big basket chair with her feet up on another, fast asleep and snoring away like an old sow. There she remained until woken by her alarm clock after 5 a m, thereby explaining a minor mystery: why all deaths in the infirmary were recorded as having occurred between 5 and 6 in the morning '.

Since this man and his wife were only allowed one full day off a month, plus alternate Sundays, and were required even then to be back by 10 p m, they finally decided 'that institutional life was not in our line', but before they left they witnessed one of the last celebrations of that once-famous occasion, Christmas Day in the workhouse:

> As Christmas approached everyone began to get excited. There was an allowance of four shillings and nine pence per inmate for extra comforts; part of this went on a small barrel of beer...

The work-shys, the mental defectives and the old men had two, sometimes three, big helpings of roast pork, parsnips and potatoes besides two generous portions of plum pudding; each man was allowed a pint of beer. I was detailed to feed the infirm, bedridden old men; they did not want a lot of food but their watery eyes shone when I filled their mugs with beer. 'I've waited twelve months for this', said one old chap. By wangling an exchange of an empty jug for a full one I managed to give the old men a double issue, and their thanks as they smacked their lips was well worth the questioning I had to undergo . . . A concert in the evening was a wash-out . . .

Boxing Day was the day for the staff dinner and dance; by the early hours of the next morning things slowed down. It was my day off duty but [my wife] had to be on duty at seven thirty. When she went I snuggled down for an extra hour's sleep but . . . she came back and said: 'You'll have to get up; none of the porters have reported for duty and there is no one to supervise serving breakfast. The milk and bread vans are waiting to be checked in and three male and one female patients have died in the night... When I had checked the bread and milk I collared a couple of work-shy able-bodied inmates and put them on to slicing bread for breakfast; then I found a nurse willing to help me remove the dead inmates to the mortuary. At last I rang the bell to let the grumbling crowed know that breakfast was ready; the porridge was burnt because the cook had a hangover, and there was no hot water as the stoker must have lost his way coming to work. In the dining hall all the able-bodied inmates looked at the burnt offering placed before them . . . I had to conform to the rule that had been in force since the building was erected that God must be thanked before and after the workhouse diet had been disposed of . . . I told the men to stand up and, with due reverrence, bowed my head and staggered those still hungry chaps by saying: 'Thank God for that little lot, and I know you could have done with more.'

The ending of the Napoleonic war in 1815 had ushered in a period of unprecedented hunger and misery, leading to the introduction of the New Poor Law. Victory in the second world war in 1945 was followed instead by a widespread demand for social justice, and the election of the first Labour government with real power, followed by the consolidation, if not the foundation, of what is now known as the welfare state. In 1946 the Family Allowances Scheme was introduced and in 1948 the Labour Government put on the statute book four great Acts: National Insurance, which unified all the existing state insurance schemes; the National Insurance (Industrial Injuries) Act, which replaced the old system of workmen's compensation; the National Health Service Act, which created a universal free medical service; and the National Assistance Act, which, when it became law on 5 July 1948, destroyed the last vestiges of the Poor Law.

Since 1948 successive governments, Conservative as well as Labour, have repudiated, one by one, all the old principles of 1834. Not merely are a vast range of benefits available, but large sums of public money are spent urging those qualified to apply for them. Rent rebates for those in full-time work, allowances even for childless widows, attendance allowance for people caring for members of their own families in their own home, Supplementary Benefit for the old, Social Security payments to deserted wives, maternity allowance and free hospital treatment for unmarried mothers—every type of aid that the men who created the workhouse most distrusted, is now provided as of right. It would be hard, too, to find a government department further removed in spirit from the Poor Law Commissioners than the Department of Health and Social Security, created in 1968, the latest in a long line of progressively more mildly-named predecessors, from the Public Assistance Board to the Ministry of Health. It would be short-sighted to pretend that poverty had vanished. But destitution and suffering on the nineteenth-century scale have certainly disappeared; today a minister or local authority is far more likely to be taken to task for spending too little on the under-privileged than too much.

As for the workhouses, those gaunt monuments to the nineteenth century's faith in the reformative powers of bare brick, simple diet and harsh discipline, those still in use, often as old folk's homes, are barely recognisable behind their carefully tended lawns and flower beds. Soon even these survivors of a departed era may vanish for in November 1971 the Secretary of State for Health and Social Security urged local authorities to prepare plans for demolishing and replacing their old, out-of-date buildings. Soon the last workhouse may vanish without trace.

It will be a tragedy if one at least is not preserved as a reminder of how the wealthier part of the British people once treated their less-fortunate fellow countrymen. The history of the workhouse surely has much to teach every citizen today: that poverty is a misfortune, not a crime; that human suffering is too high a price to pay for tidy administration; that authority in enclosed communities should be subject to constant scrutiny; that it is better for a dozen spongers to grow fat than for one deserving applicant to be turned away; above all, perhaps, that in all the affairs of life there is no substitute for compassion.

Appendix: Workhouse Architecture

by

Richard Wildman

In 1841, the architect and critic, Augustus Welby Northmore Pugin, published the second edition of *Contrasts: or a Parallel between the Noble Edifices of the Fourteenth and Fifteenth Centuries, and Similar Buildings of the Present Day; showing the Present Decay of Taste*. A new pair of illustrations, entitled 'Contrasted Houses for the Poor', showed a medieval hospital, where the bedesmen received charitable treatment, and were given a decent burial, side by side with a new union workhouse, where, according to Pugin, cells, starvation, and cruel punishments brought the pauper inmates, not to the grave, but to the anatomical dissecting-table. A further pair, 'Contrasted Towns', includes in the foreground of 'The Town in 1840' (as opposed to the same town in 1440) an identical octagonal workhouse building, only this time captioned 'the new jail'.

Pugin would have been the last to share the optimistic hope expressed by an obscure architect, R.P. Browne, that well-designed workhouses (he was thinking of his design for the 'Greenwich Union Poor-house', built in 1844) would demonstrate to pauper children that 'their Union has provided an asylum, not a prison, against their day of need'. A professional point of view closer to Pugin's was expressed by T.D. Barry, speaking to the Liverpool Architectural and Archaeological Society in 1851. He described how 'the miserable inmates of union workhouses . . . were huddled together three tiers of beds in a room's height, like the scanty provision made in emigrant ships for those classes of men whose poverty alone brands them to a fate little preferable to the worst features of slavery'.

Barry, who is otherwise utterly sunk in oblivion, specialized in the 'superintendence and designing of Workhouses' and claimed to 'have had many opportunities of examining the different systems laid down by Messrs Scott and Moffatt, by Mr Kempthorne . . . by

Mr Wilkinson, the architect at the present time to the Irish Poor Law Board, and others less publicly known.' Sampson Kempthorne was the progenitor of the new Unions, but Scott and Moffatt effectively cornered a large part of the market in workhouse design in the southern and central areas of England. They worked for about 53 unions in the first ten years of the Act, from Billericay and Great Dunmow in Essex to Flax Bourton in Somerset and Tiverton in Devon, and taking in Northampton, Oundle, Towcester, Amersham, Winslow, and Buckingham (Scott was born at Gawcott nearby).

It is a colossal irony that George Gilbert Scott, the most successful of workhouse architects, should have been converted to the Gothic Revival style through reading the works of Pugin, who detested the workhouse and all it stood for. Pugin, who abominated both the Classical and the Tudor styles customarily employed for public buildings in his time (Scott's earlier unions are Classical, his later ones Tudor) died insane in 1852, prematurely aged at 40. Scott died, knighted and worth a fortune, in 1878, the busiest architect of all time (over 750 commissions). He preferred to forget his work on the unions.

An estimated 350 new union workhouses were erected within five years of the passing of the Poor Law Amendment Act in 1834, and the architectural journals of the time are full of references to this new and flourishing aspect of professional activity. Sampson Kempthorne, 'architect to the Commissioners', and W.J. Donthorne, the Norfolk workhouse specialist, were both founder-members of the Royal Institute of British Architects.

Kempthorne supplied plans and perspective views published in the *First Annual Report* of the Poor Law Commissioners in 1835. They consisted of alternative designs for a three-storey 'Workhouse for 300 Paupers', one cruciform and the other Y-shaped in plan (with a hexagonal boundary wall), together with plans of each floor. The Commissioners' *Second Annual Report* (1836) includes Kempthorne's view and plans of a smaller, two-storey 'Workhouse for 200 Paupers, adapted for the less Pauperised Districts'. All these are general mixed workhouses, contrary to Edwin Chadwick's original intentions and Chadwick appears to have borne a grudge against Kempthorne (as well as against the Commissioners) on this account. The Andover Union was built to Kempthorne's design, published in the *Second Annual Report*.

When the first union plans appeared they were well-received by, amongst others, *The Architectural Magazine and Journal of Improvement in Architecture, Building, and Furnishing, and in the Various Arts and Trades connected therewith*, edited by the garden architect John Claudius Loudon, a pioneer of the semi-detached house. *The Architectural Magazine's* highly complimentary review declared that Kempthorne's plans in the *First Report* 'appear to us, from a cursory inspection, excellently arranged; and it is most gratifying to see the attention that has been paid by the architect to the principles of separation and classification, to cleanliness, to ventilation, and to general convenience.' The reviewer even feared that 'Such comfortable establishments . . . where labour was not constantly enforced . . . might soon create a greater demand for such communities than it would be possible to supply; but, under the vigilant management proposed . . . there will be no temptation for any to enter them that . . . can get employment elsewhere.'

Similarly rapturous was the reception afforded by the *British Almanac* in 1836 to the Abingdon union workhouse, the first to be completed, construction having begun in mid March and the inmates arriving in October. 'All the buildings are substantial erections of brick, and the entire expense was about £ 8,500', as 'large workshops . . . have very materially increased the total expense.' The average cost of the new workhouses was nearer £ 5,000. The Abingdon Union is Kempthorne's first (Y-plan) design from the *First Report*, but with an extra (fourth) storey added, resulting in variations in the internal arrangement and the *British Almanac* remarked how it provided 'with great facility, the division into six yards, for the better classification of the inmates. In the centre [of the] building are the governor's rooms, for the inspection of the whole establishment'.

The year before, Loudon's *Architectural Magazine* had noted that Kempthorne's first plans 'are arranged more or less on the panopticon principle, the master's house being in the centre, or in the focus of whatever may be the form of the plan' and this raises the whole question of the origin of the archetypal workhouse plan. According to an unsigned article, entitled 'New Poor-Law Workhouses', which appeared in the *Illustrated London News*, 7 November 1846, the official designs in the Commissioners' *First Report* (1835) and *Second Report* (1836) 'have the name of an architect attached to them, but, in fact, are tracings from designs for American prisons'. The *Illustrated London News* article reproduced Kempthorne's own perspective view of the Andover Union but with the subtle addition of three human figures, those of two paupers approaching to seek admission, and of another slouching despondently at the main door. Its author, widely believed to be Chadwick, blamed Kempthorne for much of the odium incurred by the New Poor Law. 'The young and inexperienced architect who appropriated these [American] prison plans to a purpose for which they were never intended, was not, it may be supposed, overmuch startled when Cobbett denounced the new buildings as "Bastilles".' By contrast, the *Illustrated London News* article carried a large picture of ex-Assistant Commissioner Parker's design for Canterbury workhouse, similar to those already erected at Aylesbury and Rye ('from the windows of the Aylesbury workhouse there is a delightful view of the Chiltern Hills, and from the Rye workhouse the coast of France is discernible on a clear day').

The allegation that 'American prison plans' were the source for Kempthorne's designs is hard to substantiate. The inspiration seems to have come rather from Bentham's Panopticon, or Inspection House, devised in 1787, a circular building, with rooms radiating from a central 'shaft' containing, on each floor, a control point from which an overseer could direct the labour and observe the actions of everyone ranged around him. Jeremy Bentham's brother Samuel first thought of it in Russia, where he planned to build for Prince Potemkin a circular arsenal. Jeremy thought the principle could 'serve equally well for schools, hospitals, lazarettos, poor-plan buildings [i.e. accommodation for the destitute], houses of correction, lunatic asylums, orphanages, nurseries, institutions for the blind and deaf, homes for deserted young women, factories, and even a gigantic chicken-coop'. The true Benthamite Panopticon was never built in England, though two plans resembling it were provided for prisons in America, at Richmond (Virginia) and Pittsburgh, and applied, as it often was, to the new unions, the name was inappropriate for two reasons. Firstly, the true Panopticon was to be a circular construction, not a radial one, and secondly, the idea of continuous observation of the inmates by the workhouse master received lip-service only in the official plans. The master's accommodation was placed at the centre of the plan, with the central corridors of the wards leading off from this block, but there was no visual link directly between centre and wings, especially when there were staircases on each side of the central tower.

Although each Board of Guardians was at liberty to invite designs from local architects and builders, or workhouse specialists like Scott and Moffatt, the Commissioners' designs generally supplied the basic structural arrangements, though embellishments were often added to the entrance-block, which contained the Guardians' Board Room. Relations between architect and potential clients were not always cordial, however, as Loudon's *Architectural Magazine* reveals. In 1836, a correspondent from Bishop's Stortford wrote that 'new workhouses are erecting at Saffron Walden, Lexden, and Manningtree. From the latter place, the plans were returned to the unsuccessful candidates unpacked, and completely exposed to the curious, with the descriptive particulars lost or detained. We would contrast this with the polite and gentlemanly conduct of the Stortford Union. The architects received their plans back after the decision, carefully packed, and each bearing a letter of thanks from the Board of Guardians.'

Although, for various reasons, most unions preferred to erect brand new buildings, some existing workhouses were converted under the new Act, especially those belonging to 'Gilbert unions' or other pre-1834 incorporations. A notable example is the Bedford House of Industry, now the north wing of Bedford General Hospital, designed by the architect John Wing and built 1794-96, which is described in a guidebook of 1831 as 'a handsome and extensive mansion . . . a large and regular building of brick', four storeys high (including attics) with a chapel and wash-houses forming flanking wings.

Very few small parish workhouses have survived, and the rare survivors, having reverted to domestic use, are often indistinguishable from their neighbours. The eighteenth-century workhouse at Church End, Kempston, in Bedfordshire is an example and there are others at Ravensden and Renhold in the same county. Very unusually, two early nineteenth-century parish workhouses survive in Cambridge: those of St Michael's Parish (in Gifford's Place, off Green Street), built in 1794, and of St Andrew-the-Great (in St Tibb's Row, near St Andrew's Hill), built in 1829, and sold by the Guardians of the Cambridge Union in 1838, on completion of the new workhouse in Mill Road, now the Maternity Hospital. Both these parish workhouses became shops and/or dwellings. St Andrew's is a long, three-storey building of gault brick with its original sash-windows of squat proportions. When put up for sale in 1838 it was said to have 'a sitting-room, large hall, back kitchen, cellar, yard, pump of good water and twelve good bedrooms'.

Workhouse architecture has not been the subject of serious study since the 1830s, though some of the unions built then are of considerable architectural importance, especially in their localities. Some are impressive in size, like 'the magnificent palatial-looking structure at Barn-hill, to be used as the Glasgow Barony parish poor's house', described by *The Architect* in 1850, which 'when completed, will form the largest inhabitable building in Scotland' with accommodation for 2,000 inmates. Some are interesting for their style like the union at Ampthill in Bedfordshire, designed by James Clephane in 1836, which displays Italianate influence in the form of round-arched windows in groups of three, on each floor. The whole building is a monumental design in which large square 'pavilions' of three storeys terminate each of the four arms of a cross, a fifth 'pavilion' standing in the centre of the cruciform plan. The material used is a warm, brown-red brick.

The nearest approach, an architectural inventory of union workhouses (and some earlier houses of industry, etc.) can be found in published form in Sir Nikolaus Pevsner's *Buildings of England* series (by counties), from 1951 onwards; and, in unpublished form, but very much more detail, in the Department of the Environment's *Lists of Buildings of Special Architectural or Historic Interest*, prepared under the 1947 Town and Country Planning Act. The more recent volumes of the inventories published by the Royal Commission on Historical Monuments (for example, the magnificent *City of Cambridge*, 1959) also describe the early unions (and former parish workhouses, where these survive). But even in these compilations there are, inevitably, many omissions.

The chief barrier to appreciation of the workhouse as a significant architectural species is, of course, its unpleasant associations. But as these gradually recede into folk-memory, it becomes possible for us to understand more clearly how the new unions became, in the middle of the last century, 'objects of civic pride and self-satisfaction, rather like swimming-baths or libraries today'.

A mid-Victorian poster, designed by an unknown artist for a rag-and-bone merchant, and found by E. McKnight Kauffer. The woman is saying, 'You see, Richard, the wretched state to which you have brought your wife and children through your waste and improvident habits.' (*Mary Evans Picture Library*)

A Note on Sources

A Note on Sources

The place of publication is London unless otherwise stated. Publishers are omitted, except for relatively recent books. Where a book carries no publication date—which can easily render it almost useless— I have indicated this by the letters 'n.d.'. Even when the date of publication is known, however, the events described may have taken place several years before, for workhouse visitors often described conditions 'some time ago'. Full details of a book are given only the first time it is mentioned.

General Accounts

The indispensable source is Sidney and Beatrice Webb, *English Poor Law History* (3 volumes, first published 1927-9, reprinted Frank Cass & Co., 1963), supplemented by *English Poor Law Policy* (first published 1910, reprinted Frank Cass & Co., 1963). The outstanding earlier authority is Sir George Nicholls, *History of the English Poor Law* (2 volumes, with a third by Thomas Mackay, bringing the work up to 1898, 1899). The 1904 edition includes a biography of George Nicholls by H. W. Willink, a Guardian who had known and admired him. Gilbert Slater's *Poverty and the State* (Constable, 1930) is a useful introduction to the subject. Michael E. Rose, *The English Poor Law 1780-1930* (David & Charles, Newton Abbot, 1971) provides a helpful collection of documents, informatively edited, while Brian Inglis, *Poverty and the Industrial Revolution* (Hodder & Stoughton, 1971) gives a comprehensive account of contemporary social conditions and ideas. Richard Hine, *History of Beaminster* (Wessex Press, 1914), a long and model local history, contains an interesting chapter on a typical rural workhouse. The most informative source on workhouse conditions, which includes quotations from a wide range of observers, is the *Journal of the Workhouse Visiting Society*, which appeared from January 1859 to January 1865. I have not given detailed references every time I have used it, but the approximate date is usually obvious from the context. Any descriptive passage or opinion not otherwise attributed is likely to be from the *Journal* and any factual statement from the Webbs' *History*. I also used constantly those friends of every researcher, the *Dictionary of National Biography*, the *Annual Register*, *Hansard* and *The Times*.

1 Whipped to Death

On early history of the Poor Law I used Sir Frederick Morton Eden, *The State of the Poor or a History of the Labouring Classes in England from the Conquest to the Present Period* (3 volumes, 1797) supplemented by Nicholls and the Webbs, whose Volume 1, *The Old Poor Law*, describes the effects of the Law of Settlement. On the origin of the word 'workhouse' I consulted the 1933 edition of the *Oxford English Dictionary*. The case of the old man moved from Bristol is described in *The Parish Reformers Penny Magazine*, XII (1834) and that of William Withers in G. R. Wythen Baxter, *The Book of the Bastilles or the History of the Working of the New Poor Law* (1841). The sick pauper dosed with pills was described by the Rev. Thomas Spencer, *The Successful Application of the New Poor Law in the Parish of Hinton Charterhouse* (1836). The Middlesex scale of expenses was quoted by a Late Relieving Officer in *The Poor Laws Unmasked, being a General Exposition of our Workhouse Institutions* (1859). The 'first historian of the Poor Laws' was the Rev. Dr Richard Burn, *The History of the Poor Laws with Observations* (1764) and 'one of the first Poor Law Commissioners' was Nicholls. The legal bills in the Cerne Abbas union are mentioned by Elizabeth Cockburn in 'The Cerne Abbas Union Workhouse' (*Proceedings of Dorset Natural History and Archaelogical Society*, Vol. 94, 1972), and the case of the woman sent back to Southampton by John Halcomb in *A Practical Measure of Relief from the Present System of the Poor Laws* (1926). The case of the condemned man in Canterbury is cited by Dr Joseph Rogers, *Reminiscences of a Workhouse Medical Officer* (1889) and that of the tradesman who lost his job by Mackay.

2 Much Oppressed

The early history of the workhouse is largely taken from Eden's *The State of the Poor*, as are the quotations from residents of Beverley and Maidstone. John Cary's work in Bristol is described by Nicholls and Mathew Marryott's by the Webbs' *History*, who also quote the pamphlet about the Suffolk incorporation which includes details about Nacton House and the riot. The remark that 'Suffolk is famous for its workhouses' and details of the financial failure of some workhouses come from the Rev. C. D. Brereton, *An Inquiry into the Workhouse System and the Law of Maintenance in Agricultural Districts* (n.d., c. 1823) and the material about Jonas Hanway and the Foundling Hospital from John H. Hutchins, *Jonas Hanway 1712—1786* (SPCK, 1940). The Preston man referred to is Thomas Whittaker, *Life's Battles in Temperance Armour* (1892), and the account of the premiums offered for apprentices appears in the *Journal*. On Gilbert's Act I used Thomas Gilbert, *A Bill Intended to be Offered for the Better Relief and Employment of the Poor* (1775). The text from George Crabbe can be found in *Poetical Works* (OUP, 1914). The author of *An Essay on Parish Workhouses* (1786) was Edmund Gillingwater. The descriptions of workhouses in the 1790s come from Eden. I also consulted Joyce Godber, *History of Bedfordshire* (Bedfordshire County Council, 1969), an excellent book containing much detail about the working of the Poor Law in the county.

3 The Road to Ruin

The opening quotation can be found in Rose, *The English Poor Law 1780-1930*, and the details on the Speenhamland system can be found in the Webbs' *History* and in Nicholls. There is a vast literature on out-relief before 1834. The examples of inefficiency in Kent, including the story of 'the healthy, blooming girl' and the verbatim report on Parker are taken from Sir Francis Head, *English Charity* (1835), and other information on conditions at this time is given in the *First Annual Report of the Poor Law Commissioners* (1835) which is especially invaluable for the twelve months it covers. Mackay describes the mysterious entries in parish registers, the alternating overseers, the sale of Mrs Cook and the wrangle at the altar. A similar case of enforced marriage, including a detailed tariff, can be found in the Rev. Wm Norris, *A Letter to the Inhabitants of the Parish of Warblington, Hants, on the New Poor Law, its Origin and Intended Effect* (1836). The Berkhamsted vicar is quoted by Samuel Robinson, *A Letter to Charles Hindley, Esquire, M.P. on the Subject of the New Poor Law*

(Ashton under-Lyme, 1837). The case of the Barnstaple clergyman is quoted in the *Second Annual Report of the Poor Law Commissioners* (1836). The critical accounts of out-relief were given by the Rev. Thomas Spencer, *Application*. The rector of Little Massingham was Brereton, *An Inquiry*. The critic of the magistrates' powers was a Guardian (actually Nassau Senior), *Remarks on the Opposition to the Poor Law Amendment Act* (1841). The Webbs in Volume 1 of *English Poor Law History* give a good account of the 'farming' of the poor and Eden also quotes numerous examples. The Dorset magistrate who denounced the Speenhamland system was D.O.P. Okeden, *A Letter to the Members in Parliament for Dorsetshire on the Subject of Poor Relief and Labourers' Wages, by D.O.P. Okeden, one of the Acting Magistrates for that County* (Blandford, 1830) and other information about conditions in Dorset, including wage rates and relief scales, is provided by Henry Walter, *A Letter to the Rev. H.F. Yeatman, Acting Magistrate for Dorset and Somerset* (1833). Examples of men being kept idle or employed as 'roundsmen' are given by Mackay. The paupers who stood in the pound are spoken of by J.G. (i.e. J. Godfery), *Truth Proclaimed or a Few Words to the Labourers of England on the Advantages of the New over the Old Poor Law* (1836). The paupers of Princes Risborough are described by the Rev. J. H. Gurney, *The New Poor Law Explained and Vindicated: A Plain Address to the Labouring Classes among his Parishioners*. The paupers at Pollington and the 'slave market' are quoted by Rose. The Rev. T. Mozeley, *Reminiscences, chiefly of Towns, Villages and Schools* (1885) was disillusioned at Deddington. Details of the poor rates at various dates are given by the Webbs, Volume 1, and by Brereton in *Inquiry* and in his *Observations on the Administration of the Poor Law in Agricultural Districts* (Norwich, n.d., but in fact 1822), which also describes the idleness of men on out-relief. Mackay describes the abandonment of Cholesbury and the facts can be found in Inglis, *Poverty and the Industrial Revolution*. On the 1830 riots I consulted reports of the trials in *The Times* and Barbara Kerr, *Bound to the Soil, a Social History of Dorset 1750-1918* (John Baker, 1968). I also used T. R. Malthus, *First Essay on Population* (1798, reprinted 1926 by Macmillan) and G. D. H. Cole, *The Life of William Cobbett* (Home & Van Thal, 1947), which quotes *Surplus Population*. On enclosures I followed J. L. and Barbara Hammond, *The Village Labourer* (Guild Books ed., 2 volumes, 1948). The references to Parliament before 1834 come from Mackay. The Bingham experiment and other pre-

1834 deterrent workhouses are described by the Webbs and I also used the following contemporary accounts: John Thomas Becher, *The Anti-Pauper System, Exemplifying the Positive and Practical Good realised by the Relievers and the Relieved under the Frugal, Beneficial and Lawful Administration of the Poor Laws prevailing at Southwell* (1828); John W. Cowell, *A Letter to the Rev. John T. Becher of Southwell in reply to certain Charges and Assertions made in the Introduction to the second edition of his Anti-Pauper System, recently published* (1834); Overseer (in fact George Nicholls), *Eight Letters on the Management of our Poor and the General Administration of the Poor Laws in the two Parishes of Southwell and Bingham* (1822), an indispensable source on the philosophy behind the workhouse system; A County Magistrate, *Observations on the Poor Law* (1834); the Rev. J. Bosworth, *The Practical Means of Reducing the Poor's Rate, Encouraging Virtue and for Effecting a Grand Moral Improvement in the Lower Classes of Society* (1824); John Leslie *Remarks on the Present State of the Poor Law Question with Illustrations of the Advantages arising to the Poor by Reason of the Workhouse System of Relief* (1834) and the Rev. D. Capper, *Practical Results of the Workhouse System as Adopted in the Parish of Great Missenden, 1833-4.*

4 Doing their Duty

On Bentham and his ideas I used Inglis, *Poverty and the Industrial Revolution* and on Chadwick, S. E. Finer, *The Life and Times of Sir Edwin Chadwick* (Methuen, 1952). I also consulted *The Instructions from the Central Board of Poor Law Commissioners to Assistant Commissioners* (1832). Their findings are contained in the massive *Report of the Poor Law Inquiry Commissioners* (1834) and in the shorter *Administration and Operation of the Poor Laws: Extracts from the Information received from His Majesty's Commissioners as to the Administration and Operation of the Poor Laws* (1833). The full text of each Assistant Commissioner's report appears in a series of *Appendixes* to the main *Report* (1834-5). The quotations from Head are from *English Charity*. Dr Kay's account of the palatial Suffolk workhouses is quoted in the *Second Annual Report*. On Harriet Martineau I used her *Autobiography* (1877) and *Illustrations of Political Economy* (1834). On Brougham I consulted: *Henry Peter*

(*Lord*) *Brougham, Life and Times, by Himself* (1871); George Henry Francis, *Henry, Lord Brougham and Vaux, a Critical Biography* (1853); Lander Praed, *Life of the Celebrated Lord Brougham* (1868) a short obituary pamphlet; and Frances Hawes, *Henry Brougham* (Cape, 1957), by far the best account. Brougham's nightly study of the Assistant Commissioners' reports was witnessed by Charles Knight, *Passages of a Working Life during Half a Century* (Volume 2, 1864). The quotations from Francis Place and John Stuart Mill can be found in Volume 2 of the Webbs. The life of Nassau Senior is described by F. Boase, *Modern English Biography* (Volume 3, 1901, reprinted by Cass, 1965). A useful summary intended for Guardians and magistrates is *Outline of the Poor Law Amendment Act* (1834).

5 Mr Chadwick's Cold Bath

The start of operations by the Poor Law Commissioners is described by Nicholls and Willink. Chadwick's role is described by Finer who also quotes the 'cold bath' remark. Life at the Poor Law Commission in its early days is described by W. E. Davies, *Sir Hugh Owen, his Life and Life-work* (1895). The *First Annual Report* has copies of the documents issued to the unions. Lord Melbourne's opinion of Head is quoted by the Webbs, Volume 2, and the personality of Tom Stevens is described by his friend, the Rev. Thomas Mozeley, *Reminiscences, chiefly of Oriel College and of the Oxford Movement* (2 volumes, 1882). Head's work in East Kent, including Ashford, was observed by Edward Hughes, *A Compendium of the Operation of the Poor Law Amendment Act, with some Practical Observations on its Present Results and Future Apparent Usefulness* (1836), a very helpful short account. The anecdote on the clergyman at Sutton comes from William Dennison, *Abstract of the Evidence before the Committee... into the Operation and Affect of the Poor Law Amendment Act* (1837). The stopping of the allowance to the poor can be found in Robert Blakey, *An Exposure of the Cruelty and Inhumanity of the New Poor Law Bill as exhibited in the Treatment of the Helpless Poor by the Board of Guardians of the Morpeth Union* (1837), and John Bowen, *A Refutation of some of the Charges preferred against the Poor with some Account of the Working of the New Poor Law in the Bridgwater Union* (2nd edition, 1837). Events at Andover in the 1830s were very fully exposed in the *Minutes of Evidence* bound with the *Report of the*

Select Committee Appointed to Enquire into the Administration of the Andover Union and into the Management of the Union Workhouse (2 volumes, 1846). The *Daily Dispatch* report on the treatment of the old at Hellingley is quoted by Baxter, *The Book of the Bastilles*. The change of attitude to unmarried mothers after 1834 is described in the *First* and *Second Annual Reports*, the former contributing the quotations from Bradfield and Flintshire, the latter that from Oxford. The case of the Easingwold magistrates was described by Mackay. A defence of the unpopular bastardy clauses can be found in the Rev. T. Garnier, *Plain remarks upon the New Poor Law more particularly Addressed to the Labouring Classes* (Winchester, 1835) and in Assistant Commissioner Sir Edmund Head (not to be confused with Sir Francis Head), *Report on the Law of Bastardy with a Supplementary Report on a Cheap Civil Remedy for Seduction* (1840).

6 Offering the House

The main sources for general historical background and also for the anecdotes about Chesham and those otherwise unattributed are the *First* and *Second Annual Reports*. Gilbert on union bread is quoted by Mackay; the clergyman at Bradford-on-Avon is found in Spencer, *Application* and the 'plan' to drown Sussex children in Owen Chadwick, *The Victorian Church, Part 1* (Black, 1966). The details about *Marcus* and Nassau Senior are quoted by the Webbs. The chairman of the Basingstoke Guardians was W. L. Sclater, *A Letter to the Poor Law Commissioners on the Workings of the New System* (1836). The application of the Act at Nottingham was described by Nicholls and the troubles at Huddersfield by Mackay. Joshua Holden, *A Short History of Todmorden* (Manchester University Press, 1912) describes the riot there. The setting up of registration districts is referred to by the Webbs.

7 The Pauper Palace

The case of Elizabeth Stannard appears in the *First Annual Report*; the excessive workhouse rations and Dr Kay's troubles in the *Second Annual Report*. The paupers at Heckingham are described in Mackay. On Kent I used Head and on the pre-1834 regime in other workhouses the following were useful sources: *Parochial Regulations Relative to the Management of the Poor of Bradford, Wilts, with Notes Tending to Economy and Comfort in the Workhouse* (1801); *Rules and Regulations for the Government of the Workhouse of the Parish of St Martin in the Fields and of the Infant Poor-house at Highwood Hill* (1828); and *Rules and Regulations for the Management of the Workhouse of St Luke, Middlesex* (n.d. but c. 1828). The Kent magistrate who disliked large workhouses wrote *An Address to the Board of Guardians of the Cranbrook Union on the Necessity of Building a Union Workhouse, by their late Chairman* (1839). The *Annual Reports* give details of workhouse construction, plans of model workhouses and recommended diets and include reports of individual Assistant Commissioners. A critical account of the classification scheme can be found in Anon., *On a Proposal to withhold Outdoor Relief from Widows with Families, contained in the Last Annual Report of the Poor Law Commissioners* (1840). On Samson Kempthorne I consulted Howard Colvin, *Biographical Dictionary of English Architects 1660-1840* (John Murray, 1934). The critic of various aspects of workhouse design was John Bowen, *The Union Workhouse and Board of Guardians System* (Bridgwater, 1842), a 63-page indictment. Criticism of draughts in the workhouse and the teapot-breaking incident can be found in the *Journal* for July 1864. Florence Hill, *Children of the State* (1889) criticised workhouse uniform for children. John Bowen was the critic who wrote to *The Times*; Crabbe's verses appear in *Poetical Works* (OUP, 1914) and James Withers Reynolds' verses were published in Cambridge in 1854 and 1856, while Miss E. Porter supplied me with information on his life.

8 Master and Matron

The medical officer to the Westminster workhouse, who also waged a campaign against George Catch, was Dr Rogers, *Reminiscences of a Workhouse Medical Officer* (1889). Details of the emaciated medical man at Basingstoke are given by W. L. Sclater, *A Letter to the Poor Law Commissioners* (1836). The novel *Jessie Phillips, a Tale of the Present Day* (1844) was by Mrs Frances Trollope. The hard work and poor pay of workhouse chaplains was pointed out by the Rev. D. L. Cousins, *Extracts from the Diary of a Workhouse Chaplain* (1847). Other salary scales are quoted by Louisa Twining, *Workhouses and Women's Work* (1857). The admirable master at Ashford is mentioned by Hughes and the poor candidates at Marylebone in the *Journal* (August, 1859). The short-lived master at Cerne Abbas is found in Elizabeth Cockburn. The visitor who described 'the reign of terror' was Louisa Twining in *Recollections of Life and Work* (1893), a verbose but valuable book. Events at Lambeth workhouse were exposed by Joseph Rogers and by Samuel Shaen, *Workhouse Management and Workhouse Justice* (1869). Shaen also published *The Assault at Lambeth Workhouse* (1869) but it adds little to the other accounts. The ladylike matron was encountered by Louisa Twining, *Workhouses and Pauperism* (1898), which is virtually a second volume of autobiography. The inspector who criticised the restrictions on teachers was quoted by W. Chance, *Children under the Poor Law* (1897).

9 The Poor versus the Poor Law

The Mayor of Morpeth was Robert Blakey, *A Second Letter to the Mechanics and Labouring Men of the North of England* (Newcastle, 1837). The disillusioned Whig elector is quoted by Anon., *Fallacies on the Poor Laws* (1837). The anti-Poor Law leaflet at Huddersfield is by A Friend to the Manufacturers, *The Poor Law Exposed. Is it a Whig Measure? It cannot be Re-introduced in these Districts* (1837). The allegation that the aged poor should be killed is in the Rev. Thomas Spencer, *The Outcry against the New Poor Law; or who is the Poor Man's Friend?* (1841). The diary extracts are from Charles Greville, *The Greville Memoirs* (8 volumes, edited by Henry Reeve, Longmans, 1896). The Disraeli quotation is found in Francis Hawes, *Henry Brougham*. John Walter's views are set out in John Walter, MP, *A Letter to the Electors of Berkshire on the New System for the Management of the Poor proposed by the Government* (1834), and Thomas Wakley's in an excellent, if now old-fashioned, biography, Dr S. Squire Sprigge, *The Life and Times of Thomas Wakley*. Brougham's repudiation of the story about the dead wife was reprinted as a pamphlet, *Speech by Lord Brougham on the New Poor Law in the House of Lords, 20th March 1858*. A useful summary of current charges against the workhouse can be found in William Denison, *Abstract of Evidence taken before the Committee Appointed by the House of Commons on 27th February 1837, to Enquire into the*

Operation of the Poor Law Amendment Act (1837) which highlights Walter's part in the proceedings. Less satisfactory is George Jacob Holyoake, *The Life of Joseph Rayner Stephens* (n.d. but c. 1881), a biography so irretrievably muddled that it confuses rather than enlightens. Other examples of Stephens's inflammatory oratory are quoted in Brougham's speech, cited above, and some specimens of Radical oratory can also be found in Samuel Roberts, *The Wickedness of the New Poor Law Addressed to serious Christians of all Denominations* (Sheffield, 1839), and *The Rev. Dr Pye Smith and the New Poor Law* (1839). John Bowen described events at Bridgwater in *A Letter to the King* (1835). Richard Oastler appealed to the Duke of Wellington in *Brougham versus Brougham, on the New Poor Law* (1847).

10 Scandal at Andover

On the cost of poor relief at various dates I used mainly Anon., *The English Poor Law and Poor Law Commission in 1847* (1847) supplemented by the Webbs, Mackay and the *Annual Reports*. Nassau Senior's *Remarks* was published under the pseudonym of 'A Guardian'. O'Connell's comment is found in Nicholls, Volume 1. Chadwick's disruptive role is described by Mackay and Finer. The critic protesting in 1837 was John Bowen, *A Refutation*. Bone-breaking at Eastbourne was described by Charles Booker, *The Murder Den and its Means of Destruction; or some Account of the Working of the New Poor Law in the Eastbourne Union* (n.d. but probably 1842). The main source on Andover is the *Report of the Select Committee*, which covers eight pages, and the evidence, which covers two thousand (2 volumes, 1846). A convenient summary, one hundred and twenty pages long, which includes Parker's previous contact with bone-crushing, is *The Andover Union: Extracts from the Report of the Select Committee of the House of Commons and an Epitome of the Evidence on the cases of Mr Parker and Mr Day, late Assistant Commissioners* (1847). The two men's own account can be found in H. W. Parker, *Letters to the Rt. Hon. James Graham, Bart., on the Subject of Recent Proceedings connected with the Andover Union* (1845) and William Day, *A Letter to Lord Viscount Courtenay, M.P., Chairman of the Andover Committee* (1847). I obtained some additional details on M'Dougal from Ian Anstruther, *The Scandal of the Andover Workhouse* (Geoffrey Bles, 1973), published while this book was in the press.

The later history of the Poor Law Board comes from the Webbs, Volume 2. The eminently respectable Minister was Campbell-Bannerman. I quoted Chadwick's remark from my own *King Cholera* (Hamish Hamilton, 1966). Sir George Stephens's contribution is *A Letter to the Rt. Hon. Lord John Russell on the Probable Increase of Rural Crime in Consequence of the Introduction of the New Poor Law and Railroad System* (1836). The *Poor Law Sonnets* were collected by Baxter, *The Book of the Bastilles.* Among other pamphlets defending the workhouse which I consulted are: the Rev. Herbert Smith, *A Letter to the Labouring Classes in their own Behalf* (Southampton, 1838); S.G.O., *A Word or Two about the New Poor Law Addressed to his Parishioners by a Beneficed Clergyman in Buckinghamshire* (n.d., but c. 1836); Anon., *A Few Plain Words from a Poor Man* (1838); the Rev. Thomas Spencer, *The Want of Fidelity in Ministers of Religion Respecting the New Poor Law* (1841); J. Godfery, *A Continuation of the Poor Man's Friend, being a Few Plain Words from a Poor Man who has long known their Habits* (Kings Lynn, 1836); and *Truth Proclaimed,* already cited; John Spackman. *A Death-blow to Pauperism in the Bradford (Wilts.) Union by the Introduction of the Principles of the Poor Law Amendment Act* (1836); W. H. Newnham, *Operations of the Poor Law Amendment Act in the County of Sussex. Report of the Auditors of the Uckfield Union for the Quarters ending 25 December 1835 and Lady Day, 1836* (1836), which contains tabulated returns from all the parishes in the Union; the Rev. F. Close, *Pauperism Traced to its True Source by the Use of Holy Scripture and Experience* (1837), which reached the comforting conclusion that all poverty was due to drunkenness; and A Guardian, *Remarks on the Opposition to the Poor Law Amendment Bill* (1841). The literature on the other side includes William Hussey, *A Calm and Impartial Argument on Some of the Chief Features of the New Poor Law* (Maidstone, 1837), which lives up to its title, and Sir George Crewe, Bart, *A Word for the Poor and against the New Poor Law* (Derby, 1843). Informative on other aspects of the subject are *The Report of the Board of Guardians of the Strand Union, April 1837* (1837), a useful account of the first twelve months of the Union; *Observations and Documents respecting the Petitions presented to Parliament from the Parish of Stoke Poges* (1835), which sets out the reasons for allowing the town to opt out of the 1834 Act; the *Copy of a Petition from the Board of Guardians of Stoke upon Trent* (1838), which strongly supports the Act; and A Guardian, *Stanzas for the*

Coronation day, addressed to the Guardians of the Poor of England
(1838), which rather optimistically urges fellow Guardians to 'let
mercy rule with justice'. Details about Honor Shawyer and Jonathan
Cooke are in the 1837 *Abstract of Evidence.* The dangerous life in the
Bridgwater workhouse is described by John Bowen, *A Refutation of
some of the Charges Preferred against the Poor* (1837). The pamphlet
by Samuel Roberts is *Mary Wilden, a Victim of the New Poor Law*
(1837). The classic, exhaustive account of all the Guardians' misdeeds,
real or imaginary, is by Baxter, *Book of the Bastilles* (1841). The
sufferings of Susan Barnes are described in the *Annual Register*
(1840).

11 Aged Inmates of Respectable Character

The old lady's last night in her home was described by Samuel Roberts,
The Rev. Pye Smith (1838). The farmer who met the sailor and the
84-year-old inmate was J. Godfery and the Assistant Commissioner
who felt the public needed enlightening is quoted in the *Second Annual
Report.* Dr Westlake's views can be found in the *Report of the Select
Committee* on Andover. The figures for old people in London work-
houses are given by Louisa Twining, *Recollections of Workhouse
Visiting and Management during 25 Years* (1880), an informative
200-page book. Conditions at Holborn workhouse and the gooseberry
wine incident were described by Baxter; conditions in 1872 by W.H.P.,
Our Poor Law System. What it is and what it Ought to be (1872). The
Webbs in Volume 2 describe the issue of 'Sunday best'; 'dry tea' was
discussed in *A Paper on the Conditions of Workhouses* read at the
National Association for the Promotion of Social Science Conference
at Birmingham, October 1857. The regular visitor to the Devon
workhouse was Mrs Emma Sheppard, *Experiences of a Workhouse
Visitor* (1857) which also describes the Surrey workhouse master,
proud of his mild regime. The medical officer of the Strand Union
was Dr Rogers. The visitor who disliked clothes-flavoured soup is described by H. Preston-Thomas, *The Work and Play of a Government
Inspector* (1909) which can be read purely for pleasure. The offer
of armchairs and the collection of the old from parishes are described
by Sir George Crewe, *A Word for the Poor.* The nice boarded floor is
mentioned by Mrs Emma Sheppard in *Sunshine in the Workhouse*
(1858). The Derbyshire clergyman referred to was Cousins. On Louisa

Twining's career see her *Life*. The 1872 writer describing the separation of married couples was W.H.P., *Our Poor Law System*. Improvements from 1885 are described by the Webbs, Volume 2, and the issue of tobacco, snuff and dry tea and the improvements in conditions for the old by the Webbs, Volume 1. The changes in Essex are in G. Cuttle, *The Legacy of the Rural Guardians* (1934). The verses by John Bundy are partly quoted by Joyce Godber and can be found in full in the County Record Office. Those by Thyrza Hardy are found in Arnold O. Gibbons, *Cerne Abbas, Notes and Speculations* (Longmans, booksellers of Dorchester, 1962). The Inspector who thought 'workhouse' a misnomer was Preston-Thomas.

12 Death in the Workhouse

The reaction to cut-price funerals at Bridgwater was described by John Bowen, *System*. Poor Law Sonnets are contained in Baxter. Louisa Twining in *Visiting* describes being asked for an old garment and quotes a workhouse chaplain on funerals and other matters. The Rev. D. L. Cousins in *Extracts from the Diary of a Workhouse Chaplain* describes a pauper funeral and records the case-histories of Charley, the starving man, the Author, the smuggler and the Atheist. Dr Rogers was the workhouse doctor who contributed the other anecdotes. Louisa Twining describes the shoemakers and needlewomen in *Women's Work*. The stories of Mary Ann Bull and Johnny Trott are told by Gibbons and that of the old poacher by Preston-Thomas.

13 Fallen Women

The chaplain with unhappy experience of unmarried mothers was the Rev. Herbert Smith, *An Account of the Situation and Treatment of the Women with Illegitimate Children in the New Forest Union Workhouse* (1838), and his efforts to reform them are described in *An Account of a Union Chaplaincy* (1839). The 'canary wards' and the history of the policy of distinctive dress are described by the Webbs, *Policy*, Eliza by Cousins and the dismal state of the lying-in wards by Dr Rogers; her first visit to the foul ward by Mrs Sheppard, *Sunshine*, and her later disillusionment in *Experiences*. The 'poor sinful girls', the account of the Alverstoke experiment and the reference to overworked servants can be found in the *Journal*. Mayhew's findings on prostitution are quoted by Kellow Chesney, *The Victorian Underworld* (Maurice Temple Smith, 1970). The social worker in 1889, the Guardian concerned about prostitution, the girls who used oakum to improve their figures and the riot at Kensington are mentioned by Florence Hill. The authority on Victorian prostitution was Dr William Acton, *Prostitution considered in its Moral, Social and Sanitary Aspects* (1867), and Frances Power Cobbe wrote the series of *Workhouse Sketches* which appeared in *Macmillan's Magazine* in 1861. The assault at Liverpool is mentioned in *Memorials of Agnes Elizabeth Jones by her Sister* (1871).

14 Outcasts Infants

The anecdote about Victoria Queen comes from Louisa Twining, *Life,* and the description of the wheelbarrow family is in Baxter. The children who pleaded 'let it not be me' are in G. E. Fussell, *From Tolpuddle to T.U.C.* (Windsor Press, 1948). Biddy's struggles impressed A Late Relieving Officer. The 1861 analysis of routes to the workhouse, the children from prosperous families and the 1861 inspector of a workhouse school are quoted in the *Journal.* The figures for orphans in the workhouse comes from the Webbs, Volume 2. The Poor Law official of 1838 and the 1847 General Order on Corporal Punishment is in R. A. Leach, *Pauper Children, their Education and Training, a Complete Handbook to the Law* (1890). The institutionalised children and the boy who wanted to move to the adult side are described by Florence Hill. The 'three months education in a workhouse', the Bedford controversy, the schools with uneducated teachers, the inspector visiting a school in 1868 and the report on a school in 1868 are all in Chance. The quotation 'to teach a pauper child to write', the Guardians who feared literate paupers, the Deptford teachers, the 'enthusiastic Scotch youth' and the changes in Aubin's school are mentioned in Frank Smith, *The Life and Work of Sir James Kay-Shuttleworth* (1923). The Somerset clergyman and the teacher armed with sticks are in Spencer, *Outcry* and the boys whose jaws were tied in Cousins. The persecuted girls are in Mrs Sheppard, *Sunshine.* The 'punishment of the trough' is described in Mary Carpenter, *What shall we do with our Pauper Children?* (1861), and Miss Carpenter's own experience of 'ragged schools' is in J. Estlin Carpenter, *The Life and Work of Mary Carpenter* (1879). St Asaph's school is described in great detail in *The Autobiography of Sir Henry Morton Stanley* (Sampson Low, 1909), which I supplemented from Byron Farwell, *The Man who Presumed. A Biography of Henry M. Stanley* (Longmans, 1958). A detailed description of Aubin's school can be found in the *Report of the Retiring Board of Guardians of the Manchester Union to their Successors, Elected 25th March 1841* (1841), which also covers Drouet's school, the collapse of which is described in Henry Burgess, *The Duty of the State to its Infant Poor occasioned by the Recent Disclosures respecting the Infant Poor at Tooting* (1849). The treat for the workhouse children was described in *Macmillan's Magazine* and the improved workhouse schools in Chance. Early days at Anerley were recalled in the *Journal* and Louisa Twining's visit to the badly-run school in her *Visiting*. The general history of district schools can be found in Walter Mornington and F. J. Lampard, *Our London Poor Law Schools* (1898). On Nurse Gillespie I mainly used *The Times*. The transformation of the Poplar school is described in Raymond Postgate *A Life of George Lansbury* (Longmans, 1951). The critical pamphlet referred to is Anon., *The Strand Union Pauper Children at Edmonton: A Statement of Facts* (n.d. but c. 1852). On the background of workhouse-school pupils see Louisa Twining, *Our Poor Laws and our Workhouses* (1862).

15   Friendless Girls and Boys

The downcast children were seen by A Late Relieving Officer. The young inmates of Dublin workhouse, the Board's refusal to allow a swing, the headless doll, the girls busy bed-making, the exacting routine of domestic duties described by a woman visitor, the study of 80 girls in 1860, the Industrial House, the results of the premium system, the recruits who ran aloft, the boys at Stepney, the survey of workhouse 'graduates', the benefits of military drill and the suggestion for learning other trades, are all described in the *Journal*. The critical inspector of 1884 was quoted by Leach, the toys costing 3*s*. 6*d*., by Preston-Thomas and the Webbs, Volume 2. Aubin's school is described in the *Report of the Retiring Guardians* and the later history of music in the workhouse and the problem of the 'ins and outs' by Chance. Emma Sheppard describes setting up the hostel for boys in *Experiences*. The Poor Law Board's fears about boarding out and the

Report by Mrs Nassau Senior are in the Webbs, Volume 2. The children who dreaded being sent back to the workhouse and little Dicky are in Florence Hill. The Local Government Inspector for the South and West was Preston-Thomas.

16   The Lame and the Blind

Hospital accommodation is described in the *Report of the Retiring Board.* Criticism of the 100-patient infirmary comes from Overseer, *The Vision of an Overseer (now in Office) Revealing the Fatal Errors of the Poor Laws* (1851). Dr Rogers's experiences are set out in his *Reminiscences.* The Bristol visitor is quoted by Louisa Twining, *Pauperism*, her visit to St Giles's workhouse in her *Life* and to the workhouse school in *Visiting*. Her anthology is *Readings for Visitors to Workhouses and Hospitals* (n.d.). The chaplain writing in the 1860s, the 1861 survey, the wet-nurse with consumption, the widow paralysed with rheumatism, the beds filled with decrepit old women, the improvements suggested by visitors, the 1862 visiting lecturer and the withdrawal of a shilling-a-week allowance were all described in the *Journal.* The account of ophthalmia is taken from Susan Liveing, *A Nineteenth Century Teacher, John Henry Bridges* (1926). The confiscated needlework and other items and the woman afraid to have her finger-nails cut were mentioned in *A Paper on Conditions*. The woman visitor was Louisa Twining, *Pauperism*; she described bad conditions generally in her *Letter to the President of the Poor Law Board on Workhouse Infirmaries* (1866). The figures for pauper nurses are given in *Women's Work.* On Timothy Daly and Richard Gibson I mainly used *The Times.* I used extensively *The Lancet Sanitary Commission for Investigating the State of the Infirmaries in Workhouses* (1865). The improvements made in 1865 and subsequently, and the quotations from the inspectors are found in the Webbs, Volume 2 and later developments in the Webbs, *Policy.* Changes in Essex are described by Cuttle. On Agnes Elizabeth Jones I used her sister's *Memorials.* The improvements Louisa Twining secured in nurses' living standards are described in her *Life* and *Pauperism*, which also quotes the *British Medical Journal* on Dr Rogers. On Dr Bridges I used Susan Liveing. I also consulted Dr Thomas Dolan, *Some Remarks on Workhouse Hospitals with Illustrative Cases* (1879) and Dr J. H. Stallard, *Workhouse Hospitals* (1865).

17 Moping Idiots

The most comprehensive account is William Parry-Jones, *The Trade in Lunacy* (Routledge, 1972) and the most valuable contemporary source is Dr J.H. Stallard, *Pauper Lunatics and their Treatment* (1870) which supplies the quotation on village idiots and describes the overflowing asylums of 1870, the open-day at Colney Hatch and the medical officer for Poplar. This is supplemented by Dr John Miller, *A Plea in Favour of the Insane Poor* (1859). The neglected lunatic at Bristol is described in the *First Annual Report*. The 1858 workhouse visitor was Louisa Twining, *Women's Work*. Dr Rogers provided information about individual cases and the Webbs, Volume 2, about the Lunacy Commission and efforts to secure improvements. The *Edinburgh Review* survey was quoted by the *Journal*. The Essex lunatics, mental defectives and Guardians are mentioned by Cuttle and the cases in the South West by Preston-Thomas.

18 Only at Christmas

The rules for Christmas at St Martin's in 1828 are in *Rules and Regulations*, previously cited. The Guardians at Bath and events at Bridgwater are recorded by Baxter, at Cerne Abbas by Elizabeth Cockburn, at Andover by the *Select Committee Report*, at Bedford by the *Bedfordshire Mercury* for 2 January 1860, at the unnamed London workhouse, the Strand, Brighton and the Kirkdale Industrial Schools, by the *Journal*. On George R. Sims's work I used Arthur Calder-Marshall, *Prepare to Shed Them Now* (Hutchinson, 1968) a combined anthology and biographical essay. On the Workhouse Drink Reform League and the plea to drink toasts in water, see my *The Waterdrinkers* (Hamish Hamilton, 1968). Louisa Twining's efforts to ban beer are described in *Pauperism*, the festivities at Braintree by Cuttle, at Cork in the *Journal*, at Liverpool in *Memorials*, and elsewhere in Mrs Sheppard, *Sunshine* and *Macmillan's Magazine* previously cited.

19 Tramps and Vagrants

The essential secondary source is C. J. Ribton-Turner, *A History of*

Vagrants and Vagrancy (1887), supplemented by William Newton (of Ashton-under-Lyme), *Secrets of Tramp Life Revealed* (n.d. but c. 1886), E. Vivian, *On Vagrancy* (1868), J.Theodore Dodd, *Casual Paupers and How We Treat Them* (reprinted from *Charity* 1890), and (Inspector) John Lambert, *Vagrancy Laws and Vagrants* (1868), the source of all the workhouse poems quoted except 'Dirty days', which comes from C. W. Craven, *A Night in the Workhouse* (1887), like the 'phrenological chart' suggestion. The Webbs, *Policy*, records the anxiety of the Lambeth and Colchester Unions, their *History*, Volume 2, the fate of the unhappy casual at Newcastle and the reference to 'Queen's Mansions'. The description of a casual ward, the tramps uncertain in which direction to travel, the right to search tramps on entry and their evasion of this regulation, the casual who said 'Go to hell!', the Welsh Chief of Police, the Bath police officer, the tramps who terrorised lonely farms, the figures of admissions to St Martin's workhouse, the effects of the Irish invasion, the evidence heard by the Select Committee on Vagrancy, the account of vagrants' destructive behaviour, the workhouse masters who were critical of tramps, the 'bush telegraph' and the use of false names are all in Ribton-Turner. *The Report of the Select Committee* supplied the quotations from Andover. The Poor Law Board Minute of 1848 is quoted by Rose and other details are given by the Webbs, Volume 2. James Greenwood's experiences are recounted in his *A Night in a Workhouse* (1866), 'Ellen Stanley's' in Dr J. H. Stallard, *The Female Casual and her Lodging* (1866). Lord Carnarvon's campaign against tramps is described by Sir Arthur Hardinge, *The Life of the Fourth Earl of Carnarvon 1831-1890* (3 volumes, Volume 1, 1925), the Local Government Board's efforts by the Webbs, Volume 2, and Ribton-Turner, who quotes the Gloucester survey. The 'lurks' are taken from Newton and Lambert. The 'unemployed mechanic' at Keighley was C. W. Craven, *A Night in the Workhouse* (1887), and Mary Higgs's first impressions are described in *The Tramp Ward* (Manchester, 1904) and her later experiences, including the porter who liked 'funning', in *Glimpses of the Abyss* (1906). Conditions in 1909 are described by Everard Wyvall, *The Spike* (1909) and I also consulted the Rev. George Z. Edwards, *A Vicar as Vagrant* (1910).

20   Stones and Oakum

The sources for this chapter are: Greenwood, Craven, Wyvall and Mrs Higgs.

21   Turning the Clock Back

The main source is the Webbs, Volume 2. The Inspector anxious about 'the first taste of jam' was Preston-Thomas and the Guardians who labelled their paupers' trousers are mentioned by Robert Roberts, *The Classic Slum: Salford Life in the First Quarter of the Century* (Manchester University Press, 1971).

22   Hang the Rates!

The quotation from Dr Bridges occurs in Susan Liveing. The Webbs trace the history of women Guardians, and changes in the property qualification, and they supply most of the statistics quoted. Louisa Twining's experiences at Tonbridge are described in her *Life*. I discovered no satisfactory life of Will Crooks and used *Who was Who 1916-1928* and a pamphlet for children, Ernest E. Hayes, *Up from an Orange Box* (n.d. but c. 1947). On Lansbury I used Postgate. The 'terrible sights' quotation is from the Webbs, Volume 3, and that from Mrs Webb's diary is in Postgate. I also consulted the *Report of the Royal Commission on the Poor Laws and Relief of Distress* (Cd 4499, HMSO, 1909), the *History of Poor Law Administration in Poplar, Compiled under the Direction of Mrs S. Webb*, (Cd 5072 HMSO, 1911) and the *Report on the Poplar Union* by J.S. Davy, Chief General Inspector (Cd 3240, HMSO, 1906), which also refers to the 1894 enquiry. The effect of old age pensions on Salford is described by Roberts, the changes in nomenclature by the Webbs, Volume 2.

23   The End of the Workhouse

For this chapter I used the *Eleventh Annual Report of the Ministry of Health, 1929-30* (HMSO, 1930) and *Background Material No 2 Social Security in Britain* (Department of Health and Social Security,

March 1972). The decline in the number of lunatics is mentioned by Slater. Walter Barrett wrote *A Fenman's Story* (1965). I am grateful to the publishers, Routledge, for permission to quote from this.

Appendix: Workhouse Architecture

A.W.N.Pugin, *Contrasts* (2nd edition, 1841), was reprinted by Leicester University Press, 1969; other information can be found in Stanton, *Pugin* (1971), pp. 89-91. R.P. Browne's paper on the Greenwich Union appeared in *Weale's Quarterly Papers on Architecture*, Volume I (1844) and T.D. Barry's in *Proceedings of the Liverpool Architectural and Archaeological Society* (Vol. 2, 1851-2). The review of Kempthorne's plans comes from *Loudon's Architectural Magazine* ... 2 (1835) and the complaint about the way in which plans were returned from *3* (1836), p. 481. The Abingdon workhouse is praised in the *British Almanac (Companion to the Almanac)* (1836, pp. 234-6). Bentham's influence on prison architecture is described in 'Pattern of the Law' by Thomas A. Markus in the *Architectural Review*, October 1954, and his faith in the panopticon principle by Robin Evans, *Bentham's Panopticon* in the *Architectural Association Quarterly*, July 1971. The closing quotation comes from E.C. Midwinter, *Victorian Social Reform* (1968).

Recent Publications

Since the first edition of *The Workhouse* was written a number of books in the same subject area have appeared, among them the following: Ian Anstruther, *The Scandal of the Andover Workhouse* (Geoffrey Bles, 1973, reissued 1981); Antony Brundage, *The Making of the New Poor Law* (Hutchinson, 1978); M. A. Crowther, *The Workhouse System* (Batsford, 1981); Trevor May, *The Victorian Workhouse* (booklet, Shire Books, Princes Risborough, 1997); Kathryn A. Morrison, *The Workhouse: A Study of Poor Law Buildings in England* (English Heritage, 1999). On the history and recent reconstruction of Southwell Workhouse see the *National Trust Magazine*, Summer 1998, p. 26, and Summer 2002, p. 40; The *Nottinghamshire Historian*, Spring/Summer 1998, p. 3; and *East Midland Historian*, Vol. 8 p. 3. Other information used in the Second Foreword can be found in the *Andover Advertiser*, 27 March 1997, the *Evening Standard*, 7 September 1998 and the Arts and Books section of the *Daily Telegraph*, 5 June 1999.

Index